The Making of a Salafi Muslim Woman

The Making of a Salafi Muslim Woman

Paths to Conversion

Anabel Inge

OXFORD
UNIVERSITY PRESS

OXFORD

UNIVERSITY PRESS

Oxford University Press is a department of the University of Oxford. It furthers
the University's objective of excellence in research, scholarship, and education
by publishing worldwide. Oxford is a registered trade mark of Oxford University
Press in the UK and certain other countries.

Published in the United States of America by Oxford University Press
198 Madison Avenue, New York, NY 10016, United States of America.

Library of Congress Cataloging-in-Publication Data
Names: Inge, Anabel, author.
Title: The making of a Salafi Muslim woman : paths to conversion / Anabel Inge.
Description: New York, NY : Oxford University Press, [2016] |
Includes bibliographical references and index.
Identifiers: LCCN 2016005292 (print) | LCCN 2016009355 (ebook) |
ISBN 9780190611675 (hardback : alk. paper) | ISBN 9780190611682 (updf) |
ISBN 9780190611699 (epub)
Subjects: LCSH: Salafiyah—Great Britain. | Wahhābiyah—Great Britain. |
Muslim women—Great Britain. | Women in Islam—Great Britain. |
Islam—Great Britain. | Muslim converts from Christianity—Great Britain.
Classification: LCC BP195.S18 I54 2016 (print) |
LCC BP195.S18 (ebook) | DDC 297.8/3—dc23
LC record available at http://lccn.loc.gov/2016005292

1 3 5 7 9 8 6 4 2

Printed by Sheridan Books, Inc., United States of America

To my parents.

CONTENTS

ACKNOWLEDGEMENTS

This book is the result of several years of research involving many people. It began as a short Master's dissertation in 2008, grew into a doctoral thesis, and matured into a book manuscript.

I am greatly indebted to my PhD supervisors at King's College London, Professor Madawi Al-Rasheed and Dr Marat Shterin, who provided support all the way up to publication. They immediately recognised the project's potential back in 2009, and encouraged me to write my thesis as a book from the start. Madawi's expert advice on everything from the scope and direction of the inquiry to how to navigate challenging fieldwork was essential. She and Marat opened up new areas of research, encouraging me to look beyond Islam and the veil and to appreciate the deeper commonalities between my findings and the studies of other religious groups. Marat, in particular, urged me to draw on the fruits of decades of research on New Religious Movements, and his rigorous and thoughtful readings of my writing lent it shape, clarity, and coherence.

I am truly grateful for the financial support of the Arts and Humanities Research Council, Walton Scholarship (King's College London), and King's Theological Trust, without which this research would not have been possible.

Among those to whom I owe the most thanks are individuals who prefer not to be named publicly—but they know who they are. This research would have fallen at the first hurdle had not numerous community leaders and Salafi women kept an open mind and given me and my project a fair hearing, despite negative experiences with researchers—including an undercover one. And so many went further; not only welcoming me into their mosques and *halaqat*, giving up time in their busy lives and patiently answering my many questions, but also inviting me into their homes, to weddings, and to other gatherings. They shared intimate details of their lives, which they trusted me to represent faithfully. Most were also willing to accept that I did not embrace their beliefs personally. I specifically thank AbdulHaq Ashanti, Abdul Haqq Baker, Abdi Hasan, Abu Khadeejah, and Abu Muntasir, as they waived their right to anonymity.

A book on such a sensitive subject will inevitably disappoint some within (and outside) the community, a number of whom were never enthusiastic about this project. Still, I include in my thanks those Salafis who regarded me with suspicion yet nonetheless tolerated my presence. Defensive reactions often held up my research, but they were understandable and paved the way to enlightening conversations about Islam in Britain.

Faduma (a pseudonym) took me to my first Salafi study circle in 2008 and patiently answered my questions, inspiring me to research Salafism in the first place. Dr Shelagh Weir tirelessly read and re-read the manuscript at various stages, and I cannot thank her enough for her thoughtful comments on drafts all the way up to publication, wise suggestions on research directions, and overall support throughout the project. Fahd Zafar gave sensitive feedback on drafts, kept me abreast of media articles that were easily missed and generously gave up time to help me to track down hadiths. Dr Sarah Stewart supervised my Master's dissertation on Salafism, encouraged me to take it further, and provided crucial support at various stages of the research.

My research benefited from stimulating discussions with (and general support from) Siah Elmi, Dr John-Paul King, Shane Pereira, Dr Salam Rassi, Dr Katrin Schulze, Dr Shanon Shah, and Riyaz Timol, among many others. Shanon and Riyaz also gave very helpful feedback on drafts, as did Dr Manzur Rashid and Dr Damian Thompson. The completion of this project owes much to the moral and intellectual support—and camaraderie—of Dr Julia Sei, with whom I shared almost daily sessions in the university library for most of the writing-up period.

I would like to thank, too, everyone involved with the project at Oxford University Press (US) for their time and energy. Cynthia Read and Gina Chung gave invaluable guidance and support throughout the pre-publication process. I am also very grateful to their associates Jeyashree Ramamoorthy, Shalini Balakrishnan, and Alyssa Bender Russell, as well as to the two anonymous readers for their detailed and thoughtful reviews.

Thanks also to the exceptionally talented photographer Eleanor Bentall, who was responsible for the cover photograph. During the photo-shoots, she stayed calm amid constant abuse from the general public—both Muslims and non-Muslims. I also thank my brilliant Arabic teachers, Souad Baameur and Najwa El-Abed, and Mehmood Naqshbandi for sharing his figures and insights on trends in Salafi mosques in the United Kingdom.

My special thanks for the love, support, and patience of my family and friends—including Claire Ellicott, Javier Palacios-Moreno, Saima Tarapdar, Alexander Thomson, and my sister, among many others. They cheered me on throughout the process, and provided much-needed distractions. I thank all of them deeply—above all my parents, who have supported me in so many ways that it would be impossible to list them here, nor to thank them enough—but dedicating the book to them is a start. However, I must mention that my mother read the draft closely and made helpful suggestions for improvements. In addition, profound thanks go to my grandparents, Professor Park and Jeannette Honan, both of whom sadly passed away before I completed the manuscript, but who were always supportive of my academic endeavours.

Notwithstanding these contributions, I alone bear responsibility for any errors.

NOTE ON ARABIC TERMS,
TRANSLITERATIONS, QUR'ANIC
QUOTATIONS, AND PARAPHRASING

Translations of Arabic terms were guided by *The Oxford Dictionary of Islam* (2003), edited by John Esposito. However, my main concern was to highlight the most widely used meanings within British Salafi communities, which were illuminated through participant observation and which can be narrower or altogether different from meanings the terms have elsewhere.

Arabic transliterations are according to the conventions of the *International Journal of Middle East Studies*, but without diacritics. Qur'anic quotations are from the Saudi-backed English translation, *The Noble Qur'an*, by Muhammad Taqi-ud-Din Al-Hilali and Muhammad Muhsin Khan as that is British Salafis' preferred translation.

Some quotations from circles of knowledge and informal interviews are very close paraphrases because it was not always possible to record speech verbatim—for example, when a recorder would not have been appropriate or in informal contexts—despite making every effort to achieve accuracy. Such cases are indicated with asterisks (*), and I bear sole responsibility for any inaccuracies.

The Making of a Salafi Muslim Woman

Introduction

I met Faduma in London in 2008. She was a bright and vivacious British-Somali student of religion, and I was doing a Master's degree at the same university. We enjoyed debating religious issues, and occasionally dodged the campus security guards to have long discussions on the roof into the early hours. I thought nothing of her head-to-toe black gown until she invited me along to her Islamic studies 'circle'—or gathering for religious learning—one Saturday in April that year.

The circle met at the most famous mosque in Britain: London Central Mosque, also known as Regent's Park Mosque. It seemed an unlikely place to stumble upon one of the most controversial Muslim groups in the West.

I arrived to find around sixty women—most seated on the floor, a few on chairs—all gathered around a teacher in a semicircle in the women's prayer hall. Most were in their late teens and early twenties. Nearly everyone was dressed just like Faduma, and many also had flaps of material above their foreheads. I later learned that these were *niqabs* (face veils). These were lifted during the circle, as face veils are only worn when men are present.

They were listening with keen attention to the teacher, also wearing a black gown, who was already in full swing. She was urging the women to follow Islam strictly in accordance with the Qur'an and the examples of the Prophet Muhammad and *al-salaf al-salih*—Arabic for 'the pious predecessors'. These are generally understood to be the first three generations of Muslims—the companions of the Prophet (*sahaba*), their successors (*al-tabi'in*), and the successors' successors (*tabi' al-tabi'in*).

It was not until after the lesson, when the teacher handed me a leaflet titled 'Who Are the *Salafis*?,'[1] that I realized that this emphasis on the *salaf* (early ancestors) indicated a distinctive Islamic identity and interpretation—one widely viewed in the West as extremist, misogynist, and even a potential security threat.

The women at the circle called themselves 'Salafis' to show reverence for the *salaf*, whom they regarded as exemplary Muslims. For Salafis, these early Muslims followed a pure and unadulterated form of Islam in the years before the religion became contaminated by reprehensible innovations (*bid'a*), such as local traditions and customs. As the centuries passed and Islam spread to new territories, local beliefs and practices blended with 'pristine' Islam, and *bid'a* gradually became rampant. Salafis aim to restore the religion to its imagined original form by calling others to the religious understanding and practices of the *salaf*. This brand of revivalism within Sunni Islam has come to be known as Salafism. It appears that it is now the fastest-growing Muslim faction in Britain—half of all mosques opening in 2014 and 2015 were Salafi, and this proportion is unlikely to decrease and may even go up (Naqshbandi, 2015).

During the lesson, the teacher referred to the *salaf* several times, contrasting their example with the spiritual poverty of most Muslims today. They had abandoned the path laid down for them, she said, having confused mere culture and superstition with revelation-based teaching. Despite being Arab herself, she prioritized religion above culture, including her own, when their principles clashed. Perhaps that was why her circles attracted an impressive mix of women with North African, Afro-Caribbean, Somali, South Asian, and other backgrounds, including both black and white converts (among whom, I was fascinated to learn, was a former Catholic nun).

In the sensitive political climate of that time, I had expected my presence as a non-Muslim in the mosque to raise eyebrows, or even prompt alarm. British Muslims had felt under scrutiny since 9/11, routinely becoming the subject of suspicion and negative media portrayals. This situation was exacerbated after July 7, 2005, when four British-born Muslims killed themselves and fifty-two passengers on underground trains and a bus in London. So when the lesson drew to a close, I fully expected to be questioned and suspected of hidden agendas. Would they think I was a journalist on the hunt for a sensational story? A spy, even?

To my surprise, I was treated as an honoured guest. During the question-and-answer session, the teacher prioritized my questions, and afterwards about five women surrounded me—not to interrogate me, but to earnestly request that I take their phone numbers 'in case you have questions about Islam'.

I thought that they were purely out to 'win another soul', but they were just as friendly after I told them that I wanted to study Salafism from an academic point of view. By then, I had returned to the circle twice and had decided to do my Master's dissertation on Salafism in Britain.

Over the next four months, I occasionally attended the circle, which lasted for up to eight hours every Saturday and Sunday, stopping only for prayers. The women mostly discussed matters of creed—how to worship God correctly, without engaging in *bid'a* or *shirk* (associating partners with God; polytheism). I interviewed some of the regulars. They told me that the circle had been running for about five years, attracting up to a hundred attendees every week—most of whom, intriguingly, had non-Salafi backgrounds.

A year later, in September 2009, feeling there was much more to unravel, I started a PhD and approached several London Salafi groups for permission of access. This time, however, I initially encountered suspicion, distrust, and closed doors.

Why this dramatic change in my reception?

In early 2008, Salafism in the West was still relatively underresearched, despite arousing forceful media and political commentary and debate. The face veil, in particular, had provoked controversy, yet little was known about the Salafi women's groups that promoted it, nor its highly conservative gender ideology. This all changed in September that year.

I was just finishing my Master's dissertation when a television programme suddenly subjected Salafi women in London to unprecedented public scrutiny and suspicion. Channel 4 broadcast a Dispatches documentary, *Undercover Mosque: The Return* (2008), on national British television.[2] An undercover Muslim reporter had posed as a Salafi woman in a study circle at a London mosque, hiding a camera in her billowing black *jilbab* (Muslim women's outer garment that conceals all but the face and hands). She had become a regular at the circle and convinced the women there that she was 'one of them'. She socialized with them, started wearing the *niqab*, and after a month was invited to another circle at a woman's house. She accepted, and took her camera with her.

Footage from both the public and the private circles became the centrepiece of the exposé, accompanied by the message that 'British women are being constantly exposed to hardline Saudi teachings' at the mosque. It showed teachers preaching highly conservative teachings, including brutal shari'a (Islamic law) punishments, hatred of non-Muslims, and strict gender segregation. One teacher told a woman who worked in the health service that her job was impermissible because she worked alongside men and could not wear a full *jilbab*. The documentary stressed the group's opposition to terrorism, but ended with a suggestive comment from Professor Anthony Glees: 'Separateness makes it easier for British Muslims not to regard Britain as their homeland but as the enemy.'

This Salafi study circle was the very same women's group that had introduced me to Salafism at London Central Mosque just five months previously. I realized, with a jolt, that over the past few months of attending circles for my Master's research, at any point I could have been sitting next to the undercover researcher.

Afterwards, the mosque banned the group from the premises, claiming it had never had permission to operate there in the first place. Regulars simply moved on to other Salafi circles in London.

These women, I later learned, were outraged by what they saw as a betrayal of trust and violation of privacy, particularly the fact that the reporter had filmed them without their *niqabs* (even though faces had been blurred out in the documentary). They also felt completely misrepresented. None would deny, in essence, the highly conservative, literal interpretations that had been propagated in the circle, for which Salafis remain unapologetic. These teachings are hardly secret; they are plainly described in the plethora of easily accessed Salafi websites and literature. But the women took exception to the selective editing, the sinister background music, and the overall sensationalist tone.

When I became aware of the documentary, I suddenly understood why two hitherto responsive women from the circle had not answered my messages. Clearly, the women now doubted my reasons for attending the circle. From now on, no researcher could slip into a Salafi group unvetted.

The Channel 4 documentary was the British public's first glimpse into the world of Salafi women in the United Kingdom. But its narrow remit and covert methods provided no insight into these women's lived realities, beyond the ultra-conservative rulings of scholars in Saudi Arabia and other countries. Viewers were left none the wiser about the women behind the blurred faces. Why were they learning about Islam from a Salafi point of view? Had anyone forced them to be there? What appeal, if any, did it hold for them? And how did they negotiate strict interpretations as young women living in a liberal, Western society?

These questions have largely been ignored or only superficially addressed amid periodically resurfacing debates about *niqab* bans and the ideological drivers of radicalization in the United Kingdom. While Salafi women are regularly subject to commentary in the media and politics, their own voices are almost entirely absent from the public sphere. Nor do we find them in most academic publications on Salafism in Britain, which do not provide any indepth insight into the women's side of this strictly gender-segregated community. This neglect is not justified because women have always formed a significant part of UK Salafi communities—and much more so since the turn of the millennium.

Meanwhile, the terms 'Salafi', 'Salafi-Jihadi', and 'Salafism' have increasingly appeared in the Western media since 9/11, yet remain poorly understood. Media outlets used them in connection with the terrorists behind the attacks in Tunisia and France on 26 June 2015, and again in relation to the suspects behind the Paris attacks on 13 November, 2015.

And as ISIS, the so-called Islamic State of Iraq and Syria, has grown, and thousands of would-be *mujahidin* and 'Jihadi brides' have left the West for Syria and Iraq, many commentators have branded the group's ideology 'Salafi' or 'Salafi-inspired'. Adding to this impression, ISIS women—some of whom have been photographed wielding AK-47s—dress just like Salafi women in Western countries. And, like many Salafi women, they believe that their main preoccupation is to be secluded, obedient wives to their husbands.

As a result, many in the West regard the presence of Salafi communities as a real or potential security threat. The current UK government's counter-extremism strategy appears to legitimize the latter narrative by targeting so-called 'non-violent extremists'—those who do not advocate violence but oppose 'basic liberal values' and are therefore 'providing succour to violent extremists' (Cameron, 2015).

Salafi women are typically considered to be either a sinister part of the radicalization apparatus or pitiful domestic slaves. Similarly, the wearing of the 'burqa'—often used to describe the *niqab* and *jilbab* worn together—is seen as a sign of Islamist extremism, self-segregation, and/or female oppression (Zempi and Chakraborti, 2014, p.9). It is often assumed that women who wear it only do so because they are coerced by male relatives and clerics. This assumption has fuelled campaigns to outlaw the garment in Western countries. France and Belgium have already banned the face veil in all public places, while others—Britain included—have considered following suit.

The reality, however, is much more complicated. Most Salafis in Europe—including those who feature in this study—are explicitly against violence,[3] so they should not be essentialized as a security threat. In Britain, the term 'Salafi' has been associated with non-violent, often quietist groups since at least the end of the 1990s. These preachers and organizations started to publicly condemn Jihadi ideologies and atrocities long before the emergence of ISIS and even prior to 9/11—and some have actually received government grants for counter-extremism work. Although they support strict interpretations of shari'a in theory—as do many mainstream traditionalist Muslims—they do not call for Islamic law in Britain, nor do they want a worldwide caliphate. They are more interested in proselytizing, warning Muslims against *bid'a* (reprehensible innovation), and correcting the minutiae of everyday ritual at home—prayers, manners, dress, and so on—than in international affairs.

Furthermore, empirical research suggests that Muslim veiling in the United Kingdom is largely a personal choice,[4] and this study indicates that Salafi *niqab*-wearing is no different. In fact, far from being forced by their families to cover up, I discovered that many Salafi women are subject to considerable pressure to wear *less*. The vast majority come from non-Salafi families, and became Salafis as teenagers and adults. Many are converts with other faith backgrounds; the rest are largely from less conservative or non-observant Muslim families. I have never heard of coerced *niqab*-wearing, but have met many women whose families implored them, or tried to force them—sometimes threatening violence—to discard their veils and gowns, which they saw as 'the culture of the Arabs' or even extremist.

Yet if coercion is removed from the equation, the adoption of such a restrictive lifestyle in a liberal society can seem perplexing. Why, then, do young women in twenty-first-century Britain become Salafis? If it is a devout Islamic identity they are looking for, why not pick a less restrictive interpretation? Why wear a burqa instead of a simple headscarf if no one is forcing you to do so?

This book addresses such questions through detailed ethnography in order to provide an in-depth understanding of how ordinary Salafi women see the world. I gained unprecedented access to Salafi women's groups in the United Kingdom and spent two years and four months attending their study circles, social gatherings, weddings, and many other community events. Once I had built up trust, I was able to talk to young women, community elders, and Salafi leaders at length, conducting thirty-six formal interviews and many more informal ones. Adopting this approach allowed me to capture a sense of life within the community and to pin down the small-scale dynamics of women's conversions to Salafism. I can therefore paint a far richer picture of British women's involvement in Salafism than has so far been possible.

I examine the biographical, social, political, ethnic, and local contexts that shaped the women's religious choices. I also consider the major social and other implications of these choices on young women's daily lives in London, and how they interpreted and addressed the clashes between strict Salafi teachings and social realities. My study is rooted in Britain, more specifically London—the largest Salafi base in the United Kingdom—but also contributes to an understanding of other Western manifestations of Salafism, given the strong transnational nature of Salafi thought and practice.

In the United Kingdom, Salafism appeals to women of diverse ethnic and religious origins, including a disproportionate number of black[5] Muslims. The Salafi circles and events I attended attracted many Afro-Caribbean converts from Christianity and Somalis whose parents had sought refuge in Britain during the Somali Civil War (1991–present), as well as the daughters of Eritrean refugees and Nigerian economic migrants. I also encountered many second- and third-generation South Asians, Arabs, white converts, and people of various mixed backgrounds. I even met a Pole, a Colombian, a Spaniard, and a former Sikh who had converted to Islam and embraced Salafism.

Despite their striking array of backgrounds, all of these women had reached the conclusion that Salafism was the only correct approach to Islam and were trying to live in accordance with its highly conservative teachings. They had all undergone more or less radical *conversions*, and it is this process that I sought to piece together.

Here, I use the term 'conversion' inclusively to mean the simultaneous 'transformation of one's *self*' with that of one's 'basic *meaning* system' (McGuire, 2001, p.73). This transformation comprises both cognitive and behavioural changes. Understood thus, conversion covers much more than merely swapping one faith system for another. It incorporates a range of identity transformations, including the change from the absence of faith to a faith commitment, switching religious communities within the same faith tradition, and 'born-again' experiences—that is, spiritual awakening without changing religion at all (Rambo, 1993, p.2, p.13).

Most Salafi women in the United Kingdom are technically 'born-Muslims', meaning that their parents raised them as Muslims, however loosely they interpreted their faith commitment. These women typically came to a new understanding of their religion in their teens or twenties, and this process involved both a reinterpretation of the religion of their childhood and major lifestyle changes.

Most of the born-Muslims I interviewed grew up with only a rudimentary understanding of prayer, the Qur'an, and the importance of the hijab (Muslim women's head covering). When they became Salafis, they needed to study the fundamental principles of Islam—such as strict monotheism (*tawhid*)—in depth, consulting scholarly texts and learning the scriptural proofs for their beliefs and practices. They had to adopt a stricter form of dress and sacrifice many former habits and pleasures, as well as future opportunities. The Salafi lifestyle has no place for close friendships with non-Salafis or boyfriends—or indeed any 'unnecessary' mixing with men, ruling out most careers in a non-segregated Western society.

The women from non-Muslim families tended to have already embraced Islam and to have acquired a basic understanding of the faith by the time they became Salafis. Nonetheless, they had to undergo an additional conversion process in order to bring their beliefs and practices into line with Salafism.

The process of adopting a Salafi identity and lifestyle is not instant or even linear; rather, it is often intermittent and long-term. This illustrates a crucial point that has often been missed in popular and scholarly thinking about conversion. It encompasses much more than singular transformative events, such as the articulation of the *shahada* (profession of faith) for a new Muslim, or an epiphany when someone realizes 'The Truth' and changes her life for good. Such instantaneous conversions are rare (Rambo, 1993, p.1). Rather, conversion is a *process*, with no identifiable beginning or end (Kingsley Brown, 2003, p.136).[6] The changes that accompany conversion can occur over many years—and may never be completed.

After deciding to embrace Salafism, the young women I interviewed devoted much time to internalizing the group's teachings and learning how to apply them to their daily lives. They thus developed and maintained what social scientists refer to as *commitment*.[7] During this process—itself a later conversionary stage (Rambo, 1993)—an individual's wishes and goals become aligned with those of the group. A committed follower conforms to group demands because, for her, they fulfil or express a fundamental part of herself (Kanter, 1972, p.66). She will therefore willingly adopt new practices and prohibitions, withdraw from competing social attachments, and embrace new ones.

Commitment processes are essential to ensuring and maintaining successful conversion—and, ultimately, group survival. If inadequate, the convert's initial zeal may fizzle out, possibly to the point of leaving—especially when strict demands are made on her, as in Salafism. The second half of the book considers how Salafi women struggled to negotiate these demands with the social realities they faced as young women in a Western society with non-Salafi families and educational and professional aspirations.

0.1 SALAFI BELIEFS AND PRACTICES

As mentioned, Salafi teachings are not secret. On the contrary, Salafis are typically bursting to explain to anyone who will listen why women should wear the *jilbab*, and ideally *niqab*, too; why men should grow their beards and hitch their garments above their ankles; and how all other Muslims have 'deviated' from the right path.

They are certainly unapologetic about their puritanical lifestyle. This includes endorsing traditional gender roles; avoiding any intermingling with the opposite sex; not listening to music; and accepting the (limited, but not unusual) practice of polygamy,[8] whereby a man is permitted up to four wives simultaneously, provided he can treat them equally. Far from hiding their beliefs, Salafis consider it an important religious duty to 'give *da'wa*'—that is, to proselytize—to those who in their view have not grasped 'pure' Islam, whether they are Muslim or not.

Aspects of their purist creed are shared by Islamist and Jihadi groups, and this has led to a great deal of confusion over what the term 'Salafism' refers to, who its followers are, and what its relationship to Jihadism consists of. Part of the problem is that 'Salafi' is an elastic identity label that has been invoked by a variety of groups within the Sunni Islamic tradition, including some that endorse violence (Al-Rasheed, 2007, p.3). This comes as no surprise if we look at what the term 'Salafi' means.

Linguistically, the epithet simply refers to an attachment to the pious forefathers of Islam (*al-salaf al-salih*). Stripped to its bare semantics, the label potentially has appeal for any Sunni Muslim; after all, the *salaf* included the companions and family of the Prophet, who took their understanding of Islam directly from him and are highly respected. Many Muslim groups consider that the early Muslims set an example that can inspire reform in the contemporary period, though they need not be *closely* emulated (De Koning, 2013a, p.57). For insiders, the label 'Salafi' has therefore come to denote Islamic authenticity and, as Thomas Hegghammer (2009, p.249) says, is 'often better understood as a bid for legitimacy than an indication of a specific political programme.'

However, some general observations can be made. Most Salafis 'eschew formal political and most civic forms of organization (e.g. political parties, clubs, associations)' and are primarily religious and social reformers (Haykel, 2009, p.34). Instead, they focus on nurturing distinct—and often contested— Muslim identities. As such, Salafis cannot be termed completely apolitical, but they are not 'political actors in the strict or formal sense of politics' (p.34).

In UK Muslim discourse, as elsewhere, Salafi labels have evolved and di-versified over the years, contributing to the confusion surrounding Salafi groups—particularly their position on jihad. One British group, Jam'iat Ihyaa' Minhaaj Al-Sunnah (JIMAS; meaning the Society for the Revival of the Prophetic Way), which reportedly sent at least one hundred fighters to Bosnia during the war of 1992–1995 under the banner of *Salafiyya* (i.e., Salafism; Hasan, 2014, p.9), has reinvented itself as a non-sectarian chari-table organization, and has not promoted itself as Salafi since at least 2006.[9] Since around the turn of the millennium until today, the label has been used mainly by consistently non-violent and often quietist groups, such as Salafi Publications in Birmingham and Brixton Mosque in London.

There is a complication, however. More recently, the successors of the radical UK Islamist group Al-Muhajiroun—which was banned in 2010— have occasionally used the label 'Salafi' in platforms such as 'The Salafi Youth Movement' and 'Salafi Media'. This has fuelled suspicion that Salafis are in reality Jihadi-sympathizers—wolves in sheep's clothing. However, the majority of claimants to the Salafi label in the United Kingdom con-sider groups such as Al-Muhajiroun to be arch-enemies who have grossly distorted Islam (more on this in chapter 4.3). Indeed, UK Salafi groups and Al-Muhajiroun successor groups are distinct from one another not only organizationally but also ideologically. Furthermore, Al-Muhajiroun suc-cessors use the label as just one of their many fronts. This decision can be interpreted as highly pragmatic—namely, a strategy to operate freely in the public sphere (Raymond, 2010, pp.12–13). Given the above consider-ations, in the contemporary UK context at least, it makes sense to associ-ate the term 'Salafi' only with groups that focus on non-violent religious and social reform and oppose Jihadism.

This book is concerned with this majority contingent, covering preachers, learning institutions, and, above all, ordinary women—my principal sub-jects. When I use the term 'Salafi', I refer only to this dominant non-violent tendency—whether in relation to an identity, an interpretative stance, or specific organizations in the United Kingdom today. For the sake of clarity, I employ terms such as 'Islamist' and 'Jihadi' to describe other groups and modes of thought with which Salafism is often conflated. More specifically, within this dominant tendency, the British Salafi networks featured in this book approach the more apolitical, Saudi-loyalist end of the Salafi spectrum. Not only do they shun organised forms of political participation, but they also oppose voting and strongly promote obedience to rulers.[10]

That is not to say that Salafis have nothing in common with militants who also say they want to return to the way of the *salaf* (though do not necessarily embrace the term 'Salafi'). In fact, many academics believe that certain similarities are so significant that the term 'Salafi' can usefully be applied to groups with a wide spectrum of political positions, regardless of how consistently they use the term (if they do at all).[11] Many of these studies appear to have been influenced by Quintan Wiktorowicz's (2006) typology of Salafism, according to which 'purists' (who are focused on non-violent *da'wa*), 'politicos' (who approve of non-violent political activism), and even 'jihadis' (who believe that jihad is an individual and permanent duty for all Muslims) all belong under the Salafi umbrella. The basis for this typology is that all three tendencies are said to share fundamental doctrinal principles, such as an anti-rationalist approach and a strict form of *tawhid*—though they differ widely on their application.

To be sure, this typology captures certain shared features and reference points between movements ranging from Saudi Wahhabism to the Sahwa[12] and Al-Qa'ida. However, it has been criticized as insufficiently accommodating of contextual variety, shifts, and overlaps among the three strands[13]—in particular of what is, in reality, a blurred 'purist/politico' boundary (Bangstad and Linge, 2015). It has also been suggested that certain 'politicos', such as the Sahwa movement, 'shade off into the Islamism (political Islam) of the Muslim Brotherhood' (Meijer, 2009b, p.17), raising questions about the applicability of the term 'Salafi' in such cases.

Typologies certainly have their uses: they can help us to understand the similarities and differences between groups and interpretations, and their relationships with one another. But using the term 'Salafi' inclusively to refer to such a wide range of interpretations and groups can have the opposite effect, especially if we are not meticulous in our qualification of the term.[14] This is for three reasons.

First, doing so may perpetuate widespread confusion regarding the term 'Salafi', which nowadays seems to appear in the media whenever there is an attempted or successful terrorist attack—often without qualification. This blanket use of the term puts non-violent, conservative Muslims at risk of further marginalization, and maybe even criminalization. It is particularly problematic in the Western context, where most Salafis are non-violent and often quietists.

Second, that the three Salafi 'types' share the same creed is not strictly true: quietists condemn as *bid'a* the more political groups' invocation of an additional category of *tawhid* called *tawhid al-hakimiyya* (unity of sovereignty) to justify more organized or violent activities. They also disagree on other essential aspects of creed, such as the conditions for belief and disbelief and how to understand some of God's attributes (De Koning, 2012a, p.158). This weakens the basis for classifying the three strands as all part of the same movement.

Third, by locating the only points of difference squarely in the political domain, the three-part typology encourages the mistaken belief that 'purists' are completely apolitical and lack a concrete programme of Islamic reform. In fact, like Islamists, they want to create a 'truly Islamic' society through activism—albeit only at the level of individual doctrinal and ritual reform, through the medium of *da'wa*. Such a programme, especially in a liberal, non-Muslim society such as Britain, can be considered political. Martijn de Koning (2012a) rightly points out that Salafi practices, such as the wearing of the *niqab*, though not inherently political statements, become so when 'they are transformed into public symbols that are open to contestations from different sides' (p.162). On one side, it signifies a competition with other Muslim groups and generations over the right to define 'true Islam'. And on the other side, in a society where counter-extremism is high on the political agenda and conservative Muslim groups are deemed suspect, the *niqab* has been politicized as a potential indicator of a security threat (Roex, 2014, p.52).[15] So, while Salafis tend to avoid dealing with the state, they 'turn the private into the political' (Griffel, 2015, p.190).

That is not to say that Salafis never discuss the prospect of a caliphate or the importance of shari'a. On the contrary, Salafis, like Islamists and Jihadis, consider the establishment of an Islamic state as an ultimate goal. But Salafis differ from the others in regarding the moral and doctrinal purification of society as the necessary precondition for such an event. And their bleak assessment of the current state of affairs renders, for them, even *speculation* about a future Islamic polity futile or unwise. During nearly two-and-a-half years of fieldwork, I only ever witnessed discussions about such a prospect in the context of critiques of other ideologies or, very rarely, predictions for a distant future utopia.

Rather, Salafis are 'first and foremost religious and social reformers' (Haykel, 2009, pp.34–35). They preoccupy themselves with *da'wa* and *tarbiya* (nurturing themselves and others in 'correct' beliefs and practices) in order to revive the piety of the Prophet's era. For Salafis, this process involves purging Islam of all 'cultural accretions' so that it is restored to its imagined 'unadulterated' form. This approach makes Salafis, according to some authors, 'agents of a new globalized Islam' that can transcend local space and customs (Roy, 2004; Wiktorowicz, 2006, p.210).

Salafis believe that Muslims today are in moral crisis because they have abandoned the core principles of Islam, in particular the call to worship strictly one God, and instead routinely engage in *bid'a* (reprehensible innovation). For Salafis, *bid'a* is rife in Britain today—above all, in the form of customs originating in South Asia and other migrant countries of origin. These include popular Muslim practices such as visiting holy Muslims' graves and celebrating the Prophet's birthday (*mawlid*). For Salafis, many such practices go so far as to violate the principle of *tawhid* (strict monotheism). In fact, Salafis consider that many, perhaps most, Muslims have strayed from the Prophet's path to the point of regularly committing the greatest sin of all: *shirk* (polytheism). Given these Muslims' wretched state—as well as the prevalence of disbelief beyond the Muslim community—the twin tasks of *da'wa* and *tarbiya* (preaching and nurturing others in 'correct' beliefs and practices) are Herculean.

That Salafis have such a pessimistic view of humanity's present condition is perhaps not surprising, given how easy it is to fall foul of the Salafi 'rulebook'. For Salafis, every act can be one of worship—or sin. They see Islam as a comprehensive 'manual' for living that covers every aspect of human behaviour. It includes, most visibly, strict sartorial rules—hitching a man's garments above his ankles, and fully covering a woman's shape—which they believe mirror the habits of the Prophet and his wives. But the 'manual' also covers seemingly mundane matters such as bathroom etiquette, purity rules, and the minutiae of how, where, and when to pray. Salafis claim that these rules are derived exclusively from the Qur'an and examples of the Prophet and *salaf*.

The most important rule of all is the call to worship God alone, without partners—in other words, *tawhid*—as expressed in the first pillar of Islam, the *shahada*, or profession of faith: 'There is no god but God. Muhammad is the messenger of God.' Salafis interpret this rule narrowly and strictly. *Tawhid* is therefore easily, often unknowingly, violated—even by Muslims themselves. For Salafis, acts of *shirk* encompass the extreme and obvious— such as praying before an idol—but also the everyday and mundane, such as swearing on your mother's life rather than God's name, or believing that paracetamol, rather than God, was responsible for curing a nasty headache. Calling Muslims—as well as non-Muslims—to *tawhid* is therefore paramount. In establishing *tawhid* and removing *shirk*, Salafis believe they are following in the footsteps of all of Islam's prophets.

As they obey their call to enjoin good and forbid evil (*al-amr bi-l-ma'ruf wa-l-nahy 'an al-munkar*), such as *bid'a* and *shirk*, Salafis must abstain from organized forms of political activity (for example, demonstrations and involvement in political parties) and show respect for the law of the land and its rulers. This is because as UK residents, Salafis claim they have made a 'contract' with Britain that is akin to the treaties the Prophet made with non-Muslim tribes. Since the Prophet respected these treaties, so must the present-day Muslim. The exception is theoretically in cases where obedience to a law would require disobedience to God, but in practice Salafis are often pragmatic. For example, during my fieldwork, a Salafi teacher told her students to obey the law with regard to taking out car insurance even though this entails disobedience to God because 'you can't help it, because you'd go to prison'.

Nonetheless, cordial and peaceful relations with non-Muslims should not extend to approval of their un-Islamic ways. The doctrine of *al-wala' wa-l-bara'* (loyalty and disavowal) states that Muslims should show loyalty to God, Islam, and fellow Muslims, while rejecting everything else (Wagemakers, 2009, p.81). Salafi scholars have interpreted this as condoning hatred of, and forbidding friendship with, non-Muslims—though they prescribe good treatment of non-believers (mainly because this might encourage them to convert, but also because of a common humanity).[16]

This hardline view can be found in many staple Salafi texts that are taught in UK Salafi circles, but the teachers and speakers I observed propagated it only occasionally and usually only in a qualified and softened form. They knew that many of their students had non-Muslim families and friends, and that isolating oneself from non-believers in a Western society was highly impractical, if not impossible.

Most, but not all, clarified that the prescription to hate non-Muslims was confined to hating their disbelief, rather than to hating them as people in general. For example, one teacher, Umm Mustafe, told her students to hate non-believers 'in moderation':

> When we hate disbelievers, it's not just for the sake of hating them. And it doesn't make you hate the person itself, but the action. Otherwise you're doing great injustice to mankind, like the *khawarij*,[17] who do this to justify blowing up buses. They aren't doing it for Allah's sake. When we love and hate for Allah's sake, we must do so in the way Allah wanted . . . . So we love and hate in moderation because the *Rasul* [Messenger, i.e., the Prophet] told us to . . . . That person you hate, you may have to love them some day and it will be hard to love them one day [if you hate them too much]. This also makes it harder to forgive people—and Islam is a religion of forgiveness. You can hate the *shirk* they invoke while wanting good for that person. And likewise if that person you love becomes your enemy one day, it's gonna be hard to let go of that love one day.*

Some teachers urged their students to avoid socializing with non-Muslims because they might influence them to return to the 'bad habits' they had left behind, such as listening to music and celebrating birthdays. But they gave the same warning about mixing with non-Salafi Muslims, who might tempt Salafis to engage in *bid'a*, claiming such practices are Islamic. They also told their students to treat non-Muslims with kindness and good manners.

While some of the older Salafis, who became Salafis during the 1990s, endorsed the hardline view, I found that the younger women generally favoured a 'hate the sin, not the sinner' approach. Some had left their non-Muslim friends behind after becoming Salafis but, like Fiore Geelhoed's (2014, p.64) Islamic fundamentalist respondents in the Netherlands, they did not consider non-Muslims to be basically bad people. Others had close friendships with non-Muslims, and some even had more non-Muslim friends than Muslim ones.

The Salafi *manhaj* (programme of action, way) is partly doctrinally based, partly pragmatic. The doctrinal element is based in part on analogies with the Prophet's life. Salafis claim, for instance, that he never endorsed demonstrations or political parties. They also compare the present to the Meccan period of his life, during which he relied on peaceful, proselytizing methods to spread his message. This contrasts with most Islamic political theory, which is based on the later Medinan period, when the Prophet founded an Islamic polity (Salomon, 2009, p.165).

The pragmatic element is perhaps best explained by the following story, related to me by a Salafi leader who had heard it from an Egyptian shaykh. It illustrates well how Salafis perceive their own *manhaj*, in contrast to those of other groups.

> There was this river, pure flowing river, and this small community set up by this river and they're drinking from it, taking the water for their food and suchlike. And then they become lazy and sloppy, and they start throwing pollutants into the river, basically just defiling the river as it were, and they become ill because every time they drink from the river, it's contaminated.
>
> So what then happened is they were conquered by their enemies ... Another community came and overran them and subjugated them, so they started looking at what's our problem, what did we do wrong? So one group said: 'We need to build a hospital so that when we get sick, we can be treated.' Another group said: 'No, we need to overthrow the enemy and destroy them completely, and then we'll get back to our former strength.' The third group said: 'That's wrong, what we need to do is we need to stop polluting the water and we need to clean up the water again, because that was a source of our strength, and now that we've polluted it, it's become a source of our weakness.'

Here, the groups are said to represent the Islamist group the Muslim Brotherhood, the Jihadis, and the Salafis, respectively. Salafis thus believe that until core Muslim beliefs and practices are 'decontaminated', political activism and jihad are doomed.

The Arab Spring began during my fieldwork in 2011, and the Salafis' reaction (or lack of one) provides a more concrete example. Within these networks, I could find no preacher, lay person, or written text denouncing the dictatorial regimes of the Middle East, let alone urging Muslims to take action to overthrow them. These Salafis generally avoided the subject of the uprisings, but if they spoke of them at all, they claimed they were doomed to end in further bloodshed and instability, or *fitna* (trials, tribulations). They disassociated themselves entirely from political groups in the Arab world who called themselves Salafis yet engaged with newly established parliamentary democracies, such as Al-Nour Party in Egypt.[18]

That is not to say that Salafis are pacifists. Many British Salafis regarded the first Gulf War (1990–1991), for example, as a legitimate jihad. But for Salafis, physical jihad must meet strict conditions. It must be declared by a 'legitimate' Muslim ruler, who is recognized by the local tribal leaders and the Salafi 'ulama (Islamic scholars), and it cannot violate an existing peace treaty. And once engaged in war, Muslims have to abide by certain rules: for example, they are forbidden from attacking non-combatants and carrying out suicide operations.

In their mission to inculcate themselves and those around them with 'correct' Islamic beliefs and practices, Salafis claim to be guided by two supreme sources of knowledge: the Qur'an and the sunna (the 'authentic' speech, actions, silent approval, and characteristics of the Prophet). They regard these sources as comprehensive and self-explanatory (Wiktorowicz, 2006, p.210), so they try to draw on them as literally (or, more accurately, deferentially)[19] and exclusively as possible.[20] Reason and logic have (in theory) no place in this process; the Qur'an and sunna are pure and perfect and thus can only be corrupted by any attempt to 'bash them with your brains,' as one preacher put it at a Salafi conference I attended in 2011.

During that conference, I realized just how concerned—even obsessed—Salafis were about keeping their body of knowledge uncontaminated by the intellect. I was at one of the bookstalls, and a title called *The Crime of Hizbiyyah* [i.e. partisanship] *against the Salafi Dawah* caught my eye. 'What's *hizbiyyah*?' I asked the young woman behind the stall. It was clear that she knew the answer, as she immediately started to answer in a confident voice. But then she stopped abruptly mid-sentence and picked up the book. After locating the definition, she read aloud, 'in case I get it wrong'. For her, even such an apparently simple exercise as giving the definition of an Arabic term ran the risk of polluting the 'pure' sources with human opinion. This helps to explain the literalism for which Salafis are notorious.

For Salafis, the Qur'an and sunna deserve such vigilant protection because they are infallible revelation (*wahy*) from God. By placing the sunna—the example of the Prophet, which for Salafis is articulated in the 'authenticated'[21] hadith corpus (reports of the Prophet's sayings and actions)—on a par with the Qur'an in this way, Salafis distinguish themselves from many other Muslims who regard only the Qur'an as revelation.

Since the sunna is *wahy*, it takes precedence over all other sources, apart from the Qur'an. This includes the traditional Sunni sources of Islamic law. Consequently, Salafis tend to reject the mainstream Sunni principle of *taqlid*—that the Muslim should automatically follow the verdicts of one of the orthodox schools of jurisprudence, or *madhahib* (sing., *madhhab*). There are four: the Hanafi, Shafi'i, Maliki, and Hanbali schools. They are named after the scholars who established them and who lived during the first two-and-a-half centuries of Islam. For Salafis, the sunna can override *madhhab* rulings, but the schools are considered as valuable sources of guidance, particularly as their founders were among the *salaf* (revered ancestors). The Islamic understanding and behaviour of the *salaf*, Salafis claim, can help illuminate the Qur'an and sunna because of the ancestors' proximity in time to the 'revelations' and their status in Islam as exemplary Muslims. Salafis cite a hadith in which the Prophet reportedly called them 'the best of mankind' (Bukhari 50:832).

Many Salafis are fond of summing up their approach to Islam as 'Qur'an, sunna, example of the *salaf*—and nothing else,' stressing the purity of their belief system and its freedom from human opinion and *bid'a*. But of course, these three sources do not provide unambiguous guidance on all matters. Even the most explicit Qur'anic verses and sayings of the Prophet and *salaf* cannot necessarily be easily transposed to twenty-first-century issues (Wiktorowicz, 2006, pp.214–215). Wiktorowicz (2006, p.214) gives the example of the Qur'anic prohibition on usury (Qur'an 2:275–80, 282; 3:130; 4:161). The ban itself is 'extremely explicit', but

> what does usury look like in the modern context, given the complexities of a globalized, capitalist economy? Does it include a home mortgage, car loans, or credit cards? Is it determined by the amount of interest?

Consequently, scholars ('ulama) with years of training are charged with deciphering the guidance of the Qur'an and sunna and extracting rules for everyday life. These individuals include the officially recognized 'ulama of Saudi Arabia, as well as others (based in the Gulf, Egypt, Morocco, India, and elsewhere). Probably the four best-known Salafi scholars of the contemporary era all died within three years of one another: 'Abd al-'Aziz ibn Baz (1910–1999), the former grand mufti of Saudi Arabia; Muhammad Nasir al-Din al-Albani (1914–1999), the Albanian-Syrian hadith scholar; Muqbil ibn Hadi al-Wadi'i (1933–2001), considered the founder of Salafism in Yemen; and the Saudi scholar Muhammad ibn Salih al-Uthaymin (1925–2001).

A particularly influential living scholar is Rabi' al-Madkhali (b. 1931), who is well known for his loyalty to the Saudi regime and controversial work in refuting 'deviants' (Meijer, 2011). Today, critics often label the most quietist Salafi groups 'Madkhalis' to highlight their supposed 'excessive' tolerance of 'corrupt' rulers, as well as their habit of 'refuting' Muslims with different views.

There are no 'ulama in the United Kingdom, but many of their students serve as lower-ranking preachers there. These mostly British-born preachers rely on the elite scholars' deliberations (*ijtihad*) to guide their congregations, and they maintain close contact with their superiors abroad in order to preserve the chain of 'authentication' (see chapter 4.2).

An immediate problem arises: What happens when scholars study a particular Qur'anic verse or saying of the Prophet, and arrive at different conclusions about its meaning? For example, some scholars have concluded that wearing the *niqab* is obligatory for women, while others deem it merely recommended. Which opinion should the ordinary believer follow? In these situations, the individual Salafi is responsible for researching the issue herself—she cannot simply pick the most convenient opinion, or follow her favourite scholar blindly. Upon investigation of the various scholarly opinions, she must favour the ruling that seems best supported by the Qur'an and sunna. She is excused from this duty if she is unable to access or understand the scriptural proofs, but this exemption is in practice difficult to justify in a community of educated young people with Internet access and mobile phones. Today, British Salafis can easily call or email English-speaking preachers who were taught by scholars abroad to ask for textual proofs for specific rulings. They can then 'verify' these with a few mouse clicks or smart-phone taps, thanks to the translation and digitization of the scriptures.

During my fieldwork, teachers encouraged women to approach knowledge-seeking as an individual duty (see chapter 4), and this included a responsibility to make educated judgments between different scholarly opinions. For example, one teacher, Layla, told her audience:

> There are many grey areas in the *din* [religion]—meaning discussion among the 'ulama—so therefore you need to do extra research to discover the majority opinion. If you take the first shaykh you come across, if you take his opinion, you're accountable because you didn't do your research properly.*

Here lies an inherent contradiction within Salafism: on the one hand, it purports to offer unambiguous, authentic guidance on all matters, based on the sacred texts, which minimizes the role of human interpretation. On the other, it relies on the fallible reasoning of scholars—and, to a lesser extent, ordinary believers—to address the countless grey areas. This aspect of Salafism has made Salafi groups vulnerable to fragmentation (Wiktorowicz, 2006, p.208), but has also been considered crucial to its appeal in the modern era. Academics have argued that the modern, literate worshipper is empowered by the opportunity to approach the sacred texts directly, liberating her from dependence on the interpretations of a scholarly elite (Al-Rasheed, 2007, p.4; Martensson, 2012, p.117). She is aided in this endeavour by the translation and digitization of the scriptures, as well as opportunities to engage in 'Islamic argumentation' through online forums (Becker, 2009).

Salafis respond that the apparent contradiction vanishes upon consideration of the scholars' elevated status, as stated in the Qur'anic verse 58:11. According to Salafis, the scholars continue the Prophet's mission by preserving and propagating religious knowledge (Wiktorowicz, 2006, p.212). Their status is such that God rewards them even when they are mistaken on a particular matter (albeit less than if they had been right). Moreover, Salafis argue that the Qur'an itself tells believers to seek guidance from scholars (Qur'an 21:7), so it must be good to do so.

0.2 ACADEMIC WORK ON SALAFISM IN EUROPE

Salafism has had a high profile in the European media and politics since 9/11, but academia only started to catch up over the last decade.[22] Scholarly studies have addressed a variety of subjects, but most concentrate on men, security issues, internal politics, doctrine, and texts—not the everyday, lived Salafism of its female adherents,[23] nor the group's ethnic dimensions, which are addressed in this book.

Some Europe-based studies of Salafism have included interviews with women, many of whom were more politically minded Salafis than the ones who participated in this research. These studies are mainly based in the Netherlands (De Koning, 2009, 2012b, 2013a, 2013b; Roex, 2014), Denmark (Kühle and Lindekilde, 2010), France (Baylocq and Drici-Bechikh, 2012), and Germany (Özyürek, 2015). Yafa Shanneik (2011, 2012) has also studied female Catholic converts to Salafism in Ireland.

However, the only publications that have paid attention specifically to Salafi women in the United Kingdom are an insider, non-academic account by Na'ima B. Robert (2005) and Geelhoed's (2014) study of both male and female Muslim fundamentalists in the Netherlands and Britain. The latter's research did not focus on group contexts outside of the mosque, and concentrated mainly on Dutch Muslims as it was based on only a brief period of fieldwork in Britain.[24]

There is also a significant body of literature on Muslim women in the West in general,[25] particularly converts, but this research has often focused on cognitive aspects—such as hermeneutical differences in the Western context—rather than the implications of Islamic beliefs in daily life.

The lack of close-focus studies of Salafi women is probably due to difficulties of access. In groups in which male leaders are the principal authorities and women gather in more private, segregated spaces, it is harder to obtain information about women's ideas and experiences than those of men (Silvestri, 2012, p.122). Salafi women in the West, like women from other fundamentalist traditions (Brasher, 1998, p.86), generally do not produce concrete artefacts such as books and recorded lectures that can be readily analyzed. Moreover, most UK researchers have been men, who could not gain full access to Salafi women's gatherings nor—I suspect—persuade devout women to speak to them openly on personal matters.

The political climate and focus on men has meant that many researchers have analysed Salafism through a security lens, examining its relationship with violent extremism.[26] This literature has been criticized for its narrow remit and close ties to government policy and related political, security, and sectarian agendas, and the theoretical and methodological issues it therefore poses (Sedgwick, 2010; Shterin and Yarlykapov, 2011, pp.303–304). For the above reasons, the information currently available on Salafi communities in the United Kingdom—and to some extent, the rest of Europe—is limited in breadth.

Studies have also charted the development of Salafism in Britain at the organizational level—specifically, how it spread and then divided due to bitter disputes and rifts among (male) leaders[27]—but have given little or no insight into the role of women in this trajectory. We know about the appeal of Salafi teachings in general, but not how these teachings have been interpreted and propagated by female leaders—whose existence is rarely acknowledged—nor how they appeal to or are absorbed and implemented by ordinary Salafi women.

During fieldwork in London, I seldom witnessed conversations about intra-Salafi rivalries and the associated theological debates. Although the women were not unaffected by them, they were far more concerned about how to negotiate strict Salafi teachings that directly impacted on their daily lives. Their pressing issues included obtaining a 'halal' (Islamically permissible) job, justifying going to university, pacifying anti-Salafi relatives, finding a good Salafi husband, and dealing with constant Islamophobic abuse on the street.

Another area that has received remarkably little scholarly attention in the United Kingdom is Salafism's ethnic dimensions—namely, the disproportionately Somali and Afro-Caribbean face of British Salafism, which was highlighted by Jonathan Birt in 2005 yet has never, to my knowledge, been investigated.[28] Asians, mainly South Asians, make up two-thirds of the Muslim population of England and Wales (Census, 2011), and consequently receive the bulk of attention in academic studies. There has also been a tendency among some scholars, journalists, and Islamic activists alike to downplay or ignore Muslim ethnic diversity by homogenizing Muslims as a universal, undivided, global *umma* (Muslim community). This assumption is symptomatic of the politicization of the 'Muslim' identity in the late 1980s, which triggered a shift in British discourse on minorities from race and ethnicity to religion. But in reality, ethnic differences have remained crucial to how British Muslims organize their lives (Peach, 2006).

A significant and growing number of young black people—mostly of Afro-Caribbean Christian backgrounds—have embraced Islam since the 1990s.[29] Yet black converts have not been the subject of much detailed academic research, despite the considerable body of literature on converts to Islam.[30]

Similarly, Somalis have received little academic attention, despite being the most widely documented refugee group in Britain, as the vast majority of coverage has comprised media reports and 'grey' literature (Rutter, 2006, pp.178–179). This literature is largely problem-oriented, aimed at securing resources for a community facing a host of socioeconomic issues (Open Society Foundation, 2014).

Somalis have usually been subsumed within either the 'Black African' or more general 'British Muslim' category, despite their distinct cultural and religious practices (Holman and Holman, 2003). Consequently, little is known about the religious dynamics of the community, though some authors have suggested that young Somalis are turning to highly conservative forms of Islam (Rutter, 2006, p.183). Exceptions include work by Camillia Fawzi El-Solh (1991, 1993) and McGown (1999), but their data predate the growing influence of Salafism among young Somalis in the United Kingdom since the late 1990s.

Studies of Salafism in Europe have offered explanations for the attraction of Salafism among young Muslims in general.[31] These studies stress Salafism's direct approach to the holy texts, unmediated by parents or religious leaders, plus its use of highly conspicuous identity markers, such as distinctive clothing and the use of Arabic terms in everyday conversation. They thus show how Salafism provides an empowering identity, particularly to young, new-generation Muslims, many of whom have felt alienated, rootless, even disaffected, due to being 'torn between two cultures'. Some authors have also portrayed Salafism as a response to the failure of political Islam, representing a new phase of re-Islamization where spiritual reformation of the individual trumps political participation (Adraoui, 2009; Amghar, 2007; Kepel, 1994; Roy, 2004).

Such accounts have raised important points, but it is not always sufficiently clear why young women (and men) today choose Salafism in particular from among the many other Islamic interpretations to which they are exposed in Western societies. After all, many (perhaps most) other groups require their adherents to make fewer sacrifices and take fewer risks. Salafis' strong identity markers, constant referencing of the scriptures, and claim to represent 'pure' Islam are features they share with many other Islamic trends in Britain, from Islamists to modern Sufis (Hamid, 2009, pp.396–397). Today, young Muslims across the spectrum of groups pepper their conversations with Arabic expressions, and female adherents of Al-Muhajiroun and other Islamist groups now favour black *jilbab*s and *niqab*s—the attire of Salafi women. Salafis, moreover, hold no special distinction in identifying with the aforementioned cultural, political, and identity-related grievances—these are shared by many others for whom Salafi teachings hold no appeal.

There has also been too much emphasis in some of the academic literature on alienation and disaffection as explanatory factors. This risks pathologizing Salafis and painting an inaccurate picture of passive victims of cultural, political, and (Saudi or Gulf) transnational processes, rather than portraying adherents as independent, rational agents. Scholars of Islamic fundamentalism (Marranci, 2009; Wiktorowicz, 2004a, 2005a) have criticized commentators' tendency to explore it through the prism of socio-psychological deprivation because it often leads to overgeneralizing and insufficient attention to the 'purposive, political, and organized dimensions' of groups (Wiktorowicz, 2004a, p.9).[32]

In this politicized context, such approaches also pave the way for shifts towards versions of the 'brainwashing thesis'. This was the anti-cult movement's[33] explanation for the popularity of New Religious Movements (NRMs) during the 1970s and 1980s.[34] However, as Marc Sageman (2004, p.125) says, 'five decades of research have failed to provide any empirical support for this thesis',[35] including his own research on contemporary Jihadism. Nonetheless, since 9/11, the thesis has crept back into media and political discourse in more or less obvious guises (Dawson, 2010, pp.2–3). This narrative paints participants in NRMs as vulnerable, possibly naïve, victims who are exploited by cunning leaders. 'Brainwashing' supposedly involves suspending the 'victim's' free will (Barker, 1984, p.122). A version of this narrative is implicit in the speeches on Islamic extremism of recent British home secretaries and prime ministers, in which they typically refer to the problem as an extreme 'ideology' or 'doctrine' propagated by 'ideologues' or 'hate preachers' who exploit the 'vulnerable'.

This book draws on literature beyond Salafism and even Islam in order to understand the conversion dynamics of Salafi women in the context of wider trends in contemporary religion. Such literature includes work in the sociology and anthropology of religion on conversion theory as well as studies of women in conservative or fundamentalist religious groups. I have also been inspired by the NRMs literature, and therefore join scholars such as Kühle and Lindekilde (2010), Dawson (2010), Sedgwick (2007), and Shterin and Yarlykapov (2011),[36] who believe that comparisons with new religions or 'cults' from other traditions can help illuminate certain new Muslim groups. The extensive NRMs literature reveals that these groups are commonly associated with particular characteristics. Eileen Barker (1995) discerns the following patterns: small group size, atypical representation of population, first-generation membership, charismatic leaders, new belief systems, emphasis on 'them/us' divides, and subjection to external hostility. All seven characteristics can be recognized to some extent in Salafi groups.

Drawing upon such a wide range of research has thus enabled me to identify wider trends in the phenomenon of religious conversion and in the relationship between conservative religion and gender, as well as to avoid the common tendency to exceptionalize Salafism, or indeed Islam.

0.3 THE BOOK

Chapter 1 chronicles the rise of Salafism in Britain. It begins with an account of the historical origins of Salafism, before examining how it spread to the United Kingdom and took shape there. I highlight the key turning points, trends, individuals, and organizations concerned, as well as what we know about the size and ethnic composition of the Salafi community today. I also introduce my principal case study, Brixton Mosque, an early example of how Salafism took root in the United Kingdom—in this case, among a predominantly black convert community.

In chapter 2, I explain my research methods—a combination of participant observation, semi-structured interviews, and textual analysis—and give an account of my fieldwork in London. I recount the sometimes rewarding, sometimes tense and obstacle-ridden process of gaining access, building trust, and constantly trying to negotiate a balance between neutral detachment and empathetic involvement in the life of the community.

Chapter 3 gives a detailed account of my interviewees' journeys into Salafism. I explain how, having experienced a spiritual awakening, women decided to investigate and experiment with various groups on the 'Islam market', as I call it. Gradually, they identified Salafism as the one 'correct' approach to Islam, despite often initially resisting it due to the group's 'image problem'. The conversion narratives reveal diverse ethnic and religious backgrounds and no uniform or linear pattern.

As already mentioned, conversion continues with the process of commitment. The following chapters explore the continuing effects—in families, universities, workplaces, Salafi environments, and romantic lives—of the initial steps the women took to adopt a Salafi identity and become part of a Salafi community.

Chapter 4 explains how Salafi teachers employed 'circles of knowledge'—informal study groups, lessons, lectures, and conferences—to foster commitment. I examine how teachers acquired authority and elicited loyalty from students, above all by skilled employment of the Qur'an and sunna and 'boundary maintenance'—that is, guarding the boundaries between Salafis and rival Muslim groups by emphasizing their differences. Teachers also established a framework for action that was supported by a powerful discourse of reward and punishment in the afterlife, thereby demonstrating that conformity was a matter of self-interest.

These gatherings also fostered a sense of belonging, supported by a 'sisterhood' discourse and shared etiquette, language, and dress. This chapter shifts the focus from the individual to the group and its leaders in order to illuminate how institutional contexts shaped the women's conversion processes.

As women sacrificed time, energy, money, relationships, and old habits, substituting prohibited practices and relationships for new ones, they increased their investment in their decision to embrace Salafism. Chapters 5 and 6 investigate how young Salafi women tried to implement the teachings they had learned in circles of knowledge in their lives, with varying degrees of success. I describe in detail how they navigated the thorny areas of (internal) community relations and match-making, as well as (external) familial relationships, higher education, and employment as they deepened their commitment. These chapters demonstrate how necessity forced a negotiation of theory and practice, as the women's social realities clashed with Salafi ideals.

While compromise was often necessary, the women seldom disputed the legitimacy of the teachings themselves. Chapter 6 uses the example of match-making to illuminate how the women persevered with apparently impractical and risky religious practices in the belief that only by following a divinely sanctioned 'manual' could they avoid the uncertainties that attend modern-day relationships.

Finally, I summarize this study's main conclusions and consider the likely future course of Salafism in the United Kingdom at a time of heightened political sensitivity.

CHAPTER 1

✧

The Development of Salafism in Britain

Salafism is often mistakenly assumed to be a purely modern phenomenon, or else equated with the pre-modern Wahhabi movement in eighteenth-century Arabia. Its origins, however, are more complex. This chapter begins with a brief historical account—from the early Islamic period through to Saudi Arabia's extensive propagative activities from the 1970s onwards, which facilitated the spread of Salafism to Britain and many other countries.[1]

The methodology, beliefs, and practices that characterize contemporary Salafism can be traced back to the time of the early Islamic jurist, Ahmad Ibn Hanbal (780–855 C.E.); they were also shaped by other early scholars, most notably the medieval jurist Taqi al-Din ibn Taymiyya (1263–1328). Ibn Taymiyya's impressive oeuvre can be interpreted as an attempt to purify Islamic doctrine in the wake of the major theological debates of his time (Haykel, 2009, pp.39–40).[2]

Ibn Taymiyya had a profound influence on the pre-modern scholar Muhammad ibn 'Abd al-Wahhab (1703–1792), who was from central Arabia (in today's Saudi Arabia). He believed that Muslims must return to the rigid monotheism (*tawhid*) and pristine purity of the Qur'an and sunna in order to revive the glory of Islam's beginnings. Ibn 'Abd al-Wahhab therefore regarded it as his mission to introduce a strict version of shari'a and stamp out *bid'a* (reprehensible innovation), particularly acts of worship that placed intermediaries between God and human beings, such as the veneration of tombs and trees. To do this, he needed political support.

In 1744 he formed an alliance with the tribal chief Amir Muhammad ibn al-Sa'ud, leading to the establishment of the first Saudi state. According to Madawi Al-Rasheed (2007, p.2), 'This state expanded in Arabia under the pretext of purifying faith from innovation and applying Islamic law.' Today, the state is still supported by a Wahhabi clerical establishment, which maintains considerable authority in the social sphere in exchange for its political subservience (Al-Rasheed, 2007, pp.2–4). The socially conservative, anti-rationalist interpretation they promote has become known as 'Wahhabism'—though most proponents reject this terminology—and is the dominant official religious discourse of Saudi Arabia.[3] Wahhabism became more visible both at home and abroad from the 1970s, thanks to the kingdom's new oil wealth, which funded *da'wa*-related (i.e., propagative) activities in many countries, including the United Kingdom.

Many commentators wrongly assume that the emergence of Salafi communities and organizations in Britain, among other Western countries, is simply a product of Saudi funding and influence; hence the terms 'Salafism' and 'Wahhabism' are often thought to be synonymous with one another. However, Salafis rarely use the label 'Wahhabi' as they regard it as a pejorative term. It is often used by theological opponents to signify foreign (namely, Saudi) influence, given its suggestion that Salafis follow 'Abd al-Wahhab (Wiktorowicz, 2006, p.235). The label has also become shorthand for fundamentalism or even 'dangerous' extremism in sections of the Western media. There are also significant differences between Salafism and Wahhabism, mainly with regard to *fiqh* (jurisprudence). While Wahhabism relies heavily on the Hanbali school of jurisprudence, Salafism places more emphasis on *ijtihad* (independent reasoning) in its mission to abstain from *taqlid*, or following a Sunni school of law exclusively and uncritically (Haykel, 2009, p.42).

Indeed, contemporary Salafism in the United Kingdom—as well as in some Muslim-majority and other Western countries (Lacroix, 2009, pp.77–78)— is dominated by a fervently anti-*taqlid* orientation that reveals the major influence of another trend, the *la madhhabiyya* ('non-schoolist') theology, propelled by the Yemeni scholar Muhammad al-Shawkani (1760–1834).[4] He called for scholars to consult the Qur'an and hadith corpus directly in order to derive rulings, rather than practising *taqlid* (Haykel, 2003). Muslims, he insisted, should know the textual proofs underpinning the Islamic opinions they follow.

The influence of *la madhhabiyya* ideas on contemporary Salafism owes much to the Albanian scholar Muhammad Nasir al-Din al-Albani (d. 1999), who was committed to Al-Shawkani's views on *taqlid*. He rejected the traditional Sunni view that Muslims should automatically turn to a *madhhab* for *fiqh* rulings. Instead, he encouraged a renewal of *ijtihad* (independent reasoning) via a critical re-evaluation of the hadith corpus (Lacroix, 2009). By subjecting hadiths to rigorous authenticity checks, he concluded that numerous previously accepted hadiths were, in fact, unsound. This led him to produce rulings that were at odds with both the Islamic scholarly majority and the Wahhabi-Hanbali religious establishment (Griffel, 2015, p.209; Lacroix, 2008).

Despite this, he was undoubtedly Wahhabi in creed and a formidable op-
ponent of the Saudis' Islamist adversaries. He was therefore offered teaching posts at the Islamic University of Madinah, where his ideas have had a
lasting influence (Lacroix, 2009, pp.77–78). Here, scholars teach from comparative *fiqh* textbooks that give the rulings of all four *madhahib*, rather than
just those of the Hanbali school, which they weigh up with reference to evidence from the Qur'an and sunna.[5] Given the university's prominent role in
exporting Salafism abroad (see chapter 1.1), including to Britain, it is not
surprising that Salafism has taken on this anti-*taqlid* orientation in many
countries. Also influencing the shape of British Salafism in this regard was
the fact that some of Al-Albani's Jordanian students regularly toured the
United Kingdom to give lectures during the 1990s.

Contemporary manifestations of Salafism are sometimes mistak-
enly linked to the late-nineteenth-century Islamic modernist movement
initiated by the reformists Jamal al-Din al-Afghani (1838–1897) and
Muhammad 'Abduh (d. 1905). Some scholars have called this movement
'Salafi', but there is no proof that these men used Salafi labels or regarded
Salafiyya (i.e., Salafism) as a distinct intellectual entity (Lauzière, 2010).[6]
Despite the fact that these men, like contemporary Salafis, sought to return
to the ways of *al-salaf al-salih* (the pious predecessors), they differed on the
matter of who these ancestors were and what they stood for (Griffel, 2015,
p.215). Thus, the movement with which they are credited—which was influenced by the European Enlightenment and associated with a programme
to modernize Muslim societies—should not be confused with conservative,
literalist, present-day Salafism.[7]

1.1 THE DEVELOPMENT OF SALAFISM IN BRITAIN

Salafism in Britain is a new-generation phenomenon; it did not emerge among
the first generation of Muslim migrants, most of whom settled there after
World War II in response to the rising demand for cheap labour.[8] The first generation of Muslims to have been brought up in Britain came of age during the
1980s. Fluent in English, educated in Britain, and familiar with its culture,
these young people tended to reject their elders' community-oriented, custom-
based approach to religion that was rooted in their countries of origin. For
those inclined towards Islam, an English-language version stripped of the 'cultural accretions' that preoccupied the elder generation was more appealing.

The Rushdie Affair (1989),[9] the Gulf War (1990–1991), and the Bosnian
War (1992–1995) helped to create a fertile ground for the emergence of this
new form of Muslim religiosity and its expression in Islamic activist groups,
including Salafi ones. The Muslim protests that followed the Rushdie Affair
transformed Islam into a public identity marker, no longer subsumed under

'black' politics and transcending ethnic and cultural barriers. The Gulf and Bosnian crises contributed to bitterness towards the West and a sense of vulnerability (Hasan, 2014, p.6), and were accompanied by an upsurge in Islamic activism throughout Britain (Siddiqui, 2004, p.53).

Islamic reform movements took root in Britain—notably, the Salafi group JIMAS (Jam'iat Ihyaa' Minhaaj Al-Sunnah, or the Society to Revive the Way of the Messenger); Hizb ut-Tahrir Britain;[10] and Young Muslims, which was inspired by the Jama'at-i Islami.[11] According to Sadek Hamid (2009, p.391), young Muslims were attracted to these organizations by 'opportunities to develop an Islamic identity and create communities of shared meaning and alternative religious practice structured by intergenerational change and rebellion against the Islam of their parents.'[12]

The JIMAS group was established in 1984, and can be credited with spreading Salafism and popularizing it among young people in the United Kingdom.[13] This was in large part thanks to the efforts of its founder, Abu Muntasir (aka Manwar Ali), a computer science graduate from London, who preached the Salafi message at mosques, universities, and community centres up and down Britain. The son of a Deobandi[14] Bangladeshi scholar, Abu Muntasir was determined to spread a 'purer' Islam than the one he had been taught—namely, one shorn of 'cultural accretions' (Bowen, 2014, p.60).

The JIMAS group had a steady rise in membership up to the mid-1990s, and attracted individuals who later became prominent preachers on the British Salafi scene—such as Usama Hasan, Abdul Haqq Baker, Abu Sufyan (aka Abdul Kareem McDowell), Abu Khadeejah (aka Abdul Wahid), and Dawud Burbank. The latter learned Arabic while studying with senior Salafi scholars at Saudi Arabia's Islamic University of Madinah, and subsequently became a prolific translator of Arabic texts and scholars' lectures. He and another translator, Abu Iyaad Amjad, were instrumental in introducing core Salafi texts to young British Muslims. These works included *Explanation of the Creed* by Abu Muhammad Al-Hasani Al-Barbahari and *Explanation of the Three Fundamental Principles of Islaam* by Shaykh Al-Uthaymin.

The back-to-basics Salafi message, strictly rooted in the Qur'an and sunna, was relatively new at that time, and particularly appealed to young Muslims from the main South Asian sects: the Barelwis[15] and the Deobandis (Birt, 2005, p.174). While reading the Qur'an was familiar to them, *understanding* its meaning in English—let alone using hadiths to interpret verses—was, in the words of one former JIMAS member, 'completely unheard of' to these young sons and daughters of Indian, Pakistani, and Bangladeshi immigrants. Abu Khadeejah recalled:[16]

> When we as Salafis started saying to the people that this speech of the Prophet Muhammad is found in Bukhari or Muslim or Abu Dawud [i.e., hadith

collections], people would say: 'What's Bukhari? What's Muslim? What's Abu Dawud?' Because they'd never heard of it. . . . Barelwism, Deobandism and Tablighi Jamaat [i.e., a missionary offshoot of Deobandism]—they weren't credible in terms of opposition to us. . . . You're talking about a premier league team playing football against a local pub team. . . . For years, we were the lone voice out there that no one could defeat.

The credibility of JIMAS was also enhanced by its links to well-known scholars abroad, particularly in Saudi Arabia, the country of Islam's two holiest cities. Salafis have often idealized Saudi Arabia as a country in which Islam is practised in its 'pure' form, where respected 'ulama are the law-makers and a rigidly orthodox lifestyle is enforced—in contrast to the over-permissiveness of Western society (Adraoui, 2009, p.369). The kingdom's acquisition of enormous oil wealth since the 1960s was regarded by many as a divine reward, 'confirming' Saudi Arabia's conformity with 'true' Islam.

As mentioned earlier, Saudi Arabia's new prosperity had enabled it to launch a worldwide *da'wa* mission to promote the spread of Wahhabism, thereby reinforcing the state's own legitimacy, both at home and abroad (Al-Rasheed, 2005a; Birt, 2005; Hasan, 2007). Since 1975, the Saudi government has allocated an estimated two to three billion dollars per year for this purpose (Alexiev, 2002). The governments of and various non-governmental organizations (NGOs) in Kuwait and Qatar made similar outreach efforts.

Leaders of JIMAS, Brixton Mosque, and Salafi Publications have categorically stated that they have never received any Saudi or other foreign governmental or NGO funding.[17] So where did the money go, and to what extent did it shape the development of Salafism in Britain?

One well-known recipient of Saudi funding was the Muslim World League (established in 1962), a state-sponsored global organisation, which disseminated Saudi funds for *da'wa* purposes worldwide, including to Western institutions such as cultural centres and schools. The London Central Mosque in Westminster and the East London Mosque in Tower Hamlets were among the 1,500 mosques and 210 Islamic centres abroad wholly or partly financed by Saudi Arabia during the reign of King Fahd (1982–2005) (Bin Abdul Aziz, n.d.a.; Eade, 1996, p.219).

According to Birt (2007), much of the Saudi funding was 'pretty benign' as it was directed towards 'infrastructural projects' and included the mosques of sectarian rivals. However, Al-Rasheed (2005a, p.154) points out that these were the 'visible' projects that are mentioned in official Saudi publications. Evaluating funding directed towards 'less prestigious organizations' is much more difficult because, she says, such donations 'tend to be covert, as they pass through personal networks and connections, which people are reluctant to disclose'.

Saudi Arabia also financed the translation of Islamic publications into many languages (Wiktorowicz, 2001, p.125), and produced 138 million copies of the Qur'an in more than twenty languages between 1984 and 2000. These were then distributed 'through embassies, overseas information offices and Islamic organizations', and many found their way to Britain (Bin Abdul Aziz, n.d.b.). The Saudi English translation by Muhammad Taqi-ud-Din Al-Hilali and Muhammad Muhsin Khan, which some Muslim scholars have criticized for excessively conservative translations and interpretations,[18] is the version that Salafis in the United Kingdom favour.

Salafi organizations further benefitted from the stream of returning British graduates from Saudi Arabia's Islamic University of Madinah (established in 1961), which allocates around 85 percent of its places to non-Saudis (Birt, 2005, p.170) and gives them generous living allowances to study there (Madinastudent, n.d.). There can be no doubt that the proselytizing of these returning graduates was a powerful factor in the introduction of Salafi ideas to Britain, among other countries, such as the United States.[19] Although the university's British students 'gained a reputation for unreliability and laziness in their studies, with many failing to complete their degrees', hundreds are thought to have graduated from Madinah since the 1980s (Birt, 2005, p.171).[20] Many trained at the Faculty of Da'wah, where they learned how to preach the fundamentals of Islam (p.71).

One alumnus, Dawud Burbank, formed a breakaway group from JIMAS in 1996, which led to the establishment of one of the most visible and influential faces of British Salafism today: Salafi Publications (Birt, 2005, p.172).[21] Burbank and others, notably Abu Khadeejah, had grown concerned that other JIMAS members were compromising the Salafi *manhaj* (programme of action, way) and giving way to political and revolutionary Islamic ideologies. Having grown so quickly, JIMAS had attracted the attention of not only Salafi scholars and organizations abroad but also Jihadi groups that had emerged from the Soviet-Afghan War of the 1980s (Bowen, 2014, p.60). Jihadi voices, such as that of the Kashmiri group Lashkar-e-Taiba (LeT)—which was blamed for the 2008 Mumbai terror attacks—competed with political and pietistic ones for influence within JIMAS, each claiming that they were the true Salafis (pp.60–62).

This led to divisions within the British organization, especially after leaders of LeT were invited to the JIMAS annual conference in 1995, while the Bosnian War (1992–1995) was underway. They urged all able-bodied Muslims to join the jihad in Kashmir and Bosnia as a matter of religious obligation. It appears that pietistic factions within the audience forced them to retract their comments at the time, but already JIMAS members were growing concerned that the organization was undergoing an ideological shift. The JIMAS leader Abu Muntasir was himself a veteran mujahid of the Soviet-Afghan conflict, and his organization sent at least a hundred fighters to Bosnia, according to Usama Hasan (2014, p.9).

However, JIMAS's unity started to crumble in earnest when members became belatedly aware of the divisions among Salafi scholars in the Gulf over the Saudi regime's decision to permit the presence of US troops there during the Gulf War of 1990–1991. The then grand mufti of Saudi Arabia, Shaykh Bin Baz, had issued a fatwa (advisory opinion) in support of this decision, which was criticized by popular scholars, such as Shaykhs Safar al-Hawali and Salman al-'Awda (known as 'the Awakening Shaykhs'). While JIMAS shifted in favour of the latter camp, Burbank and his group, along with Brixton Mosque, remained staunch supporters of Bin Baz and other pietist scholars—and severed ties with JIMAS.

Burbank's faction formed the Organisation of Ahl al Sunna Islamic Societies (OASIS), before replacing it with Salafi Publications six months later, with Abu Khadeejah among the leadership. Their decision to incorporate the term 'Salafi' in the organization's title was significant: they felt that it was time to propagate openly under the Salafi banner, even if it put other Muslims off (Abu Khadeejah, 2013).

As its name suggests, Salafi Publications was established as a publishing house, but its remit has since grown. Today, Salafi Publications comprises a bookstore, publishing house, primary and secondary schools (both fee-paying), and two mosques in Birmingham, as well as a network of thirteen affiliated centres and organizations throughout England, including six in London. Salafi Publications lecturers regularly preach in the United Kingdom and abroad.

The organization has maintained an exclusivist Salafi stance in alignment with Saudi 'ulama. Indeed, Salafi Publications' rigid insistence on maintaining the 'purity' of Salafism, which they regard as the one 'saved sect' (see chapter 3.3), is manifest in its constant 'refutations' of 'deviant' groups and preachers and refusal to share platforms with individuals whose Salafi credentials it deems suspect. As a result, its adherents have become known by the derogatory label 'Super Salafis'. Meanwhile, JIMAS has reinvented itself as a non-sectarian Muslim educational charity that runs community projects for those of all faiths and none (JIMAS, 2015; JIMAS, n.d.).

The reactions of JIMAS and Salafi Publications to the terrorist attacks of 9/11 in the United States and of 7 July 2005 (7/7) in London highlighted their differences. With the spotlight on Salafism as a potentially violent ideology, Salafi Publications seized the opportunity to present publicly the mainstream, non-violent face of Salafism. Notably, they subsidized the translation and circulation of a 1998 fatwa by Bin Baz in which he denounced tactics used by Al-Qa'ida, such as suicide bombing, terrorism, and hijacking (Hamid, 2009, p.399; Vallely, 2007).

Meanwhile, JIMAS's leader Abu Muntasir unexpectedly broke down in tears and made a public apology at an event hosted by the City Circle, a network for Muslim professionals, a few days after the 7/7 bombings. Ten years later, following the rise of ISIS, he spoke on camera of his deep regret at having inspired and recruited many young Muslims to take part in jihad in Afghanistan, Kashmir, Burma, Bosnia, and Chechnya during the 1980s and 1990s (Jihad—A British Story, 2015). The JIMAS group has not promoted itself as a Salafi organization since at least 2006.[22] Usama Hasan, meanwhile, is no longer associated with JIMAS and works at the Quilliam Foundation, a UK-based counter-extremism think tank.

Attempts publicly to distance Salafism from terrorism should be seen in the context of rising suspicion in the West towards Salafis in the immediate aftermath of 9/11—no doubt related to the fact that fifteen of the nineteen hijackers were Saudis. This stance contrasted sharply with pre-9/11 Western attitudes towards Saudi Wahhabism. According to Al-Rasheed (2007, p.8), many Western scholars had appreciated it as a politically stabilizing force, despite reservations about its social conservatism.

Following 9/11, Western governments, journalists, think tanks, and academics scrutinized Salafism for possible links to violent extremism. The 9/11 Commission Report's verdict was damning: it actually lumped Wahhabism and 'Al-Qa'eda ideology' together, stating that they draw on the same 'long tradition of extreme intolerance within one stream of Islam', a position that 'can only be destroyed or utterly isolated' (2004, p.362).

In the United Kingdom, various events combined to intensify suspicion towards Salafi communities. First, it came to light that the 'hate preacher' Abdullah El Faisal,[23] 9/11 plotter Zacarias Moussaoui,[24] and 'shoe bomber' Richard Reid[25] had all been associated at some point with the Salafi mosque in Brixton, south London. However, the mosque denied it had played any role in their radicalization (see section 3, this chapter).

Then, in 2002 an armed passenger suspected of attempting to hijack a plane claimed he had been on his way to a Salafi Publications conference in Birmingham. At the time, Abu Khadeejah told journalists that Salafis were 'anti-terrorist, anti-fundamentalist', so the suspect either had 'no connection to us' or else 'was trying to harm someone at the conference' (Dodd, 2002). Following the London bombings of 2005, some commentators claimed the perpetrators had been Salafis, or that they had been 'Wahhabis' before becoming Jihadis (Gardham, 2011; Malik, 2007; Vallely, 2011).

Following the Channel 4 *Undercover Mosque* documentaries of 2007 and 2008 and the disputed Policy Exchange report, *The Hijacking of British Islam* (2007), public focus shifted to the socially conservative teachings propagated in UK Salafi communities. These undercover investigations shocked the British public by 'exposing' the intolerant and patriarchal teachings taught in Salafi groups and texts.

The UK veil controversies of 2006, 2010, 2011, and 2013 also highlighted deep public concern about the *niqab*. The first 'veil affair' was ignited by the MP Jack Straw when he wrote a column in the *Lancashire Telegraph* expressing his discomfort at meeting fully veiled constituents; the most recent came after a defendant named Rebekah Dawson refused to remove her *niqab* in court (Camber, 2013). Following each controversy, women who wore the face covering were portrayed in the media as religious fanatics or potentially dangerous extremists (Piela, 2014). Meanwhile, their own voices were almost totally absent from the public sphere (Zempi and Chakraborti, 2014, p.11). Photographs of fully veiled women—frequently sinister-looking, recycled stock images—became common, even when they had no direct relevance to the stories they accompanied.

The prevailing public perspective that was shaped during these years was that Salafism—though opposed to terrorism and Jihadism—fosters an intolerant, misogynist worldview that can fuel violent extremism. The predominance of this view, at least in political circles, was in large part due to the efforts of the counter-extremism think tank the Quilliam Foundation, which gained substantial government funding. It sent a secret (later leaked) list of 'Wahhabist-influenced groups and mosques' (among other groups) to the Home Office in 2010, suggesting that the government should be wary of working with them (Ali Musawi, 2010; Nawaz and Husain, 2010).

However, the notion of Salafis as contributory factors to Jihadi violence was complicated when it emerged that Salafi leaders had been proactive in *counter*-radicalization efforts. In fact, successive governments in the mid- to late 2000s had recognized Salafi expertise in this area by funding at least three Salafi-led organizations: STREET (Strategy to Reach Empower and Educate Teenagers) in Brixton, Inner City Guidance in Birmingham (Mercury, 2008), and IMPACT (Initiative for Muslim Progression and Advancement of Community Tolerance) in west London.[26]

In 2011 the newly formed Conservative-Liberal Coalition Government cut funding to various organizations it suspected of fostering so-called non-violent extremism—that is, not directly promoting violence, but allegedly propagating the ideology that fuelled violent extremism. The organizations STREET and IMPACT consequently lost their government funding. That same year, the former head of the Metropolitan Police's Muslim Contact Unit, Robert Lambert, and STREET director Abdul Haqq Baker each published books that detailed the counter-extremist activities of Salafis in Brixton.[27] They argued that Salafis, far from aiding the Jihadi cause, were the ones with the determination, expertise, and credibility to counter the influence of Jihadism among British Muslims. Theirs remains a minority view today.

1.2 BRIXTON MOSQUE: A HUB FOR BLACK CONVERTS IN SOUTH LONDON

One old Salafi base stands out for its longstanding involvement in counter-extremism work and its association with a black convert community: Brixton Mosque in Lambeth, south London, my principal fieldwork site. This is one of Britain's first Salafi mosques, as well as one of the first mosques in the country to be managed by converts.[28] Its success in attracting Afro-Caribbean converts led it to become known as 'the revert[29] mosque' and 'the Jamaican mosque'. Mosque records indicate that it oversaw more than 1,500 conversions of young people between 1997 and 2001 alone (Lambert, 2011, p.174). Even today, despite the estimated 100,000 converts in Britain (Brice, 2010), Brixton Mosque remains one of just six mosques in the United Kingdom (0.3 percent of the total) that has converts in charge (Naqshbandi, 2015).

The Brixton Mosque community can be traced back to around 1975, though it was not officially Salafi until around 1993. A group of West African and Afro-Caribbean Muslims—including converts and two University of Madinah graduates—started congregating in each other's homes in south-east London. Prominent among them were Shaykhs Saleh Jannah (Sierra Leonean imam and Madinah graduate), Abu Bakr (Jamaican), and Mohammad Kamaludin (Jamaican). At that time, there were few 'black' mosques—despite the fact that West African (especially Nigerian, Ghanaian, and Sierra Leonean) convert communities had been emerging in London since the 1970s. These founders had felt unwelcome and culturally alienated at their local South Asian and Arab mosques, and decided that the time had come to establish a 'black-friendly' Islamic space.

Kamaludin, who is now chairman of the mosque, recalled that these founders started 'calling the Afro Caribbean people to Islam, which led them to Brixton' (Kamaludin, 2015). There, they met one of the leaders of the Rastafarian community. They engaged him in discussion for more than three days, trying to convince him of Islam's truth, before he agreed that 'the Rasta religion was made up by man, and the Islamic Religion was based upon Revelation from God' (Kamaludin, 2015). He subsequently converted, adopted the name 'Omar', and offered his home in Stockwell Gardens, south London, as a base for the nascent community. According to Kamaludin (2015):

> From [Omar's] home the dawah spread to many brothers, sisters, and families who accepted Islam including his brother . . . and within the first five years there were about one hundred and twenty practicing Muslim families belonging to our community.

As the community grew, the self-appointed committee of elders moved their base to Omar's new, larger house in Bellefields Road, which could accommodate more than 150 worshippers. 'In those days,' writes Kamaludin, 'we were mainly concentrating on learning the basic fundamentals of Islam, the five daily prayers, Ramadan, Eid, and Da'wah to Tawheed' (Kamaludin, 2015).

In the mid-1980s, they established a monthly news magazine, an office in Brixton to deal with community affairs, and the first Muslim housing association in Britain, called 'Ash Shahada' (referring to the first pillar of Islam, the *shahada*, or profession of faith). When the association obtained its first property in Ferndale Road, the community moved their base there for a brief period, before moving again in 1990 to a council-owned community centre on nearby Gresham Road. The building, a Victorian villa, had been left derelict and was populated by squatters and drug dealers. This became the permanent site of the mosque.

Initially, even major sectarian differences were tolerated at the mosque and a strikingly broad spectrum of Muslims worshipped there, including Sunnis, Shias, Sufis, and even Nation of Islam[30] members. However, conflicts arose over certain issues, particularly the correct way to pray (Lambert, 2011, p.169). In 1992 the mosque banned Shias and Nation of Islam followers at the request of Salafi youth, who 'had become an integral part of the community' (Baker, 2011, p.24). Then, a year later, a Salafi leadership was elected, heralding the gradual establishment of a unified theology at the mosque (Baker, 2011, pp.26–27) that was influenced by scholars such Bin Baz, Al-Albani, Al-Wadi'i, and Al-Uthaymin. Throughout the 1990s, students of the great hadith scholar Al-Albani visited the mosque at least once a year.

One of the mosque's teachers, an African American convert named Sirat Abdul Malik, was particularly instrumental in introducing a 'purified' Islam—effectively Salafism, though he apparently never referred to it directly. He conducted classes at the mosque and in his own home, and arranged *'umra* (the lesser pilgrimage to Mecca) trips for Brixton Salafis between 1991 and 1993, which included opportunities to meet shaykhs (Masjid Ibnu Taymeeyah, 2012, p.40). Sirat also sold incense in Brixton that was produced at his factory in West Norwood, south London, and helped many fellow male Brixton worshippers to get into that trade, as well as helping with other employment, education, and marital issues (Masjid Ibnu Taymeeyah, 2012, p.40).

In 1994 his wife, 'A'ishah Abdul Malik, also an African American convert, cofounded Iqra Independent, a girls' school that was attached to the mosque and had a Salafi ethos. Its slogan was 'Training for this life . . . And the hereafter.' She was joined by three cofounders: Maryam, a white British convert; Naseem, a British-Pakistani; and Amatullah, a black British convert. At the time, Iqra had Salafi teachers who taught girls aged up to about fourteen, but it has since become a mixed, voluntary-aided primary school.

Umm Reemah, a woman who converted to Islam in the late 1980s and worshipped at the mosque from 1990 onwards, described the transition into Salafism on the women's side:

> We were just used to wearing hijab and civilian clothes, so to put on an abaya [women's robe-like dress] and then a *jilbab* and stuff, that for us, that was a bit of a—I think we did it in stages some of us; a few of us did it just [clicks fingers] like that.

She said that previously, the women had been given a small pink book explaining how to pray, while the men were given a blue one. However, after the mosque became Salafi, the women started to attribute this gendered prayer style to the Hanafi *madhhab*, rather than the 'authentic' sunna. She described the buzz in the community when Al-Albani's book, *The Prophet's Prayer Described*, was translated into English, 'proving' that their way of praying was actually incorrect:

> Learning how to pray properly was one of the biggest things, and . . . when [that] book about prayer first came out, how to pray according to the way the Prophet (*s.a.w.*)[31] prayed, it was just like wow! Where's this been?

Gradually, Brixton Mosque became known for its uncompromising adherence to a socially conservative version of Islam—Salafism—as well as its equally uncompromising opposition to Jihadi groups, who presented a major challenge for British Salafis during the mid- to late 1990s (Hamid, 2009, pp.393–396). These groups had become notorious in British Muslim communities for pronouncing *takfir* on (i.e., declaring them non-Muslims) the leaders of Muslim countries, such as Saudi Arabia, Jordan, and Egypt, claiming that they did not rule by the shari'a. Some even declared any Muslim who did not share this view—the Salafis included—to be apostates, and therefore deserving of the death penalty. Nonetheless, some Jihadi preachers saw the mosque as a fertile recruiting ground and tried to use the space to gather followers (Baker, 2011, p.32).

For example, according to one leader, representatives of the notorious former Al-Muhajiroun leader Omar Bakri Muhammad tried to promote their group at the mosque at least twice during the 1990s. Abdul Haqq Baker, who has worshipped at the mosque since 1990 and was its chairman between 1994 and 2009, said that only one representative came on the last occasion. Baker said he was dealt with 'quite abruptly—and, unfortunately, forcibly—when he tried to distribute leaflets'.

The mosque leadership has been actively involved in efforts to limit the influence of Jihadis since the early 1990s.[32] Although Abdullah El Faisal preached at the mosque in the early 1990s, the leadership banned him from the premises after it became clear that his ideology had taken a Jihadi turn. They then successfully thwarted his attempt to seize control of the mosque in 1993. They also challenged Abu Hamza Al-Masri[33] at his talks on numerous occasions, then identified youths who attended his lessons and tried to persuade them that his views contradicted Islam.[34] They even explained the ideology of these groups and their differences with Salafism to the police and local council at community meetings (Baker, 2011, pp.226–227), but were left 'disillusioned by an apparent lack of interest from police' (Lambert, 2011, p.184). Indeed, they had the impression that the police did not much distinguish between them and those they were trying to undermine.

The mosque itself came under suspicion in 2001, following an attempt by its former worshipper, the so-called shoe-bomber Richard Reid, to blow up a commercial aircraft. Reid, who reportedly converted to Islam while an inmate at Feltham Young Offenders Institution, had become actively involved in Brixton Mosque after his release. However, according to Abdul Haqq Baker, he later started attending external, 'militant' classes and drifted away from the mosque (BBC News Online, 2001).

More recently, in 2009 mosque leaders confronted Anjem Choudary[35] and other Omar Bakri Muhammad[36] followers, attacking them for their lack of Islamic credentials when they tried 'to propagate their views in Brixton' (As-Salafī and Al-Ashantī, 2009). Brixton leaders also published a lengthy refutation of the teachings of Abdullah El Faisal, *The Devil's Deception of 'Abdullaah Faysal al-Jamaykee* (2006), which became a book (2011), along with book-length critiques of Al-Muhajiroun (2009) and Anwar al-Awlaki[37] (2011), among others. As these publications illustrate, the general approach of Brixton Mosque towards Jihadis has been to present them with textual proofs from the Qur'an and sunna to 'demonstrate' that their beliefs run counter to Islamic teachings.

Brixton Mosque leaders have also been involved in more organized anti-extremism efforts. After 9/11, they established a partnership with the Metropolitan Police's Muslim Contact Unit, which was eager to harness the mosque's long experience in combating the influence of Jihadis in the community. And in 2007 Baker launched the youth outreach project STREET,[38] which used government funds to engage with 'disenfranchised Muslim youth' in the local area. Mosque representatives joined Baker to address issues affecting young people in south London, especially the influence of Jihadi propaganda, through social activities and projects designed to challenge the extremist narrative (STREET, n.d.). However, STREET was forced to scale down its projects in 2011 following government cuts.

The mosque itself is a charitable trust that is entirely reliant on public donations. One major donation, from El-Rahma Charity Trust, made it possible to buy the Gresham Road property in 1998. The premises, which have recently been expanded following a major community fundraising campaign, are divided into a male section and a female one, which is much smaller due to the Salafi teaching that congregational prayers are obligatory for men but optional for women. These two sections have separate entrances in order to preserve strict segregation at all times. The rooms are minimally decorated, with no art, photographs, or even calligraphy on the walls. The same is generally true of Salafi homes. This reflects Salafis' austerity and concern to minimize the possibility of distraction and idol worship. There is also a bookshop and a madrasa (Muslim religious school) for children aged five to mid-teens.

The mosque is situated in the heart of Brixton, a vibrant inner south London district that often conjures images of gun and knife crime, gang culture, run-down housing estates, racial tension, and riots. The area was a flashpoint of the 2011 England Riots, which erupted halfway through my fieldwork after police shot dead a black man called Mark Duggan in Tottenham, north London.

The area also has a positive reputation for what is seen as its buzzing, multicultural vibe. There is a well-established population of Afro-Caribbean descent, as well as an increasing number of white middle-class residents, among others—testament to Brixton's gradual process of gentrification from the late 1970s onwards (Mavrommatis, 2011).[39] The market is still lined with Afro hair-care and cosmetic outlets and stalls selling Caribbean-style clothing and jewellery, interspersed with CD stalls blasting reggae music. But delicatessens, vintage clothing shops, and small art galleries have also sprung up, contributing to a bohemian atmosphere that attracts young people from all ethnic backgrounds.

The make-up of the mosque congregation—mainly from the Borough of Lambeth—reflects the large local Afro-Caribbean community, but in recent years, Somalis appear to have overtaken Afro-Caribbeans as the largest ethnic group in the mosque. The leadership, however, is still dominated by Afro-Caribbean converts. This includes the imam, who studied at Saudi Arabia's Islamic University of Madinah.

Somalis started to worship at Brixton Mosque in significant numbers from the late 1990s, but did not become Salafis immediately. At first, they largely retained Islamic beliefs and practices associated with Somalia, despite disapproval from fellow worshippers who saw such activities as *bid'a*. But in the mid- to late 1990s, a small number of Somali women in their twenties became Salafis. Many learned about Salafism through their children, whom they had sent to the mosque's school, Iqra Independent. Some of the elder sisters of Somali Iqra pupils followed their sisters into Salafism, and by the early 2000s, a large number of young Somalis had embraced the *da'wa*. Over the same period, other London Salafi centres witnessed similar surges in the number of young Somalis attending lessons and events.

During my fieldwork, I noticed that the older-generation Somali women, dressed in colourful Somali clothing and conversing in Somali, congregated in the downstairs part of the women's section of the mosque. Their daughters and granddaughters, on the other hand, mostly sat upstairs, where Salafi circles of knowledge were held in English, and wore head-to-toe black garments like the Afro-Caribbean converts and others who congregated there. These included Afghan, South Asian, French, Albanian, and African Muslims—particularly Nigerians and Eritreans.

1.3 THE CHANGING COMPOSITION OF THE UK SALAFI COMMUNITY

After the bitter internal splits, plus external pressure from Jihadi recruiters and a suspicious British public, has Salafism managed to maintain its appeal? Has it become a major trend that enjoys cross-ethnic, countrywide appeal, or is its success in Brixton, the location of my main case study, atypical?

There are few reliable figures, but Salafism has undoubtedly attracted an increasing number of followers throughout the United Kingdom since the 1990s, particularly in the cities of London and Birmingham, which have large minority Muslim populations. And we know that Salafi communities comprise a growing number of women, Somalis, and (mostly black) converts.

Mosque numbers provide an indication of Salafi growth and spread. Mehmood Naqshbandi, who has been recording information on British mosques since the 1980s, estimates that there are 168 Salafi mosques out of a total of 1,857 mosques in the United Kingdom—that is, approximately 9 percent of all UK mosques.[40] Many of these were originally breakaways from traditional South Asian mosques. According to Naqshbandi, the overwhelming majority of Salafi mosques in the United Kingdom are quietist, and the rest are open to a degree of non-violent political activism—but none promotes militancy.

The relatively low proportion of Salafi mosques does not, however, include the many informal and transitory networks that meet in private homes and at universities. Nor does it take into account the fact that some Salafi teachers host circles in non-Salafi mosques or other buildings, such as community centres.

Moreover, the proportion of Salafi mosques in Britain is set to increase. Based on trends in mosque numbers over the past fifteen years, Salafis are the fastest-growing Islamic faction in the United Kingdom. Naqshbandi expects Salafi mosque numbers to continue to rise rapidly every year, while older-generation Deobandi and Barelwi mosques and their organizers will decline in influence. He said:

[Salafis'] ability to attract [the] younger, less traditionally dogmatically inclined, and the burgeoning numbers of dissenters from the Asian Sunni mainstream traditions (Barelwis and Deobandis), mean that these new Salafi masjids [i.e., mosques] will attract a lot of young talent that has been stifled in the traditional masjids.

He projects that there will be more Salafi mosques in the United Kingdom than those of any faction other than the Deobandis by 2023.

The cities of London and Birmingham are the main hubs of Salafi activity in the United Kingdom. Birmingham has a large concentration of Muslims, and is home to Salafi Publications and at least six Salafi mosques (Naqshbandi, 2015). London has historically had a high concentration of Muslim residents—12.4 percent of Londoners identified as Muslim in the 2011 Census, significantly more than the overall figure of 4.8 percent for England and Wales. Naqshbandi has identified twenty-eight Salafi mosques in London.

There are pockets of Salafi activity all over the capital. Some, as in Brixton, are mosques; the others are organized groups of Muslims that meet in community centres, which I call *da'wa* groups. One of those that I frequented regularly is Al-Athariyyah in Newham, east London, which was established in 2002, though the community started meeting informally in the early 1990s. Al-Athariyyah, which is affiliated to Salafi Publications, purchased a church and converted it into their first mosque, Masjid Abdul Aziz Bin Baz, in 2014.

While the two major networks Brixton Mosque and Salafi Publications both subscribe to quietist Salafism, they are by no means a united front. They have had longstanding disagreements about Salafi principles that continue to divide them and render any collaboration unthinkable. In particular, there have been differences over what kind of associations—with arguably non-Salafi scholars and Muslim organizations—compromise an organization's Salafism. These ongoing claims and counterclaims, which can be sampled by visiting their websites, could themselves form the subject of a book, so I cannot do justice to their complexity here.

As for the number of Salafis in Britain, leaders of two of the most prominent Salafi centres in the United Kingdom estimated their numbers of worshippers as follows: 1,800–2,000 (Brixton Mosque) and 11,500 (Salafi Publications and its affiliates; of which at least 4,000 are in London). The total number for the United Kingdom may be much higher. For practical and ideological reasons, it is impossible to give even an estimate.

First, there is no Salafi membership form; community leaders base their estimates on conference registration lists, mailing lists, and simply counting the rows at a Salafi Eid prayer—the only annual event every Salafi is religiously obligated to attend. Second, estimates based on mosque attendance are unreliable due to overlaps and absences. Muslims may attend Salafi-managed mosques, for instance, without ever adopting a full-fledged Salafi outlook. Similarly, many Salafis attend non-Salafi mosques out of convenience. Third, hard-line Salafis exclude from their estimates more liberal-minded Salafis and other Salafi groups with whom they have little or no relationship.

By all accounts, however, the overall number of Salafis has grown significantly since the 1990s, though they remain a modest component of the country's approximately 2.7 million Muslims (Census, 2011). Today, Salafism in Britain is still dominated by young people in their teens and twenties, but there are also many followers who became Salafis in the 1990s and are now in their thirties and forties.

How to account for the increase? First, the number of female Salafis has risen. Abu Khadeejah estimated that 70 percent of British Salafis in the 1990s were male, and that it was only in the past decade or so that the gender ratio had evened out. The fact that 95 percent of UK Salafi mosques have women's facilities (Naqshbandi, 2015)—the highest proportion for any Sunni faction in Britain—indicates a significant female component.

In addition, an increasing number of converts have embraced Salafism, at least in the south London area. Converts of Afro-Caribbean origin in particular have been a substantial part of the British Salafi community since the early 1990s, particularly in Brixton Mosque. During the mid-2000s, converting to Islam became fashionable among young people in south London—predominantly those of Afro-Caribbean origin—and many of these newcomers became worshippers at this mosque (see chapter 3.2).

More recently, a significant number of French, Belgian, and Dutch Salafis—both converts and Muslims of North African origin—have migrated to English cities, mainly Birmingham. This pattern is related to increasing tensions surrounding strict Islamic practices in their native countries, particularly the wearing of the *niqab*, which was banned in public places in France and Belgium in 2011. During my brief visit to the Salafi mosque in Birmingham in 2011, I met several French and Belgian women. One told me that her migration from France to Birmingham had been a *'petit hijra'*, implying that she felt she would be freer to practise her religion here.

Her use of the word *hijra* was significant. In Salafi discourse, in addition to describing the Prophet and his companions' journey from Mecca to Medina in 622 c.e., it refers to the migration from a land of disbelief to one where Islam prevails in order to facilitate religious practice—that is, to a *Muslim* country. But this woman's use of *hijra* reflects a recent move by Shaykh Ubayd Al-Jabiri, a Saudi scholar, to encourage Salafis who are 'put to trial' in their countries of residence but unable to migrate to Muslim lands—for example, due to visa restrictions—to move to Birmingham and affiliate with the Salafi mosque there (Salafitalk.net, 2011). This is an intriguing new development that is beyond the scope of this research, but it will become clearer as the number of *petit muhajirun* (emigrants) rises.[41]

Most significantly of all, there has been a surge in the number of young Salafis of Somali origin over the past decade or so, particularly in London, where most Salafis were previously from South Asian and Afro-Caribbean backgrounds. Umm Mustafe, a Somali Salafi preacher based in London, claimed that 'virtually all' Salafi mosques in the capital are now 'dominated' by Somali teenagers and young people. This relatively young and recent Somali contingent has not yet produced many preachers—I came across only two during the course of my research—but this will likely change in the coming years.

Somalis have had a significant presence in the United Kingdom since the late nineteenth century, when transient seamen's communities developed in the port cities of London, Cardiff, and Liverpool. Subsequently, many Somali men served during the First and Second World Wars and stayed on in the United Kingdom. The most recent Somali arrivals, however, are refugees, not economic migrants. Thousands fled to Britain after the outbreak of civil war in 1991, following the overthrow of General Siad Barre's government by a group of clans.

At the time of the 2011 Census, approximately 99,484 Somalis were resident in the United Kingdom—most (65,333) of whom were living in London—making it the largest Somali community in Europe (UNDP, 2009). These figures are probably an underestimate because the Census did not take illegal immigration into account. In addition, there was no 'British-Somali' box on the Census form—meaning that Somalis may have crossed 'British-African' rather than specifying their country of origin. A 2006 International Organisation for Migration report estimated the number at between 95,000 and 250,000 (p.5).

Abu Khadeejah told me in 2011 that he had observed an emerging Somali presence at Salafi events in London since the late 1990s:

> If I sat in a lecture 15 years ago [in London], it would have been predominantly Afro-Caribbean and Pakistanis, with scatterings of Bangladeshis, no Somalis whatsoever—now I'm talking about 1994 . . . up to 1997. The first sprinklings of Somalis that I began to see was probably 1998: one in a lecture, two in a lecture. From about 2005 onwards, you could sit in a lecture and it will be predominantly Somali now.

Many of these young people were born in Somalia, fled the civil war at an early age, and have spent many of their formative years in Britain. While some were comfortable assimilating into a liberal youth culture, others—particularly young women—developed a heightened religious sensibility.

Rima Berns McGown (1999) observed in the late nineties that rather than abandoning their faith, Somali teenagers in London and Toronto were starting to renegotiate the religious practices of their birth culture to suit the new environment. This involved addressing issues such as the correct ways to dress and behave around the opposite sex. Fifteen years on, it is clear that many young Somalis found answers to these questions in Salafism—though this was not usually the religious orientation of their parents.

One young Somali Salafi I interviewed described a funnel-like process, intensified by the migration experience, whereby Islam has been defined ever more narrowly down through the generations. Other Somalis I spoke to agreed. The young Somali Salafis understood their religious identities in rigid, specific terms—as Salafis—while their parents were usually content with the 'Sunni' label. Grandparents, meanwhile, saw themselves as simply 'Muslims', an identity inseparable from being Somali and speaking the Somali language (El-Solh, 1991, p.544).

Many of the young Somalis do not remember the disruption and difficulties of living through the civil war and initial resettlement. But they were inevitably influenced by those who did remember: parents (often single mothers), other relatives, and fellow Somalis in the diaspora, many of whom became increasingly conscious of, and attached to, their religion as they sought to re-establish themselves in unfamiliar environments. As McGown (1999, p.98) puts it, Islam provided 'an oasis of tranquillity amid the dislocation of refugee straits and the turmoil of adjusting to a new culture, trying to learn a new language, and attempting to find jobs', as well as facing racism. Somalis could no longer take Islam for granted as an all-pervading societal force, so in order to preserve religious practices, they had to actively seek out such things as halal meat and remember prayer times.

In these insecure circumstances, many Somali migrants turned to the Qur'an and hadith to retrieve credible rules for conduct in the new environment (McGown, 1999). Mothers often became more committed hijab-wearers—even adopting conservative forms, such as the *jilbab*—than they had been in Somalia. They also dedicated themselves more to studying Islam and attending the mosque. This was partly related to their concern to pass on cherished values to their children amid fears about the impact of alien influences. One such mother was Umm Mustafe, who went on to become a Salafi preacher (though she is unusual for her generation). She said that when she arrived in Britain, 'Islam was my survival'.

Some, including Umm Mustafe, were influenced by the Somali Islamist movements, such as the Salafi-inspired al-Ittihad al-Islami, some of which promoted a stricter style of hijab and a degree of isolation from mainstream non-Muslim society. Operating in the host countries allowed them to acquire greater authority than in Somalia, as they became known for assisting community members with resettlement, rather than primarily for their political entanglements (McGown, 1999, p.96).

Mothers were particularly influential given their role in raising children and the absence or diminished authority of Somali husbands. Many never arrived—some because they were killed in Somalia, others because their families were separated (Rutter, 2004, p.3). And those who did come often had to cope with a worse financial status or unemployment in the United Kingdom. A Somali man's authority in the family was linked to his primary provider role in Somalia, so this was threatened by difficulties in obtaining employment in the West (McGown, 1999, pp.17–18). Somali women, in contrast, enjoyed increased opportunities (Hopkins, 2010, p.524). Social welfare payments were also channelled through them, giving them control of the family finances (Olden, 1999, p.220).

The new economic independence of women altered their relationships with their husbands (Olden, 1999, p.220) and was probably a factor in the community's reportedly high rate of divorce and family breakdown (DCLG, 2009, p.43; Hassan, 2002; Holman and Holman, 2003). The Somali population of England and Wales has the highest percentage of lone-parent families—60 percent of families with a Somali-born 'family reference person', compared to 18 percent in the population as a whole (ONS, 2014, p.1).

Girls, perhaps in part due to their close relationships with their mothers, have tended to be more religiously observant than boys. The latter have, in general, achieved much worse results at school, with many struggling later to find employment and falling into gang crime (Aspinal and Mitton, 2010, p.42; DCLG, 2009, p.8; Holman and Holman, 2003, p.2).

Salafi mosques, such as Brixton, offered a welcoming space where teenaged and young Somali women could pray, study Islam, and socialize with like-minded others. Somalis tend to regard mosques as spaces for women as much as men; places where women may spend hours relaxing with their families and exchanging news with friends, rather than just popping in for a quick prayer. Yet Somali women often found that many of the South Asian mosques, which still dominate the Sunni Muslim landscape in the United Kingdom, either disapproved of their presence in the mosque or excluded women altogether. There were also major cultural differences, including those of language, diet, and dress (Open Society Foundations, 2014, p.24). Somali-established mosques are now starting to appear, and may prove to be more welcoming to Salafi Somali groups.

Today, Somalis are probably the largest ethnic group represented in London's Salafi congregations, and they form a considerable, though minority, component of other Salafi communities in the United Kingdom. The trend of young, mostly female Somalis embracing Salafism shows no sign of abating, and this might well prove crucial to shaping the future of Salafism in Britain.

CHAPTER 2

༺

Fieldwork

The notorious Channel 4 documentary, *Undercover Mosque: The Return*, highlighted both the need for in-depth, comprehensive research on Salafi women and the major obstacles such a project would inevitably now face. In the aftermath of this documentary, I realized that any fresh attempt to research Salafi women would be greeted with suspicion. It was therefore critical to plan my research approach carefully.

This chapter is about where and how I conducted my research. I explain the methods I used and how I adapted them to suit the geography, loose organization, emerging themes, and sensitive political context of the Salafi community in London. I then give an account of my experience of fieldwork in a community that was highly sceptical about outside researchers: how I entered the community, gradually built up trust, and sought to balance close involvement and objective detachment.

My main aim was to understand the world of Salafi women in rich detail; thus my research method was qualitative rather than quantitative. I combined long-term participant observation, formal and informal interviews, and textual analysis. During fieldwork lasting two years and four months (June 2010 through October 2012), I participated as fully as possible in the life of the community, and was therefore able to capture a broader range of information than typical topics in the headlines, such as shari'a and sharing husbands.

I concentrated my field research in different sites in London. In the summer of 2011, I also went to Birmingham, British Salafism's 'second city', where I visited the home of Salafi Publications: the mosque Masjid As-Salafi and its bookshop. There, I interviewed the leaders—many of whom regularly lecture in London—and also met members of the local Salafi community.

My principal fieldwork site was Brixton Mosque in Lambeth, south London. As mentioned in chapter 1, it is one of the United Kingdom's longest-established Salafi communities, so it held a variety of lessons and events and had many regular worshippers. Its ethnic mix—mainly young converts of Afro-Caribbean origin and Somalis—meant that I could investigate the attraction of Salafism for black Britons, an aspect of Salafi communities that was neglected in previous studies. I also attended numerous study circles and other events at the *da'wa* group Al-Athariyyah in Newham, east London, which, by contrast, attracted mostly Muslims of South Asian origin.

I had originally intended to concentrate my fieldwork on two religious centres and their immediate environs, but soon realized that such a narrow focus would not reflect the individualized and informal nature of women's involvement with Salafism. In a city that can easily be traversed within an hour or so, and in the age of the Internet, religious adherents seeking a 'base' can prioritize an institution's or network's ideological affiliation over its geographical location. This was certainly the case for many Salafis. I soon discovered that it was common for a woman to attend, for example, *jum'a* (Friday midday congregational prayers) at Brixton Mosque, a weekly lesson at a Salafi mosque in west London, and the occasional Salafi conference in east London or even Birmingham. Meanwhile, she would regularly go online to browse articles and download lecture recordings at several Salafi websites.

Moreover, like others who have conducted research on Muslim women, I quickly realized that women's participation in the group was generally more informal than that of men (Abu-Lughod, 1999; Silvestri, 2012; Torab, 1996). Women, unlike men, were not obliged to pray at a mosque and were excluded from official leadership roles. Thus Salafi women often seized the opportunity to host their own loosely organized study circles in private homes. I regularly attended two of these.

There were also what I call 'semi-formal' networks—somewhere between the formal circles described above and the informal circles at private homes—that had no permanent base but met regularly and were always led by the same person. I stumbled upon one such group that had no name, which I call 'Sisters of Tawheed'. It was led by a Somali teacher, Umm Mustafe, and attended almost exclusively by young Somali women. Umm Mustafe preferred that I did not mention the group's location in London, partly because they were in the process of finding a permanent base.

My research therefore took me all over London—to mosques, homes, and community centres. All networks, from the formal to the informal, tend to organize special events every now and then—whether they be educational (e.g., conferences), social (e.g., community *iftar*—the breaking of the fast at sunset during Ramadan), or for charity fund-raising purposes—and I attended these whenever I had the opportunity. In addition to attending organised lessons and events, I hung around parks, restaurants, banquet halls, shops, and homes. I shared meals, picked up children from school, danced at wedding parties, popped into local fried-chicken shops, shopped for wedding dresses, and joined in picnics.

By these means, I gained a first hand, intimate understanding of the culture and identified sensible questions to ask. I also built up a rapport with my participants and gradually became less conspicuous. This, in turn, meant that people behaved more normally around me, which increased the validity of my data.

At the same time, I had to remove myself from my surroundings and relationships in order to maintain a critical distance from my data and record them as objectively as possible. I wrote down details of seeming trivia, of the apparently mundane and everyday, and not just the loud arguments and festivities, as all contributed to a comprehensive picture of the culture. I wrote notes on the physical arrangements and ceremonial activities at Salafi events. But I also took in the informal, far less predictable aspects. For example, how did women tie their hijabs? Where did they sit and with whom? What language did they use? What books did they carry around with them? Also, I observed interactions. For example, when was humour used? How were rule-breakers rebuked? Who seemed to be in authority?

Whenever possible, I handwrote field notes on-site—for instance, during study circles, when most women took notes anyway—or else as soon as I could afterwards, usually during my journey home. As my fieldwork progressed and I started narrowing down my areas of interest to particular themes, I became more discriminating in my note-taking.

Sometimes it was possible to record lessons with near 100 percent accuracy. During Umm Hamza's class, for instance, she wrote her entire lesson on a whiteboard for her students to copy down, which I duly did. Initially, I had considered digitally recording other classes, since many Salafi women did so, but I abandoned the idea because I did not want to invite the suspicion that I was eavesdropping on conversations under the pretext of recording lessons. Thus I relied on handwritten notes.

But I quickly developed strategies for ensuring accuracy and comprehensiveness. For instance, when note-taking seemed inappropriate, I tried to write down key words on a note-pad or on my mobile phone as an aide-memoire. And whenever I failed to record speech verbatim, I indicated this in my field notes with the letter 'P' for 'paraphrase'. My notes were all typed up within the week; organized according to time, date, and location; and stored securely on a home computer in encrypted files.

All groups spoke English as their primary language, though Arabic was sometimes spoken, particularly when quoting classic texts. Hardly any of the young Salafis were fluent Arabic-speakers, so when teachers used Arabic they generally translated it immediately afterwards. Yet Arabic had a special value in these Salafi groups (see chapter 4), and had crept into these Britons' everyday speech since they had become Salafis. For example, a young British-Somali woman ordering at a take-away run by a British-Pakistani Salafi said: '*Al-salamu 'alaykum* [peace be unto you], I'll have a burger with chilli sauce and burger sauce and fries, and *khalas* [that is all]. . . . *Jazak Allahu khayra* [may God reward you].' I therefore took Arabic lessons at my university, the better to understand the key concepts and phrases.

I also examined staple Salafi texts, leaflets, pamphlets, popular websites, and audio recordings of lectures. Salafi literature in English is now so extensive that I had to be selective. I prioritized topics that affect the lives of ordinary Salafi women in London (e.g. *20 Pieces of Advice to my Sister Before her Marriage*), and studied the texts and websites that seemed most likely to be accessed by the women I encountered. I made a point of examining books that teachers encouraged their students to read; free leaflets and pamphlets that were distributed or readily available at Salafi institutions; books that women often recommended to me; and websites that women told me they consulted or that were linked to the Salafi groups I was studying.

These texts, which are listed in my bibliography under 'Primary Textual, Online and Audio Sources', enhanced my research in several ways. First, they clarified and elaborated upon Salafi teachings to which I was sometimes exposed only in a limited or fragmented way during lessons and conversations with Salafis. In particular, these sources enabled me to understand Salafism's key tenets from the insider's perspective, rather than relying on—often inaccurate—outsider accounts.

Second, such texts helped to illuminate the appeal of Salafism, as they included those mentioned by women as part of their conversion narratives. Some of these texts were free materials that were handed to me as a newcomer at Salafi events. These materials usefully highlighted one of the ways in which women are welcomed into and learn about the group. And there were other texts that explained some of the key issues facing Salafi communities, which provided helpful context to my case studies. Such issues included concerns about factionalism within Salafi groups and the influence of Jihadi propaganda.

Another vital source of information was Blackberry Messenger. This mobile phone instant messaging application was very popular among Salafi women at the time of my fieldwork because it allowed them to 'broadcast' messages to many other users simultaneously and for free. These frequent messages included religious 'reminders'—usually Qur'anic verses, hadiths, and quotes from famous scholars. There were also requests for Islamic proofs for certain rulings, invitations to social gatherings, advertisements for personal businesses, requests for charitable donations to help impoverished 'sisters', requests for supplementary prayers for the sick or recently deceased, and even personal advertisements from men looking for brides.

Upon entering the field, I bought a Blackberry, and the numerous 'broad-casts' I received helped to illuminate the dynamics of the Salafi 'sisterhood'.

2.1 INTERVIEWS

In addition to the above field research, which consisted of numerous infor-mal interviews,[1] I conducted more formal, extended interviews with thirteen community leaders—such as imams and Islamic studies teachers—and with a sample of twenty-three young (aged nineteen through twenty-nine) Salafi women.[2] I kept in touch with most of these women, so was able to update their information (for example, marital status) as time passed.

The community leaders I interviewed were based at Brixton Mosque and other Salafi da'wa networks in London, as well as at Salafi Publications in Birmingham. I interviewed most of the leaders on several occasions, which allowed me to pose new questions as they arose during fieldwork. A few were reinterviewed in the second half of 2015 in order to ascertain their views on more recent developments, such as ISIS.

To gather participants, I used the snowball method. This meant starting with a few participants who acted as 'seeds' (Bernard, 2006, p.194), including leaders who had given me permission to access the community and women in the study circles I attended. These participants then told others about my research—often, but not always, at my request—and encouraged them to take part. As my sample of women grew, I tried to ensure that the age range and ethnic mix of interviewees corresponded to my own and community leaders' estimates of the demographics of these Salafi centres. The snowball method, though not conducive to creating random samples, is ideally suited to hard-to-reach groups like this one because it keeps research low-profile and promotes trust.

The majority (twenty) of the twenty-three women in my sample associated themselves with Brixton Mosque (though many also attended the circles of other networks). I also interviewed three women who regularly attended the circles of Sisters of Tawheed, which has close ideological and social links to Brixton Mosque ('Brixton'). At least three of my Brixton interviewees were also involved with this network, and the two networks often exchanged speakers at their respective events. The interviews with the Sisters of Tawheed usefully complemented those of my Brixton sample.

All of the women interviewed identified as Salafis but, interestingly, only nine of the twenty-three women said that they openly and unre-strictedly used the Salafi label when among non-Salafis. Most feared that by identifying themselves as such, they would be dismissed outright or ridi-culed. They also felt that using the Salafi label would hamper their efforts to call others to 'true' Islam.

The religious and ethnic backgrounds of the interviewees varied (see Tables 2.1–2.7). Most (18) were from Muslim families; the rest (5) from Christian, nominally Christian, or agnostic backgrounds. Nearly half (11) were of Somali background. The others had originally come from Eritrea (4) and Nigeria (3), with one from Jamaica, South Asia, East Africa, and Southern Africa, respectively.[3] One convert, Firdaws, preferred not to disclose her (rather unusual) ethnic background because she thought that it would identify her. More than half were either born in Britain or struggled to remember living elsewhere because they had been less than six years old when they arrived in the United Kingdom. The rest had come between the ages of nine and sixteen.

These different backgrounds raise conceptual and ethical issues: should interviewees be referred to by their ethnic origin, by nationality or citizenship, or in terms of a hyphenated identity such as 'British-Eritrean'? The problem is particularly difficult in the case of women who have spent much of their childhood abroad but are now British citizens. I have opted to

Table 2.1. INTERVIEWEES BY AGE

19	20	21	22	23	24	25	27	29
1	2	3	4	5	2	3	2	1

Table 2.2. INTERVIEWEES: BORN-MUSLIMS AND CONVERTS

Born-Muslim	Convert
18	5

Table 2.3. INTERVIEWEES' COUNTRIES OF ORIGIN

Somalia	Eritrea	Nigeria	Jamaica	South Asia	Kenya	Southern Africa	Not disclosed
11	4	3	1	1	1	1	1

Table 2.4. INTERVIEWEES' AGES WHEN THEY CAME TO BRITAIN

Born here	Too young to remember/1 or less	3	5	9	10	11	13	15	16
4	5	1	3	4	2	1	1	1	1

Table 2.5. INTERVIEWEES' MARITAL STATUS

Single	Engaged	Married (with children)	Divorced
15	3	4 (2)	1

Table 2.6. INTERVIEWEES' OCCUPATIONS

Full-time job	Part-time job	Student & no employment	Student & part-time job	Student & volunteer	Housewife
5	3	6	5	2	2

Table 2.7. INTERVIEWEES' HIGHEST EDUCATIONAL QUALIFICATIONS (INCLUDING COURSES CURRENTLY COMPLETING)

BTech	Access course	NVQ	Diploma	Foundation degree	BA	BSc	MA
3	1	1	2	1	9	5	1

describe participants in terms of their ethnic and national origin—for example, 'Somalis' and 'Nigerians'—partly as a shorthand and partly because this is how they referred to themselves and to other women in Salafi institutions. However, this is not to say that they are not British citizens.

At the time of the interviews, all but four women were unmarried. Unmarried women predominated in my sample for practical reasons— single women were generally much more forthcoming (more on this later). This focus unexpectedly opened up a fascinating new area of research: Salafi match-making, the subject of chapter 6.

The women in my sample lived all over London, but mainly in the south— namely, the boroughs of Lambeth, Southwark, and Croydon—which was expected, given their proximity to Brixton Mosque. Most lived with their parents or guardians, though the four married women lived with their husbands. Four lived with friends or cousins, and two lived alone.

Sixteen of the twenty-three women had grown up with a minimal (or no) relationship with at least one of their parents. This absence had been due to death (eight), parents living abroad (seven), and/or uninvolved fathers (three). Two of the Somalis had lost parents in the civil war. The women came from working- and middle-class backgrounds, and one was the daughter of a late colonel in Somalia. Their parents were now mostly in lower-skilled jobs or unemployed, and included Somalis, Eritreans, and Nigerians who had been farmers and owners of small businesses prior to migration.

The women had a relatively high level of educational attainment.[4] It is difficult to evaluate whether or not they are typical in this regard. On the one hand, one leading Salafi preacher told me that the 'vast majority' of Salafis in London have progressed to higher education; on the other, Anne Sofie Roald (2001, p.53) claims that Salafism in Europe 'tends to attract Muslims with little formal education'. My own impression was that most young Salafi women in Britain—especially Somalis—go to university at some point. Sixteen of my interviewees had achieved (or were in the process of completing) university-level education. One had a Master's degree, while the rest were completing or had completed a Diploma or Bachelor of Technology qualifications. Thirteen were currently students, and the others were all employed full-time or part-time, apart from two full-time housewives.

The great majority favoured the 'Salafi' attire of the *jilbab*, sometimes accompanied by the *niqab*, as their everyday dress. Eighteen wore the *jilbab* full-time, with three additionally wearing the *niqab* full-time and four wearing it part-time—for example, when not at work or university, or specifically for trips to Salafi mosques or conferences. Two wore the *jilbab* part-time because they were in the medical profession so had to conform to regulations governing professional attire during working hours; two wore the less-enveloping abaya; and one, at an early stage in her practice of Salafism, wore an abaya for mosque visits and loose Western clothing and a headscarf the rest of the time.

Each individual interview was between two and five hours long and conducted privately, though male interviewees often preferred others to be present. Most interviews took place in cafés, but others were in deserted areas of mosques, participants' homes, parks, offices, restaurants, and twice in participants' cars. My priorities in choosing interview locations were to put interviewees at ease (so that women felt able to remove their *niqabs*, for instance, if they wore them) and to ensure as much privacy as possible.

I expected interviewees to be reluctant to have their words digitally recorded due to the sensitivity of the research topic. However, I was proven wrong, with just two exceptions (and one of those women was happy to be recorded for the second half of the interview once she learned what to expect). The vast majority of my interviewees actually felt reassured by my digital recorder, which they seemed to regard as a sign of my professionalism—that I took accuracy and context seriously. I quickly learned that the women felt more relaxed once I had explained to them that I would permit nobody else—and certainly no men—to listen to the recordings, as I would be doing all of the transcriptions myself. To Salafis, a woman's voice is part of her *'awra*—that is, the intimate parts of her body that should not be exposed to men for reasons of modesty—so this reassurance was crucial. Inevitably, using the digital recorder meant that some women were initially self-conscious. But any awkwardness quickly vanished once I was able to engage them in relaxed conversation. Indeed, using a recorder freed me to make eye contact and use open body language, which helped to make the interviews more intimate.

My interviews were semi-structured: I had a list of questions that I posed to every woman, but also let conversations develop and go off on tangents. Having consulted the literature on Muslim and fundamentalist women, I initially included several questions on gender roles, obedience to husbands, polygamy, and dress, supposing they would be relevant. These are, after all, the issues that most preoccupy the media and mainstream public opinion when it comes to conservative Islam.

Yet these questions did not animate, or resonate with, the Salafi women as much as the others, many of which I formulated after nearly a year of participant observation in the community. Since these were single women in their early to mid-twenties, it was not surprising to find that the primary challenges they faced were not marital issues. Rather, they spoke passionately about the difficulties of getting a degree, securing a job, pacifying anti-Salafi parents, and finding a good husband in the first place, given the constraints imposed by Salafi teachings and external factors, such as the economic recession.

Although I was guided by a list of themes and questions (see Interview Question Guide for Salafi Women), in general my approach was non-directive in order to encourage my interviewees to take the lead and thereby identify the 'important' issues themselves and in their own terms. For example, I asked open-ended questions, such as: 'What makes your approach to Islam different to those of other Muslims, who may interpret their religion in different ways?,' rather than referring to sects or mentioning the term 'Salafi'. This was in order to understand how the woman herself interpreted her affiliation, and whether indeed 'Salafi' was a label with which she felt comfortable. And whenever there was time, I encouraged people to talk for as long as they liked; hence interviews could take up to five hours and span several sessions.

From the start, I concentrated on how Salafi women expressed themselves, including the language they used and the issues they were most concerned about. In taking this approach, I assumed that—contrary to popular conceptions—Salafi women have agency and power over their lives like anybody else.[5] Adopting this starting point allowed me to pursue other research questions—issues that have been neglected in the scholarly literature on fundamentalist and Muslim women in the West.

Such an open approach had many advantages, but also limitations. Naturally, people remember selectively, sculpting their past lives according to their current circumstances and what they want the researcher to know. This was most evident when women used terminology and phrasings favoured by Salafi teachers or rooted in the Qur'an and sunna to interpret past decisions and events. As Karin van Nieuwkerk (2006c, p.98) found with the Muslim converts she interviewed, the women 'created a common script' through their interactions with one another. Similarly, Kate Zebiri (2007, p.103) found that the converts she interviewed used 'phrases and concepts which were reminiscent of phrases and concepts from the Qur'an, and to a lesser extent the hadith'.

Another constraint was manifest in some Salafis' reluctance to dwell on the triumphs and struggles of becoming Salafi, due to Islamic teachings about humility and hiding one's sins. Yet such limitations are in themselves valuable data, suggesting an internalization of a Qur'anic 'worldview' (Zebiri, 2007, p.103). Moreover, through participant observation, I was able to confirm and, in some cases, question the lifestyle changes, beliefs, and issues described in interviews.

2.2 ENTERING THE FIELD: A NON-MUSLIM ANTHROPOLOGIST AMONG SALAFI LONDONERS

'Why do you want to study Salafiyya?' 'Who's your supervisor?' 'Who's funding you?' 'What's your religion?' 'What do you think of Islam?' 'What do you think of the government's counter-extremism agenda?'

I usually faced a barrage of such questions when I arrived for the crucial first meetings with leaders of London's principal Salafi communities. But in the recently intensified political climate, that did not surprise me. After all, only a year or two had passed since an undercover reporter had secretly filmed the notorious documentary on Salafi women.

However, as I explained to my would-be gatekeepers at the time, my interest in Salafism had started before the sensationalist programme was broadcast. In fact, it had been a Salafi 'sister' who had first introduced me to the subject, and my interest had grown after meeting many women with fascinating and stereotype-busting stories to tell. This answer was accepted.

Their curiosity was understandable, regardless of the sensitive context. There I was: a non-Muslim, English, white researcher with a middle-class, educated accent, requesting permission to 'hang around' in predominantly black, highly conservative milieus. I did not come equipped with surveys and clipboards; I was there to do 'participant observation'. Completing this bizarre impression, I had draped myself rather inexpertly in a hijab, which felt as if it might unravel at any moment, and donned some loose-fitting clothing. I arrived with no personal connections, apart from a limited acquaintance with a few leaders whom I had interviewed during a short project for my Master's degree.

I explained that I wanted to understand Salafism from the women's own viewpoint, rather than accept unquestioningly accounts in the media. I showed them some consent forms and a letter from my university's Research Ethics Committee, proving that my project had undergone a thorough vetting process. My methods would be overt, I said, and I would anonymize participants' comments and gain their informed consent before proceeding with extended interviews. Crucially, I would keep even the fact of interviewees' participation confidential within the community and beyond.

These ethical research procedures helped my subjects to distinguish me from the *Undercover Mosque* journalist and made them feel more comfortable talking to me. Such ethical codes were also reassuringly familiar to Salafis who had learned academic research skills or written dissertations at universities themselves. As awkward and tense as these vetting meetings often were, they always ended with my being granted permission to go ahead.

But that was just the first hurdle. Much harder was gaining acceptance among the rank-and-file Salafi women. In this strictly segregated community, most had little or no contact with the predominantly male leadership, so my chances of acquiring some ready-made trust through my connections with the men were limited. Moreover, many women were baffled by the 'participant observation' model of research. For those women, I was, at best, a snooper; at worst, a spy.

The women of Brixton Mosque, my principal fieldwork site, apparently had good grounds to be suspicious. On my second visit, one of them told me that the Brixton women had experienced researchers who had 'not been very upfront with us.' Many of them had actually been among the blurred faces in the *Undercover Mosque* documentary, or knew someone who had been. These wounds were still raw, and I knew I had to tread lightly. Thus, I tried to strike a precarious balance between being unobtrusive while also being transparent and consistent.

Having obtained permission from the leaders, I began by attending Islamic studies circles that were open to the public—arriving on time and not hanging around afterwards. This meant, of course, that my field notes initially consisted of rather bland accounts of the lessons themselves ('The seven conditions of the *shahada* [profession of faith] are as follows . . . ') or of the make-up of the audience ('about 40 women. Mostly Somalis, a few Afro-Caribbean converts').

I restricted myself to unforced small talk—nothing too personal—before and after lessons, and always mentioned my researcher role if the conversation went beyond a quick comment on the class or the weather. I was open about my (non-)religious identity, and happy to converse on personal subjects, such as my family, university, and life experiences. Reciprocal exposure can be vital in sensitive fieldwork—as many other researchers have found (Al-Rasheed, 1998, p.8; Atay, 2008, p.46; Bolognani, 2007). I waited for these conversations to warm up naturally before I broached the subject of extended, one-to-one interviews. But the months crept on and, though people were generally friendly, I was still without a single interviewee.

Occasionally, my hopes rose when my usual request—'Fancy being interviewed?'—was answered with the apparently more acquiescent '*insha'Allah*' (God willing), but to no avail. I gradually realized that this was just a polite way of saying no. When I finally did get a couple of women on-board, they cancelled at the last minute, using their husbands as excuses (a Salafi wife must obey her husband in all things halal, or permissible).

Concerned at this lack of progress, I shifted my attention to the unmarried women, who were about the same age as me, and found that they were much more forthcoming. Far from being suspicious and reserved, they enjoyed chatting about my research, which fascinated them (most were students themselves). We also had entertaining—and cathartic—woman-to-woman discussions about how hard it was to find a good man. Meanwhile, remarks were made about my diligence in consistently attending lessons and learning Arabic, which seemed to convince people of my sincerity and lack of hidden agendas. Finally, I secured my first interview.

After that, one interview led to others. I started receiving invitations to social gatherings and private circles in Salafis' homes. I was introduced to Umm Mustafe, an assertive Somali preacher who taught a popular women's circle that was only advertised by word of mouth. She said that she had been approached by many other researchers and journalists, and all were turned down. After a long chat over a cup of coffee, she astonished me by giving me permission to join her lessons whenever I wanted. By this point, hardly anyone seemed to remark on my presence at fieldwork sites in anything other than positive terms.

Many women who had initially kept a slight distance were conversing with me naturally now. The most extreme example of this was Aliyah, a bright primary-school teacher in her early twenties, who was initially rather reserved. After a few encounters, and many questions on her part, she explained that she had felt uncomfortable talking to me because she had assumed I was an MI5 agent. At this point, we both burst out laughing. Despite the rocky start, we became friendly—and one day, she startled me by proposing that I should become her co-wife (i.e. fellow wife in a polygamous marriage). I declined, but thanked her for the thought. She laughed.

Indeed, once initial suspicions related to my 'non-Muslimness' faded, I could embrace the advantages bestowed by my gender. As a woman, I was able to have intimate conversations with women and access areas that had previously been off-limits even to Muslim researchers on Salafism in Britain, who to my knowledge have been almost exclusively male (Baker, 2011; Birt, 2005; Hamid, 2009; Lambert, 2011).[6] This did not, however, prevent me from conducting interviews with male leaders, who perhaps regarded me as an 'honorary male'—a common experience among female anthropologists. In all, I obtained interviews with nine men. They often insisted on having another person present. (In fact, so important was this social norm to some that once, when my 'chaperone' left for five minutes to get coffee, the imam I was interviewing left his own office to wait outside in the corridor for his reappearance.)

But at no point in my almost two-and-a-half years of fieldwork could I take my acceptance by the community for granted. More than a year in, after one of my regular lessons had finished, the teacher beckoned me into a side room. '*I* don't have a problem with you,' she began, ominously. I braced myself. Some women, she said, had expressed concerns that I might be 'spying' on them—and had reminded her of the fate of the teacher who had starred in the *Undercover Mosque* documentary. According to this teacher, her fellow teacher had been banned from every mosque in the country following the broadcast.

My heart sank. I thought of the consent forms my gatekeepers had signed over a year ago: they had included a standard statement about the right to withdraw consent and data at any time before the research was completed. Was all this fieldwork, all these hundreds of pages of notes, about to come to nothing? I also flushed at the realization that, despite my best efforts, I had made some people feel uncomfortable—though I knew that I would never know who had made the complaint, nor how many people were involved. But the teacher went on: 'I told them I do not believe what you are doing is spying, and that you came with the right paperwork, and I gave you an interview.'

I was touched by her openness and loyalty, and said that I understood the women's point of view. But it was difficult to come back to her lessons after that. I did so, reminding myself of the teacher's support and redoubling my efforts to be as unobtrusive as possible. I avoided sitting near groups of women with whom I was not already on friendly terms, lest they thought I was eavesdropping, and the matter was never mentioned again.

My physical positioning in Salafi spaces was just one aspect that I had to consider carefully. Participant observation, by definition, involves a delicate balance of participating and observing, neither role extending too far. Overemphasis on observation at the expense of participation would make it harder to access the field and experience the lives of Salafi women intimately; but too much participation could compromise my academic 'objectivity' and ethical research guidelines, not to mention my own personal morals. I needed to get close enough to empathize, not sympathize. Moreover, if I became a 'total participant', this would fuel any suggestion that I was doing covert research.

I decided to take notes in circles of knowledge just like the other students— which usefully complemented my 'observer' role, anyway—and even sat a short test that one of the teachers had set for them. But I never participated in prayers, always shifting instead to the back and making myself useful by becoming a babysitter for a few minutes. I chatted freely and informally to everyone, but always got out my consent forms when it reached the point of a formal interview. This could be problematic: while community leaders used to dealing with the media and researchers were not put off by the forms, ordinary Salafi women often found them corporate and intimidating and were consequently more hesitant to participate.[7]

There was also the delicate matter of dress. When I first entered the field, I had to make a crucial decision: should I wear Western clothes, despite spending time in places of worship, or opt for some form of Islamic dress? If the latter, how far should I go? In the end, I decided on a plain headscarf and loose-fitting long-sleeved top, and alternated between baggy trousers and long, khaki-coloured peasant skirts. My aim was to strike a balance between respect for religion and openness about my researcher role (the undercover reporter in the documentary had worn a full *jilbab* and *niqab*). I also assumed that men would be more willing to be interviewed if I did not wear tight or even modestly flesh-baring outfits. I found the headscarf uncomfortable and never got used to it, but with hindsight, I think it helped me to build trust and secure in-depth interviews with men. I am also certain that I would have been asked to cover up had I not done so anyway, as this happened to another female researcher conducting similar fieldwork in London (Geelhoed, 2014, p.40).

Yet another careful balance had to be struck between appearing knowledgeable and knowing 'too much'. This is a typical anthropologist's conundrum: on the one hand, she needs to appear professional, well-informed, and genuinely interested in the community. But if she displays an extensive knowledge, down to the fine details, she risks being taken for a know-it-all or, much worse, a spy. Paul Dresch (2000, p.114), a British anthropologist who did fieldwork in Yemen, writes: 'Knowledge itself was problematic. To be worth talking to one has to know things, but the question then arises of how on earth one knows them.'

I learned this the hard way. The first time I was asked, 'Why are you interested in Islam?' during an initial meeting with an imam, I gave a detailed answer, referring to various religious teachings. He looked at me in astonishment and said: 'Are you sure you weren't present at my lecture last Sunday—I was saying those exact words!' I told him that I had not been to the lecture (as I was yet to be granted permission). Unconvinced, he repeated his question twice. I realized that my knowledge of Islam had made him slightly uneasy due to the fact that I am non-Muslim.

However, one area where I was expected to be reasonably well-informed was in the rules of Islamic conduct. Salafis are very strict when it comes to social conventions such as greeting people with '*salams*', eating with the right hand, not walking in front of praying Muslims (this invalidates the prayer), and avoiding any 'unnecessary' intermingling with the opposite sex, particularly in the vicinity of the mosque. Within the first few months, I suspect that I broke every one of these rules. But due to the ambiguity of my 'participant observer' role, this was only occasionally remarked upon. As a researcher, I could, for instance, talk to male community leaders relatively freely without either party attracting comments. But there were limits, as I learned one Friday afternoon outside Brixton Mosque.

Midday prayers had just finished and streams of men and women, myself among them, were pouring out of their respective entrances. I caught sight of Khizar, an unmarried community leader with whom I had been in contact while negotiating access to the mosque. 'Oh, hi Khizar!' I called out, smiling. 'Hi, Anabel!' he replied. 'It's been a while—look, I've been meaning to tell you, I've got a new number.' 'Oh, what is it?' I replied, getting my phone out automatically. 'No!' he said, waving my phone away frantically and looking around to check if anyone had seen. It had been an entirely innocent exchange, but I suddenly understood how it must have looked. We walked away from the mosque, without looking at one another, until we were at a safe distance and could continue the conversation.

Many women tried to make sense of my ambiguous 'participant observer' role by ascribing me the role of 'potential convert'. As Nicola Goward (1984, p.112) says, communities tend to define ethnographers in terms familiar to them. This particular ascribed role is common for anthropologists studying proselytizing groups.[8] This led to many difficult exchanges in which I had to explain sensitively that, although as an agnostic I had an open mind to Islam's truth claims, I had entered the community as a researcher with an academic interest in Salafism. Most accepted this, but some women continued to refer to my supposedly imminent conversion in such phrases as: 'When you are a Muslim . . . ' (in an affectionate tone); 'Have you taken your *shahada* yet?' (curious); and 'What is preventing you from taking your *shahada*?' (aggressive).

A few persevered in their *da'wa* efforts, growing frustrated with my obstinacy and giving me dire warnings about the torment that awaited me in Hell if I did not listen. Some even claimed that the devil was 'whispering' in my ear, telling me not to embrace Islam. On these occasions, it was difficult to remain composed, especially when the tone was aggressive and I was confronted in front of others. It was often presumed that if I was interested in Islam enough to do a PhD on it and to spend so much time studying in Salafi circles, I would eventually come to the inevitable conclusion that Islam was the one true religion. My stubborn agnosticism was therefore a discomforting anomaly to some. Others were philosophical, remembering that 'Allah misleads whom He wills and guides whom He wills' (Qur'an, 14:4), meaning my fate was out of their hands.

On the other hand, this ascribed role was an academic advantage because it gave me access to the feelings and experiences of a newcomer to the community. I, like other newcomers, was escorted to study circles I had not tried before; corrected when I broke rules; and handed leaflets, CDs, books, and even an abaya (in my size) for Eid. I am sure I was not the first newcomer to feel a sense of irritation when older Salafis told me off for reading the 'wrong' Qur'an translation, nor the first to feel gratitude towards the women who helped me to tie my hijab comfortably. Many ethnographers keep a fieldwork diary to supplement their participant observation notes, but I combined the two, realizing that my impressions as a newcomer could constitute data in themselves.[9]

Moreover, as an agnostic with no Muslim background whatsoever, I could never be accused of having a sectarian agenda. Salafis were aware that they were unpopular with the wider Muslim community—in fact, many seemed to take pride in their marginal status[10]—and would surely have been cautious before allowing a non-Salafi Muslim in their midst. After all, the *Undercover Mosque* reporter had herself been a Muslim.

In fact, I bumped into the teacher who had starred in the documentary a year or so into my fieldwork, quite unexpectedly. After telling her about my research, I broached the subject of the exposé and the reporter. She exclaimed her shock at the deception, adding that at a time of so much '*hizbi-yya*' (partisanship), she preferred the idea of a non-Muslim researcher, who would be 'new to it' and could 'keep an open mind'.

Another advantage of being an 'outsider', from an academic perspective, was my daily exposure to non-Muslim circles in my social life, at work, and at university. This allowed me, at times, to reverse perspectives and understand what it was like to be a visibly Muslim woman at a time of widespread alarm about so-called creeping Islamization. I saw the startled expressions on my friends' faces when I met them for coffee immediately after a mosque visit, still wearing a headscarf (I could not bring myself to unwrap it in full view on the street). I received hostile stares and occasionally comments on the way to study circles. On one occasion, I was verbally abused by a young man sitting next to me on the Tube.

Despite my personal dislike of the *niqab*, I found myself defending women's right to wear it at dinner parties, especially around the time of the French ban on face coverings in 2011. I was called upon to explain my research so often that, by the time I started my fieldwork, I had acquired a full appreciation of many non-Salafis' chief concerns those with illegitimate the group. People told me that most, if not all, women who wore the *niqab* in Britain were forced to do so by their husbands or male relatives. Brixton Mosque, in particular, provoked associations with terrorism. I often found myself explaining Salafis' opposition to Al-Qa'ida and Jihadism.

However, these explanations did not always convince: 'Do you really believe them when they say they are anti-jihad?' asked a journalist at a dinner party. Others raised concerns about the 'ghettoization' of Salafis, who try to avoid socializing with non-Muslims. Yet I quickly realized that such concerns, though understandable, were largely reducible to issues about women's rights and terrorism. When I mentioned other, non-Muslim Londoners who are prone to similar separatism, such as Haredi Jews in Stamford Hill, north London, less concern was aroused by such behaviour. The asymmetry in perceptions was clearly due to the political context.

Nonetheless, being an 'outsider' certainly had its limitations, both academic and practical. On the academic side, it was difficult to maintain a coldly neutral, let alone empathetic, stance when controversial topics were discussed in the field. As an independent, career-minded woman, I found the patriarchal norms to which I was exposed—such as the obligation to obey your husband and acceptance of polygamy—hard to stomach. Also, the teachers in Salafi circles occasionally advised the women to distance themselves from non-Muslims. It was discouraging to be reminded that even the women who invited me to dinner in their homes and met me regularly for coffee may have believed that any friendship with me and other non-believers was wrong.

Sometimes such friendly behaviour seemed downright contradictory. One woman with whom I got on well would occasionally talk about non-believers in unflattering terms while at the mosque—for example, saying that non-Muslim women lacked *haya* (modesty, shyness). But one day, she made a point of telling me that when she said such things, 'I don't mean you', and that she always worried that I might take her words personally. Such ambivalence made me uneasy, but I tried to regard these exchanges as welcome fieldwork data, as they revealed a gap between theory and practice. What Salafis said in the mosque, and how they conducted their relationships outside it, were not necessarily consistent with each other.

On the practical side, it is likely that Salafis at times altered their behaviour and responses in front of a non-believer, at least at first. H. Russell Bernard (2006, pp.241–242) refers to the 'deference effect', which occurs when people tell you what they think you want to know in order not to offend you, and this may have been an issue. Zebiri (2007, p.13) notes how the Muslim converts she studied were more likely to use the term *kafir* (non-Muslim), a term often seen as derogatory, in interviews with her Muslim research assistant than with herself. And in my own interviews, it is possible that Salafis moderated their responses to a non-Muslim researcher because they feared a 'bad write-up'.

This is an inevitable limitation of empirical research by 'outsiders', but precisely why long-term participant observation is such an essential tool. This way, the ethnographer can gradually reduce the effect of her presence in the field as much as possible, while observing her participants' lives closely yet outside the more artificially constructed context of interviews. Participant observation also allows the researcher to confirm what is said in interviews, as well as to observe dissonance between self-portraits or pulpit preachings and everyday realities—as in the contradiction described above.

Overall, the potentially 'problematic' aspects of my identity proved manageable, thanks to a strong emphasis in Salafi communities on welcoming and assisting all those who are interested in learning about Islam. After all, a very cornerstone of the Salafi identity is discharging one's duty to enjoin the good and forbid the evil—to revive the sunna of the Prophet by setting a good example and by purifying and correcting the 'misguided' ways of others. Paradoxically, it was the openness of this insular community that made my research possible.

CHAPTER 3

❧

Becoming Salafi

Although the first generation of born-and-raised British Salafis started to emerge in the early 2000s, the vast majority of Salafis in the United Kingdom today were not born into the group. Rather, they were raised in families with varying degrees of religious consciousness, both Islamic and otherwise.

My sample includes five women who grew up in non-Muslim households and for whom Christianity was the most familiar religion until at least adolescence. The remaining eighteen women had Muslim backgrounds. Of these, most had parents or guardians who were lax in their religious observance or who infused their practice with customs from their countries of origin to which their children, who had mostly grown up in Britain, could not relate.[1]

Thus the women in my sample all consciously rerouted their religious identities at some point, joining a group that often seemed either alien or 'extremist' to their families. Such was the transformative and all-encompassing nature of this process that even some of the women with Muslim backgrounds described it using conversionist language. A few referred to 'becoming Muslim' or 'reverting', striking an interesting similarity with 'born-again' Christian narratives. Before embracing Salafism, Safia, a Somali, said she had been 'blind', never having learned about or practised Islam fully. Similarly, Madeeha, of South Asian origin, felt as though she was 'learning from scratch.' Both said that they felt like 'reverts'. Others said they had been lost, or would feel lost, without Salafi Islam.

Salafi teachings actually encourage followers to understand their journey into Salafism as a radical identity renegotiation. They specify such strict conditions for a person to be considered 'truly' Muslim that even some of the women who had been brought up as Muslims no longer believed that they had deserved to be identified as such. Manal, an Eritrean of Muslim background, said: 'I wasn't Muslim for a while in my life . . . because I wasn't praying . . . that [according to Salafi teachings] can take you out of the fold of Islam.' Moreover, it was common parlance among both converts and women of Muslim backgrounds to hark back to their *jahiliyya*—meaning 'pre-Islamic age of ignorance'[2]—when referring to their pre-Salafi days.

I therefore treat the transformations of both the 'total converts' and the 'born-Muslims' as conversions. While all of the women in this study had learned about and practised Islam to some extent before becoming Salafi, to describe this change as a mere 'reaffiliation' or 'reaffirmation' would belittle both the transformations they underwent and how they understood them.

Similarly, the American fundamentalist Christian women of Brenda Brasher's study used conversionist language, though most had a history of involvement in Christianity, so she opted to describe them as 'total converts' (1998, p.37). The case of Salafi women in Britain is less straightforward since, for many women, there was a substantial degree of continuity of belief and practice. Yet it would not be an exaggeration to describe the socioreligious change most of them went through as 'conversion'. I follow De Koning (2009), Baylocq and Drici-Bechikh (2012), and Geelhoed (2014) in this regard. However, since only a minority of Salafi women from Muslim families seem to call themselves 'converts' or 'reverts', I reserve those terms to distinguish those of non-Muslim background from the others.

This chapter examines the antecedents and dynamics of the initial stages of this conversion process. It illuminates how young women from a range of backgrounds chose Salafism from a variety of competing offers, and why they found it appealing.

Conversion is a complex process, and accounts of it should not overemphasize any single component (McGuire, 2001, p.77). My analysis combines the two approaches Nieuwkerk (2006b, p.10) outlines as necessary for a comprehensive understanding of conversion. The first is the functional approach, which focuses on conversion as the fashioning of a new identity and biographical context—personal routes, susceptibilities, and motives. Certainly, a person's prior socialization, relationships, and life experiences may dispose him or her to conversion (Wohlrab-Sahr, 2006, p.75). As Rambo (1993, p.5) points out, conversion occurs in 'a dynamic force field of people, events, ideologies, institutions, expectations, and orientations'; so I highlight the social, political, local, ethnic, and biographical contexts in which conversion took place.

The second approach is discourse analysis, which analyzes the discourse or ideological content of the religion, as well as how this message is spread and appeals to individuals. A combined approach is essential because, as my data illustrate, neither biographical factors, such as social networks and emotional upheavals, nor ideational factors alone are sufficient for a woman to embrace Salafism. I start, however, with some biography: the women's early years and how these shaped their route into Salafism.

3.1 EARLY YEARS

The eleven Somalis of my sample were less than five years old when civil war broke out in Somalia in 1991 (and one of them was born in 1992). Since most of them fled the country shortly afterwards, they have no clear memories of the conflict. However, the experience of forced migration was usually fraught with complications and severe emotional strain, which had a profound impact on the women for years to come.[3] In some cases, this had encouraged the women to worship God from an early age, as they found they could derive relief and support from a relationship with Him.

For the most part, their parents had initially fled to a nearby country—usually Ethiopia, Kenya, or Saudi Arabia—or to a Western one then known for 'lenient' policies on refugees, such as Denmark or Norway. Migration to the United Kingdom came later, sometimes after brief stays in other countries where families struggled to find a comfortable environment. Fowsiya was the exception: she came directly to Britain in 1989, aged one, after her UK-based grandfather, who had worked for the British navy, successfully applied for the rest of his family to join him under the family reunion programme.

The refugees regarded the United Kingdom as an ideal destination for several reasons: its education system, which was well regarded and considered to provide good access to higher education for immigrants (unlike, for example, in Saudi Arabia); its reputation for treating refugees better than some other Western countries; its multiculturalist orientation and environment, with plenty of mosques and halal meat; and, finally, the fact that it (and London in particular) was already host to substantial Somali communities. Eritrean immigrants, discussed later, drew similar conclusions.

However, obtaining asylum in Britain was rarely straightforward. In fact, some Somalis strategically settled in a European country where it was comparatively easy to gain refugee status, with the aim of eventually securing a passport in order to reach their final destination—Britain. Others split up their families, sending one parent or child to join relatives already based in the United Kingdom, due to the difficulty of obtaining visas. Bilan's mother left her children with relatives in Kenya and came to Britain alone. She then worked up to three jobs at once in order to send remittances to her family, until she finally obtained visas for them all under the family reunion programme six years later.

As many as six of the Somali interviewees came to Britain without their parents and grew up under the care of aunts, grandmothers, and cousins, sometimes being moved around between relatives. This is not uncommon: many of the Somalis who have sought asylum in the United Kingdom have been unaccompanied children. The number peaked at 345 in 2002 and remained steady up to 2010 (Aspinall and Mitton, 2010). Some of my interviewees had lost their parents; in other cases, their parents were still alive but unable to obtain or afford visas for all of the family. In Warsan's parents' case, they were simply disinclined to leave Africa yet determined that their daughter should have the best opportunities in life (they remained in Kenya).

Deqa and Nadia had been chosen to accompany aunts and uncles to the United Kingdom after their families respectively only managed to obtain one visa each. Why them and not one of their siblings? Deqa was deemed the most resilient among her siblings, and Nadia most resembled the girl in a fake passport picture. Sagal had lost both parents during the war and fled Somalia with her aunt. Safia's mother had sent her three children to Britain to live with their grandmother because she could neither support them financially nor obtain a visa for herself. In some cases, the women were reunited with their parents, but often after suffering psychologically as a result of their prolonged absence during these formative years, as well as suffering ill-treatment by relatives in some cases.

My non-Somali interviewees either had far less traumatic migration experiences or had been born in Britain. In most cases, however, they maintained a clear sense of the culture from which they originally sprung; indeed, it helped shape their sense of personal identity. All four Eritreans were born in Saudi Arabia, which had been a popular destination for Eritreans escaping the long, bloody war of independence with Ethiopia (1961–1991) and seeking better employment opportunities.[4] All four came to Britain as babies or young children with their families between 1989 and 1990. At that time, according to Manal, Eritreans had started leaving Saudi Arabia as employers sought to replace them with Saudi nationals. Parents had also been concerned about their children's future prospects in what they saw as a two-tier society where non-Saudis could not go to university for free nor secure good jobs without sponsors. Also, some had relatives already in the United Kingdom.

The Nigerian 'born-Muslims', on the other hand, had enterprising parents in business who came for purely economic reasons—plus, according to Maryam, the status attached to living abroad. Despite this, Maryam's parents—in common with many of the migrant parents from other backgrounds—found themselves having to accept a lower socioeconomic status in Britain than in their countries of origin. The rest of the women were either born in the United Kingdom (four) or were unsure of their parents' reasons for migrating.

None of the women from my sample could identify a time when they had not believed in God. All of those from Muslim backgrounds had had a clear sense of being Muslim from a young age, yet for some this identification had few practical implications beyond, for instance, fasting during Ramadan and celebrating Eid. Just two of those who were born into Muslim families (both Somalis) had what could be termed 'religious' upbringings in the sense that their parents had tried to practise Islam's five pillars consistently and had raised their children to observe them.[5] Those families had also enforced a strict form of hijab-wearing and gender segregation.

The vast majority of the upbringings of those from Muslim families fell somewhere in the middle of the religiosity scale. In nearly all cases, their parents had sent them to madrasas linked to their ethnic communities, where they had learned how to read the Qur'an in Arabic to the exclusion of almost anything else. Since Arabic was no one's first language and no translations were provided, this amounted to little more than a recitation or limited linguistic exercise. Thus the women often regarded these classes as a chore—for some, a daily one—and did not take them seriously. Amina said she had considered her Eritrean Arabic school as effectively a 'social club', and Saidah would skive off her Arabic classes at the local Nigerian mosque, using the money her father had given her for the teacher to buy snacks instead.

The fact that their parents had 'outsourced' Islamic education to religious teachers was, some women suspected, more due to a desire to counteract the influence of non-Islamic schooling than to a commitment to raising practising Muslim children. Little religious instruction was provided at home beyond general advice to be honest and modest. According to Shukri, there is a cultural expectation among Somalis that children be taught to pray, read the Qur'an, and be truthful and obedient to their parents—but this is often the extent of Somalis' propagation of Islam to their children (as was the case for Shukri herself). Even non-practising Somali parents often send their children to Qur'an school because, as Fowsiya put it, 'for [parents] to say "my child knows the Qur'an" is something big'.

In general, the parents and guardians of the women of Muslim backgrounds encouraged them to pray, wear headscarves (at least when attending mosque), and abstain from 'too much' free-mixing (i.e., intermingling between the sexes) with men. Boyfriends, for example, were definitely a no-no, though socializing with male cousins was usually fine or even encouraged. Explanations for various practices and prohibitions would take the form of: 'You're a Muslim, and Muslims wear x,' or 'It's not from Islam to do y,' or something similar.

Thus, unsurprisingly, very few women reported embracing Islamic practices with enthusiasm before they rediscovered their faith in their mid- to late teens. Indeed, some admitted to praying only when forced to, and to removing their headscarves when out of sight of relatives. Deqa, for instance, wore a headscarf as a child because this was expected of her—but did not care if it fell off while she was out playing—and attended madrasa because 'my mum's gonna beat me up if I don't go'.

Meanwhile, there was also an emphasis on integrating into mainstream society to an extent—for example, by relaxing dress codes and celebrating Christmas—especially by refugee parents who were focused on making a comfortable life in a new country. The girls' limited religious instruction often left them feeling confused about the meaning and boundaries of their Islamic identity. They had similar feelings about their 'British' or 'Western' identity, particularly once they started to have non-Muslim friends and classmates who sometimes questioned their unfamiliar practices. Some of the women came to regard Islam as a religion merely of 'don'ts', against which they wished to rebel.

> We only prayed when we went to the mosque, and we wore our little headscarves and stuff when we went to the mosque. But then, when we went out, my mum would do my little pigtails to the school. It was part of who you are, but at the same time, you had to fit into society. So it was quite confusing. (Fowsiya, Somali)

> I was confused about what being a Muslim entails after praying, reading your Qur'an, and not lying! [Laughs]. . . . 'Cause I was like OK, so is my hijab compulsory upon me, you know, can I still go out to party with it and come back and pray, you know? (Shukri, Somali)

> Being in that kind of environment [growing up as refugees in Norway] it kinda— I dunno, you can't find your identity. So although you're trying to mix with the people and be part of the community, you're still gonna feel like an outsider 'cause you don't blend with how they look like, what they do. (Filsan, Somali)

Most of the women of Muslim backgrounds claimed that their religious instruction was not only limited but also misleading. A common narrative was to point out that the Islam they had been taught by their parents was infused with cultural 'innovations' rooted in their countries of origin. The women later became convinced that these rituals and prohibitions were not from the Qur'an or sunna, and consequently adjusted their practices.

Fowsiya learned that it is permissible to eat outside, despite what her Somali parents had told her. Nadia realized that her Somali mother's practice of seeking intercession via dead shaykhs constituted *shirk* (polytheism). Somali Abyan had been taught that if she died, she would become her aunt's 'guest' the following night—but later dismissed this as *bid'a* (reprehensible innovation). Madeeha discovered that many of her South Asian family's religious practices were rooted in hadiths that were 'not authentic'. Amina later learned that socializing with her male first cousin counted as free-mixing, though her Eritrean parents had always said: 'Oh, he's like your brother.' And Saidah later learned that her Nigerian parents' tradition of dressing up for the mosque on Sundays, rather than Fridays, was a 'cultural innovation' due to local Christian influence.

Meanwhile, Somalis Bilan and Sagal—the only two with 'religious' upbringings—had slightly different experiences. Although both had periods of rebellion—they were known as troublemakers who got into fights as young adolescents—they prayed and covered fairly consistently from a young age. Bilan was also the only one to mention madrasa as a positive experience. Both sets of parents incorporated relatively high levels of religious practice into their lives, in contrast to the others. For instance, they prayed regularly themselves and ensured that the girls copied them, and Bilan's uncle had even paid for her to be educated at a subsidized Islamic school.

For the converts, Christianity had been a significant part of their childhoods. Wafa, Humayrah, and Iman were taken to church regularly as children; Firdaws went to a Church of England school (her parents were agnostic); and Hayah started attending church at the age of eleven of her own accord. As they grew up, the girls became sceptical about Christianity, struggling with two aspects, above all.

First, three said they had been troubled by the concept of the Trinity, particularly the idea of worshipping a man who was simultaneously God. Humayrah said that despite being a regular churchgoer, she had always prayed to God, not Jesus, because worshipping the latter did not make sense to her.

Second, three mentioned Christianity's perceived lack of a coherent and consistent soteriology, since Christians had not always given them clear answers to questions about the afterlife. When they did, they referred to the doctrine of universal salvation, which was 'weak' and 'too easy'. As Firdaws put it: 'So even though I knew I was like a bad person and I was doing everything wrong, I thought: "Ah, it doesn't matter if I kill somebody—I'm still going to Heaven, I don't care."'

Thus all of the women previously had some involvement with religion or at least belief in God before they became 'practising' Muslims. The following section illuminates this process of becoming 'practising', which can be regarded as a conversional stage, seen in hindsight by Salafis as a transitional one as it led to the critical conversional stage—becoming Salafi.

3.2 BECOMING PRACTISING

The women generally had their spiritual awakenings between the ages of sixteen and twenty-two, a time commonly associated with formation and identity crises, and often coinciding with a diminishment of parents' authority and an increase in peer influence (McGuire, 2001, p.62). Nearly all of the women were at college or university at the time—often just beginning their studies in a new environment. Many mentioned peer influence in their narratives—although, interestingly, it was sometimes referred to as the catalyst for a woman suddenly to feel ashamed of her 'sinful' lifestyle. This led some to resolve to stop hanging around with their friends, who were seen as a corrupting influence.

I could not identify a typical pattern of 'becoming practising', and the process often took many twists and turns over several years, shaped by social, political, local, ethnic, and biographical factors to varying degrees and at different stages. The path to becoming what the women referred to as a 'practising Muslim'—by which they generally meant someone who tries to implement the five pillars of Islam consistently, plus some form of hijab—was never simple and linear. Usually, there were setbacks along the way. Many women admitted to having temporarily removed their hijabs during low points, for example. Sometimes, under the influence of practising peers or boyfriends, they would take on the hijab before they were ready, then remove it when their friends did or when they broke up with their boyfriends. During my fieldwork, I often heard the expression to be 'off *din*' (i.e., 'off' the religion) in reference to this pattern.

The example of Safia illustrates this dynamic. During her teens, Safia, who had been raised Muslim, intermittently tried to practise because she knew she 'should', but kept returning to music, boyfriends, and low-cut tops. 'You're thinking: "I've got all the time in the world,"' she explained. Separated from her Somali parents as a child refugee, she had felt neglected and battled with depression as she moved between relatives' households. Gradually, however, she had become more conscious of her religion, especially as a source of comfort during difficult times. She then became friends with some 'good sisters' who encouraged her to practise, and this proved to be the push she needed to make a lasting change to her lifestyle.

As previously indicated, the women had varying degrees of religious consciousness and knowledge at the time of their spiritual awakenings. It is therefore not surprising that their narratives range from the less dramatic trajectories of those who had always had a sense of an Islamic identity, which would have to be examined and self-consciously practised at some point, to those who identified a sudden event that triggered the transition from a distinctly haram (forbidden) lifestyle to a pious one.

Most, however, were unavoidably influenced by two key trends in the 2000s that raised the profile of Islam and thus heightened curiosity about the religion in Britain in general and south London in particular. Only a minority of women mentioned these trends as having directly influenced their decision to become practising Muslims, but the trends were so far-reaching in their impact that they provide crucial context to the spiritual awakenings of all of the young women.

The first was Islam and Muslims' heightened public profile in the wake of the events of 9/11, the ensuing War on Terror, and the London bombings of 7/7. The attacks shocked non-Muslims and Muslims alike, prompting many

to examine more closely the religion that had apparently inspired the atrocities. The media attention that followed led people—including non-observant
Muslims—to ask questions about one of the world's most widely practised
religions, adhered to by friends, relatives, colleagues, and neighbours, and
some were pleasantly surprised by the answers and attracted to the faith.
Salafism and particularly Brixton Mosque had a high profile during this
period (see chapter 1).

This post-9/11 pattern of rising interest in Islam was also observed in the
United States, where several reports found a significant rise in conversions
to Islam, particularly among women. One Muslim leader said: 'Not even a
billion dollars to support da'wa [propagation] would have made it possible to
reach as many Americans with the message of Islam' (Haddad, 2006, p.19).

The second influential trend had a much more direct effect on Salafis in
London, and has to date only been partially documented. A curious 'fashion'—as Salafis termed it—for converting to Islam gathered pace during the
early to mid-2000s, predominantly among youth of Afro-Caribbean origin
in south London. Women at Brixton Mosque recalled that during the early
to mid-2000s, peaking in 2003–2006, scores of teenagers mainly from Afro-
Caribbean backgrounds became Muslim, while many of their peers from
Muslim backgrounds became more Islamically conscious, too. Although there
are no official statistics on converts, let alone reliable breakdowns of factors
such as ethnicity and location, there is evidence of a pronounced increase in
conversions during the 2000s. A 2011 report estimated that the number of
converts in Britain had risen from 60,669 in 2001 (Scottish Census, 2001)
to 100,000 in 2010, and that roughly half of mosque-based conversions took
place in London (Brice, 2010).

This local trend apparently overtook the fashion for adopting aspects of
the Rastafari Movement, particularly among youth from Jamaican backgrounds, that prevailed from the 1970s onwards (Reddie, 2009, p.194).
It is worth noting that the fact that Bob Marley had joined the Rastafari
Movement, which had a following in Brixton, had demonstrated to young
people the compatibility of a religious lifestyle and street credibility (Lambert,
2011, p.169). Like the Rastafari Movement, Islam had come to be perceived
as at odds with white British culture and 'middle England' (Githens-Mazer,
2012, p.55).

'Muslim Chic', as Reddie (2009, p.194) describes it, seems to have originated in the early 1990s, when Spike Lee's film *Malcolm X* (1992) was
released. Calling one's children Islamic names became fashionable, and
some black men replaced their usual 'respect' greeting with the Islamic
al-salamu 'alaykum. Islamic clothing, too, became trendy, even in non-
Muslim circles. Jonathan Githens-Mazer's (2009, p.55) interviewees,
who were associated with the Finsbury Park and Brixton Mosques, recalled 'individuals first coming to the Mosque to find out how they could

buy thobes (the outfit worn by Salafi men), and only subsequently becoming interested in Islam'.

Yet it appears that Muslim Chic did not peak until around 2003–2004. Abdul Haqq Baker, chairman of Brixton Mosque (1994–2009), informed me that, at that time, even non-Muslim black youth were using 'Islamic' lingo—such as the greeting *al-salamu 'alaykum* and *ak* (derived from the Arabic word *akh*, meaning 'brother'). In the Brixton area, black-and-white and red-and-white *kafiyyat* (traditional Arab headdresses), worn on the head or around the shoulders, became popular markers of this new Muslim identity.

This trend was lent impetus by gangs who wished to appropriate the fearsomeness that had come to be associated with the 'Brixton brothers'. Indeed, the Salafis, said Baker, had acquired a reputation locally as 'brothers who feared only Allah'. Their street credibility had been enhanced by a series of confrontations with police and community members during the 1990s, in which the 'brothers' demonstrated their defiance and combativeness in the face of perceived injustice. For example, according to Baker, there was an incident in 1996 when

> police ... chased a Muslim suspect of Algerian descent into the mosque without a warrant nor consent and arrested him. .... Approximately 30 to 40 of us ... proceeded to the police station and took over the foyer, demanding the man's release. .... I received calls from brothers across west London who had started to come across to Brixton. However, I dissuaded some of them, being aware of what they had equipped themselves with. .... The duty sergeant ... was clearly very worried by what he'd seen and invited me to visit the man in the holding cell to assure me that he had not been harmed in any way. He also arranged to release the man without charge, remarking that this was the quickest release he'd ever done.[6]

This perception of Muslims as a force to be reckoned with was amplified by 9/11 and the counter-narrative of resistance it represented to some of those who considered themselves as the underdog. Osama bin Laden was seen by some as a modern-day David taking on Goliath.

Subsequently, some gang members came to regard the Islamic identity as an intimidating weapon that could help facilitate their criminal activities. Some were influenced by gang leaders who had converted in prison. Others were spurred by Jihadi preachers, such as Abdullah el-Faisal, a Jamaican-born convert, who claimed it was justifiable to commit violent crimes against non-Muslims on the streets of London (Lambert, 2011, p.174). According to Githens-Mazer (2013), 'Al-Faisal regularly combined discourses of race and Islam in order to instil a sense of obligation to confront injustice against Muslims'.

Stories circulated about 'new Muslims' engaging in criminal activities, such as robbing drug dealers. Gangs dominated by Muslim converts emerged—most notably South Man Syndicate (also known as South Muslim Soldiers), Peel Dem Crew (also known as Poverty Driven Children or PDC), Organised Crime (OC), and GAS Gang (a younger offshoot of PDC and OC, linked to at least six murders).[7] These became collectively known in the media as 'the Muslim boys'.[8] Some such gangs became notorious for instigating 'conversions' at gunpoint.

According to one Brixton Mosque leader, Kareem, these gangsters never used the 'Salafi' label, but a few became Salafis later on. Nonetheless, he said, their appearance—black, bearded men wearing *thawbs* (Muslim men's robe-like garment, raised above the ankles)—meant that they were automatically associated with Brixton Mosque in the minds of locals, journalists, and the police.

When a local named Adrian Marriott was shot five times in the head in 2004, allegedly after refusing to convert, then-chairman of Brixton Mosque Abdul Haqq Baker spoke to the media to distance the mosque from gangsters (Cohen, 2005). In an effort to reduce inflamed community tensions, the mosque's imam also went with other staff to Marriott's family home to try to make his relatives understand that what had happened was contrary to what Islam, and Brixton Mosque, stood for.

This south London 'fashion' for converting quickly gathered pace, becoming a wider trend that was no longer limited to male gang members. In this, it was undoubtedly aided by the simplicity of the Islamic conversion process—expressed outwardly by the recitation of the *shahada* (profession of faith).

In many cases, whole friendship circles at schools and colleges became Muslim in quick succession. Sometimes younger siblings would follow their elders into Islam. Girlfriends and boyfriends, too, would influence one another. According to Baker, it got to the point where almost everybody in south London seemed to have a friend or relative who had become Muslim.

The role of Brixton Mosque in these developments was highly significant due to its location and reputation as 'the revert masjid'. Throughout the period, it was particularly receptive to newcomers—especially Afro-Caribbean converts and newly practising Muslim youth. Leaders said that at the peak of this trend, the mosque oversaw at least three hundred conversions during May and June 2004 alone, and that on some occasions as many as five young people would embrace Islam in one sitting.

In some cases, conversion was undoubtedly the result of social pressure or even a desire for protection from Muslim gangs, rather than genuine religious seeking. One leader at the mosque recalled 'kids coming in and saying, "Yeah, he wants to become Muslim," and it appeared that there was an element of peer pressure to become Muslim, in some cases.'

In more extreme cases, young people converted amid threats by Muslim gangs. Baker recalled the account of an agitated young man who had turned up at the mosque declaring that he wanted to convert. After being questioned by mosque staff, who were concerned by his tense manner, the young man admitted that a gang to which he owed money had warned him: 'The only thing that will save you now is if you take your *shahada!*'

Such cases, said Baker, led the mosque's *shura* (consultation committee) to decide that 'we've got to put the brakes on this'. In 2004, to make matters worse, police alerted the mosque to (unconfirmed) reports of people hiding weapons on the premises. In one notorious incident, a gun fell out of the pocket of one worshipper as he bowed in prayer.

Thus the mosque took steps to address the situation. One step was to condemn the gang culture in the mosque's Friday *khutba* (sermon). In addition, would-be converts could no longer obtain quick, 'walk-in' conversions; they had to sit down and listen to staff members explain Islam in greater detail. Yet, according to Baker, this did not hinder the majority from becoming Muslims.

Despite such measures, it appears that many youths did not take their new religion seriously. Some merely adopted a superficial and intermittent Islamic lifestyle, adorning themselves with Islamic symbols by day and drinking alcohol and raving by night. Others embraced an Islamic lifestyle with zeal, but then abandoned it just as suddenly. As one London Salafi leader put it, in the case of young people who converted to fit in with their friends, 'their Islam is as lasting as, for example, the latest phone or the latest trainers'. Umm Reemah, a long-time worshipper at Brixton Mosque, recalled an 'influx' of young women into the mosque around 2006 who had 'come in on a hype [i.e., overexcited]'. She said they were

> fasting *hard* and they were praying and everything, and then one by one they stopped coming to the mosque. And you're like what's happened to this one, what's happened to that one? 'Oh that one, she's had a baby, that one's in prison, that one's doing this, that one's doing that, that one's turned the other way.'

For many, interest in Islam was a fleeting phase. But for those who remained practising Muslims, this period was crucial in stimulating their curiosity about Islam and Muslims and thus their quest for more information about the religion. For some, such as convert Humayrah, the sudden appearance of so many new Muslims in their midst led them to question assumptions they had made about Islam since 9/11.

The 'fashion' also prompted some youth who were raised in Muslim families to reflect on their own religious identities and to adopt visibly Islamic symbols and practices with pride. Indeed, Brixton Mosque leaders said that the trend helped to 'reignite' the local Muslim community. Saidah, who had previously felt embarrassed to admit she was Muslim, started covering her hair for the first time when all of her friends became Muslim in her first year of college: 'We used to wear normal clothes [jeans, tracksuits, trainers] and then get a headscarf and wrap it round the back [i.e., a head-wrap], and that used to be like, "Yeah, we're Muslims!"'

Converts Humayrah, Iman, and Firdaws said that many or most of their friends or classmates converted or became Islamically conscious at one point, and often encouraged others to follow suit. But they initially resisted such attempts due to a perception that the trend was mere 'hype'. Firdaws said that she had simply thought: 'How can you be so dumb to want to be part of such a dumb religion like Islam with all its rules?' Gradually, however, all three women did some research on their own, and realized that many of their problems with Islam were based on misconceptions and converted. Iman said that one of the friends she converted with later became a Christian, and another struggled to start practising Islam because she missed dressing up and going to raves.

These two trends at most acted as 'curiosity triggers' or facilitated spiritual awakenings by popularizing Islam. But there were many other forces at play. When asked about their initial transition to 'practising' Muslims, the women from Muslim backgrounds fell into two categories. There were those who seemed to have internalized Islam from a young age to the extent that they had always known, consciously or not, that they *ought* to practise their religion fully at some point. This had regulated their lifestyles to some extent before they had become practising. Others described having led 'haram' lifestyles until something happened to make them reassess their life choices. Both groups often mentioned social networks—the inspiration of practising friends, boyfriends, siblings, cousins, or neighbours—as influential in encouraging them to stick to their choice.

The first group tended to describe the transition as a fairly seamless one that occurred once the circumstances were right. It was not the case that an event—such as a personal crisis or something that produced acute tension—had turned them into a religious seeker, as suggested by the conversion models of Lofland and Stark (1965) and Rambo (1993). These women used phrases to convey this sense of inevitability, such as 'I used to think about it [becoming practising and wearing "proper" hijab] all the time before that so when I did it, it was kinda like—it seemed like it was due time' (Abeer). Bit by bit and often with the inspiration and encouragement of friends or young relatives, the women investigated the religious beliefs and practices of their childhoods in detail, learning for the first time about the meaning of the hijab, for instance, then adopting it with conviction.

But most of the women suggested that there had been a disjuncture between their '*jahiliyya*' time and practising stage. They stressed that before practising, they had been aware of their 'sinful' lifestyles, but unable to resist joining their peers in going out and having fun. Two patterns emerge: they gradually became bored with their lifestyle, and started feeling guilty about doing 'un-Islamic' things to 'fit in'; or a crisis occurred that led them to re-assess what they were doing. Wiktorowicz (2005, p.20) has recognized the power of crisis in turning individuals into religious seekers: it can, he writes, produce a 'cognitive opening' that 'shakes certainty in previously accepted beliefs and renders an individual more receptive to the possibility of alterna-tive views and perspectives'.

In the first group were Dania, Manal, and Madeeha, who focused on having fun in their late teens—going out for shisha, clubbing, smoking can-nabis, and so on—until boredom set in as they reflected on the 'emptiness' of their lifestyle, coupled with a sense of guilt because they had internalized the 'correct' way to behave as Muslim women from a young age. Madeeha, for in-stance, dropped out of college and hung around 'drinkers and drug-dealers', smoking cannabis 'every other day' for three years and getting thrown out of 'practically every club in the West End', until she became fed up with her destructive habits, disturbed by unwanted male attention, and concerned by paranoia and memory lapses that had set in as a result of her drug use. She resolved to cut off all of her friends and start attending Islamic lessons.

In the second group were those who were prompted by crises, varying in in-tensity, to use the resources of the religion in which they were raised to make sense of their experiences and lend them purpose. For these women, their crises generally fell into two categories. First, some became more dependent on God as a source of comfort and support during difficult times. Saidah and Warsan relied on God especially after illness and death in the family. Deqa, a refugee whose parents stayed behind, said that she had started attending mosque and became closer to God because she was lonely. Safia and Nadia, who both grew up without their parents, had felt neglected in their youth as they moved between relatives' households, lacking the warmth of a parent-like figure. Nadia said:

> Instead of asking my mum or dad, I didn't have that so I turned to God from a young age.... When things got difficult, I've always asked Him, and I always felt that He'll always find a way out for me, even if I don't see it now.

Second, some interpreted the destabilizing event as a 'sign' from God to start taking Islam seriously. For Warda, it was her underperformance in her GCSEs—UK qualifications typically taken by school students aged 14–16—that convinced her that she was being punished: 'I knew it was something to do with God . . . because it wasn't logical for someone to fail and they worked hard.' And for Maryam, it was the London bombings of 7/7: 'I thought to myself that day. . . . If I do not wear the hijab today, it will start getting difficult for me, in the sense that there will be more trials.' For Amina, it was constantly being let down by friends that made her realize God was telling her: 'I'm here. . . . You should rely on Me.' And Filsan was 'hanging out with the wrong crowd' at eighteen, but reevaluated her lifestyle after a man tried to rape her. 'I'm thinking, I could have not gone out clubbing and went with this guy,' she said. 'I'm like, if I was practising, I wouldn't be in that situation. I wouldn't be in an environment where I feel I'm scared now.'

As for the converts, all five mentioned other Muslims as being the initial curiosity-triggers that led them to do independent research on Islam, which then corrected any misconceptions while raising doubts about the claims of Christianity. This was generally enough to convince the women to pronounce the *shahada*. Practising the religion, however, often came years later, prompted by the influence of social networks and/or dramatic events. For example, both Humayrah and Iman had been complacent in their religious practice for some time after converting—until the sudden deaths of Humayrah's close friend, who was shot, and Iman's mother prompted them to take Islam more seriously. Iman contemplated suicide, but then she began to 'think about where I'm going, like do I wanna die like this? Nah, I wanna die with Allah being pleased.'

3.3 NAVIGATING THE 'ISLAM MARKET'

Having resolved to take their religion seriously and start practising, the women realized that they would have to remedy their ignorance of Islam. But where to start? They were eager to learn about their religion, but ill-equipped to distinguish between the different interpretations in their midst. They therefore tended to enter an experimental phase in which they learned almost indiscriminately from any source with an 'Islamic' aura. For most, their starting points were chosen simply out of convenience: the local mosque, college prayer room, university Islamic society, religiously observant Muslim friends, or a combination of these.

The initial source could even be virtual: Humayrah admitted that, at first, 'I'd just type in what I wanted [to know about], just go into Google and just type it in,' after which she would follow whatever links looked informative. Shukri Googled 'Islamic talks' and found that the late Yemeni-American Jihadi preacher Anwar Al-Awlaki came up as the first result. Impressed by his knowledge and oratory, she listened to his lectures devotedly for some time before turning to Salafism.

Yet, interestingly, even those who encountered Salafism early on in this experimental phase—for instance, because Brixton Mosque was their local mosque or most of their friends were Salafis—mostly did not experience a quick and smooth transition into Salafism. Rather, like the others, they described a gradual process of looking into different groups and, in many cases, initially wrestling against Salafism.

At this early stage of investigation, the young religious-seekers were often overwhelmed by what I call the crowded 'Islam market'. In the consumerist, liberal, modern society, it has become common to analyze conversion as occurring in a 'religion market'—an array of competing religious 'products'— in which individuals may freely 'shop', weighing up the pros and cons of the various options (Wohlrab-Sahr, 2006).

The young women faced a choice between a considerable number of groups and preachers that operated in London, as well as online, all competing for their attention. These had distinct approaches to creed, jurisprudence, and politics, and made reciprocal refutations of each other.[9] Raising the stakes further, many had competing claims about which was the 'saved sect',[10] or *al-firqa al-najiya*, implying that joining other groups would put even believers on the path to Hell.

Even women of Muslim backgrounds had very little, if any, prior knowledge of the origins and interpretations of the various schools and groups beyond a basic acquaintance with the Sunni/Shia divide. Safia and Saidah, both from Muslim families, had no concept of different 'Islams' until their college classmates started to convert in large numbers and to investigate different groups.

> At first ... I found that [the different 'sects'] really confusing.... Growing up, I've never realized there were so many different sects until people started reverting. People that were coming into Islam, going to these different sects and I didn't even know nothing about it. So I just thought, I'm interested.... The word 'sect' did not exist in my head. (Safia)

> It was only when I got to college I realized there was different types of Muslims, you know—I'm being serious! I didn't know this!... It was something that I was not taught. (Saidah)

Many women described an earnest sense of intense confusion during these early practising years as they grappled with many different sources of information—websites, videos, lecture recordings, books, Islamic Society talks, friends, relatives, boyfriends—all promoting different ideas about how a Muslim woman ought to live. During this period, many learned about Islam simultaneously from various mosques, websites, books, conferences and Islamic Society events, which were often linked to groups or approaches plainly at odds with one another. They were often guided simply by what 'feels right' or 'wrong', as well as by how 'Islamic' a preacher appeared.

For example, Manal experimented with groups whose approaches ranged from Sufi to Islamist to Salafi. She attended lectures almost indiscriminately, despite occasionally hearing things that 'didn't feel right', because 'I was at a very naïve stage where I was like, OK, I'll take the good and leave the bad'. Shukri also took this 'pick-and-mix' approach when she started practising during her first year at university, listening 'to any person who said they're Muslim'. Warsan, too, recalled: 'When you don't have that knowledge, you take from anyone with a beard.'

In a few cases, this naïveté led the women to experiment with radical groups, such as the successors of the banned group Al-Muhajiroun. I spoke at length with three Salafi women who had become involved with versions of this group, and they said that they knew other former Al-Muhajiroun followers who were now Salafis. One of them, Asmaa, said: '*Loads* of the people that I knew from . . . [Al-Muhajiroun] are *al-hamdulillah* [praise God] on the Salafi *da'wa* now.' This group, which has been linked to around half of the terrorist plots carried out or foiled by Britons since 2000 (Kennedy, 2015), was banned by the UK government in 2010 but continued to operate under various aliases, such as Islam4UK, Need4Khalifah, and even Salafi Media and The Salafi Youth Movement. The preacher Anjem Choudary, who has represented the group through its various mutations, has become notorious for his praise of the 9/11 terrorists and for other inflammatory statements.

But when Layaan, Asmaa, and Nadia stumbled upon the group, they were ignorant of its true identity—as well as of some of the basic principles of Islam itself. They lacked Islamic points of reference against which to judge the group, so were initially persuaded by its claim to represent 'true' Islam, based on the Qur'an and sunna.

Layaan, a university graduate in her mid-twenties, had just decided to practise her birth religion after a few turbulent years. With no practising friends, she had no one to turn to for advice on which Islamic lessons to attend and which to avoid. Instead, she went to her local mosque, hoping to find a lesson. None was currently running, but while she was there, an attractive flyer caught her eye. It simply said: 'coffee mornings, Wednesdays 10.30 am–12 pm' and 'evening talks, Mondays 5–7 pm'—with no reference to particular preachers or Islamic interpretations. The following week, she tried out the evening lecture, which took place in a community centre in east London.

When I went there, there was a lot of sisters all from different backgrounds and reverts. They were all so lovely and welcoming—I really felt connected to them. One sister said to me on my first day: 'The best thing about this place is we don't follow any *madhhabs* (i.e., schools of jurisprudence), only Qur'an and sunna.' I thought, great! That's exactly what I've been searching for. So I continued going on and off for about six months. A lot of their talks was about politics, law, prisons [i.e., Guantanamo Bay], freeing Babar Ahmad [a British citizen extradited to the United States on terrorism charges in 2012, released in 2015], demonstrations. That was the first time I heard the name of that prison [Guantanamo Bay] . . . I didn't have the slightest clue who they actually were. I didn't even know what Al-Muhajiroun was.

Nadia and Asmaa were just sixteen when they were approached by Al-Muhajiroun recruiters, who invited them to attend talks—without referring to the group by name. Asmaa, a university student in her early twenties and Brixton attendee, had only just started practising her religion, and naturally turned to her college prayer room as a first step. There, she met a Jamaican man who reprimanded her for wearing nail varnish before giving her books and inviting her and a friend to lessons that turned out to be affiliated with Al-Muhajiroun. She trusted him because

> he had the big beard, trousers were above the ankles, he was much older than us, he seemed like he was much more knowledgeable than we could ever be, and we were just these two little girls.

The confusion the women described experiencing during this early stage in religious seeking seemed particularly acute in the case of converts, who naturally had even less knowledge of different approaches to Islam. Converts may also have a still greater concern to learn from the 'correct' source, as to do otherwise would demean the sacrifices they made to become Muslim.

Humayrah, for instance, did not even understand the difference between Sunnis and Shias when she converted, and had to trust her instincts when both a Shia and a Salafi gave her *da'wa* at college. She decided to trust the Salafi because, unlike the Shia, she seemed knowledgeable, gave proofs from the Qur'an and sunna, condemned 9/11, and never said 'I think' when explaining Islam.

A particular source of initial confusion for converts that favours their entrance into Salafism is the tendency of Sunni Muslims to take jurisprudential rulings only from the *madhhab* associated with their country of origin—a tendency that Salafism opposes. For instance, South Asian Muslims, who make up the majority of British Muslims, favour the Hanafi school, while Somalis traditionally follow the Shafi'i one, originated by the famous imams Abu Hanifa and Al-Shafi'i, respectively. Thus British mosques, as well as Islamic lessons and books, are often oriented strictly towards just one *madhhab* to serve these ethnic communities. Some of the schools' rulings directly contradict each other, forcing a new Muslim to choose between them. For example, she must decide whether to pray in the Hanafi way or the Hanbali way—she cannot do both simultaneously.

Converts notice how born-Muslim peers often follow *madhahib* (schools of law) purely in imitation of their parents, whose approach is predetermined by their countries of origin. But converts with no Muslim family background are not naturally drawn to any particular *madhhab* (unless, perhaps, they marry someone who is). Lacking knowledge of the intricate differences between the schools, they face a perplexing choice.

> These people in college, they used to say to me, 'I'm Maliki', 'I'm Hanbali', 'I'm this', 'I'm that'. This is me: 'Why don't you just follow all of them if they're all so good!' . . . I didn't get why you had to be one! [Laughs] 'Cause like 'you have to be what your parents are upon'. And I goes, 'Yeah, but my parents aren't upon all this—what's this, I've never heard of it.' And he goes, 'Choose one.' So what, I'm going to research every single one of these things and then go, OK, this is what I like most? D'you know what I mean? (Wafa, convert)

> All that thing about the *madhhab* confused me anyway 'cause I was like, hold on, why am I gonna follow an imam called Abu Hanifa when he wasn't the Prophet (p.b.u.h. [peace be upon him]) and the Prophet (p.b.u.h.) didn't tell me to follow him? (Firdaws, convert)

Going to university exposes the Muslim student to intra-Sunni clashes head-on, since various Muslim groups—notably, Islamist or Muslim Brotherhood–inspired groups, Hizb ut-Tahrir, Sufi groups, and Salafis—operate on British university campuses, often through their links to student societies. For many women, in common with other freshers, it was a time when they faced deep questions of identity. University is an opportunity for a fresh start, a chance to reinvent oneself and reevaluate goals. Many of the women I interviewed, for instance, were considering adopting the headscarf or a stricter form of hijab when they arrived; at a new institution at which they were unknown, it was easier to make this transition.

They arrived with few or no friends, often living away from home for the first time, and the university prayer room provided a social, as well as religious, space where they could meet like-minded people—mainly fellow Muslim women. These new friends encouraged them to experiment with different interpretations. Most of the women found the dominant drinking culture of British universities unappealing and alienating; consequently, their opportunities to meet new people beyond the prayer room were limited, since alcohol was present in most other social spaces on campus.[11]

Three women also mentioned involvement with their university Islamic Societies (ISOCs) as an important part of their religious journey. With such a simple and apparently universal label—'Islamic'—ISOCs attract Sunni students of all doctrinal and ideological persuasions. But in reality, ISOCs often promote certain Islamic interpretations at the expense of others. The committees of ISOCs consist of elected students who have their own particular religious and political leanings, which inevitably influence members' exposure to the teachings of different groups. Also, other university groups, individuals, and societies—sometimes ISOC splinter groups[12]—promote their own approaches. Rivalry between groups can be fierce, as cliques defend their own 'shaykhs' and refute those of others.

In recent years, ISOCs in UK universities have been accused of propagating conservative interpretations and even of radicalizing Muslim students to support violent extremism. Above all, the revelation in 2009 that the 'Underwear Bomber', Umar Farouk Abdulmutallab,[13] was formerly president of the University College London ISOC, prompted the government and think tanks to take a renewed interest in campuses as potential 'breeding grounds' of Islamic extremism. Some reports accused ISOCs of hosting 'extremist' speakers who promote fundamentalist views on women, politics, and relations with non-Muslims, for instance.[14]

Responding to these concerns, the government made it a legal requirement in 2015 for universities and other public bodies to monitor and report extremism, whether suggestive of violence or not (Gov.uk, 2015). However, the evidence that universities and specifically ISOCs foster 'radicalization' is disputed,[15] and, as Miri Song (2012, p.156) has pointed out, 'the specific activities and aims of each ISOC may be quite diverse, and cannot be simplistically characterized as a body which facilitates radical extremism'.

Two women I interviewed had been particularly proactive in their ISOCs, which had at that time promoted an Islamist interpretation focused on raising awareness of perceived injustices against Muslims worldwide. They said they even met people there who approved of suicide bombings of civilians under certain circumstances.

When Fowsiya arrived at university, confused about her religious identity and determined to start practising, her ISOC enabled her to meet like-minded, similarly dressed women. It also hosted talks by lively speakers who always moved her—and others—to tears on emotive subjects such as the plight of the Palestinians. She started to have doubts when she realized that, despite learning a lot about current events around the world, she was not progressing much in terms of *Islamic* knowledge. At the recommendation of a friend, she then attended an Al-Athariyyah Salafi class in Forest Gate, east London, that focused on the fundamental concept of *tawhid* (Islamic monotheism), and she suddenly felt as though she was learning her religion directly and in pure form.

A similarly political and emotive ISOC experience initially stirred Warsan, who described a process of earnestly seeking her purpose in life during her university years. Along with a group of Muslim girlfriends, she went from talk to talk—all of them, she said, were 'trying to find themselves' and to resolve their Islamic identities. Confused by the 'melting pot of ideologies' they encountered on campus, they tried to make sense of it by researching Islam together. Those considered more knowledgeable or more 'Islamically' dressed would answer the others' questions. The friends would then transfer allegiances when 'it didn't sound right' This eventually led them to a Salafi

ISOC splinter group, which convinced Warsan that she knew so little about the basics of her religion—such as *tawhid*—that remedying this ignorance was more urgent than 'saving the *umma* (i.e., worldwide Muslim community)' through political activities.

In this context, even those who were less proactive than Fowsiya and Warsan in engaging with Muslim groups on campus would be drawn into heated discussions among friends in which they debated the truth claims of each other's 'shaykhs'. Amina said:

> There'll be a group of us just sitting round in a shisha café and we'll be talking about Islam, and one person would say 'Yeah, I'm upon *Salafiyya* [Salafism], I'm a *salaf*, I'm this'—[another says] 'No, but I'm a Sunni'—and I'll be so confused 'cause I was never raised in any sort of way of Islam, I was just raised as a Muslim full-stop. . . . A lot of people will say, 'No, we're not going to this talk—this shaykh's been refuted, he's not even a shaykh.' And then again it started confusing me even more, and I'm like, 'What's the term "refuted"? How can someone say that about a shaykh?' To me, a shaykh is a shaykh, and no one can say anything about a shaykh.

Amina's confusion became so great that she isolated herself from all of her friends, changed her phone number, spent much more time at home with her family, and gradually started investigating the different groups independently—a process that eventually led her to Salafism.

Others stumbled upon different groups in other environments, including some who were actively engaged with Islamist groups before becoming Salafi. Manal and Filsan experimented with Islamist strains that were focused on political matters; and Shukri was initially an avid listener of the Jihadi preacher Anwar Al-Awlaki.

Indeed, the general picture the women presented was one of delayed involvement in Salafism, with various other Islamic experiments along the way. At least half of the women encountered Salafism at an early stage in their religious seeking—their 'experimental phase'—yet did not embrace the group until later. Often they made forays—some more prolonged than others—into other Muslim groups, which were initially more attractive.

The reasons for this delayed involvement were related primarily to Salafis' poor public image, and the women had to resolve these issues before they could consider embracing Salafism. Within many British Muslim circles, Salafism has acquired a reputation as, at best, a group that unnecessarily divides the *umma* and, at worst, a 'cult' or fashionable new group that imposes draconian restrictions on its followers—particularly the women—and has little to do with genuine Islam. Three women admitted that this had been their initial impression of Salafism.

The tendency of Salafi leaders constantly to refer to Salafism as 'the saved sect', while branding all other groups as 'deviated', contributes to this image. In addition, the 'hype' surrounding Brixton Mosque during the mass-conversion era of the early to mid-2000s left some with the impression that Salafism was no more than the latest fad for rebellious youth. At first, Manal saw the Salafi 'craze' as a passing fashion—partly due to the sexual appeal of the 'Brixton brothers' among young women. '[Brixton Mosque] was like the place to be seen,' she explained. 'The way everyone would hang around outside the masjid, and you'd see numbers being exchanged or this and that.' Flirtatious behaviour at the mosque entrance among a minority of worshippers had been a cause for concern among the mosque leadership—so much so that they highlighted it in Friday *khutab* (sermons).

Some women were also put off because they had heard that Brixton Mosque was 'in league with' the government. Certainly, its staff had cooperated with the police during the 'Shoe Bomber' affair,[16] and in 2006 its chairman launched a counter-radicalization programme that later received government funds. When Filsan first heard about Salafism, she was actually told that Brixton Mosque was run by government spies—an allegation she later dismissed as false.

But by far the most damaging issue for Salafism's image in Muslim communities has been the harsh attitude and bad manners of some of its followers. Although Salafi leaders frequently advise adherents to give *da'wa* in a gentle and humble manner, numerous women said—often reluctantly, sometimes only after repeated reassurances of anonymity—that the judgmental and unwelcoming attitude of a minority of women initially kept them away from Salafism and Salafi environments. Indeed, during fieldwork, I soon realized that this was a common sentiment among both non-Salafi and Salafi Muslims alike.

Salafi teachings require followers to enjoin good and forbid evil, with the greatest spiritual reward for those who repudiate evil by intervening in some way, rather than merely disapproving silently.[17] Salafism also promotes a clear distinction between the 'halal' and the 'haram', allowing far less ambiguity about the permissibility of different types of hijab, for instance, than other groups.

These two aspects of Salafi groups mean that there is great potential for heated confrontations between Muslims. Indeed, three women said that they had felt judged and intimidated when they first sat in the women's section of Brixton Mosque, clad in colourful hijabs and make-up. Hayah had been reluctant to become involved with the mosque because 'I felt that you had to be in all black with *niqab*, you know, you had to be holding the banner of Salafi to be accepted.' Manal and her friends were upset by comments from converts there who 'felt we were a bit too done-up' and, she suspected, were wary of young, pretty girls who might have entered the community to become second wives to their husbands.

I bumped into an old university friend, a non-Salafi black Muslim convert called Aisha, outside Brixton Mosque one Friday afternoon, who had a similar impression. A Salafi friend had encouraged her to go there for Friday prayers. Aisha said she had felt uneasy there after being told by the women not to wear an abaya decorated with 'ethnic colours', as she described it. 'In Salafi environments, it can feel like a pressure cooker,' she added.

Compounding the 'holier-than-thou' impression, a significant number of Salafis would mistakenly refer to themselves as *salaf*s, rather than Salafis, suggesting that they placed themselves on a spiritual par with the pious predecessors themselves. I am convinced that this error was entirely innocent—their intention was to signify an *attachment* to the *salaf*, which is, after all, the meaning of the term 'Salafi'—yet it was nonetheless damaging. By the time of my fieldwork, this habit had become a cause for concern among Salafi leaders, who occasionally expounded upon the linguistic differences between the two terms in lectures.

Furthermore, Salafi leaders are known for not mincing their words about Islamic preachers and groups that are considered 'deviated'. This encourages a culture of refutation[18] among Salafis in general that can be offensive to outsiders, particularly when combined with harsh and tactless manners. Three of the women I interviewed described upsetting confrontations with Salafi women during lectures when they took issue with the former's attachment—at the time—to non-Salafi preachers:

> They could be very ill-mannered, so they hear *masha'Allah* [i.e., 'whatever God wills', expression of joy] maybe so and so's been refuted, and they'll come to you and be like, 'Well he's refuted, why're you listening to him? *You're* refuted, *you're* upon *bid'a*'—and you're like, wow! I don't think I wanna associate with you. (Shukri)

> They'll come up to you and be like, 'Oh I don't know your face, are you familiar here, sister, where are you from?' And you're like, 'Oh I live in so and so.' 'Oh, d'you come here often?' And then 'I go to so and so's masjid'. 'Oh, *those*? Those people are deviant, those people are this and this and that'—and you're already being attacked. And it's like, oh my gosh, what is wrong with these people. . . . It was just a constant attack. (Abyan)

Similarly, Sagal was introduced to Salafism when a Salafi friend objected to the books she read and talks she attended, telling her they were not Salafi and therefore not 'safe'. When Sagal asked how her friend knew this, she simply said: 'Someone else told me.'

These issues are aggravated by the 'street mentality' that, the women claimed, some Brixton Mosque attendees—who included some ex–gang members and ex-convicts—never fully shed when they became Salafis.

AbdulHaq Ashanti, who has worked in the mosque's administration team since 2002, agreed that Salafis have had a 'reputation of being very harsh and blunt and hard-nosed' since the 1990s, partly because some of them 'came into Islam from the gang culture, hip-hop culture, that kind of thing'.

Some women described experiencing a cold and confrontational manner when they first tried to become acquainted with others at the mosque. They also had the impression that the women's section consisted of closed cliques, rather than the warm and welcoming sisterhood they had envisioned when they had started practising. Hayah described a frosty and intimidating 'let me look you up and down attitude' that initially put her off going to the mosque. Manal, Filsan, and Abyan had similar experiences at Brixton Mosque and Salafi events elsewhere, contrasting with their experiences of other groups. Filsan said of her early days at Brixton:

> The whole process of getting to know new sisters, so you'd be like, do they wanna get to know me? . . . You would see the older sisters just by themselves, you will see the young sisters, and then you'll see the Somalis at another corner, and you'll be like, what's going on? But then in Acton [Mosque in Ealing, west London] everyone is sitting together, everyone is talking, it's just friendly, but then here it's just one group to another to another. You'll be like, so who do I talk to, then? No one is actually passing *salams* [i.e., Islamic greetings] to you.

She persevered only because she had married a member of the mosque, and eventually managed to make friends.

Asmaa attended some Salafi conferences during her experiment with Al-Muhajiroun but was not tempted to switch allegiances until much later, for similar reasons. Unlike the Salafis, the Al-Muhajiroun women were

> very helpful. If they find out that your husband's in prison or, you know, you're struggling, they clearly show a lot more sympathy than the Salafis, in a way. They'll be there for you, they'll cook for you, they'll clean for you, they'll show you love. . . . I wasn't drawn to the Salafi *da'wa* because—it was almost cold. . . . *They* [Al-Muhajiroun] were friendly and welcoming. . . . They welcome you, they take you and they take your number, they become friends with you, and it's just it was a lot more open. The people were a lot more open, the people seemed to be incredibly much more compassionate.

Listening to these strong objections to and unpleasant experiences of Salafism, I wondered how on earth these women were won over in the end. In what follows, I explain the pushes and pulls that led the women to choose Salafism over competing interpretations and groups.

3.4 CHOOSING SALAFISM

When I asked the women how they had become interested in Salafism, they often spoke first about their negative perceptions and experiences. Ironically, it seems that these factors could—eventually—*promote* their entrance into Salafism. Some women said that hearing other Muslims' criticisms of the group, and observing the rigidity of Salafi mentalities and behaviours, had stirred their curiosity and prompted them to investigate Salafism thoroughly for themselves.

Safia, for instance, was initially baffled by the strictness of Salafi dress, which she saw at the time as *bid'a*. However, she decided to investigate it because she reasoned: 'Why would they put themselves through that unless there's wisdom behind it?' Salafism, it seems, was *reassuringly* challenging. Hayah, meanwhile, battled with herself for a while before concluding that the fact that she had had negative experiences when exploring Brixton Mosque, unlike at other mosques she tried, was actually a sign that it promoted 'true' Islam. This was because, she said, God tests His followers when they take steps towards Him, while the *shaytan* (devil) beautifies deviancy.

Negative stereotypes and experiences may have brought Salafism to the women's attention, but many other factors were necessary to counteract its bad public image and win them round. 'Push' factors were particularly apparent in the accounts of the women who initially became supporters of Islamist and Jihadi groups, but who became disillusioned and started to seek alternatives.

Above all, they said that the other groups emphasized politics and social issues at the expense of providing a substantive theological education. As newly practising women, keen to compensate for their lack of religious instruction while growing up, the women were disappointed that fundamental issues such as how to pray seemed to take second place to political ones. Layaan, who had attended Al-Muhajiroun–linked lessons because she was told that they taught 'only Qur'an and sunna', was disappointed to find that the talks—which focused on issues like Guantanamo Bay and Palestine— did not have 'any relevance in my life'. Politics, she said, was not 'something I was particularly interested in'.

Manal had regularly attended lessons at Al-Maghrib Institute, which runs intensive Islamic studies weekend seminars in several countries. She said that the institute exaggerated the religious import of its events, promoting its speakers as 'shaykhs', charging around £60 for a weekend course 'on Islamic finance and what have you'—rather than focusing on 'the important matters of the *din* [religion]', such as *tawhid*—then providing certificates upon completion.

Another major factor was the women's unease with specific radical teachings. In particular, some groups' approval of 9/11, or of terrorism against civilians under certain circumstances, conflicted with a belief that the women had internalized from a young age—that killing innocents is wrong. Nadia and Asmaa, who had attended Al-Muhajiroun lectures, found that they could not justify the group's extreme antagonism towards non-Muslims, with whom the women had had positive experiences. Nadia, a Somali, had always believed that 9/11 was wrong, and certainly could not approve of terrorism against the country that had given her sanctuary. Like Asmaa, she also could not accept that even children could be legitimate targets in jihad.

Layaan went to Al-Muhajiroun–linked talks on and off for six months, but stopped after watching a disturbing documentary in which she recognized some of the Muslims featured. In the BBC 3 documentary, *My Brother, The Islamist* (2011),[19] the director tried in vain to reconnect with his brother, who had become deeply immersed in the extreme interpretation promoted by the preacher Anjem Choudary. Layaan was shocked by the harsh views expressed—and above all to see her acquaintances openly associating with the notorious Choudary.

[I] recognised some of them. [They] were husbands of the sisters at the talks. I was disgusted by the way Anjem Choudary spoke to the reporter—it was shocking! I also clocked that one of the sisters was Anjem Choudary's wife! I knew anything to do with Anjem was bad news, and these were definitely not the people I wanted to associate with, and they were definitely not following Qur'an or sunna. So I left and never looked back—except at how naïve I was. After that, I stopped going to talks altogether, feeling lost, not knowing who I could actually trust.

The three women's unease with elements of Al-Muhajiroun's ideology was heightened by the secrecy of the group, which restricted some lessons to core members and, according to Asmaa, withheld venue information for larger events until three hours before the start in order to avoid police intervention. Layaan was also disconcerted by how most members kept their real names private, introducing themselves only as 'Umm *x*' (mother of) or 'Abu *y*' (father of).

As for pull factors, previously existing social networks had a significant role, as in many studies of joining patterns in New Religious Movements (NRMs) and Muslim groups.[20] As Wiktorowicz (2005a, p.15) points out, groups that are stigmatized as 'extremist' and involve 'high-risk activism' are likely to rely heavily on social networks for recruitment because 'personal relationships facilitate trust and commitment'. And, predictably, personal relationships figured in the narratives of all of the women I interviewed, though to widely varying degrees.

Several women had regarded Salafism as a cult-like sect with unnecessarily strict rules and ill-mannered adherents until a friend, cousin, boyfriend, or fiancé had 'corrected' this impression. Indeed, encouragement and accompaniment was often necessary for the women to take the crucial step of attending a Salafi mosque, lesson, or conference, which they might otherwise have avoided given Salafism's reputation as 'extremist'. Researching the highly controversial Unification Church, Barker (1984, p. 99) similarly found that the influence of a friend or relative was sometimes necessary to persuade individuals to attend a Moonie workshop in the first place.

The character of the messenger, her or his Islamic knowledge, relationship to the woman, and method of giving *da'wa* were important in several cases. Three women mentioned being inspired by the good character of the messenger; two specifically said that they were impressed by the messenger's knowledge of Islam; and three mentioned that the messenger had tactfully prodded them gently over time without once referring to 'Salafis' in order to overcome their prejudice. At least six women seemed to have such close relationships with their messengers that it seemed almost inevitable that they would give Salafism serious consideration.

There was also a role, albeit limited, for affective ties. Upon investigating Salafism, at least seven women were affected by a sense of 'sisterhood', of belonging to a united 'family' of believing women who supported one another and worshipped together. This notion of 'sisterhood' was promoted by Salafi teachers, as chapter 4.5 shows, and it fostered a sense of belonging that no doubt contributed to the women's decision to take Salafism seriously.

When Deqa stumbled upon the Salafi study circle at Regent's Park Mosque that featured in the documentary *Undercover Mosque: The Return* (2008), she felt as though she had finally found a social space where she did not feel alien. 'They were very nice, they were like me, they dressed like me—I didn't feel any different,' she said. When Deqa was sixteen, her Somali parents—who had fled to nearby Kenya—sent her by herself to live with her aunt in London, where she had felt lonely and rootless.

Wafa, a Nigerian convert from north London, had thought that she was 'the only black Muslim in the world' until she visited Brixton Mosque, a hub for black converts. She said:

> The Asians, can't relate to them, but I can relate to these black people because they spoke the same, had the same background-ish. They were a bit more rowdy, you know, piercings and all of that, had children already, that kind of thing.

Amal, an Afro-Caribbean convert in her mid-twenties, told me that when she had a son out of wedlock, the people from her church distanced themselves from her, while the Brixton sisters welcomed those with illegitimate children from their '*jahiliyya*' time.

This sense of sisterhood seems to intensify during Ramadan, which encourages a heightened piety and higher attendance at mosques. The holy month and the social activities it fosters played a key role in five women's narratives. This aspect accords with research on NRMs that emphasizes the role of intensive interaction between members of the group in successful conversions (Dawson, 2006, p.78; Lofland and Stark, 1965, p.871). Such experiences helped to establish the plausibility structure[21] necessary to make a marginal group and 'extreme' practices seem acceptable.

Sagal, Saidah, and Amina said that they adopted the *jilbab* after being surrounded by women wearing it at Brixton Mosque or a Salafi conference, which made them realize that they 'had no excuse'. Others said that being around women who covered made it easier to take that step.

However, the role of social networks and affective ties in Salafi joining patterns should not be overemphasized, for three reasons. First, the crucial encounters that steered the women towards Salafism were often fleeting, and were seen as significant only on later reflection. For instance, the essential encounter for Hayah appears to have been a conversation with a Salafi woman she had met at her child's playgroup, who later emailed her a statement by Shaykh Al-Albani explaining why it is important to differentiate oneself as a Salafi Muslim. Maha Al-Qwidi (2002, p.178) noticed a similar pattern with the encounters that set her convert interviewees on the path to Islam.

Second, embracing Salafism placed many women at odds with most of their close friends and relatives at the time. Five said that becoming Salafi caused them to lose friends—usually, there was a mutual drifting apart— and another seven took the difficult and, for some, extremely painful decision to sever ties with friends and even relatives because their divergent beliefs and practices would 'hold them back'. Most said that they had had a mixed group of friends, composed of non-Salafi Muslims and often non-Muslims, but that their own transition to Salafism had frequently upset the dynamics of these friendships.

Third, in many cases, these losses were not compensated by new friendships with Salafis. As mentioned earlier, several women struggled to build relationships with women they met in Salafi environments. Those who *were* influenced by friends to become Salafi often mentioned that these relationships alone did not suffice; rather, individual research—usually via articles and lectures on the Internet—was necessary to convince them. Saidah, for instance, was captivated by the 'sisterhood' at Brixton Mosque and started practising during Ramadan—but 'didn't wanna become a Salafi until [she] really understood it'.

Some women explored the group in relative isolation, while others did so among a group of like-minded close friends. However, what all of them had in common, as a precondition for embracing a Salafi identity, was the need for a coherent belief system that made intellectual sense to them. This accords with studies of conversion to Islam that stress the intellectual aspects and an 'active', as opposed to 'passive', model (Al-Qwidi, 2002; Roald, 2004).

My most consistent finding, mentioned directly by twenty out of twenty-three women and by innumerable other women I met, is that Salafism is seen by adherents as the only group that teaches the Qur'an and sunna *purely*. Indeed, words such as 'pure', 'authentic', and 'original' featured prominently in many narratives. This reflects the core aim of Salafism to restore Islam to its imagined original form, free from *bid'a*.

Salafis attract followers by portraying Salafism as the one group that preserves a sense of authenticity, free from opinion, personality, emotion, tradition, and culture. An important example of this is Salafism's opposition to *taqlid* (following a school of law exclusively and uncritically); instead, Salafis claim that the sole criterion for their acceptance of a particular *fiqh* (Islamic jurisprudence) ruling is its level of proof in the Qur'an and sunna. In short, its accordance with any particular *madhhab* is irrelevant or coincidental.

Eleven women mentioned that Salafi literature and individuals, such as friends or teachers, offered proofs from the Qur'an and sunna to support rulings. This made for a compelling case, since most Muslims would not dispute the authority of these two fundamental sources. Maryam, who was introduced to Salafism by the teacher of the circle at Regent's Park Mosque that was filmed in the 2008 *Undercover Mosque* documentary, was attracted by how she related everything back to the Qur'an and sunna—because 'when you hear the Qur'an and sunna, you don't wanna reject it because this is the command of Allah'. This contrasted with her experience at the 'West African' mosque, Masjid-ul-Qudus, near Brixton Mosque, where she said she was given instructions without explanation or proof.

Shukri said that it took one lesson on Al-Albani's book, *The Prophet's Prayer Described*, to convince her because all of the points on how to pray were backed up with evidence from the practice of no less than the Messenger of God himself. Humayrah was impressed to find that the Brixton Mosque imam 'will *never* tell you, "This is what I think that you need to do"; the imam will give you evidence in the Qur'an, "This is what you do."'

This strong scripturalism particularly appealed to those who had experimented with more political Muslim groups, as it contrasted with their lively speakers' blatant attempts to arouse emotion in their audiences. Others appreciated that Salafis, unlike other Muslims—including, they claimed, their own parents—focused on the text without 'corrupting' it with elements of Muslim or Western cultures. Bilan said that many non-Salafi British Muslims celebrate birthdays, but this was not from the Qur'an or sunna. Wafa said she liked that Salafis were 'not like the people who dilute it and want to integrate and you know, want to modernize it or believe it's pragmatic. No! What are you doing?'

In a similar vein, four women stressed how Salafism's emphasis on the Qur'an and sunna bypasses the issue of which *madhhab* one ought to follow, which had been a source of confusion, particularly for the converts (see previous section). This rejection of a law school–based approach to *fiqh* in favour of an emphasis on the 'original' sources seems common among converts in general. Many of Roald's (2004, p.113) interviewees took this approach in their search for a 'purified' (not necessarily Salafi) Islam, shorn of cultural biases.

This uncompromising, purist approach is reflected in the inflexibility of attitudes and behaviours that religious seekers encounter upon entering Salafi environments. But this, too, while initially off-putting, can serve as a confirmation that the group takes Islam seriously. Four women said that they were impressed by the refusal of Salafi women to make any concessions to Western dress codes, for example, or to moderate their beliefs for the sake of convention or politeness. This created an impression of remarkable confidence and courage that suggested the women had indeed discovered 'authentic' Islam.

> When you see a sister in a light blue abaya, you know with her yellow hijab—to me, it's like she's trying to fit into society, you know. Where you know from the Salafi sisters, when you just see the black black black black black *niqab niqab niqab*. . . . I would see them as very *firm* and not trying to conform to society at all. It's like, 'I'm not even *bothered* about what you think of me.' . . . In life, you want to be strong, you want to be firm—you know, who wants to be weak? . . . So you wanna be with the stronger crew; you don't wanna be with people that's gonna be with the loser. (Hayah)

> The way I look at sisters with *jilbab* and *niqab*, I truly am inspired by them. I truly believe they're strong as women, 'cause to be able to wear that, to face all the battles that you'll—all the assaults that will get thrown on a day, all the abuse, all this *fitna* [trials, tribulations] you have to shield yourself from, you have to stay *firm* upon it. (Safia)

Similarly, Maryam was struck by how her teacher at Regent's Park Mosque never minced her words.

> She's quite forceful in her opinions, which is what I like . . . someone who's happy with themselves and happy with what they're doing—if they know they're saying the *haqq* [truth], the right thing, they're happy saying it even if ten people die because of that.

Of course, no matter how literally, strictly, and exclusively Salafis rely upon the Qur'an and sunna, they are compelled, like every other Islamic group, to rely extensively on other sources because the Qur'an and sunna do not directly and unambiguously tackle every issue. These sources include, above all, the example of the *salaf* and the *ijtihad* (independent reasoning) of scholars. Yet the women had come to believe that these additional sources could actually clarify and protect—rather than corrupt—the 'pure' teachings of the Qur'an and sunna.

Four mentioned that the *salaf* are useful role models because they lived at the time of the Prophet, so were well placed to understand how to put the revelations into practice. Two said that the Qur'an itself endorses the *salaf* as worthy of emulation. According to the women, the contemporary Salafi 'ulama also had an aura of 'authenticity', for two reasons. First, most of them have lived and/or studied in the land of Mecca and Medina, Islam's two holiest cities—Saudi Arabia. Second, they have studied for long periods under other established, well-known scholars. Salafi 'ulama—particularly famous names such as Bin Baz, Al-Uthaymin, and Al-Albani—actually enjoy considerable scholarly authority among Sunni Muslims in general. At least two women I interviewed, as well as other Salafis I met, seemed unaware that established non-Salafi 'ulama even existed.

The women felt they could trust Salafi interpretations of the Qur'an and sunna because of the reputation and interconnectedness of the Salafi 'ulama. For example, Asmaa, who was initially convinced by Al-Muhajiroun's pro–suicide bombing stance, later revised her views because Salafi 'ulama had given Qur'anic evidence against it, and they had 'studied Islam for 70 years'. And Hayah said:

> They're [i.e., Salafis] gonna be more upon what is right than what is wrong; they're not just going with so-and-so because they've studied in this back bush of, you know, Syria, with this so-called lovely shaykh—I don't know who, and we don't know who taught him. It all goes back to very well-known scholars, seekers of knowledge, you know, these people. So you can follow, follow, follow the chain back.

Framing Salafism as the group that adheres most closely to the Qur'an and sunna in their original form not only underlines its Islamic validity, but also paves the way for Salafi preachers to convince undecided religious seekers of the necessity of aligning themselves with Salafism alone. In this they are aided by a much-debated hadith. The Prophet is reported to have said: 'And this *Ummah* will split into seventy-three sects, all of them in the Hellfire except for one. . . . They are those who are upon that which I and my Companions are upon today' (Tirmidhi 2565; also Abu Dawud 3980, Ibn Majah 3982–3983).[22] Having constructed themselves as the group most devoted to following the example of the Prophet and the *salaf*, among whom were the companions of the Messenger themselves, Salafis can lay claim to the title of 'the saved sect' with great effect.

Aware that they are operating in a competitive 'market', Salafi preachers repeat this narration at lessons and conferences again and again, establishing clear boundaries and suggesting to religious seekers that picking and mixing is no longer an option. This can cement an individual's commitment to Salafism once she is convinced of its Islamic authenticity, as she will come to see Salafism as the referent of the hadith and thus the only route to Paradise. Indeed, this narration was crucial in pushing at least four women towards making a commitment to Salafism. Three are quoted here:

> I was very aware of the [hadith]. . . . When I read that hadith, that's when I was kind of thinking: 'Hold on a second, what am I supposed to follow?' (Firdaws

> If there's gonna be seventy-three [sects] and only one of them is gonna get into *janna* [Paradise] *insha'Allah*, then you'd think it's important to differentiate what you are—you can't be general. . . . It's common sense, literally! (Saidah)

> The whole thing about being, on the day of *qiyama* [judgment] there's going to be seventy-three sects of Islam—so why not try and pick the path that is so close to the way the Prophet (*s.a.w.*) lived his life? So that to me was a *big* influence, just reading that hadith. (Amina)

Once a religious seeker has recognized the authorities on which Salafism relies—the Qur'an and sunna upon the understanding of the *salaf* as elaborated by Salafi 'ulama—she will appreciate the comprehensiveness and explicitness of Salafi teachings and fatwas, which address everything from major creedal issues to the mundane and everyday. A quick browse of virtually any Salafi website shows that Salafis attend to rulings on everything from lavatory etiquette to the conditions for excommunication (*takfir*).

Seven women spoke of their ease at having clear-cut guidelines on everything from manners to how one should interact with 'deviant' Muslims to precisely when one should and should not fast. Salafi scholars and teachers address common issues facing Muslims in the West, such as the circumstances that permit consumption of non-halal food products or engagement in usury. They also provide answers—framed by the Qur'an and sunna—to questions about which different groups and *madhahib* disagree, such as whether or not eating gelatine is permissible. Salafism teaches that believers must avoid grey areas and leave them to trusted scholars to determine. Consequently, several women were regular visitors to websites, such as fatwa-online.com, that provide guidance from major scholars on a wide range of common issues.

Having observed the way in which Al-Muhajiroun seemed to change their position on certain matters, such as the punishment of the grave,[23] Asmaa was relieved to discover that Salafism seemed to offer

> a clear guideline. . . . There's like five other opinions that I could follow [on a given matter] and nobody really knows if this opinion [is true] 'cause this opinion changes. . . . [But] the truth is so clear in *da'wa Salafiyya*, and it's just, like, OK—this is it.

During my fieldwork, several women expressed to me their dislike of 'grey areas', which effectively vanished when they embraced Salafism.

Many spoke of a sense of 'inner peace' or 'tranquillity' at having finally found an approach that generated 'correct' (since they were evidence-based) answers to every question. Several mentioned that it was reassuring to know that if they stuck to Salafi teachings, all of their actions could potentially be blessed by God because they would be practising Islam in the way He had originally intended.

Saidah spoke of having a 'manual', a complete set of instructions to life that, if meticulously followed, would guarantee the optimal result—God's pleasure and, ultimately, Paradise. Conversely, following a different or incomplete set of instructions would mean that one's efforts to implement Islam in an often hostile environment were futile.

> It's authentic: you're doing it according to the way of the Prophet (p.b.u.h.). If you're not doing it according to the way of the Prophet, no matter how many good deeds you do, they don't amount to anything, so at least you know this deed that you do, it has the potential to be accepted. . . . You can have a recompense in the hereafter. Whereas if you do all these good things and you don't follow the right way, then the outcome is nothing. So that kinda, like—I wouldn't say guarantees, but that's kinda like knowing that, why else would you follow anything else? (Warsan

> The best thing about *Salafiyya* is knowing that the way I'm trying to practise Islam isn't going in vain. . . . Their *dalil* [evidence or proof from the Qur'an and/ or sunna] proves to me that I'm doing things correctly or I can—I know if I *wanna* do things correctly, they're the resource I would go to, you know? (Abeer)

The influence of the 73-sect hadith is apparent in many women's narratives; evidently, they had come to see 'shopping' in the 'Islam market' as a zero-sum game (Wiktorowicz, 2005a, p.185). While adhering to Salafi teachings, God willing, guarantees Paradise, implementing a different approach guarantees Hell.[24] Saidah captured this attitude perfectly:

> We [Salafis] only do what we're told to do. If you do what you're told to do, you're guaranteed to pass. If you do something else apart from that, you're guaranteed to fail. And to me, that just sums up the whole Salafi *minhaj* [i.e., programme of action, way].

Salafism thus represented God's will as rational and discernible in its entirety by the ordinary believer, not merely by a spiritual elite. It therefore offered these young women a surer, more achievable route to salvation than the obscure teachings into which they had previously been socialized.

This was a crucial element of the women's 'conversion' narratives, reflecting Bryan Wilson's (1982, pp.17–18) observation that NRMs can provide a level of soteriological reassurance that is lacking from 'old religions'.

Having such a refreshingly clear sense of purpose in life was undoubtedly fulfilling for the women. Some said that they no longer felt 'lost', or that they would feel 'lost' without Salafism; others spoke of finally achieving a sense of 'inner peace', thanks to their newfound certainty. Maryam said: '*Subhanallah* [glory to God], I feel more at peace and tranquil, in the sense that I am trying my utmost in trying to implement the religion, because I have evidence to support me.' Having finally identified the 'correct' approach, the women felt justified in shunning all non-Salafi lessons and literature and liberated from their former doubts. Shukri said she felt a sense of

> calmness now where you don't feel like the uneasiness about what, OK, who are these sects, where are they, what do they talk about—you're not so confused about it, now you actually know. . . . I'm more firm in where I'm getting my knowledge from in the sense that . . . I'm more confident about it, whereas before, I could easily go to one lecture, listen to that lecture say something, go to another lecture, and that lecture that I had gone to before was now refuted, and I would be *so* confused.

Another pull factor was the women's positive experiences of learning about Islam at Salafi lectures, conferences, and circles. Thirteen women highlighted the way that Salafi lessons and literature focus on intensively learning the basics of Islam, such as the five pillars and *tawhid*. When the women started to attend lessons, they felt a sense of relief that they were finally compensating for their lack of in-depth Islamic instruction while growing up or while attending the talks of other Muslim groups.

> I went to many places for classes and stuff like that, and I wouldn't feel that essence of I'm being taught—I don't know, I just wouldn't feel it. Even, like, sometimes, I've gone to places, the *khutbas* are OK, you know—they might say some beneficial things that leave me thinking. But when I go to Brixton, it's a much more stronger, in-depth passion or—I dunno, it just touches me more. (Hayah)

> When I went there [Al-Athariyyah Salafi lesson], I felt like . . . I was actually learning with a book and a pen and I was learning the fundamentals of the *din* and proofs. (Fowsiya)

Most of the women had grown up with little, if any, understanding of the meaning or conditions of the *shahada*, Islam's first and most important pillar, or of the prayers that many had been encouraged to utter every day. For those determined to revive or initiate their religious practice wholeheartedly, it was crucial to start with the foundations of Islam—such as the nature of the Islamic belief in one God—in order at last to understand what it means to say 'I'm Muslim'. Salafism's back-to-basics approach compared favourably with those of other groups with which they had experimented, and Muslim communities in which they were raised, many of which seemed to prioritize 'secondary' matters, such as politics or Qur'anic recitation.

> If you compare them to other Muslims, they [Salafis] constantly seek knowl-edge. . . . Other masjids . . . they'll go there on a Friday but they just like lit-erally pray and they learn Arabic so they can read the Qur'an, but they don't actually study, they don't study Islam in depth. (Firdaws)

> I didn't know what *tawhid* was—after three years of attending [politically ori-ented Islamic] talks at uni! . . . *Tawhid* is the reason we were created—it says it in the Qur'an. It's the reason for the prophets. It's the reason for Islam. Our Prophet called to *tawhid* alone for thirteen years. It's the first pillar of Islam. We need it in order for our supplications to be accepted. (Warsan)

A final point, raised by two women, is the fact that Salafis usually offer conferences and lessons free of charge, unlike many other Muslim groups in London today. While other organizations popular with Muslim youth, such as the Islamic Education and Research Academy, might charge around £10 per ticket for one-day conferences held in plush Central London halls or hotels, Salafi conferences tend to be free (or very cheap); run over two days or more; and take place in more modest venues, such as school gymnasiums, in outlying areas. Not only does this make Salafi events more affordable for young people, but it can also create the reassuring impression of austerity and sincerity of purpose. Furthermore, booking was usually not required, reducing the burden of commitment to those with busy lives. Manal said of Al-Maghrib Institute, whose seminars she used to attend:

> Why are you charging me so much money when you know it's [i.e., seeking knowledge] an obligation on me? Make it easier for the people. . . . It doesn't need to be glamorous, it doesn't need to be in the most beautiful location—humble yourselves, you know. And it was a thing where I felt like they had an agenda in that they would always, it's like they were self-promoting—you are still students of knowledge!

3.5 CONCLUSION

The young women I encountered during my fieldwork had varied paths into Salafism, but some overall themes have emerged. All had been religiously conscious from an early age, yet confused by the inconsistencies and ambiguities of the belief systems within which they were raised, and which often placed them at odds with their liberal, multifaith environments. Some women were separated from their parents at an early age and had felt alien within their own households.

Such difficulties, however, had eventually prompted them to convert to Islam or to practise with a heightened sense of purpose and resolve. This process of becoming practising was stimulated by destabilizing life events and social networks, and occurred within the context of Islam and Salafism's raised public profile during the years following 9/11 and the related south London 'fashion' for converting. Yet it must be noted that the women's conversion narratives were not linear or uniform, and some lacked the elements of tension or crisis that are often thought to precede religious seeking (Lofland and Stark, 1965; Rambo, 1993).

Determined to take their religion seriously, the women took steps to try finally to understand what being a Muslim 'really' meant. Yet they often found themselves overwhelmed by the zealousness and sheer number of 'Islams' they encountered at college, within friendship circles, and at university. Thus began an experimental phase of religious seeking.

Although Salafism usually caught the women's attention at an early stage in their religious seeking, the process of becoming Salafi was not straightforward, and often included experiments with other Muslim groups that initially seemed more persuasive. In general, the women painted a picture of delayed, even resisted involvement, due to Salafism's 'image problem'.

Interestingly, involvement with Salafism frequently came *despite*—rather than because of—social encounters with adherents, who were often unwelcoming. This is at odds with the traditional 'passivist' model of conversion, in which the individual—often made vulnerable by emotional upheavals— is persuaded to join as a result of social-interactive pressures from within the group.

While social networks were often crucial for the women to take the first steps towards joining a group that they might otherwise have avoided, becoming Salafi generally came at a social *cost*, rather than gain. They made some friends, but lost others—and many struggled to form attachments to fellow Salafis. These data support much of the literature on conversion to Islam, which has tended to downplay social factors, often finding that encounters with Muslims—whether through preexisting social networks or newly formed bonds—are not necessarily pivotal to the conversion process, though they usually facilitate it (Al-Qwidi, 2002; Köse, 1996; Roald, 2004). For example, Köse's interviewees 'were already oriented towards a religious quest at the time of their contact' (1996, p.193).

On the other hand, the findings contrast with much of the literature on NRMs, which emphasizes the roles of social networks, affective ties, and intensive interaction in successful conversion. As Dawson (2006, p.78) says, 'On these ... three points ... there is little disagreement in the academic literature.' Some have even suggested that affective bonds are a *necessary* condition for conversion (Lofland and Stark, 1965, p.871).

The pattern that has emerged here suggests another form of conversion, specific to liberal, religiously diverse societies in which a religious seeker is free to 'shop' in a religion 'market'. I term this pattern '*delayed conversion*'. Here, an individual resists affiliation with a group after initially encountering it, due to something off-putting. Involvement occurs only after exploration of and/or experimentation with other groups has proven disappointing, prompting a reinvestigation of the original group, which subsequently emerges as more attractive. This is a more intermittent, interrupted version of Lofland and Skonovd's (1981) 'experimental' conversion motif, in which an individual actively explores religious options and 'tries out' a group before becoming fully committed and making sacrifices.

Eventually, Salafism proved to be the most credible and attractive option, due to its constant and literal appeal to the holy texts, with elaborations from highly regarded individuals: the *salaf* and well-known 'ulama. By thus underlining their Islamic legitimacy, Salafis position themselves to take full advantage of the 73-sect hadith in order to demand wholehearted and exclusive allegiance from adherents. Once the women had accepted that only Salafism led to Paradise, they could not justify associating with other groups—however friendly they might be. Hayah and Abyan, who were initially attracted to other groups that were much more welcoming, said:

> You have to understand, on that day [i.e., the Day of Judgment], we're all gonna be judged individually. You know, you can't always be focusing, focusing on the people ... because for example, you can go to a masjid now and *bid'a*, yeah, *full* of innovation—they're doing this, they're jumping around, they're clapping their hands. ... When you walk in, they *hug* you—'ah al-salamu 'alaykum, ah this that'—yes, they greet you with all this niceness. (Hayah)

> In a very like selfish way, I just wanna get to *janna*, I just wanna get to Paradise, and I just want to be good and follow the sunna and that's just all I'm concerned with. *Al-hamdulillah* [praise God] I have loads of family, I have loads of friends, so I don't come to any [Salafi] events to form friendships with any Muslim women. ... My mission is just to learn and just to follow the Qur'an and sunna, and here's the truth and I'll just follow the truth. That's it. (Abyan)

Yet Salafism's appeal does not lie merely in the promise of future reward; my data show that women also derived considerable psychological benefits from becoming involved—namely, a sense of relief, fulfilment, and 'inner peace' at finally being taught their religion clearly, comprehensively, and 'accurately'.

Having accepted the authorities upon which Salafism rests, they felt they could justifiably ignore the teachings of other groups and the 'cultural' practices of relatives in favour of one clear and complete set of life instructions that would, God willing, guarantee eternal spiritual rewards. Centred on in-depth study of Islam's most fundamental and pivotal tenets—and free of charge—the Salafi learning experience proved to be a refreshing change from the madrasas of their childhoods and their experiences of more political Muslim groups.

As the next chapter demonstrates, this learning experience, which mostly takes place in mosques and community centres, was crucial both in arousing initial interest and in encouraging the women to assess their lifestyles and align them with Salafi teachings.

CHAPTER 4

✧

Commitment and Belonging

The Role of Circles of Knowledge

Once a woman has identified Salafism as the 'correct' approach to Islam and taken the first steps towards adopting a Salafi identity and lifestyle, there are two likely outcomes. She will either become more deeply involved, or her attachment may wane—possibly to the point of leaving. After all, many New Religious Movements (NRMs) struggle to retain their members for a significant period of time (Barker, 1984, p.146), with research suggesting that more than 90 percent of joiners leave their groups within two years (Dawson, 2010, p.7).[1]

One defection trigger, according to research, is the making of overly strict demands on members (Stark, 2003, pp.262–264). Certainly, Salafi groups in the West demand great sacrifices from their followers. Women must proudly use the controversial identity label 'Salafi', regardless of any alienation that may ensue. They should also actively participate in the community by regularly attending events (such as lessons and conferences), making financial contributions (in the form of regular zakat and *sadaqa*),[2] giving *da'wa* (preaching) to encourage others to become Salafi, and eventually marrying someone from the community—and potentially accepting a polygamous marriage.

More generally, they must be seen to adhere to Salafi teachings on dress, gender segregation, prayer habits, and so on. Meanwhile, they have to withdraw from the company of non-Salafis where such relationships could negatively influence their religious observance. That includes friends and relatives, as well as non-Salafi environments, such as lessons given by other, 'deviant' Muslim groups.

They also have to accept the accompanying material risks of becoming a visibly Salafi woman in the United Kingdom. There is the risk of Islamophobic attacks—a more frequent occurrence since 9/11 (Allen and Nielson, 2002; Lambert and Githens-Mazer, 2010) and reportedly rising in recent years (Ameli and Merali, 2015). Then there is the risk of being unemployed, either due to discrimination by the employer or because the job-seeker herself restricts her opportunities to avoid engaging in any *haram* (see chapter 5.4). So, although Salafism in Britain often disassociates itself from politics in the strict and formal sense, it nevertheless demands a kind of 'high-risk activism', comparable to that of more politicized groups such as Al-Muhajiroun (Wiktorowicz, 2005a, p.45).

Securing this degree of commitment from young women in twenty-first-century London is the challenge that Salafi leaders set themselves. Here, a young Muslim woman will be exposed to a range of Muslim groups competing for her 'business' in the 'Islam market', as well as a variety of Muslim and non-Muslim perspectives on women's place in society. And she may become doubt-ridden and disillusioned after her initial enthusiasm subsides and she grasps the reality of the sacrifices she must make.

So, from the group's point of view, effective recruitment strategies must be followed by effective *commitment* processes in order to prevent initial zeal from fizzling out and new problems from undermining the belief system. These mechanisms also serve to ensure that adherents contribute to maintaining the group, rather than simply 'free-riding' on the efforts of others (McGuire, 1997, p.85; Wiktorowicz, 2005a, p.15). To return to Rosabeth Moss Kanter's (1972) definition (see introduction), commitment involves the harmonization of individual self-interest with the demands of the group. As a later stage in the 'conversion' process, commitment also implies participating 'more deeply in the life of the group, its values and goals,' while withdrawing from 'competing allegiances and alternate ways of life' (McGuire, 1997, p.83).

According to Kanter (1972, p.69), there are three types of commitment that help to maintain a group—and thus, by implication, successful conversion. *Instrumental* commitment: 'When profits and costs are considered, participants find that the cost of leaving the system would be greater than the cost of remaining.' *Affective* commitment: the result of 'strong emotional bonds' between members, who 'stick together', even when confronted by threats to the group's existence. *Moral* commitment: 'When demands made by the system are evaluated as right, moral, just, or expressing one's own values, obedience to these demands becomes a normative necessity, and sanctioning by the system is regarded as appropriate.' This chapter reveals how Salafi leaders attempt to foster all three forms of commitment in Salafi 'circles of knowledge'[3]—lessons, lectures, and conferences.

These are the Salafi leadership's main points of direct contact with women (and men), and thus the principal sites for promoting commitment. Some of the leaders are women, both young and middle-aged, who are permitted to teach women-only circles by virtue of being deemed 'knowledgeable' in the community. Hence these circles are also of interest as one of the few areas of community life where women may acquire substantial sacred authority. This organizational form of transmitting knowledge, based on the informal teacher-scholar relationship, lies at the heart of Salafi propagation efforts, and was one of Al-Albani's great legacies (Meijer, 2009b, p.9). This contrasts with other Islamic groups, such as Muslim Brotherhood–inspired groups, which are additionally focused on community work, political activism, and other activities.

The preference for this form of propagation reflects Salafism's characteristic emphasis on *tarbiya* (nurturing individuals in correct beliefs and practices), and on the cultivation of a pious self above other priorities. Salafis also cite a hadith in support of such gatherings, in which the Prophet reportedly said that God's angels 'travel around seeking out the gatherings of Remembrance, so when they come upon them they surround them'.[4]

This chapter is based on the many Salafi circles of knowledge that I attended between June 2010 and October 2012. It describes their structure, content, teachers, and audience, and shows how preachers employed them to solidify commitment. Shifting the perspective from that of ordinary Salafi women to that of teachers and leaders, the chapter illuminates more fully the processes by which they portray the group as the only one with the correct understanding of the Qur'an and sunna, and therefore the only one saved from Hell. The chapter also explains the role of circles in fostering a sense of belonging and deeper identification with the group. These processes promote both recruitment (as seen in chapter 3) and commitment.

4.1 LONDON'S SALAFI CIRCLES OF KNOWLEDGE

As mentioned in chapter 2, I attended circles of knowledge linked to different Salafi networks at various locations, especially Brixton Mosque, where I attended a variety of women-specific classes for nearly two years. I also regularly attended circles at Al-Athariyyah (Forest Gate, east London) and Sisters of Tawheed for much of this period.

Circles of knowledge usually involve a group of women (or men) sitting on the floor and listening to a teacher speak in English for one to four hours (normally one hour), with breaks for prayers if necessary. Attendance is not formally monitored and lessons are free of charge, although voluntary donations to the mosque or *da'wa* group are frequently encouraged (sometimes a collection bag is passed around at the end of the class).

Gender segregation is always strictly upheld: if the teacher is male, he will either sit with the men in a separate room from the women (as Abu Ahmed of Al-Athariyyah did) or in the same room but separated from the women by an opaque curtain (as Kareem of Brixton Mosque did). In fact, segregation was taken so seriously that when the fire alarm went off during one of Abu Ahmed's classes, the men waited for all of the women in the next room to evacuate before attempting to do so themselves. The women lost potentially crucial seconds as they hastened to put on their *jilbabs* and *niqabs*. Fortunately, it was a false alarm.

As Table 4.1 illustrates, the lessons I attended attracted audiences of varying sizes, consisting of women from different backgrounds and age groups. While Umm Mustafe could draw an audience of forty to fifty young women every week, other circles attracted as few as five regular attendees.

Unsurprisingly, the classes that took place during the week were more likely to attract housewives in their mid-twenties and above, while the weekend circles were more popular and largely consisted of women in their late teens and early to mid-twenties, among whom were many college or university students. Weekend circles were usually at a more basic level and slower pace, so those who had not had further education or studied Islam for long could also follow them.

The ethnic composition of the classes reflected their locations: Brixton Mosque has many Afro-Caribbean convert worshippers, whereas Al-Athariyyah in east London drew many South Asians, and Sisters of Tawheed's circles were local to a large Somali community. Regular Salafi circles always focus on one or two books, usually relating to Salafis' most emphasized subject, creed. Teachers painstakingly go through these texts, line by line, so students are encouraged to bring their own copies. In this way, it is not unusual for weekly circles to spend three years on a slim volume.

I was also invited to two informal, irregular circles that took place at women's homes. One was in south London at the home of Nabila, a married Somali and Brixton mosque attendee in her mid-twenties; this attracted around eleven young women each session, mostly Somalis from north-west and south London. The other circle, of similar size, took place in different locations—the women would take it in turns to host—and attracted a surprising array of ethnicities and ages: from North Africans to Polish and Jamaican converts, ranging from the young and unmarried to those with grown-up children. Such circles were by invitation only, and regular attendees would make a particular effort to invite newly practising or newly Salafi women along.

These gatherings were very loose in structure, but usually one woman—the host and/or the one deemed most knowledgeable—would take the lead and go through a passage in a book. The women were encouraged to bring home-cooked dishes, and there were regular breaks for eating and praying together.

Table 4.1. INFORMATION ABOUT THE REGULAR CLASSES I ATTENDED

	Women only?	Teacher	Women's attendance (approx.)	Ethnic composition	Age group	Main books studied
Weekday class (1), Brixton Mosque	Yes	Kareem	5–16	Mostly Afro-Caribbean converts, some French-Algerians	Mostly mothers, mid-twenties upwards, some with babies and toddlers	*Kitab Al-Tawhid* by Muhammad ibn 'Abd al-Wahhab (creed) and *Al-Adab al-Mufrad* by Imam al-Bukhari (Islamic etiquette)
Weekday class (2), Brixton Mosque	Yes	Kareem	5–11	Mostly Afro-Caribbean converts and some Somalis, among others	Mostly married women, mid-twenties upwards	*Explanation of the Creed* by Abu Muhammad Al-Hasani Al-Barbahaaree, *Fiqh* by 'Abdul-Azeem Badawi (jurisprudence), and *The Book of the End* by Ibn Katheer
Weekend class, Al-Athariyyah	No	Abu Ahmed	17–30	Mostly South Asian; some Somalis; a few white and Afro-Caribbean converts	Young: teenagers, women in their twenties and thirties; a few young families	*Kitab Al-Tawhid* (see above)

Weekend class, Sisters of Tawheed	Yes	Umm Mustafe (occasionally Layla)	35–50	Almost entirely Somali	About half were teenagers of school age (sometimes with their mothers); the rest were young university students or women in their early twenties	*Tafsir* of Ibn Kathir and *Kitab Al-Tawhid* (see above)
Weekend class, Brixton Mosque	Yes	Umm Hamza	6–30 (usually around 20)	About half Afro-Caribbean converts; some Somalis and West Africans, with a few North Africans and a Spanish convert	Mostly 19–25, including some students, employees, and housewives, some with small children	*Beneficial Speech in Establishing the Evidences of Tawheed* by Muhammad bin Abdul Wahhab al-Wasaabee (creed)

I also often attended Friday prayers at Brixton Mosque, which included a *khutba* (sermon) delivered by a male preacher, lasting approximately thirty minutes. These were transmitted via loudspeaker into the women's section. During sermons, preachers would address issues that were pertinent to the community at the time. For instance, during the summer 2011 England Riots—which took place in Brixton, among other areas, during the month of Ramadan—a preacher delivered a strongly worded sermon that emphasized Islam's opposition to looting and vandalism of private property:

> *Any* Muslim who finds themself involved in such activities, then one needs to make *tawba* [i.e., seek repentance] to Allah (*s.w.t.*),[5] and more so to be involved in such practice in the month of Ramadan is even more disgusting.

Saidah told me that the weekly *khutba* was eagerly—and sometimes ner-vously—anticipated by Brixton Mosque attendees, who expected to gain an insight into 'what he's [the imam] seen on the streets, what's going on, the phone calls he gets', though names were never mentioned. I also attended occasional charity fundraisers all over London, at which there was always a short Islamic talk.

Conferences (or 'seminars') are regular fixtures in the Salafi's calendar, so I went to those organized by Brixton Mosque, Tottenham Da'wah, (a Salafi Publications-linked group in north London), Al-Athariyyah, and Sisters of Tawheed (see Figures 4.1–4.4). The conferences in London are promoted by SMS message, email, Twitter, Facebook, and word of mouth. They attract large numbers from different parts of the capital—I estimated anything from 30 to 170 women per conference[6]—and a disproportionate number of Somalis and young people, especially teenagers and students. Conferences were usually free, unless they were organized partly for the purpose of fundraising—for example, for plans to extend Brixton Mosque.

Women and men were, of course, separated. Sometimes they were assigned to different areas of the building; at other conferences, they shared a large hall that was divided down the middle by a high black screen. Loudspeakers were always erected on the women's side to ensure that they could hear the preachers, who were male and therefore on the men's side. The exception was the very occasional 'sisters' seminar'; these excluded men and hosted only female preachers.

Most events had a stalls area in which women sold hot food and soft drinks, bags of sweets for children, natural beauty products, cheap make-up, perfumes (including non-alcoholic concoctions designed to imitate famous brands), books and CDs of lectures (all Salafi, of course), Islamic dress (*jilbabs*, abayas, hijabs, *niqabs*, gloves, and other accessories)—and even sexy night-wear (silky camisoles and negligées). Conferences were also seen as oppor-tunities to stock up on Islamic products, as well as to support fellow Salafis' small businesses.

Figure 4.1: 'Purification of the Soul Series': 2011 event publicity, Brixton Mosque.
P. Addae

The atmosphere was usually buzzing with excitement: small children (most dressed in Islamic clothes for the occasion) ran to and fro between the women's and men's sections, and women greeted each other warmly (*al-salamu 'alaykum ukhti* [my sister]!'). Yet while conferences were clearly social occasions—opportunities to catch up with friends, as well as meet

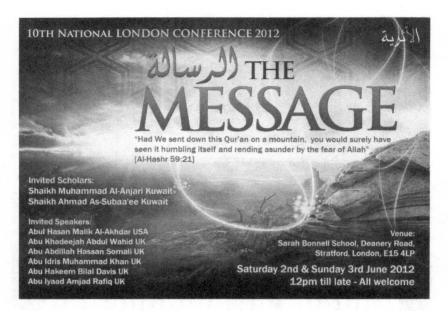

Figure 4.2: The 10th National London Conference 2012: event publicity, Al-Athariyyah [Front Side].

Salafi Publications, Birmingham

Figure 4.3: The 10th National London Conference 2012: event publicity, Al-Athariyyah [Back Side].

Salafi Publications, Birmingham

Figure 4.4: 'Remaining Steadfast in Times of Trial': 2011 event publicity, Brixton Mosque.
P. Addae

new Salafi women—they had been designed with the primary purpose of serious learning.

The schedule was demanding: typically, there were three to six lectures per day, usually lasting between forty-five minutes and two hours each, followed by a lengthy question-and-answer session. If the speakers were male, women wrote their questions on slips of paper that were passed through to the men's section. There were short breaks for prayers and food, but it was often necessary to sit on hard floors for hours at a time. And at every conference there was usually at least one 'telelink'—often crackling and very difficult to hear—with a scholar from Saudi Arabia or another Muslim country, whose words were translated phrase by phrase from Arabic.

Meanwhile, '*da'wa* packs' were often made available for all, or at least for the regulars to distribute to newcomers. These generally consisted of eye-catching leaflets addressing potentially controversial issues (for example, 'Who are the Salafis and are they from Ahlus Sunnah wal-Jamaa'ah [i.e., people of the sunna, of the Prophet]?' (see Figure 4.5); 'Women in Islaam: Separating Fact from Fiction'; and 'The Corruption of Terrorism & Suicide Bombings: Exposing the Perpetrators of Evil'), CDs of previous lectures, and sometimes English translations of the Qur'an.

Of course, circles of knowledge constitute only one of numerous ways in which Salafi women learn about their religion. There are also Arabic and *tajwid*

Figure 4.5: 'Who are the Salafis?' Leaflet regularly distributed at conferences, especially to sceptics.
Salafi Publications, Birmingham

(Qur'anic recitation) classes, audio CDs of past lectures, YouTube videos, online articles, and—still very much in business—printed books. However, focusing on circles of knowledge (and their associated books) enabled me to make unmediated observations of how the women engaged with ideas and each other. I was also able to witness how the group managed to foster a sense of social belonging that can be crucial to commitment processes.

4.2 TEACHERS AND THE CHAIN OF 'AUTHENTIC' KNOWLEDGE

The narratives in the previous chapter revealed that the appeal of Salafism was closely tied to the certainty it bestowed, thanks to its grounding in the 'pure' sources of Islam. At the time of their conversion, the interviewees had come to trust that their Salafi messenger—whether it was a friend, a mosque teacher, text, or a combination—was an 'authentic' conveyer of the Qur'an and sunna, distinct from the many other Muslims with similar claims. This section sheds further light on how such credibility is built up by examining how those who teach circles of knowledge acquire authority among their students, thus fostering conversion and deeper commitment. After all, studies of social movements and NRMs have repeatedly shown that followers' positive perceptions of those who transmit the message can enhance its reception.[7]

Above all, Salafi teachers acquire authority by virtue of their participation in a long chain of 'authentic' knowledge transmission (hereafter referred to as the 'chain of knowledge'), stemming from the Qur'an and sunna, and based on informal teacher-pupil relationships[8] (see Figure 4.6). The chain also functions as a hierarchy of sources, with each link of the chain subordinate to the authorities above it, which are closer to the 'pure', original sources of the Qur'an and sunna.

Many of the Salafi teachers in the United Kingdom are 'students of knowledge'—meaning they have studied for several years with recognized 'ulama abroad, mostly in Saudi Arabia. My own teachers at Brixton Mosque and Al-Athariyyah, Kareem and Abu Ahmed, respectively, both studied with 'ulama at the Islamic University of Madinah (Madinah University). The scholars above them are deemed fit to interpret the Qur'an and sunna, but must consider the example of the *salaf, ijma'* (the preceding scholarly consensus), and *qiyas*[9] (analogical reasoning) when giving rulings. Despite these scholars' elite status, their authority hinges, for Salafis, on their faithfulness to the 'pure sources' and preceding *ijma'*; a scholarly ruling is binding on a person only if supported by scriptural evidence.

The vast majority of contemporary scholars and teachers in the chain of knowledge are male, despite the fact that Salafis admire many great female scholars of the past, such as 'Aisha bint Abu Bakr, the Prophet's third wife.

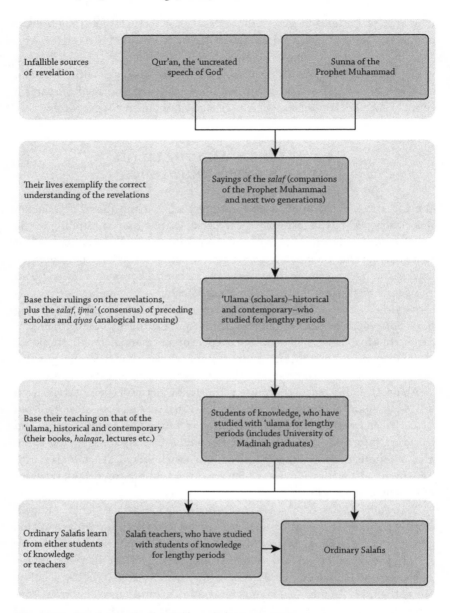

Figure 4.6: The chain of 'authentic' knowledge transmission.

This is at least partly due to the practical difficulties for a woman to study with 'ulama, particularly when it involves travelling abroad: women are expected to organize their time around their family duties, and cannot travel long distances without being accompanied by a *mahram* (husband or male with whom they have a close blood relationship).

However, the chain of knowledge allows a space for women who cannot travel abroad yet who diligently learn from local 'students of knowledge' over a significant period of time (usually understood to mean several years). Umm Hamza had consistently attended circles taught by Kareem and other students of knowledge at Brixton for more than fifteen years. Layla, a Somali university student who occasionally gave talks at the Sisters of Tawheed circles, was only in her early twenties but had been an eager student at various mosques since she was sixteen. Umm Mustafe had learned from an Egyptian *'alim* (scholar) for many years (though most of her studies were online), so she technically fell into the 'students of knowledge' category. However, as a mark of humility, she refused to consider herself as part of their ranks.

Other, usually young Salafis hosted their own informal circles of knowledge at each other's homes after even less training—though some Salafis disapproved of this. Wafa, for instance, called such women 'mess-about sisters', and always declined their invitations because she felt that they were inadequately qualified. 'I mean, who are you? I don't wanna get *your* opinion!' she said.

Salafism has no formal, specific, or universal system of ratification (Wiktorowicz, 2001, p.137). Teachers simply had to have studied under recognized Salafi authorities for an unspecified period of time; there were no agreed-upon minimal requirements or qualifications.[10] Salafism's simple and relatively shallow hierarchy of scholarly authority is related to its emphasis on directly interfacing with the sources of revelation and preserving their 'purity' (Haykel, 2009, pp.35–36). A more layered hierarchy would expose the 'pure sources' to a greater risk of contamination by fallible transmitters.

When I asked women how they knew that their teachers were authorized, some were more precise than others, and had taken pains to investigate teachers' credentials in detail before attending their circles. Yet many others were rather vague on the issue, and seemed content with little information. For example, a newcomer turned up at Abu Ahmed's circle and asked a regular female attendee about the teacher. The regular replied: 'It's a brother who went to Madinah.' No further information—such as his name, how long he had been teaching for, whether or not he had graduated, the duration of his studies, or his specialization—was given or requested. The fact that the teacher had studied at Madinah University seemed to settle the matter of his credibility.

This informal ranking system has two important implications about how sacred authority is acquired in Salafi milieus. First, it is relatively easy for individuals to rise to authority positions. As Bernard Haykel (2009, p.36) points out, 'as an interpretive community Salafis are, in contrast to other Muslim traditions of learning, relatively open, even democratic.' Second, authority is potentially precarious because there is space for subjective judgments to influence the process of acquiring authority. In practice, the status of having learned from 'legitimate' authorities was not enough—in order to build a following, Salafi teachers also had to constantly signal to their students their connection to the 'authentic' sources through the content and style of their teaching.

All teachers took great care to weave their lessons tightly around the 'authentic' sources to which they were subordinate—whether that was the scholarly book under study or the Qur'an and sunna themselves. They strayed only occasionally from quoting from and paraphrasing texts. Usually, this only happened when they answered questions about day-to-day issues and gave examples to elaborate and clarify—particularly contemporary ones with which audiences could identify. For instance, when he explained the rulings on brigandry in *The Concise Presentation of the Fiqh of the Sunnah and the Noble Book*, Kareem compared the phenomenon to 'gangs with guns and weapons' who are 'creating unease in [our] society'—a pertinent reference in a part of London (Brixton) known for its gang crime.

Everybody was expected to 'know their place' in the hierarchy of sources—high-ranking scholars included. The books used in the lessons—such as *Kitab Al-Tawhid* by the renowned Salafi scholar Muhammad ibn 'Abd al-Wahhab, which three of my teachers taught—were peppered with Qur'anic and hadith references. Contemporary works such as *Beneficial Speech in Establishing the Evidences of Tawheed* by Muhammad bin Abdul Wahhab al-Wasaabee, which Umm Hamza taught, often read like a series of annotated quotations from the Qur'an and hadith.

Meanwhile, students of knowledge could not offer their own interpretations; they had to defer to the superior knowledge of the scholars above them. Kareem occasionally declined to answer students' questions, saying, 'Let us wait until the 'ulama speak on this' or 'I will put this to the [more experienced] students of knowledge, insha'Allah'. 'Ignorant leaders, on the other hand, will 'always try to give an answer', he said. Occasionally, scholars would visit Brixton Mosque and other Salafi centres to give talks; and whenever they did, Kareem would cancel all of his classes for the week as a mark of respect.

At the bottom of the chain, the female teachers who were neither scholars nor students of knowledge had to ensure that their lessons conformed to what they had learned from those above them. Like Kareem, Umm Hamza declined to answer questions if she was not absolutely sure of her references. Rather than losing the respect of students, this actually helped to build up her credibility: 'If she doesn't know, she doesn't tell you,' said Dania, one of her students; 'she doesn't act like she knows . . . so you can trust her then'.

In fact, Umm Hamza took the chain of knowledge so seriously that, when teaching, she generally stuck to the notes she had taken in Kareem's class when he taught her the same book several years ago. In preparation for each class, she would type up these notes, indicating any additions from other books with different-coloured text, and email them to Kareem. As a student of Salafi scholars abroad, he could be trusted, she felt, to check that these additions conformed with the rulings of the 'ulama and the 'pure' sources. 'It's important that people don't see it as, "Well, she's just coming with her own thing,"' she explained to me. 'She's actually getting it from someone who's studied and etc., so it's authenticated.' Her comment illustrates clearly the rationale behind this system from the Salafi perspective: by respecting the chain of knowledge, you limit the possibility of contaminating 'pure' Islam with opinions, emotions, and cultural traditions.

The system illustrates an approach to religious learning that Salafis share with fundamentalists from other faiths.[11] In short, they regard 'correct' religious teaching as a technical transmission of 'authentic' information directly—or indirectly via 'trustworthy' mediators—from the 'original' sources to students.[12] Therefore the material cannot be questioned; it can only be retrieved, read out, explained, memorized, and applied. In effect, teachers and scholars see themselves as archaeologists, *retrieving* information that they then convey (Wiktorowicz, 2006, p.210). This approach to education has been institutionalized at the Saudi Arabian Islamic universities, as Qasim Zaman observes:

> It is remarkable ... that few people associated with these universities write commentaries of the sort sometimes still produced in the madrasas of Pakistan or the hawzas [seminary where Shi'a Muslim clerics are trained] of Iran and Iraq. Instead, numerous master's theses and Ph.D. dissertations take the form of annotated editions of medieval collections of hadith and of works of law.... What they ... illustrate ... is a changed view of the Islamic tradition: the concern here is not to engage in an ongoing conversation with interlocutors from the past ... but rather to selectively *retrieve* and disseminate particular facets of what is implicitly recognized as a bygone rather than a continuing tradition. (Zaman, 2007, pp.257–258, italics original)

Of course, if the students of knowledge and teachers themselves could not engage in critical debate, this was certainly forbidden for ordinary Salafis. Umm Hamza told her students:

> Whatever argumentation we have amongst each other, we should return to the Qur'an and sunna.... What you see today is people saying, 'I think this', giving their opinions, but with no *dalil* [evidence or proof from the Qur'an and/ or sunna] ... on the Internet.... Well, Islam isn't about your opinion!

Most circles ended with a question-and-answer session. Both questions and answers followed narrow, specific formats. The most common type of question was: 'What do you do in such-and-such a situation?' These questions reflected modern realities. For example, 'With photographs, can you take them and hide them, or is it always impermissible?' (Answer: generally impermissible except when it is a legal requirement, e.g., passports); 'Should you reply to the *salam*s of a "person of innovation" [i.e., someone who engages in *bid'a*]?' (Answer: Don't reply to their *salam*s, to show that you disapprove of their ways); and 'Can you travel [long distances] with your non-Muslim brother [as your guardian]?' (Answer: Yes). Answers included, whenever possible, references to the Qur'an, sunna or the words of a respected scholar, and never included subjective phrases such as 'I think' or 'in my opinion'.

The other format was: 'What is the proof for such-and-such ruling?' Specifically, students would ask for Qur'anic or hadith references as evidence for what they were being taught, which they could then verify for themselves. Indeed, they were encouraged to question their teachers' sources. Once, after giving a definition of the first pillar of Islam, the *shahada*, Umm Hamza actually rebuked her students for not demanding scriptural evidence: 'Who am I? I'm not the *rasulullah* [Messenger of God]. . . . You need to get into the habit of asking for proofs—someone should've asked me, "What's your proof for that?"'

All these limitations made it difficult for all but the most gifted orators to make their circles engaging and dynamic, and many teachers were at best modest in their delivery, at worst ineloquent and long-winded. While a few preachers displayed impressive oratorical skills—varying pitch and volume and employing fiery and emotive rhetoric that could draw tears from audiences—they were all fond of long sentences, definitions, textual references, and numbered lists of conditions and types.

Humour was employed only very occasionally; speakers often simply read directly from texts, dwelled on passages at length, and repeated themselves. They also generously peppered their talks with respectful expressions such as '*salla Allahu 'alayhi wa-sallam*' (meaning 'May Allah honour him and grant him peace', following mention of the Prophet's name), as well as Qur'anic and hadith quotations—both in Arabic and then in English—making it tiring to concentrate until they finally got to the point.

At first, I wondered how these preachers maintained a regular audience. After speaking to many women about their favourite teachers, however, I realized that this somewhat tedious style was, to some extent, deliberate, as it could actually seal authority. By restricting the content, structure, and delivery of their teaching in this way, teachers signalled their participation in the chain of knowledge transmission that connected them to the 'pure sources', the authority of which no one would dispute.

The constant presence of the Qur'an and sunna in circles—along with explanations by more 'learned' Muslims ('ulama and *salaf*)—was to reassure students that they were being taught 'authentic' Islam. And the teachers' use of Arabic, the language of the Qur'an, could have a similar effect; they all used it liberally throughout their lessons, even when they were not quoting scripture. Abu Ahmed, a native English speaker, even sprinkled his talks with expressions such as *tayyib* ('OK'), *ya'ni* ('you know', 'meaning'), and *la!* ('no!').

The use of Arabic helped to seal a preacher's position in the chain of knowledge as it was a good sign that she or he had studied with 'ulama 'abroad'—typically understood to mean a Salafi institution in Saudi Arabia, another Gulf country, or Yemen. Leaders could further promote this impression by securing well-respected scholars as speakers at conferences.

The 'authenticity' effect was also enhanced by skilful boundary maintenance. Teachers warned students to be suspicious of preachers from rival groups who appealed to the emotions yet quoted scripture sparingly. 'You can't follow someone because they speak eloquently, or 'cause you like the exciting way in which they speak; it has to be based on *dalil*—proof,' Umm Hamza told her students. 'People follow someone 'cause they're from the same race, or they excite you when they speak, or they have a huge following,' she continued, adding that some scholars on Arabic television have a level of popularity that even major scholars such as Saleh Al-Fawzan (b. 1933), a well-known Saudi scholar, cannot match. 'I say to sisters, "Don't follow your friends—do it [i.e., learn] for yourself."'

Other factors—such as personal characteristics—influence the process of authority acquisition, too. Whether or not a leader is seen as morally upright, a gifted orator, likeable, approachable, or has a shared background with his or her followers has an impact on his or her ability to garner authority. This was where female teachers were at a particular advantage, as they had far more in common with their students and were permitted much more intimate contact than male teachers were. In this area at least, female teachers could acquire significant authority that did not depend on a subordinate relationship to higher, male authorities.

In some cases, the fact that a teacher had a similar background to the women was particularly significant. Unlike many of the 'imported' imams in community-based mosques and madrasas, these teachers could understand and sympathize with the issues that most concerned the young women—and in their own language. Usually, the teachers came from non-practising or non-Muslim families, so they could relate to their students' difficulties in gaining acceptance from relatives (see chapter 5.2).

Umm Mustafe and Umm Hamza had daughters of similar ages to their audiences. Thus they could demonstrate an awareness of the issues facing today's youth, and refer to celebrities, social media, and up-to-date slang to illustrate points. For example, Umm Hamza told the women that slang such as 'I swear down' shows how '*shirk* [i.e., polytheism] creeps into our lives every day', presumably because 'down' means 'Hell'. She also attacked the conventional paradigm for beauty among young women—scantily clad celebrities: 'Look first at how they're dressed ... Lady Gaga looks like a *shaytana* [female devil] ...Beyoncé—sorry, but a tart.'

Umm Hamza, who had left school at sixteen, was proof to her students— some of them early school-leavers—that a lack of formal education need not hinder an Islamic one. She could also relate to women with *jahiliyya* pasts; for example, she told them that, in the past, 'Music was my thing—I used to listen to it morning, day, and night,' before she resolved to stop because it was 'haram'.

Umm Mustafe, as a Somali, tried to instil in her almost entirely Somali audience a pride in their origins: 'We are travellers, gypsies here.... We will go back.... You're the future of the nation of Somalia.' At the same time, she urged them to prioritize their religion over national and tribal identities and to feel free to ask her questions because she understood how 'Somali youth have a lot of problems due to culture clash with their parents.' Rather than patronizing and berating the young women, she showed that she understood the realities of combining cultural and religious identities with life in Britain.

Layla, a young university student, could relate to the women more directly and provide a role model. For example, when advising the women on the subject of going to university, she said that she herself had been shocked to find that her university Islamic Society held non-segregated events. She had said to the woman who had invited her: 'Why would I wanna be in a place where the curse of Allah is upon it?' And all of the female teachers could relate to the common experience of verbal or even physical harassment on the streets due to their highly visible attire.

Other significant qualities in teachers were patience and approachability. Umm Hamza, for example, would laboriously write out her lessons on the whiteboard so that students who found dictation difficult could catch every word—and she made herself accessible both in and out of class to those with questions. Salafi teachers generally allowed their mobile telephone numbers to be passed around so that people could call, text, or instant-message them with personal queries—which women, in particular, took advantage of. Abu Khadeejah, a leader at Salafi Publications in Birmingham, said he constantly received calls from Salafis up and down the country, and estimated that 80 percent were from women. This imbalance was probably related to the difficulties women face in speaking to male leaders in person, due to gender segregation.

As for Umm Mustafe, she told her students that not only could they call her mobile 'any time' but that she would also be happy, if necessary, to pass their queries on to 'ulama abroad with whom she was in contact. Kareem, too, made himself available to those with queries. Saidah said, admiringly:

Sisters call him any time. If he misses your call, call back in about ten minutes and he'll pick up and be apologetic for missing your call, unless he's praying. . . . He is so cool, he is.

4.3 BOUNDARY MAINTENANCE IN A COMPETITIVE MARKET

Boundary maintenance was not only crucial for bolstering a leader's authority. It was also an essential tool for fostering greater commitment to the group and to a Salafi identity in general. Teachers devoted much class time to praising knowledge-seeking from 'authentic' (i.e., Salafi) sources and warning students against associating with other, 'deviant' Muslim groups. They also said it was *wajib* (obligatory) to seek religious knowledge (*'ilm*) regularly and by any available means—for example, by reading books or listening to lectures online. But they stressed that attending circles in person is particularly beneficial for obtaining in-depth knowledge and clarification in the event of confusion.

This emphasis is not surprising since regularized group contact— especially if face-to-face—is itself a commitment mechanism that many other communities have employed to help achieve communion (Kanter, 1972, p.98). Moreover, teachers said that attending one-off talks is not sufficient; one must also attend regular lessons that tackle books from beginning to end. A weekly lesson on one book can go on for years.

Significantly, women and men are equally obligated to seek knowledge, provided that this does not conflict with their other religious duties, such as (for women) child-rearing. This contrasts with the experience of some fundamentalist women, such as the ultra-orthodox Jews studied by Tamar El-Or (1994), who were discouraged from studying their own sacred texts. Salafis cite (among other proofs) a hadith in which the Prophet set aside a day for giving women 'religious lessons and commandments' (Bukhari 101) to demonstrate that Islam is in favour of women's religious education.

For Salafis, studying Islam should be a major preoccupation. One teacher even suggested that one ought to spend 'an hour for your *akhira* [afterlife], an hour for your *dunya*,' meaning that one should spend an hour learning about Islam for every hour spent learning about worldly matters, such as at university. Other teachers invoked an old saying that one should 'seek knowledge from the cradle to the grave'; the knowledge-seeker's journey, they insisted, continues throughout her life, never completed. In emulation of the *salaf*, who were avid knowledge-seekers, students should study with *ikhlas*—the sole intention of pleasing God—and be consistent, regularly take notes, and ask questions for clarification. Asking for *dalil* was particularly encouraged.

Outside of class, students were expected to revise their notes and occasionally do a small amount of homework.

Lessons were deliberately structured in order to create an atmosphere of serious and effective learning. Umm Hamza told me: 'I expect study, writing, memorising, etc., etc., and you come back next week and you've understood what was taught, ready to build on that.' At the beginning of each class, she would ask us to recap out loud the content of last week's lesson. She even gave us an hour-long written test at one point, with such detailed questions as 'Ayn Allaah—where is Allaah; give an aayaah [Qur'anic verse] to prove this.'

To encourage attendance, teachers often emphasized the spiritual rewards on offer. Seeking knowledge, they pointed out, carries reward in the afterlife—just like other *wajib* [obligatory] acts, such as fasting in Ramadan and wearing the hijab—while failing to do so incurs punishment. Aware that their students had taken time out of busy schedules to attend, teachers also stressed that all time spent sitting in circles of knowledge with *ikhlas* earns reward.

At the beginning of a conference at Brixton Mosque, a speaker observed that there were not yet many attendees—but no matter, they will get less reward, whereas 'our reward starts now'. On another occasion, at a mid-week Tottenham Da'wah mini-conference, a speaker brought the event to a close as follows:

> May Allah reward you for attending, even though it's late and in the middle of the week, many of you are working. . . . We hope to get the highest reward through our *da'wa* and classes, which is to see the face of Allah (*s.w.t.*) on the Day of Judgment.*

Students were often reminded about another, continuing reward from regular attendance: they would better understand how to perform further acts of worship, which themselves carry reward and contribute to the likelihood of entering Paradise. At the 2011 Al-Athariyyah conference, a speaker likened the pursuit of knowledge to the use of GPS before setting off on a journey. Seeking knowledge, he explained, is like checking for directions that will bring us to our goal—Paradise. In addition, teachers pointed out, a student who travels across London and beyond to seek knowledge follows the example of the *sahaba* (companions of the Prophet), who endured hardship in their journeys to faraway lands to collect hadiths. Moreover, one who acquires knowledge and passes it on to another is rewarded for her student's good deeds, as well as her own.

Another incentive is that there is a certain amount of prestige attached to someone who is known to have knowledge. This is marked by the label *talib al-'ilm* or 'student of knowledge', which is applied informally to those who study consistently. Knowledge gives you a 'high rank', as Layla told an

audience of teenaged Somalis at a Sisters of Tawheed conference. 'If you acquire knowledge and for the sake of Allah, then you are above the average
Muslim.'

Urging students to attend classes regularly was not sufficient; teachers
also had to ensure that they attended *their* circles, and not those held by
the many other Muslim groups in London. This was achieved by constant
boundary activation, sometimes in highly explicit ways that descended
into derogatory remarks about other groups and their leaders. Constantly
reinforcing the purity and authenticity of Salafism, while portraying all
other beliefs and practices as deviated and sinful, was a crucial strategy not
merely in encouraging attendance at circles of knowledge but also to help
nurture resilient Salafi identities. Thus teachers often referred to Salafis and
their scholars as the 'people of sunna' or the 'people of *'ilm*', and seldom did
a conference take place in which the hadith about the 'saved sect' did not
feature prominently.

Preachers employed the hadith to make it seem impossible for students
to 'sit on the fence' (see chapter 3.4). In other words, once it is clear that only
one sect will be saved from Hell, it becomes a matter of urgency to pick one.
For example, Umm Mustafe told her students: 'People say, "Oh, there are so
many Islamic groups, how do I know who to follow?" But Allah will not excuse
you on *yawm al-qiyama* [the Day of Judgment] [for that reason].'* However,
teachers cited the hadith even to audiences made up almost entirely of those
who had already accepted Salafism, highlighting how reference to the one
'saved sect' was thought to reaffirm beliefs and solidify commitment.

Teachers also emphasized the necessity of publicly proclaiming the
'Salafi' identity label, rather than hiding behind general, more publicly acceptable terminology, such as 'Muslim' or *ahl al-sunna wa-al-jama'a*. They
hardly needed to devote lesson time to the issue because, at almost every
conference, there would be an opportunity to reinforce the message in the
question-and-answer-session. 'Why can't we say we follow the sunna without calling ourselves Salafi?' was the question frequently asked. In reply, the
teacher would refer to examples of major scholars advocating the use of the
term, the hadith in which the Prophet told his daughter Fatima that he was
'for you a blessed *salaf*' (Bukhari 2652)—'He didn't say "I'm a blessed Shia to
you", or something else' (Umm Hamza)—and the importance of differenti-
ating oneself from the many other groups calling themselves 'Muslims' or
'people of sunna', as illustrated by the 73-sect hadith.

Time and time again, teachers would stress that the majority of Muslims
had gone astray, and that the straight path is trodden by a minority of
Muslims. Reading between the lines, they were suggesting that their students should not be put off by the relatively small numbers some Salafi circles attract. If anything, the lack of mass support was testimony to the truth
and authenticity of the Salafi *da'wa*.

There's a lot of people upon *bid'a* in this country. . . . Don't just follow the majority—Allah says in the Qur'an that the *haqq* is with the minority. (Umm
Mustafe)

Yet far more class time was dedicated to undermining Salafism's rivals
than to bolstering the group's own credentials. This became starkly apparent
when I categorized my notes from circles of knowledge; I had accumulated
about six times as much information about undermining rivals. As mentioned, British Salafism operates in an intensely competitive 'Islam market'
and in a liberal Western society generally at odds with many of its precepts. It
is subject to external pressure from rival Islamic groups popular with young
British Muslims, older-generation Muslims with culturally infused beliefs
and practices, and the liberal (Muslim and non-Muslim) youth culture in
wider society. All three areas of competition were regularly challenged in
circles of knowledge, yet the first received by far the most attention.

More specifically, teachers targeted the Muslim groups closest to the
margins and boundaries of Salafism—in those areas in which Salafi beliefs
and practices overlap with or bear striking similarities with those of other
groups. Teachers spoke little of the Shi'a, for example, whose transgressions
reach the point of *kufr* (disbelief), according to Salafis. This is unsurprising;
Nancy Ammerman (1987, p.75) shows how fundamentalists tend to focus on
patrolling the boundaries that divide them from their closest neighbours.
As she wrote of the American fundamentalist Christian community she was
studying: 'The pastor's righteous indignation is far more likely to be directed
at the clergy and members of other Christian churches than at thieves, mur-
derers, pagans, or atheists.'

Such areas of ambiguity are a matter of concern for Salafis because they
can impact negatively on Salafism's numbers and public image in two ways.
First, people may unwittingly be led to the circles of others, thinking they are
part of the same group. And second, people may be put off Salafism if they
cannot distinguish it from groups that have adopted similar identity markers, such as Al-Muhajiroun, whose followers are (even more) widely considered to be 'extremists' by Muslims and non-Muslims alike.

The most dangerous rivals were those who had tried to appropriate the
label 'Salafi' or some of Salafism's most visible identity markers, such as
beards and attire, so these boundaries were patrolled most vigilantly of
all. One such group was Al-Muhajiroun. This UK-based group was banned
in 2010, but successor organisations continue to operate under different
names (see introduction). The members of this group prompted particular
concern due to their provocative behaviour and resultant high media profile
in recent years.

Consequently, men linked to Brixton Mosque published a lengthy 'refutation' of the group in 2009, which was sold in the mosque bookshop. This

book aimed 'to diametrically separate the Salafis from the deviant group' by outlining their divergent beliefs in fine detail and challenging their leaders' credentials (As-Salafī and Al-Ashantī, 2009, p.13). This text, and other book-length refutations, were occasionally distributed free of charge to the women at Brixton Mosque circles.

The authors claim that Bakri Muhammad's followers used to be 'clean-shaven, Levi jeans sporting juveniles', but have now 'gowned the majestic attire of the Sunnah, and have embraced numerous qualities of the Salafis' (As-Salafi and Al-Ashanti, 2009, p.14), such as the beard, *thawb* (Muslim men's robe-like garment), and Salafi label (Bajwa, 2009, p.11). The same shift was apparent on the women's side, according to women at Brixton who had been Salafis since the early 1990s. They claimed that Hizb ut-Tahrir and (later) Al-Muhajiroun women had mostly worn hijabs, skirts, and abayas in the 1990s. Today, however, they look almost identical to Salafis, favouring *jilbabs* and *niqabs*. Salafis see this apparent shift as proof of their own credibility within the British Muslim community, which others have envied and tried to appropriate.

Tablighi Jamaat, a missionary offshoot of the Deobandi movement, was another group that could easily be mistaken for the Salafis due to their conservative practices and attire (men typically have beards and women often wear *niqabs*). 'One has to be on our guard against them,' Kareem warned his students. He said that Tablighi Jamaat activists wear 'the clothes of the Muslim' but 'the Muslim should not be fooled by them'. Shaykh Bin Baz, he added, had warned believers against the group.

Often preachers would speak more discreetly about 'claimants to *Salafiyya* [i.e., Salafism]' or 'so-called Salafis' who have 'infiltrated our ranks' and are 'causing division', without naming the offenders. The confusion, leaders maintained, had been intensified by academics who have referred to 'purist', 'politico', and 'jihadi' Salafis, suggesting that a whole spectrum of divergent groups merit the label 'Salafi' (see introduction). 'Enemies of Islam and enemies of *Salafiyya*,' said a speaker at the 2012 Al-Athariyyah conference, try to 'compartmentalize *Salafiyya*. . . . We reject all these labels. . . . A Salafi is a Salafi.' Those who fall outside the narrow definition of a Salafi were variously termed *'ahl al-bid'a'* (people of innovation), 'callers to misguidance'; *'hizbis'* (partisans); *'ahl al-batil'* (people of falsehood); or similar. Salafi teachers warned their students to be alert to their cunning tactics to attract them.

The clever amongst them try hard to display good conduct. . . . They're from amongst us, look like us and sound like us, yet they are calling to misguidance.* (Kareem)

In this day and age, non-Muslims are not able to distinguish between the Muslims, 'cause there's so many people trying to resemble us now [for example, using the beard and *jilbab*]. . . . Muslims upon *hizbiyya* [partisanship] are using it to recruit. . . . They even quote some of the same scholars.* (Abu Ahmed)

A lot of people are ignorant of the sunna and think it's OK to go to places of *bid'a*. They think they have a big shaykh on their website, a big shaykh came to see them. This is what they do—they get someone to come [in order] to gain their reputation. A lot of so-called Salafis do that. *Ahl al-batil*, they learn how to beautify the *batil* . . . just like a fisherman beautifies bait to catch fish. . . . This is the way of *ahl al-bid'a* from now 'til *yawm al-qiyama*.* (Umm Mustafe)

Mary Douglas (1966) showed how communities employ the body as a symbol of society, where bodily orifices possess power to pollute the body just as marginal beliefs, behaviour, and other pressures pose a danger to the social order and, ultimately, group survival. Salafi preachers were fond of using bodily metaphors to strengthen boundaries with other groups and intensify their warnings about the dangers of associating with sectarian rivals.

In Salafi circles, such ideas about bodily 'pollution' are readily employed when describing how bodily orifices can literally invalidate a Muslim's purity status, requiring him or her to perform *wudu* (cleansing rituals) before praying. For instance, a person who leaks urine or blood must repeat his or her ablutions. But Salafis also use these ideas as metaphors for how evil and sin can corrupt a person's morality or, indeed, Salafism as a whole. Richard Gauvain (2013) has analyzed such ideas and practices extensively in relation to Salafi ritual worship (*'ibada*) in Egypt, including how prohibitions can be strengthened through the use of purity language (p.78).

During my fieldwork, Salafi teachers frequently referred to the 'purity' of Salafism, which had been 'infected' by 'poisonous ideologies'. A speaker at the 2011 Al-Athariyyah conference said that 'some of those who have ascribed themselves to *Salafiyya* have been infected with a disease that races through their veins' and drives them to seek 'fame and status' by trying to bring about 'the downfall' of the Salafis. This is a phenomenon Salafis cannot 'cure', so such people should be excluded from 'our ranks'.

Such metaphors are liberally employed in Salafi literature, too. Abū Ameenah 'AbdurRahmān As-Salafī and 'AbdulHaq Al-Ashantī (2009, 2011; Sloan and al-Ashantī, 2011) pathologized Jihadi preachers such as Abdullah El Faisal in a series of critiques for the Brixton Mosque-linked publisher, Jamiah Media. Tongue-in-cheek, they claimed such clerics suffer from an 'extreme condition' called 'excessive-compulsive takfeer disorder (ECTD)' (2009, p.21), referring to their reputation for making *takfir* (pronouncing as non-Muslim) on Muslim scholars and rulers. The authors conclude their 'refutation' of El Faisal with advice from the scholar Abu Muhammad Khalf al-Barbahari (d. 941) to '[e]xamine the speech of every one of the people' before accepting it. This 'antidote', the authors claim, can 'immunise against all strains of deadly misguidance' and result in preachers like El Faisal being 'swiftly contained, quarantined and prevented from spreading their noxious teachings' (pp.332–333).

Seeking knowledge was often portrayed by Salafi teachers as the 'remedy' to areas of doubt and potential or actual harm that result from the plethora of 'deviant' ideologies. Kareem spoke of knowledge as a 'protection' from the many misunderstandings and sects that had developed since the Prophet's time. And Umm Mustafe told her students to refrain from unfamiliar practices until they learned more: 'What you don't know, you leave it until you know'—just as they would be careful of 'what you put in your body'.

Thus teachers constantly advised students to be wary of whom they associated with, particularly of those engaged in *bid'a*. As teachers often said, while the company of Salafis brings benefit, like the odour of the perfume-seller, the company of 'deviants' brings harm, just as the blacksmith exposes others to poisonous fumes—a reference to a famous hadith (Bukhari 2101, 5534). They warned students of the various tell-tale 'signs' of such people: they do not emulate the *salaf*; they speak ill of the people of sunna, such as Ibn Taymiyya, Ibn 'Abd al-Wahhab, and Bin Baz; and they may invoke an additional category of *tawhid*, *tawhid al-hakimiyya* (unity of sovereignty), in order to justify a political emphasis, rather than focusing on the other components of *tawhid* (see section 4, this chapter).

Rival Islamic groups that promoted engagement with politics, such as Muslim Brotherhood–inspired groups, came into focus during the Arab uprisings, which began in December 2010. Salafi teachers reacted either by apparently ignoring the developments or by suggesting that those who campaign and demonstrate are slaves to their desires and emotions, rather than the evidence of the Qur'an and sunna, which—they claimed—do not endorse such activities.

Another typical way of undermining other groups was by highlighting their leaders' lack of 'Islamic' qualifications. Teachers urged students to ask questions before attending other circles or even picking up an Islamic book, such as: Did the teacher or author study with 'legitimate' scholars? Did he or she graduate from a recognized Salafi institution? Is he or she known to call to the Salafi *da'wa*, as a morally upright individual who practises the sunna? Many of the most popular preachers, they claimed, such as those who present satellite television shows, had qualified as doctors, engineers, and solicitors—but not as Islamic teachers, so their rulings could not be trusted.

This boundary policing was not confined to warnings; it could be enforced, too, as Salafis made efforts to discharge their duty to enjoin the good and forbid the evil (see chapter 3.3). Occasionally, I observed how leading community members literally patrolled the lines between 'correct' and 'deviated' groups or ideologies.

One Friday afternoon at Brixton Mosque, a young woman wearing a hijab and abaya—not a full *jilbab*—started distributing flyers to the women promoting a 'Ladies Night' with 'live entertainment' and an 'Islamic fashion show'. Some of the Salafi women congregated there were muttering that this event, which had clearly been organized by another group, was in 'imitation of the *kuffar*' (non-Muslims) and not permissible. Then, one of the longest-standing worshippers asked the young woman if she had obtained permission from the mosque authorities. She reacted defensively—'it's a public place!'— but soon left.

Boundary policing could also be enforced in the virtual world. One evening, I received a general SMS message from Muna, a middle-aged Moroccan I had met at an informal circle, promoting a conference whose speakers included Murtaza Khan, Abdul Raheem Green, and Waseem Kempson. These individuals were known in the community for advocating a more 'political' approach. Several hours later, I received another group message from Muna that bore the marks of boundary policing: 'Asalaam waleykum sisters, the message I sent you about the talk. The speakers are not salafis. Please let the people that you have passed it on to [know]. Sorry for the inconvenience.'

Furthermore, 'deviant' literature was not tolerated in Salafi spaces. Sagal told me privately that she would risk an argument if she brought to Brixton Mosque any of her books by authors who were not recognized Salafis. I myself was advised by a middle-aged woman at a circle I attended in Tottenham that my translation of the Qur'an, by Yusuf Ali, was 'full of errors'; she promptly directed me to www.freekoran.co.uk, which supplied free copies of the Saudi-sponsored translation. And some of Umm Mustafe's students would actually bring in their new book purchases to run them by her to check the authors' credentials.

4.4 BUILDING FOUNDATIONS: *TAWHID* AND *AHKAM*

The greatest thing that Allah has enjoined upon us and the first obligation . . . upon us is *tawhid*. . . . Some new sisters come [to the circle] and are like: 'Oh, *tawhid* again?' They haven't really got it. (Umm Hamza, speaking to her students)

Salafism places the utmost emphasis on teaching *tawhid*. This is the doctrine of absolute monotheism as testified in the first part of the *shahada*—'I testify that there is no god worthy of worship except Allah'—the Muslim declaration of faith and first pillar of Islam. Indeed, *tawhid* was the focus or at least an element of most of the classes and talks I attended over two years and four months, and I gradually realized that this was a clue to Salafis' most important commitment strategy.

Salafi scholars divide *tawhid* into at least three categories in order to make it comprehensible. *Tawhid al-rububiyya*—roughly, 'uniqueness in lordship'—asserts that God alone created and governs everything in the universe. *Tawhid al-uluhiyya* relates to worship, stating that all worship should be of God alone, without involving partners or intermediaries. And Salafis teach that worship, or *'ibada*, is a 'comprehensive term that includes everything Allah is pleased with, loves from speech and actions, done internally and externally' (Umm Hamza). In other words, a vast range of acts can potentially be acts of worship if done for the sake of pleasing God.

These include making an oath, cooking your husband's dinner, or even getting a good night's sleep so that you are ready for dawn prayers. Indeed, the list of 'acts' that have the potential to become worship is long: slaughtering, vowing, supplicating, trusting, fearing, loving, hoping, repenting, desiring, revering, giving charity, fasting, seeking aid, and so on—yet all must be directed towards God alone. The exception is instinctive acts, such as love of one's children or fear of darkness, which fall under the category of 'natural' love or fear. These are not considered blameworthy unless one allows them to take precedence over one's obligations to God.

Third, *tawhid al-asma' wa-al-sifat* relates to God's names and attributes, asserting that God be described only in the terms authorized by Himself or the Prophet—for example, the name *al-Haqq* ('the Truth') or the description that He 'rose over the (Mighty) Throne (in a manner that suits His Majesty)' (Qur'an 20:5)—without distortion of words or meaning. It also states that believers must not doubt the possibility of God possessing such attributes (by asking, for instance, how He can have two right hands?); nor should they draw similarities between God's attributes and those of His creation (for instance, by comparing God's eyes to those of human beings, the better to understand them).

Salafi leaders asserted the centrality of *tawhid* by constantly portraying it as the 'ticket' to Paradise, while describing *shirk*, its opposite, as the pathway to Hell. More specifically, students were taught that those who commit major *shirk* (*shirk al-akbar*) take themselves out of the fold of Islam; and unless they retake their *shahada* and repent, they are destined to Hellfire for eternity.

Major *shirk* includes voluntarily supplicating to others besides God, believing in horoscopes, or sacrificing an animal in the name of someone besides God. Minor *shirk* (*shirk al-asghar*) applies to sayings and actions that lead to *shirk*, without reaching the level of worship. This includes praying to show off, giving to charity in order to brag about it, or even saying that medicine rather than God cured an illness. Umm Hamza warned her students not to say things like 'Oh, I took Nurofen [Ibuprofen] and it really helped me'—rather, say: ' "By the will of Allah"—it's Him that helped you.' Those who commit minor *shirk* and do not repent will be sent to Hell temporarily, if God so wills.

Teachers portrayed *shirk* as a grave sin, which believers must avoid at all costs. *Shirk al-akbar* is considered the worst offence of all, as it is the only one that God does not eventually forgive. 'The issue of *tawhid* is the heaviest issue on the balance of *yawm al-qiyama*,' as a speaker at a 2011 Brixton conference put it. Thus a large proportion of lessons was devoted to laying out meticulously the various forms *shirk* can take so that students could ensure they did not commit it. Indeed, Abu Ahmed spoke of little else in his classes.

Tawhid al-uluhiyya was by far the most emphasized component of *tawhid* in the circles of knowledge I attended. This was not only because it is 'what all the prophets called to . . . the main call of Islam' (Umm Hamza), but because instilling a sound understanding of how it is fulfilled and violated paves the way for higher commitment levels in *all* spheres of life. Violations of *tawhid al-uluhiyya* are wide-ranging and easily committed—it is not simply a matter of praying before an idol. For instance, if fear must be directed towards God alone, then all fear of things besides God has the potential to reach the level of a major sin, and possibly one that could bar a believer from Paradise for all eternity.

To put this in context using an example that Salafi teachers were fond of, a woman who does not wear the *jilbab* because she fears the reaction of others has not only disobeyed God's commandment to cover herself fully, she has also committed *shirk*. Indeed, *shirk*, particularly *shirk* of *uluhiyya*, is so comprehensive that it can be committed all the time if due caution is not taken.

'We have to be very, very careful 'cause *shirk* is something Muslims fall into every day,' Umm Hamza warned her students. And Umm Mustafe went so far as to say that 'everything that takes us away, occupies us away from Allah, it's a *shirk*'. Thus teaching *tawhid* was thought to promote students' obedience to God in matters that went far beyond those of belief and prayer.

Emphasis on *tawhid*, particularly *tawhid al-uluhiyya*, can also drive commitment in other ways. Students who understand and accept the full extent of *tawhid* will be driven to perform their acts of worship with sincerity for fear of falling into *shirk*. An unacceptable alternative would be performing them to show off or fit in with peers—clearly a more precarious basis for commitment. For example, a young woman who wears a *jilbab* because her friends wear it, rather than consciously as an act of worship purely for God, is likely to consider abandoning the garment if her friends do so. And, by concentrating on *tawhid*, rather than more controversial issues such as the hijab or polygamy, teachers were less likely to put off newcomers, many of whom were Christian converts and could relate to the principles of monotheism.

This is Salafis' most emphasized commitment strategy and one of which they are proud because it is thought to reflect the Prophet's approach in calling to *tawhid* for the first thirteen years of his prophethood. Therefore rival groups that overly concern themselves with other matters, such as politics and violent jihad, are 'deviating' from the prophetic paradigm. 'Start with learning *tawhid* and repeat and repeat these affairs until they stick,' said a speaker at the 2011 Al-Athariyyah conference:

Other groups need a three- or five-day conference on the hijab or *riba* [usurious interest]. The *sahaba* just [accepted these rulings]. . . . It was enough that they were commanded to do it or not to do it. Why? Because the *foundations* were built.*

Teachers advised students to take the same approach when giving *da'wa* themselves. Umm Mustafe said that with new converts, 'teach them gently— *tawhid* first . . . there is no point saying "Put a hijab on," and she may want to come to the mosque and wear trousers and we drive her away.'*

Alongside their focus on *tawhid*, Salafi teachers promoted a discourse of quantifiable rewards and punishments, enhanced by vivid descriptions of the end of the world and the afterlife, to demonstrate that adherence to Salafi norms was a matter of rational self-interest. On the Day of Judgment, teachers explained, everyone's good and bad deeds will be individually measured on a scale, which determines their eternal destiny. Since death could come at any point, Salafis need to evaluate constantly their deeds and strive to perform more acts of worship to ensure entrance to Paradise. Students learned that every deed has a positive, negative, or neutral effect on one's balance of deeds, depending on its *hukm* (ruling).

There are five categories that acts can fall into: *wajib* (obligatory), *mustahabb* or sunna (highly recommended), *mubah* (permissible), *makruh* (hated, detested), and haram (forbidden). *Wajib* acts—such as the five daily prayers, wearing the *jilbab*, and obeying one's husband—carry reward if performed and punishment if not performed. *Mustahabb* or sunna acts—such as fasting on Mondays and Thursdays and performing two *rakat* (prostrations and words accompanying ritual prayers) before *fajr* (the dawn prayer)—carry reward if performed but entail no punishment if not performed. *Mubah* acts—such as wearing a grey (rather than black) *jilbab* and eating a veggie (rather than halal beef) burger—carry no reward or punishment. *Makruh* acts—such as talking while going to the lavatory and drinking water while standing—carry reward if abstained from and no punishment if performed. Finally, haram acts—such as drinking alcohol, smoking, and *zina* ('illicit' sexual acts, especially sex outside marriage and adultery)—carry reward if abstained from and punishment if performed.

It was significant that avoiding *makruh* and haram acts carried reward, as these categories included many habits that the women had left—or, in many cases, were still struggling to leave—behind in their *jahiliyya*. Umm Hamza, who openly told her students about her difficulties in giving up music, encouraged them to see these prohibitions in a positive light:

If you walk down the street and refrain from smoking or showing your hair, you get a reward. Don't look at it [the haram] like 'I can't do it'. Look at it in the positive way, rather than the negative.*

Teachers often quantified rewards and punishments explicitly so that students could better understand them and grasp the value of afterlife reward and the severity of afterlife punishment. Umm Hamza said that reciting the Qur'an brings a reward of '10' per letter, and that saying 'al-salamu 'alaykum' to another Muslim brings 10 rewards, with an extra 10 if one adds 'wa rahmatulla' ('and the mercy of Allah be upon you'), and an extra 10 if one further adds 'wa rahmatulla wa barakatu' (. . . 'and His blessings').

Quantifying reward seemed especially popular in the context of charity fundraising speeches. A speaker at a fundraiser for the 2010 Pakistan floods at a Salafi-run Moroccan-themed restaurant in north-east London appealed to the women by reciting hadiths about a man who was promised 700 camels in Paradise because he gave one for the sake of God (Ahmad 4:121; Muslim 3:1505; Al-Nasa'i 6:49), showing that rewards are 'multiplied by 700' in proportion to the amount given to charity. Similarly, Umm Hamza encouraged the women at a Brixton seminar to donate to the mosque because zakat brings at least 10 rewards, adding, 'Stinginess is from *shaytan*. We cling to our wealth to get a pair of Nike trainers or Iman make-up. But giving *sadaqa* and zakat will not decrease your wealth. It's for your *akhira*.'

Some teachers referred to the process of gathering good deeds as one of 'adding' to your 'account' with God. For example, Umm Mustafe said that for those converts who were chaste before coming to Islam, 'Allah will add them [the good deeds] to your account.' In general, teachers encouraged their students to see their pursuit of piety in terms of simple benefit/cost calculations. Layla urged her audience:

> Every day, aim to total your good deeds for that day, and be honest for yourself—for example, did you *salam* (give Islamic greetings to) another Muslim? Did you smile at her? Did you attend the funeral of someone you didn't know? Did you recite the Qur'an? Create a tick-list. . . . Evaluate yourself: am I in *janna* today or am I in *nar* [(Hell) fire] today? . . . Evaluate: do you spend enough time on your *din* [religion], enough time on evaluating your hereafter? It has been suggested that you spend an hour for your *akhira*, an hour for your *dunya*. . . .Set yourself a target, for example, finish the Qur'an every month.*

Teachers repeatedly emphasized the importance of looking beyond temporary, material matters to the eternal life beyond death, enhancing the message with modern references.

> No matter driving test, GCSEs, A-levels or any other tests—this is the real test. (Speaker, 2010 Tottenham Da'wah conference)

> How many of us spend our time listening to the radio, reading newspapers, using media? . . . If we knew what awaits us, the questioning we will get, we wouldn't get distracted by this *dunya*, by our wealth.* (Brixton Mosque *khutba*)

You're only going to your grave with your deeds . . . we're not going to our graves with Louis Vuitton! (Umm Hamza, circle)

These warnings were supported by vivid descriptions of the afterlife, namely the terror of the Day of Judgment, the torment of Hell, and the bliss of Paradise—and talks on these subjects often drew tears from audiences, as well as the speakers themselves. Entrants to Paradise are promised flowing rivers, perfect health, beautiful spouses, wine that does not intoxicate, no need to go to the lavatory, and eating for pleasure rather than sustenance. And for those who achieve the highest level of Paradise, *firdaws*, there is the ultimate reward of literally seeing the face of God. Meanwhile, the forms of torment that entrants to Hell can expect were often horrifyingly specific, such as the 'burning of the part of the body that enjoyed the *zina*' (Umm Hamza) for those who indulged in illicit sexual intercourse.

Kareem taught his students *The Book of the End* by Ibn Katheer, which is full of descriptions of the signs marking the approach of the Day of Judgment; these, he maintained, still apply today. By making the end of time seem close, he intensified the urgency of performing good deeds and abstaining from sin. For example, commenting on Ibn Katheer's signs of widespread ignorance, rampant fornication, the prevalence of alcohol, and perishing of men that herald the Day of Judgment, he decried the lack of (Islamic) knowledge today, with the result that

people are giving information based on ignorance, not *'ilm*. So then you find evil becomes widespread. . . . We're seeing the spread of *zina* and men are killing each other and the likes. You see this in Mecca—men coming and a whole group of women is with just one man.

Moreover, one of Ibn Katheer's signs of the end was that 'women will be dressed yet undressed, and we live in that time,' said Kareem, undoubtedly referring to the flesh-baring outfits of modern Western women.

By devoting most class time to establishing this framework, teachers could then simply inform students that obeying one's husband is *wajib*, polygamy is sunna, and free-mixing is haram—and there would be little need for further discussion. Once the foundations for understanding acts of worship and disobedience and their eternal consequences were in place, students would come to regard it as a matter of self-interest to take heed of the *ahkam* (rulings).

Circles therefore did not often explore the specifics of controversial and difficult topics that affected the women in their daily lives, such as gender roles in marriage, polygamy, higher education, employment, dress, traveling without a *mahram*, and relationships with non-Salafis. The exception was during the question-and-answer sessions. At that point, women did frequently ask about the permissibility of certain actions—such as taking out a student loan, praying in a multifaith prayer room, or eating Christmas dinner with one's non-Muslim parents—and teachers would respond with the *hukm* (if they knew it), at which point the discussion would be closed.

Even if their students accepted this clear-cut reward/punishment discourse, teachers recognized that there would be times when the sacrifices the women had to make and struggles they faced threatened to overcome them. So the teachers employed theodicies[13] to help women to endure difficulties and hardship, put them into perspective, and even regard them as positive evidence of their piety.

Students learned about the concept of God's *qadr* (decree); that God knows exactly what will happen to each individual and has everything under control. God's will is benevolent, so one can be sure that He allows suffering to occur because it brings good outcomes. Moreover, the women were taught, if you sacrifice something for God's sake—such as a job that involved haram activities— He will replace it with something better, as stated in the hadith Ahmad 5:363.

Shortly after the devastating Japanese earthquake and tsunami of 2011, I attended an informal gathering of eight women at the home of a French-Algerian woman, at which Umm Muqbil, who was leading the circle, said that the disaster was '*qadr* Allah' (God's decree). It was, she said, a test for some people and a punishment for others. Afterward people had filled the mosques of the Arab world—albeit temporarily—because they suddenly feared God as they ought, she added. 'See, something good comes of it!' said another woman.

Labeling even the most shocking, devastating occurrences as '*qadr* Allah' lends meaning to them, even if it is not understood. As Umm Hamza told her students:

> Once you understand the *qadr* of Allah, your life becomes open. . . . You get upset for maybe a day, but you accept, '*qadr* Allah!' . . . When I came to an understanding of it, it settled my heart a lot.*

Students learned that suffering is a Muslim's test of faith: Will she turn her back on her religion, shedding her *jilbab* after her relatives ridicule her, or will she turn to God in supplication and trust in His decree? Moreover, with every test comes the expiation of past sin, purifying the Muslim and decreasing her total of 'bad' deeds that will count against her on the Day of Judgment.

4.5 FOSTERING SISTERHOOD

As Kanter (1972, p.72) points out, achieving group cohesion and solidarity requires that an 'individual commits himself to the group as his primary set of relations; his loyalty and allegiance are offered to all the members of the group, who together comprise a community.' Such is the importance of this commitment mechanism that 'where strong ingroup loyalty is present, a community can stick together even though it is forcibly removed from its home, loses its crop, or is threatened with a lawsuit.'

Circles not only provide a forum for regularly instilling Salafi teachings, but also foster closer ties between Salafi women. More specifically, these gatherings promote a deeper sense of belonging to the group, as well as plausibility and support structures.

Some women follow or accompany their friends into Salafism, so they arrive at a Salafi venue with a ready-made friendship network; but for others, the initial process of becoming Salafi is one that involves alienation from old social networks and entering unfamiliar environments (see chapter 3). Therefore attending Salafi circles is a chance to meet fellow Salafi women who face the same challenges and to gain a sense of shared identity—and new friends.

In my experience, Salafi circles of knowledge and conferences usually start later than advertised, so there is a chance for women to say *al-salamu 'alaykum* to each other—normally accompanied by a handshake or three cheek kisses—and chat before the lessons and talks begin. Informal circles at private homes were followed by meals, during which there was ample opportunity to become better acquainted with one another. At more formal circles, it was common for friends to sit together and speak only to one another. But whenever a newcomer attended a lesson, others would usually warmly introduce themselves and explain the content of the lesson and the book(s) being studied.

Sometimes new converts would attend Umm Hamza's class, since it was billed as a 'basic' class, but no one seemed to mind if they arrived without an all-enveloping gown or even a headscarf, at least for their first lesson. This friendliness—though not always forthcoming—is important because attending a Salafi class for the first time can be an intimidating experience, particularly if one is alone and lacking the 'proper' attire in the midst of a sea of black clothing (as I know from personal experience).

Given the emphasis teachers place upon giving *da'wa* to encourage others to become Salafis, it was unsurprising that plenty of women took pains to become acquainted with newcomers, offering their phone numbers and BlackBerry Messenger PINs so that they could invite them to other events and include them in group messages with religious 'reminders' (hadiths, Qur'anic quotations, and so on).

Particularly at the beginning of my fieldwork, I was often seen as a potential convert and occasionally found myself surrounded by women curious to hear my 'story' and eager to swap phone numbers and invite me to other circles. Sometimes, women offered to accompany me to circles to encourage me to come, and I was frequently invited to homes for circles, meals, and *iftar* (the breaking of the fast at sunset) during Ramadan and laden with gifts such as books, pamphlets, audio CDs, and even an abaya (in my size) to wear for Eid. Other newcomers related experiences that matched mine.

The circles fostered ties between women not only by their actual content but also by the atmosphere and shared etiquettes, language, and attire they promoted. As is common in NRMs, familial metaphors were used to promote intimacy and loyalty (Barker, 1984; 1989: Daschke and Ashcraft, 2005, p.12; Palmer, 1994). The women referred to one another—and were labeled by the teacher—as 'sisters', and they often called their female teachers 'auntie'. Teachers frequently stressed sisters' reciprocal duties: respond to your sister's Islamic greetings, attend to her when she is sick, answer her invitations, respond to her with the correct *du'a* (supplication) when she sneezes,[14] give her *nasiha* (sincere, Islamically sound advice), and, if and when the time comes, attend her funeral. They also urged women to assist and encourage one another, taking heed of the hadith in which the Prophet said that believers support one another like the components of a building (Bukhari 2446).

You must put aside your differences and love your sister purely for the sake of Allah, the women were told, rather than for other reasons, such as a shared race, tribe, or nationality—or because, as Umm Hamza put it, 'she looks pretty and you look good beside her'. Rather, she said, you should love her because you 'see that person striving for her *din*' and long to be closer to her as a result.

In the event of a dispute between sisters, it is impermissible to go longer than three days without speaking to one another (Bukhari 5727; Muslim 2560). 'Fix that which lies between you and your brother *al-salafi*, or your sister *al-salafi*,' implored a guest speaker at the Al-Athariyyah circle. 'Each one of you should be an example of what this *da'wa* is about.'

An important aspect of love between sisters is that they do not turn a blind eye when the other falls into sin and ignorance. As Umm Hamza told her students: 'A sister who *truly* loves me is the one who corrects me and says: "Umm Hamza, you shouldn't have said that," because otherwise that's gonna be a sin for me on *yawm al-qiyama*.'* Conscious of Salafis' reputation for harsh manners, teachers stressed that *nasiha* should be given gently, tactfully, in private, and with reference to the Qur'an and/or sunna. In addition, if a sister is considering or engaging in something haram, one should suggest a halal replacement when advising her—for example, henna rather than permanent tattoos.

Umm Mustafe urged her students to be gentle ambassadors to all— including fellow Salafis:

How many people left the *din* of Allah because of the harshness of the people? One of the things people say about Salafi people is that they have bad manners, they think they're better than everyone. We should be an example for every-one—we've got to be kind like our Prophet. He wanted to save people from the fire. Some *sahabas*, like Omar Ibn Al-Khattab, took ten years to become Muslims. We are only ambassadors, we don't guide anyone—Allah does.*

A similar message was delivered powerfully by a newly practising Somali in her early twenties, who gave a talk on 'sisterhood' at a conference in Woolwich for about seventy mostly Somali women. She recalled being patronized by more longstanding sisters when she first started to practise, and warned the women that rudeness to others—particularly converts—can result in their leaving the religion and moving on to 'Sufism, Shi'ism or Judaism'.

Another aspect of sisterhood that was stressed was the prohibition of *ghiba*—that is, back-biting or telling someone something about another sister, without her knowledge, that she would not like to be passed on. Indeed, teachers regularly lamented the prevalence of back-biting in the community, likening it to eating 'the flesh of [your] dead brother' (Qur'an 49:12), and reminding the women that it is a major sin and thus carries a prescribed punishment in the hereafter.

Umm Hamza was disturbed by how new technology appeared to have worsened the problem, telling her students:

> The *sahabas* used to think for ten seconds before they responded . . . but nowa-days people just ping, ping, ping![15] 'Yeah, she gets on my nerves, innit.' Or just quick click on an email, slandering the scholars. . . . Ask them anything about Islam, they can't tell you, but ask them about 'Aisha's' business, how many times her husband left her . . .

Some teachers cited a hadith in which the Prophet said that those who guard their tongues and private parts are guaranteed Paradise (Bukhari 6807), and they warned the women that even listening to back-biting is sinful. In such circumstances, the young Somali speaker at the Woolwich conference advised that women should say something like: '*Subhanallah*, I don't wanna hear this,' and refuse to listen.

The circles also fostered an atmosphere that encouraged women to dis-play uniform etiquette, language, and dress, thus promoting a sense of a shared identity and reinforcing their distinction from others. The teach-ers sometimes emphasized this through the content of their lessons—for example, explaining what constitutes 'correct' and 'incorrect' hijab—but above all, by example. They always observed strict gender segregation themselves: Kareem would draw the curtain separating him from the women right to the end to seal off any gaps before starting his class; and the female teachers always wore loose-fitting, black *jilbabs* that dragged along the floor.

Teachers peppered their speech with Arabic expressions, such as *insha'Allah, al-hamdulillah, masha'Allah*, and *wallahi* (I swear to God), and used the Arabic for Islamic terms wherever possible, even when one English word would have sufficed (for example, *din* instead of 'religion'). They also meticulously observed Islamic etiquettes, such as those related to greetings. For example, Umm Hamza always said *al-salamu 'alaykum*, smiled, and shook hands with every woman in the room before starting her class, even if it took several minutes. She also frequently reminded the women that returning 'salams'—by saying *walaykum al-salam* ('and unto you peace')—was *wajib*. And she exemplified this by doing so even when mid-flow during a lesson, each time a woman walked into the room. Over my twenty-eight months of attending lessons, I observed how gradually—sometimes suddenly—newcomers would adopt the shared language, incorporate Salafi codes of behaviour, and disappear behind ever more enveloping swathes of dark fabric.

This homogenization of dress and conduct is most conspicuous at conferences, where the large numbers of attendees and intensity of the experience encourage an implicit competition in piety. Women who did not normally wear the full *jilbab* or *niqab* often did so at conferences, I noticed, and they made a particular effort to use Arabic expressions. As my field notes from the 2011 Al-Athariyyah conference recount:

> Many of the women clearly already knew each other, and the Somalis mainly sat with only fellow Somalis. Yet there was, in general, an atmosphere of getting to know new people—and the paper programme that was distributed did, after all, urge everyone to 'make each other welcome and establish the ties of brotherhood (and sisterhood) throughout the conference'. It seemed common to walk down the corridor to the hall and be '*salam*-ed' by every woman who walked past, whether they knew you or not, and even for some to stop for a second to ask: 'How are you?' I would always respond: 'I'm fine, thanks, how about you?' to which they always replied: '*Al-hamdulillah.*' Even in the bathroom, if a woman was passing as I entered, she would say: '*Al-salamu 'alaykum*, excuse me *ukhti.*' Because of this, it was difficult to get around quickly. Frequently, women would ask me and each other: 'What did you think of the talk?' 'Did you benefit?' '*Masha'Allah!*' (A positive answer would always invite this exclamation.) Most were all in black, including *niqabs* and often gloves, but I knew for a fact that some were not normally *niqab*-wearers—it was just for the conference.
>
> Nabila, a young Somali I knew from Brixton Mosque, was wearing a black *jilbab* for the occasion, complete with black *niqab* and gloves—exactly the same outfit as at least 70 percent of the women here—though I knew she normally favoured a navy blue or brown *jilbab*. At the end of the day, her phone died and she asked to borrow mine to call her husband. She spoke to him in a rather irritable tone. It seemed he was concerned about finding his wife once she made

her way outside to meet him by the main entrance to go home. 'Identify your-self somehow!' he pleaded. Nabila told me she was adamant that she would not compromise her modesty by drawing attention to herself and looking around to see which brother was which. I said she ought to have worn one of her coloured *jilbabs*. 'No way!' she said. 'Why not?' 'Everyone here is wearing black—I would be the odd one out!' '*I'm* wearing a green skirt,' I pointed out. 'Yeah, but you're different, innit!' We laughed, then set off with three other women, also wearing black *jilbabs* and *niqabs*. I saw a line of bearded men, all in white *thawbs*, waiting awkwardly outside the women's entrance for their wives and sisters. Fortunately, Nabila's husband managed to identify her (perhaps thanks to my green skirt).

[Later, I wrote:] I felt exhausted today by the palpable pressure to display piety in what seemed like a competitive way—for example, sprinkling one's sentences with as many *masha'Allah*s and *al-hamdulillah*s as possible. As the conference went on, it seemed that conversations and mannerisms were becoming more and more homogenized and predictable—'Did you benefit from the talks?' 'There's a really good class at Shepherd's Bush on Saturday, *masha'Allah*, you should come some time.' 'Did you buy any books?' There was no doubting, no silliness, few 'frivolous' conversations.

Newcomers also learned from observing their teachers and other long-time Salafis to behave discreetly in the presence of men and avoid interac-tion with them whenever possible. I often noticed how women made quite a performance of observing gender segregation in public—whether waiting outside a fried chicken shop for Muslim men to leave before entering, re-questing a screen in a Muslim-owned restaurant to shield themselves from view, or leaping out of sight whenever a man accidentally glimpsed a women-only area. Such performances helped promote intimacy among women, as they all experienced the awkwardness of such situations on a daily basis—something outsiders could not understand.

For instance, at a circle at the house of Fatima, an Algerian in her thirties, we were in the hall, preparing to leave, when our host's husband returned home from work earlier than expected. There was a sudden rush to the near-est room. Four of us crammed into the bathroom so that he could pass with-out catching a glimpse of us. As we looked at one another—four fully grown women shut up in a tiny room as though playing a game of Sardines—we had to fight hard to restrain the urge to laugh.

Salafi etiquette, language, and dress are identity markers that sharply distinguish women from non-Muslim society, as well as many other Muslims and Salafis' own *jahiliyya* pasts. Therefore when these markers are promoted and shared in circles of knowledge, they can foster a sense of belonging and greater commitment to Salafi norms. Once a Salafi woman learns and adopts these markers, she can deepen her identification with the community in other contexts, too. For example, when she spots a similarly dressed woman in the street, each will instantly recognize the other as her 'sister' and forge a (perhaps momentary) connection, symbolized by the uttering of the greeting of *salam*. In addition, once such habits are learned and adopted, it can be uncomfortable to discard them—and difficult to do so without this being remarked upon in the Salafi community. Thus, shared identity markers can also act as deterrents for those considering reducing their commitment by, for example, not always wearing the *niqab*.

In addition to dress, behaviour, and language, Salafi women share the experience of being a small minority within a society, and indeed world, of 'falsehood'. Teachers often reminded students of Salafis' status as members of an elite religious group, willing to make sacrifices and endure suffering and rejection from wider society, friends, and relatives for the sake of 'authentic' Islam. During Ramadan 2011, Kareem taught his students an entire book on the subject, *The Journey of the Strangers* by Ibn Rajab al-Hanbali and Abu Bakr al-Ajurri, which describes the plight of the Prophet and early Muslims. They

> were viewed as strangers in their individual localities and strangers amongst their tribe members. They would be forced to conceal their Islam and would be ostracised by their own families, they would be humiliated and belittled but would bear all they met with patience and constancy. (Al-Hanbali and Al-Ajurri, 2009, p.34)

Kareem said that today, the Muslims who are 'practising in the correct way' are 'still in the minority', but that they will be rewarded after death for their steadfastness.

This idea helped to cement a sense of belonging for women who faced daily frustrations and struggles as they tried to implement religious practices at odds with their friends, neighbours, and even their own families (see chapter 5.2). At one of Umm Mustafe's circles, for instance, a young woman of Ghanaian (Muslim) origin gave an emotional talk about her loneliness and struggles within a family that had rejected her Salafi practices. With tears rolling down her cheeks, she described how her mother would rip off her hijab, and spoke of the 'tests' women endured in a society at odds with their religion.

> We are all striving in a society that doesn't understand us. We are all strangers. We may have *kuffar* friends, but they will never be your true friends as they will never be happy until you become like them.*

As she talked, gradually raising her voice to the point of shouting, several women burst into silent tears, and the sense of solidarity and harmony in the room was palpable. When the young woman had finished, Umm Mustafe, her voice hoarse and croaky with emotion, added:

> Here, we are strangers, we don't belong. Every day, people tell you to get out of here. And then when we go back to our own countries, we are strangers, too. Why are we strangers to our own family, our own brothers, our own sisters? 'Cause we put the hjiab on and we want to worship Allah. . . . You walk down the street and people are calling you 'Bin Laden' or 'suicide bomber' and making fun of us, just because we believe in Allah, but the day [i.e., the Day of Judgment] will come.*

Rejection by fellow Muslims could be a particularly effective source of unity. Most Salafis were used to having their practices routinely questioned or even ridiculed by Muslim friends and relatives, and were aware of hostility toward their presence in non-Salafi Muslim spaces, such as mosques (which Salafi groups sometimes use due to the shortage of Salafi-owned premises).

One circle I attended took place in this type of space. Then one day I arrived, a little late, to find the students gathered around the teacher with stunned looks on their faces. It transpired that the non-Salafi Muslim authorities had just announced that the classes were being discontinued until further notice, and had demanded details of what was being taught and by whom. The atmosphere was emotional, and the young women were comforting one another, some in tears. One of the elder women who helped to organize the circle embraced me in a hug and said, defiantly, 'We will overcome it; *shaytan* is everywhere, even [here].'

Then the teacher beckoned the women to sit on the floor. She told them that it might be better to abandon the premises for good in the face of such *hizbiyya* (partisanship) and relocate elsewhere. 'Yes! Allah is our provider!' came the seemingly unanimous response, reflecting a unity of purpose in persevering with their *da'wa* despite these setbacks.

4.6 CONCLUSION

Recalling Kanter's (1972, p.69) typology of commitment, it is clear that the Salafi teachers employed circles of knowledge to further all three forms of commitment: instrumental, affective, and moral.

By constantly signalling their participation in a chain of 'authentic' knowledge transmission, stemming from the Qur'an and sunna, teachers could convince their students that the rulings they taught were *morally* binding. They did so above all by limiting their lessons to references to the Qur'an, sunna, and 'authentic' mediators as far as possible—though there were many

other factors at play that allowed teachers, particularly female ones, to acquire authority.

While hierarchical and restrictive in nature, this approach to religious
learning is also empowering to the ordinary literate worshipper. It reflects
a world where—partly due to mass education and mass communication—it
is no longer the exclusive privilege of the scholarly elite to access and interrogate the meaning and authenticity of religious teachings. Certainly, ordinary Salafis' hermeneutic freedom is severely limited, and the scholar's word
on a particular issue has great weight. However, a Salafi can always dismiss
one scholar's view in favour of another on the basis of textual evidence. And
she can 'authenticate' what her teacher or a scholar says with a quick Google
to track down Qur'anic verses, alternative scholarly opinions, and even less
well-known hadiths.[16]

As indicated by the narratives of the previous chapter, the simplicity of
this 'authentication' system—in which, in the Salafi view, only the word of
the 'original' texts counts—is key to understanding Salafism's appeal among
young Western Muslims who, detached from Islamic historical and cultural
contexts, may lack the tools to engage critically with centuries of debate and
tradition.

Having established the authority required to secure *moral* commitment, teachers could elicit *instrumental* commitment by introducing the
ahkam framework for action. This was supported by a discourse of quantifiable reward and punishment that was enhanced by vivid descriptions of
the afterlife. In this way, teachers attached eternal consequences to every
(non-*mubah*) action imaginable, demonstrating that conformity with Salafi
teachings in all spheres of life was a matter of self-interest.

The doctrine of *tawhid* and its violations were particularly stressed to illuminate the heavy consequences of even seemingly trivial acts and omissions.
Crucially, teachers tried to deter students from straying by characterizing
attendance at Salafi circles itself as rewardable, while undermining the credibility of other groups and their lessons.

Circles of knowledge could also advance a deeper sense of belonging
and support structures among women, furthering *affective* commitment.
Teachers reinforced boundaries between Salafis and non-Salafis and
strengthened intragroup bonds by encouraging women to consider themselves as 'strangers' to the rest of society and 'sisters' to one another. To
this end, they also promoted uniform and distinctive etiquette, language,
and attire.

Nonetheless, the teachers recognized that even the most committed
Salafis would struggle at times to implement the teachings in a liberal,
non-Muslim society. Thus they employed theodicies to bestow meaning

upon even the most incomprehensible suffering and to enable students to interpret their own difficulties as opportunities to improve their situation after death.

Despite these systematic commitment strategies, however, the processes had mixed results; this is the focus of the next chapter.

CHAPTER 5

༄

Applying Salafism

Negotiating Teachings and Lived Realities

The previous chapter showed how Salafi teachers employed circles of knowledge to promote commitment by encouraging women to understand all of their decisions as cost-benefit calculations based on a classificatory system of rules (*ahkam*). The circles also fostered a shared identity and sense of belonging by means of a warm and supportive discourse of 'sisterhood'.

Once a Salafi woman has internalized this framework, she will start to scrutinize her lifestyle critically for areas that fail to live up to Salafi ideals and then adopt new practices and prohibitions. In so doing, she may decide to detach herself gradually from her former lifestyle, thus increasing her investment in her decision to become Salafi and deepening her commitment.[1] As Kanter (1972, p.76) points out:

> Sacrifice operates on the basis of a simple principle from cognitive consistency theories: the more it 'costs' a person to do something, the more 'valuable' he will consider it, in order to justify the psychic 'expense' and remain internally consistent.

For a Salafi woman, an obvious place to start is her sartorial habits, since regularly being in the company of fully veiled women will serve as a constant reminder that she has yet to adopt the *jilbab*. Galvanized by teachers and others into taking her place in a loving 'sisterhood' of God-fearing 'seekers of knowledge', she will probably try to become more involved with the community and to take her Islamic studies seriously. Mindful of Salafi prohibitions on free-mixing, she may start to distance herself from (non-*mahram*) men socially, at work, at university, and even in her family. And she may even reconsider her educational or career ambitions.

Yet beyond the controlled environment of the study circle, she will often find that the dynamic and challenging realities of everyday life present a far more complex picture than the neat, systematic rulings seem to anticipate. This chapter investigates several areas in the lives of young Salafi women in London—community, household, higher education, and employment— where clashes between Salafi ideals and social realities frequently occurred. It illustrates how teachers attempted to resolve common dilemmas, and how women responded with compromises and creative solutions.

5.1 IN SEARCH OF SISTERHOOD: DWINDLING PARTICIPATION AND ESTRANGEMENT

I feel that there's a lack of knowledge amongst all of us as sisters, there's a lack of commitment to Islam.... It all stems down to knowledge: people being in-genuine with regards to their behaviour, their sisterhood. (Umm Hamza to her students)

The amount of people coming to *Salafiyya* [Salafism] may be greater I think than before, but ... the commitment to learning [in the early days] was very high. Today, not that as before. (Kareem)

As shown in chapter 4, circles of knowledge were important to ensure not only the internalization of the Salafi framework for action but also the strong ties between Salafis that were necessary to deepen attachment to, and participation in, the community. Yet despite teachers' encouragement, atten-dance at most circles was poor and inconsistent. Umm Hamza's circle was the most popular among the young women at Brixton, yet it only attracted around twenty women per week, and attendance was patchy. And rarely did Kareem's circles attract more than a few women under thirty.

With all circles, there was usually a surge in numbers right after Ramadan, when women were particularly conscious of their religion and eager to rec-tify spiritual shortcomings. But this would gradually reduce over the follow-ing months. *Jum'a* at Brixton, on the other hand, usually attracted a signifi-cant crowd. However, this seemed partly related to the social function of the event—it was a weekly opportunity to catch up and possibly go for lunch— as remarkably few young women would linger for the circle that took place there later in the afternoon.

Umm Hamza's circles had been set up in 2008 with the express aim of reaching the younger Salafi generation (aged about twenty-nine and under), many of whom could not follow the more complicated texts taught by Kareem. She said these new circles used to attract 'at least thirty-five [young] sisters every week—you couldn't stretch your leg out'. However, around mid-2010, 'one by one, they fade away—I don't know [why]'. Indeed, only twelve of the twenty-three women in my sample regularly attended at least one circle of knowledge, though all recognized the importance of regular knowledge-seeking.

In addition, noise levels on the women's side at conferences were often distractingly high—much more so than on the men's side, I heard. On some occasions, the volume was such that the chatting could be heard from the men's section and the speaker would scold the women for talking. 'Sisters, what can I say?' said one conference speaker, reminding me of school. 'Whether it be Birmingham, Leeds, London, Toronto, it's always the sisters chattering to their neighbour, or even worse sometimes the person three places down.' I asked the speaker to elaborate on his concerns about the women's behaviour at conferences:

> Patience in seeking knowledge requires that you basically turn your phone off, put everything to one side, send your children to a babysitter that day, send them to your mother for those two hours that you're at the lecture, sit in the lecture, open up your notebook and write notes. That *very* rarely occurs now. I mean, I do lectures in London and I'm getting messages—in a lecture I'll get two, three messages saying, 'Please can you tell the sisters to be quiet'—so where's the patience in seeking knowledge?

At Brixton, women (particularly young teenagers) often talked over the Friday *khutba* (sermon) and especially the Eid sermon, sometimes making it difficult to catch any of it, despite occasionally being sharply reminded by other women of the hadiths that prohibit speaking during the *khutba* (Bukhari 934; Al-Nasa'i 1577; Ibn Majah 1:5:1111). My research revealed a variety of factors that combined to discourage women from attending or engaging fully with the lessons.

Many of those who could not attend regularly cited other commitments, particularly work and family, as the main reason. Two of the women in my sample had to devote a lot of time to looking after relatives in poor health, and others had working patterns that made travelling to circles of knowledge a struggle, even on weekends. One cohort, married women with children, had a noticeably low turnout at circles, for obvious reasons. Although many such women did go out to seek knowledge, their attendance was often erratic or restricted to one-off events like conferences, which had less quiet areas to which one could bring restless children.

This raises the issue of the compatibility of Salafi teachings on women's roles as wives and mothers with teachers' insistence that women should go out to religious classes regularly—an apparent paradox that has preoccupied other researchers of female piety in conservative religious groups (El-Or,

1994; Limbert, 2010). Although women and men are equally obligated to learn about their religion, this requirement can clash with other obligatory duties particular to women, which, in practice, take precedence; namely, those of looking after the house, child-rearing, and obeying one's husband.

To illustrate, at the 2010 Tottenham Da'wah conference, a woman passed a slip of paper to the men's side of the hall with the following question for the (male) speaker: 'If a Salafi husband says to a Salafi wife that she can't go to a lecture, can she go?' The response ran thus: If the husband forbids his wife from attending the mosque itself, or is a 'person of innovation' (that is, a non-Salafi Muslim), she may disobey him. However, as he is Salafi, he may have a good reason for preventing her from seeking knowledge—namely, that she has not fulfilled her duties in the home and towards their children. If the wife *has* fulfilled these duties, then her husband should not prevent her from seeking knowledge from a Salafi source (though it was not clear whether she should disobey him in this instance).

To clarify the hierarchy of duties further, I asked Umm Hamza how a woman ought to juggle her knowledge-seeking obligations with her wifely and motherly ones. She said that 'looking after the children and the husband's home would be the priority', with the proviso that, if she can't attend lessons, her husband ought to give her books and tapes in order to study from home.

Thus it seemed that wifely duties took priority over knowledge-seeking, as well as over attending *jum'a* (Friday midday congregational prayers), which is compulsory only for men. Umm Hamza told her class: 'You've got to *prioritize* that which is *wajib* [obligatory].' Plenty of women come to prayers every Friday, she said, 'but have they cooked their husband's dinner? Which is more *wajib* on you?' The answer, she said, is being an obedient wife. Despite this, she encouraged women with babies and small children to attend her class, and indeed most teachers were very patient with noisy children.

Other aspects of Salafi teaching made attendance and effective learning in circles of knowledge difficult for women. Women were taught not to stay out until late without *maharim* (male guardians)—preferably no later than sunset—though few seemed to adhere to this strictly. Yet some circles finished late, such as that of Abu Ahmed, which finished at 9.30 p.m., and conferences normally finished between 7 and 10 p.m. in the evening. This posed problems for some unmarried women or those whose *maharim* could or would not escort them. In addition, many women worked or attended university so they were unable to attend circles during the day.

Even if they were willing to ignore Salafi teachings and attend late circles anyway, the possibility of inviting remarks from others may have deterred them. When I told a group of young women at Brixton of my intention to go unaccompanied to a circle finishing late in another part of London, they looked at me disapprovingly. One declared: 'Oh, I can't be doing those late circles. Not until I'm married and I can go places by car!'

Many, I learned, had self-imposed curfews, partly due to fear of Islamophobic attacks on the street. Women were also limited by the distance they were permitted to travel, even for the purpose of knowledge-seeking, without being accompanied by a *mahram*. Although most of the women I asked were hazy about the precise number of miles that would be deemed excessive, they usually drew the line at within the London area. Thus those without *maharim* to escort them, such as unmarried converts, barred themselves from conferences held outside of London.

There was also the fact that conferences and circles run by male teachers required the women to engage with someone they could not see, often while tending to boisterous children, which could diminish the learning experience. Inevitably, male speakers were less engaged with their female audiences—who were usually in a separate room or on the other side of a high screen—than with their male ones, who were directly in front of them.

In the question-and-answer sessions at conferences, women were not permitted to ask questions out loud; instead, they had to write down their queries on slips of paper that were then passed through to the men's section. At two conferences I attended, the men forgot to fetch the slips of paper from the women to pass on to the speaker and their questions were not aired at all. In addition, as there was no roving microphone, rarely could questions on the men's side be heard by the women, who were left guessing what the question had been from the answers.

These disadvantages partly explained the tendency of many women to chat at conferences, occasionally drowning out the speaker. Yet it was also evident that, for all Salafi teachers' talk of the value of knowledge-seeking, many women treated circles as social events. Salafi women do gather regularly to socialize, both at home and less often for special events such as *wala'im* (marriage banquets) and charity fundraisers, but circles of knowledge provided a more frequent and dependable opportunity to meet and make friends. The ensuing noise greatly irritated the more diligent students, as well as the teachers. After one particularly rowdy spring conference, Wafa declared to me that this would be her last one.

Easy access to information through the Internet also seemed to have affected attendance, since it is often no longer seen as necessary to be physically present in circles of knowledge, despite teachers' encouragements. In our interview, Umm Hamza explained how this had contributed to the gradual dwindling of attendance at all community events since the early 1990s:

It's made people [think]: 'If I don't wanna come to class, I'll just listen on the Internet.' All these kinda things, it removes people away from the togetherness, you know, lots of things that we used to do together. It's now—like e.g., when the shaykh [Fahad al-Fuhayd, Imam Mohammed Bin Saud Islamic University, Saudi Arabia] was here [at Brixton] last week [giving a lecture], I stayed at home and listened on the Internet 'cause I was busy, while back then I'd never have done that, regardless of what was—I would've come 'cause otherwise I missed it. So I just could click on Paltalk, turned it on, and there it was. So it makes people more fragmented, you know. The scholars, they have talks on the Internet a lot these days; while before, you only heard scholars when they came. So if there was a scholar coming, you couldn't even—the buses couldn't even get along the road, the amount of cars. It was—I could not even tell you how full.

Several of the women in my sample said they used the Internet, usually reading articles on websites or downloading audio lectures, to try to compensate for their absence in circles of knowledge. Popular websites included abdurrahman.org, salafipublications.com, fatwa-online.com, salafimanhaj. com, islamqa.info, and madeenah.com. All such sites provide short, digestible articles by respected scholars and preachers addressing topics that affect Salafis' everyday lives—from free-mixing to finance—supported by references to Islamic texts. Some also provide free or cheap downloadable audio lectures and recordings of past conferences. Hadiths and Qur'anic verses can also be accessed at the touch of a button and in English, and many of the great Salafi texts by prominent authors such as Ibn 'Abd al-Wahhab can be ordered cheaply in the English translations.

In addition, Paltalk, an instant messaging service, allowed Salafi organizations to broadcast conferences live to up to two hundred people at no charge, thus reaching those unable to attend. This was a convenient option for women who were constrained by family responsibilities and travel restrictions. For example, Filsan, a wife, mother, part-time student, and part-time employee, said she struggled to juggle all of her responsibilities, so she tried to listen to lessons over Paltalk and visit websites regularly from home.

In facilitating access to what were previously relatively inaccessible texts and circles of knowledge, the Internet may also have reduced their *value* to adherents. Access to them is no longer a privilege, reserved for those prepared to travel and sacrifice other commitments—or indeed to learn Arabic. As recently as the 1990s, when the first generation of British Salafis was emerging, Salafi circles of knowledge and English translations of texts were scarce. Yet today they are not only plentiful, but also accessible in bite-sized form on the Internet—without the need to leave home. Umm Hamza described these changes and their impact on commitment levels one afternoon at Brixton Mosque to Zaina, a twenty-year-old convert, and myself:

UMM HAMZA (UH):   When we came to Islam [in 1990–1991], there were hardly any books—there was Bukhari and Muslim [i.e., hadith collections] and Qur'ans with 'thou art' etc. that were impossible to understand, but the knowledge and the sisterhood was *high* [gestures with her hand].

ZAINA (Z) [surprised]:   There were no books on *tawhid* or explanations or nothing?

UH: No, there was just one book on *tawhid* by Bilal Philips. I remember when Albani's book on the prayer came out . . . I was running to get it. A brother was selling them out of the boot of his car, and by the time I arrived there, there were none left and I had to run and look in every single Islamic bookshop I could find, and eventually I found it.*

The depreciating value of the texts and learning experience can, in turn, reduce motivation to put in the concentration and effort required to become a dedicated student of knowledge. Indeed, several women admitted to me that it was merely laziness, rather than a busy schedule, that stopped them from attending regularly.

But there was another factor that helped to explain the lack of participation of young women in community life. As my fieldwork progressed, I began to realize that a significant number of women felt estranged from the Salafi community as a whole or in parts. As chapter 3.3 described, some had entered the community with an idealized vision of a unified and supportive 'sisterhood', and were disappointed to find this vision hampered by the presence of cliques. Some had learned to lower their expectations in this regard, and limited their community involvement to occasional circles that they found beneficial, without lingering to socialize afterwards. Others persevered and managed to form strong friendships.

Few women made direct comments on this issue, but what they did say was very suggestive (see chapter 3.3 for more details). It was also striking that, although most of the women in my sample made some positive comments about the Salafi sisterhood, the only ones to do so unreservedly were three women who had been part of the community for only a few months.

One woman who was very open on the subject was Manal, who no longer attended any circles because she felt alienated by the converts at Brixton, whom she found judgmental of those who wore make-up or whose attire fell short of Salafi standards. Manal, a pretty, unmarried Eritrean in her twenties who wore a black abaya and hijab with make-up, was particularly upset by one incident at the mosque: she had said '*al-salamu 'alaykum*' to a convert who was younger than her and wearing a *niqab*, to which the latter replied '*wa 'alaykum*', without completing the greeting ('. . . *al-salam*'). This Manal took to be a grave insult, as the abbreviated form of the reply is the response some Salafis give to non-Muslims who give the Islamic greeting. She elaborated on her concerns about the sisterhood:

The attitude and the behaviour of people, like, 'Who are you, you don't belong here?' And I'm like, hold on, I've been Muslim all my life, I've been here before you even knew what Islam was and yet I'm seen as the stranger in the masjid [mosque]. In my mind, it's because when I started to try to practise, I had this idea of . . . sisterhood in my mind, and maybe it was a dream, but I had this hope that it would be a beautiful sisterhood. And there were people that were nice at times and stuff like that, but . . . they're so quick to judge you on your appearance and think you're, you know, you're a certain type of person 'cause you look a certain way, or because you might have make-up on your face, or because—I'm not here to get your husband! [Laughs] . . . I was trying to establish Islam in my life as a full-time thing, I wanted sisterhood so bad and didn't get it. . . . They didn't like us [me, my sister, and my Eritrean friend] for some reason . . . and we didn't do anything to them. . . . They [the converts] were really rude. . . . It's [the sisterhood] very cliquey, and if you're not in, you're not in, and if you don't look a certain way . . . if you're not covered in a certain way, you're not in.

Differences between 'culturally' Muslim communities, among whom Somalis were the largest group, and the (largely Afro-Caribbean) converts were occasionally evident. At Brixton Mosque, elder Somalis preferred to sit in the downstairs room, while black converts and younger Salafis of all ethnicities sat upstairs. However, this arrangement was as much based on linguistic, generational, and religious differences as it was on cultural ones. Many of the elder-generation Somalis did not speak English, so had their own programme of activities downstairs in Somali. Meanwhile, the younger-generation, English-speaking Somalis—many of whom were not fluent in Somali—would normally join the Salafis upstairs, whose religious practices they deemed to be less 'cultural' and more in line with 'pure' Islam.

Yet I could not help but notice how even the young Somalis and Eritreans, for example, often sat only with those with a shared ethnic background. Moreover, cultural differences occasionally became apparent in uncomfortable exchanges. One such occasion was after a Ramadan *iftar* (breaking of the fast at sunset) at Brixton, at which there was an unusual and generally friendly intermingling of 'upstairs' and 'downstairs': young black converts and Somalis of all ages gathered around platters of home-cooked chicken, rice, salad, and cakes laid out on the floor. But a middle-aged Somali turned to me, looking rather affronted, after an exchange with a convert. She said she could not understand the bad manners of some of the British-born women in the mosque. 'When you don't like the food, don't say so because it's bad manners—just say *jazak Allah khayr* [i.e., may God reward you], I'm full.'

On the converts' side, and in line with Manal's account above, I occasionally suspected a degree of impatience with displays of religious laxity, such as colourful or patterned adornments, though this could equally be directed at fellow converts who fell short. On one occasion, a convert reprimanded a group of Somali teenagers who had disturbed Kareem's class thus:

No disrespect, but you guys were talking when Kareem was giving us a lesson. Do you talk when your *mu'alim* [teacher] is giving a lesson? No! So why do you talk when Kareem is giving a lesson? You do it every week yet when your *mu'alim* is talking, you guys are silent. You should respect *everyone*, not just people from your culture.*

Some Somali Salafis admitted to me, admiringly, that the converts were generally more 'firm' in their religious practice than those from Muslim backgrounds, having so dramatically turned their backs on their *jahiliyya* pasts.

There were also clues in the frequent reminders during Friday *khutab* at Brixton to love your fellow Muslim brother or sister for the sake of Allah, regardless of his or her nationality, tribe, or race, and that 'back-biting' and 'slandering' one another was prohibited. In one *khutba*, the speaker revealed that people had come to him to say that they did not feel welcome at the mosque because people were in cliques, so he urged the congregation to unite and always to *salam* one another. Everyone should remember, he said, that one of the 'minor signs' of the end of the world is that Muslims stop giving *salam*s to those they do not know.

Of course, the tendency to clump together with fellow ethnics is extremely common in wider society, and by no means necessarily indicative of any racist sentiment. Yet such a pattern is thrown into sharp relief in Salafi spaces, which are more ethnically diverse than many of the established traditional Muslim communities. Moreover, it suggests that regardless of the universalist thrust of Salafi teachings, which promote a 'pure' Islam that overrides cultural attachments, these still determine social relationships to some extent.

Another line of division that had been causing growing concern was a generational one. Some of the older Salafi women at Brixton, mostly converts in their thirties and forties who had become Salafis in the 1990s to early 2000s, had increasingly felt disrespected by some of the younger women, many of whom had entered the community during the 'fashion' of the early to mid-2000s that saw numerous young people turning to Islam, often in groups (see chapter 3.2). Some of the newer Salafis had struggled to adhere to the teachings on make-up, the correct hijab, and gender segregation. The 'immodest' appearance and behaviour of some had, according to the older women, tarnished the previously honourable reputation of Salafi women at Brixton and encouraged some of the 'brothers' to disrespect even the more 'practising' sisters by talking to them in the street—something they apparently never used to do.

Some of the community elders had tried to 'correct' the younger Salafis, but their words were not always well received. Some of the younger women, particularly those who were new to Salafism, found some of the long-time Salafis to be judgmental and aggressive when giving them *nasiha* (sincere,

Islamically sound advice). One told me that some older women would criti-
cize the younger women for embracing different scholarly opinions on issues
such as halal food. For example, while many younger women were fond of
eating at McDonald's—which they considered to be food from the 'people of
the book' (i.e., Christians and Jews) and therefore permissible—some older
women took issue with this view, though it is held by some Salafi scholars.
'But there are so many halal chicken shops!' the older women would retort.

On the other hand, some of the younger women undoubtedly overreacted.
Umm Reemah was an old-timer convert with a warm and friendly disposi-
tion, yet she took seriously her duty to enjoin good and forbid evil. She said
that when she advised some of the younger converts to stop talking to their
boyfriends because 'they'll pull you back', either the women refused to listen
or they stopped talking to *her* instead.

She later found out that they were making negative comments behind
her back, such as, 'That sister's always going on, she gets on my nerves, she's
always telling me what I can't do.' Worse still, one threatened her with violence and another tried to push her down the stairs of the mosque. She suspected that some of the younger women, who were often absent from circles
of knowledge, were lazy and disliked being told what to do by those who had
studied for much longer.

Umm Hamza, meanwhile, followed up brief reminders about these issues
in her classes by helping to organize women-only conferences at which she
spoke about *zina* and the related topics of correct hijab and modest behaviour,
with contributions from Umm Mustafe. Among the criticisms she spelled
out were 'getting the waist taken in' on abayas or 'putting a belt round it',
and wearing make-up, false eyelashes, and nail varnish. Anticipating hostile
reactions, perhaps, she followed up her remarks by saying that 'this is not
from us up here; this is from the 'ulama [i.e., scholars]. . . . I'm not saying this
to offend, but because on *yawm al-qiyama* [the Day of Judgment], we're gonna
be asked these things.'*

She and Umm Mustafe claimed that the worst sartorial offences were
committed at *wala'im*, women-only marriage celebrations, where women
felt free to dress as skimpily as they liked. But in fact, they told the young
women, there were strict rules even for how to dress in front of women, and
ignoring them had actually encouraged 'lesbianism' in the community:

UMM HAMZA (UH):   On many occasions, I see sisters dressing in miniskirts
  high up on their thighs so that they come just under their bum, and they
  think it's OK because 'I'm wearing tights'. I've been seeing this over the last
  three, four years. That's for your husband *only*. . . . And you don't wanna
  be like 'haram, haram!' [forbidden] etc. at someone's *walima* [i.e., marriage
  banquet]. D'you remember [to Umm Mustafe] one Eid we did that and we
  got slated by everybody, so . . . [they smile at each other].

UMM MUSTAFE (UM):   We as Somalis have a culture we have inherited
for hundreds of years. Why is it Somali girls [who are doing this]? See-
through stuff and miniskirts. Where has that [culture] gone? What about
the parents? What are they doing [allowing this]?

UH: I think it comes from the *kuffar* [non-Muslims]. . . . And one thing I've
heard has happened in the community is lesbianism. Don't think it can't
happen in front of you because when we show parts of our bodies in front
of each other, if someone has a disease in her heart, it leads to lesbianism.
Skin-tight clothes [in front of women] is not OK.

UM: [Recounts a story she found on the website of a Salafi scholar] A Salafi
sister gave *da'wa* to a sister and she became Salafi. She became friendly
with her, talking on the phone for hours and hours, then touching occurred and then kissing on the lips. So let us not think, we're Salafis,
we don't commit *zina* . . . we're Salafis, *we* don't have lesbians . . . 'cause
you know we have this mentality—we Salafis, we don't commit haram.*
(Brixton Sisters' Seminar, 2011)

Many of the teachers' comments in circles reflected concerns about a general culture of back-biting and bad manners that was causing division and
discord within the sisterhood. This even appeared to be discouraging women
from becoming Salafi in the first place, as seen in chapter 3. As Umm Hamza
told her students at Brixton:

> If one sister, Khudija, has a problem with 'Aisha, Khudija will go and talk to
> all of her friends and say, 'I don't like her, she gives me bad looks,' and then
> they're all looking at her with dirty looks. *Wallahi*, this never used to happen
> in the past. It becomes like thirty or forty sisters don't talk to each other in the
> mosque for no reason. And it's *so* common. *Shaytan* is behind it. It's a big *fitna*;
> you find so many factions in the mosque of today—that group doesn't give
> *salams* to that one—and this is not Islamic.*

Such was her concern that Umm Hamza took a break in the middle of
explaining a book about *tawhid* to devote five circles to the topic of *ghiba*
and *namima* (slander). She explained the rulings on the matter, including the associated rewards and punishments, permissible exceptions to
back-biting, and procedures for repentance—citing evidence from the
Qur'an, sunna, *salaf*, and scholars. 'Everything we utter is recorded and
it can be in our favour or it can go against us,' she wrote on the board.
These circles were particularly well attended, with more questions than
usual—questions, moreover, that seemed to be related to real situations,
such as 'If someone slanders you, should you try to clear your name?' and
'If you're in conflict with a sister and you want advice, can you mention
negative things?'

In fact, numerous speakers, including all four of my regular teachers, spoke at various points about the 'evil' of back-biting. One called it a 'disease' that had 'crept into this masjid' and 'comes into most gatherings now' (khutba, Brixton); another said it was an 'illness' in the community (lecture, Tottenham Da'wah, 2011); one young speaker said it was something she was 'very worried about, something that hardens our hearts'* (Woolwich conference with Sisters of Tawheed, 2011); Kareem said it 'added a foul smell' but is nowadays so common that we do not smell it, for 'it occurs even in the masajid [i.e., mosques]' (circle, Brixton); and Umm Mustafe said that 'lots of people are telling tales', and warned her students gravely that 'nothing will send women to the Hellfire more than men except this [points to her mouth]'* (circle, Sisters of Tawheed).

Despite these concerns, a supportive, united sisterhood was manifest at times (see chapter 4.5), even among women who were not acquainted with one another and who appeared to have nothing in common other than Salafism. Numbers were swapped with ease; cars shared after conferences finishing late; useful religious reminders circulated via social media, such as BlackBerry Messenger. Women of all races, ages, and cultural backgrounds intermingled, particularly on special occasions, such as community iftar, Eid parties, charity dinners, conferences, and wala'im, which (with the exception of conferences) were designed for the purposes of socializing and having fun.

Newer Salafis, above all, said that they were extremely grateful for the support, guidance, and friendliness of longstanding sisters, though I was left wondering if this would fade over time. Personally, I was touched by many acts of generosity, such as being given books and invited for meals at people's homes. Sometimes these gestures were from women who were barely acquainted with me or my research. For example, during the England Riots in August 2011, Wafa and I found ourselves near a riot flashpoint after a Salafi-hosted tarawih (night prayers conducted during Ramadan), and a woman we had just met insisted we take her money for a taxi home.

5.2 HOUSEHOLD CHALLENGES

As mentioned in chapter 3, the parents of the women I interviewed were generally much more relaxed in their practice of Islam than their Salafi daughters, if indeed they were Muslim or religious at all. The Muslim parents belonged to a generation that mostly considered Islam primarily as a determinant of ethnic or cultural identity. Thus both parents and daughters tended to regard the latter's Salafi transformation as a departure, even rebellion, from familial values and practices, and as signifying a rejection of parental authority in favour of another.

The converts' parents had a variety of religious perspectives: agnostics (Firdaws); nominal Christians (Hayah); Anglican mother and 'laid-back' Muslim stepfather (Humayrah); non-practising Catholics (Iman); and Pentecostal mother (who died when she was young) and non-practising Muslim father (Wafa).

The remaining eighteen women had Muslim parents, and most (fourteen) said that their parents would categorize themselves further as 'Sunni', with only three further distinguishing themselves—by *madhhab* (two Hanafis, one Shafi'i). Bilan, a Somali, was the only one whose parents had embraced a Salafi approach. Most of the women characterized their parents as 'practising'—ten said both were practising, four said one was (including Abeer, who did not know about her father's religious practice)—by which they tended to mean an adherence to the five pillars of Islam, such as fasting in Ramadan and praying.

Interestingly, a few of the Somalis said that the family's migration to Britain was followed by an increase in their parents' Islamic consciousness. Some mothers, for instance, had started to take hijab-wearing more seriously upon settling in London. This supports the findings of McGown (1999), Hopkins (2010), and Tiilikainen (2013), who observed that many Somali refugees had become more committed to their religion upon migration to London, Toronto, and Helsinki, for various reasons. Having lost so much that was familiar and dear to them—friends, relatives, homes, money, and status—the migrants often clung to their religion as a source of meaning and stability as they sought to re-establish themselves in a new, challenging environment. As McGown says (1999, p.98):

> What was valuable about it [Islam] was the very ritual of stepping outside the daily struggle, five times over the course of the day, to concentrate on the prayers that never alter, in rhythmic language that linked them to a community of believers that was theirs no matter where in the world they were.

Moreover, in the new multifaith society, it was no longer possible to take Islam for granted; effort was required to preserve Islamic practices and to ensure that they were passed down to children, who could otherwise be 'lost' to 'alien' cultures.

Yet both the Somali and other Muslim parents took core Islamic teachings—such as prayer and modest dress—much more lightly than their daughters, though most of the mothers did wear some form of hijab. For example, Deqa said that her parents saw the religion as a 'way of life', but did not 'submit to Islam fully' because they prayed and covered merely out of habit; they did not, for instance, care about praying on time.

Parents also retained practices from their countries of origin that, according to their daughters, had no basis in Islam. These included free-mixing within extended families, visiting soothsayers, and seeking the intercession of deceased holy Muslims. Many of the women said that their parents were not aware of any sectarian differences beyond the Sunni-Shia divide, let alone Salafism.

All four married women had husbands who were Salafis (or open to Salafism but not yet practising it, in one case). A few of the Somalis had shared houses with unsympathetic cousins at some point. All of the women had siblings—some had many, particularly the Somalis—and fifteen out of the twenty-one with Muslim siblings said that none of them practised Salafism, though Amina said that one of her sisters believed that it was the correct approach.[2] Most had at least one sibling who practised Islam to some degree, and three had siblings who had adopted rival approaches to Salafism—Madeeha's sisters were staunch Hanafis, and Fowsiya and Bilan each had a brother with a more politicized Islamic outlook who took issue with Salafis' apparent passivity in the face of Muslim suffering worldwide.

A common reaction from Muslim parents when their daughters started to practise Islam was joy and pride. Yet this often gave way to reservations and even outright opposition once they realized the full extent of strict Salafi practices. For example, Warda said that her parents

> were happy and everything at first, isn't it. But when they saw me really prac-tising, it wasn't as easy as it used to be. I would do things like the *jilbab* and everything, and they were like: 'Oh yeah!' They knew it was a good thing. They knew the salat [compulsory prayers conducted five times a day], praying salat, you have to do it, you know. But as in certain things like the way I would pray, for example . . . because usually you find people they would pray salat the way their parents taught them, not the way the Prophet did it.

While a few (Amina, Abyan, Sagal, Bilan, and Filsan) had parents who were open-minded or even sympathetic to Salafism, others found them-selves being labelled as 'extremists' or 'brainwashed'.[3] Safia's family doubted her sincerity, suspecting her of adopting Salafism only 'for fashion', at a time when Brixton Mosque had overseen many conversions to Islam.

When Nadia embraced Salafism, the aunt and cousins with whom she lived thought she 'might be crazy', and an older cousin physically attacked her:

> I remember a cousin of mine came over . . . and she was all like, 'There's a place you should go and they will teach you about the four *madhhabs* [i.e., schools of Islamic law]'. . . . And I was like, 'I know a bit of them, why do I need to go?'—'No, no you should go there.' I'm like, 'No, what's your agenda, you have a motive, what is it?' She's like, 'Listen, what you're saying is ridiculous, you know it's annoying, it's wrong, so you need to be educated.' . . . So I just let her talk. Instead of talking, she got violent, and I was like, OK—I left her to it.

Five areas of disagreement between the women and their families repeatedly came up in interviews. These were the issues of free-mixing with extended family members, dress, prayer habits, where one can seek 'authentic' religious knowledge, and which special occasions (for example, birthdays and weddings) should be marked and in what manner. I focus on the first two, as they arose on a regular, in some cases daily, basis in the women's lives.

Many Somali and Eritrean Salafis struggled with their families' laid-back approach to free-mixing with extended family members. Since childhood, the women had been encouraged by their families to socialize with male cousins regularly and to see them as 'brothers' and close friends, but now the women deemed these relationships un-Islamic.

Suddenly starting to cover in front of those whom they had always regarded as 'brothers' or 'uncles' could be very awkward and provoke family arguments. Once, when Shukri darted into the next room after catching sight of her cousins entering the house, her aunt exclaimed: 'Oh my God! You're hiding from your brothers—I can't believe this! This is crazy, this is crazy, you know!'

The issue was obviously heightened in households shared with extended family members—not uncommon among Somalis. Some young Somalis, such as Nadia and Deqa, had fled the civil war alone or with just one parent and joined relatives already living in Britain. Deqa described the tension that could occur:

> In every Somali culture, it is an issue: stepdad, uncle, dad, *everyone* in the house, like ten people in one house, and when you walk without hijab, you go around, you do this, you jump up and down—and suddenly my cousin's like [coming in]. . . . I'm like, 'He's a man, he can marry me, you know, don't look!' . . . And I put on my scarf. . . . He used to come to our room and we all sat on the bed, we'd talk, and I'm like, 'What are you doing, get out!' And he's like, 'What's wrong with you?' . . . My auntie was like, 'What's wrong with you?' And I'm like, 'Auntie, it's haram 'cause cousins can marry,' and they're like, 'But you grew up together from a young age, all of you, blah blah blah.' And I'm like, 'I know, but it's not my culture, it's Islam.'

As the women started gradually to distance themselves from their male cousins, close childhood bonds were awkwardly and painfully disrupted, often leaving the non-Salafi party confused and hurt. Deqa, for instance, said that her cousin/'brother' 'stopped being open with me like he used to'. And Shukri was still struggling to stop speaking to a cousin whom she had once regarded as 'my very, very closest friend'—while the cousin, not a practising Muslim himself, was puzzled by her distant behaviour.

However, for families, the most controversial aspect of the women's transformation was usually their adoption of the *jilbab* (twenty women wore it) and *niqab* (eight women). The Qur'an (24:60 and 33:59) tells Muslim women to cover themselves with the *jilbab*, often translated as a long outer garment. Yet Salafis follow a particularly conservative interpretation of *jilbab*, taken from reports from various *salaf* that suggest a head-to-toe, loose-fitting, shapeless robe, which women should wear whenever among non-*mahram* men.

Furthermore, Salafi scholars insist that the *niqab* is at least recommended and possibly obligatory due to reports from *salaf* such as Ibn 'Abbas and 'Aisha that refer to the covering of women's faces. 'Ulama also infer that since the face is one of a woman's most attractive and seductive features, covering it conforms to the Qur'anic (24:31) injunction for women to 'protect their private parts (from illegal sexual acts, etc.)'.[4]

Crucially, for parents, these garments are highly visible, acting as constant reminders of their daughters' new religiosity—and immediately alerting neighbours, family friends, other relatives, and the general public. By contrast, men do not have to proclaim their new religiosity so visibly. Firdaws' conversion to Islam followed her elder brother's, yet his transformation did not provoke anything like the storm hers did within the household—'because, with him, it's just, like, a beard, so he can hide it'.

A common experience among those from Muslim families was that while parents or guardians accepted or even praised the hijab, and often the abaya, more enveloping garments such as the *jilbab* were regarded as worrying signs of extremism. In addition, parents—particularly Nigerians—were uneasy with the Salafi preference for the colour black, which they associated with Arabic culture. While a degree of Islamic covering was familiar in these families, indicating a continuation of traditions passed down from previous generations, there were culturally specific 'stretch points' where visual indicators of Islam exceeded 'acceptable' limits (Badran, 2006, p.205).

> My mum's like, 'Isn't abaya enough for you? Abaya and hijab?' And it's like, no, we have to cover from head to toe. So that's another thing that my mum doesn't seem to understand. To her, wearing hijab is just wearing the scarf on her head and covering her bottom and her hips and wearing a long top. (Amina, Eritrean)

> 'What you wearing, all this black, black, black? Islam doesn't say you should cover up like this—this is the custom of the Arabs. Why can't you just wear long sleeves and a long skirt? You're becoming extreme—don't go to the Brixton Mosque again.' (Wafa, describing the reaction of her Nigerian Muslim family)

There were also more extreme reactions. Abeer's mother threatened to throw her *jilbab* out of the window if she ever wore it, and Saidah's parents summoned the imam of the local Nigerian mosque in a vain attempt to talk her out of wearing one:

> He was like, 'Oh I understand what you're doing . . . but you have to understand, it's not part of our culture.' . . . I was like, 'Um, what's culture got to do with religion, like d'you know what I mean?' I told him, 'You go into the Qur'an and find out where, how it describes how a Muslim woman should dress and then get back to me. Until then, I don't hear nothing from you.' I heard nothing from him!

Over time, Saidah's parents gradually accepted her new dress, and Abeer's mother even got used to her daughter wearing the *niqab* after she got married. But while Muslim parents and guardians saw the *jilbab* as a misinterpretation of the religion, non-Muslim parents regarded any form of Islamic dress as alien. At one end of the scale, Hayah endured sniggering and mockery; at the other, Firdaws was threatened, assaulted, and nearly forced to leave the family home.

When Firdaws first brought an abaya home to wear while praying, her father threatened to throw her 'out the window' and to kick her out of the house. Her mother said that if she saw 'those black rags' lying around, she would 'cut them up and put them in the bin'. When Firdaws defied her parents and wore her abaya to college, her father burst into her bedroom, throwing the schoolbooks she had been studying across the floor. He slapped her and spat at her, yelling 'Fuck your religion!', while her mother punched her from behind. They eventually accepted her choice, but relations remained very frosty.

Reactions to the *niqab*, of course, were often particularly dramatic due to greater perceived associations with extremism, as well as parents' concerns about their daughters' safety and access to education and employment. While only three of the women wore the *niqab* full-time, and a further five part-time (for example, only when outside of the workplace), several others had experimented with it at some point—typically soon after embracing Salafism.

Anticipating furious reactions, four admitted to having concealed their *niqab*-wearing from relatives. When Nadia started wearing it, her cousin threatened to beat her up and 'rip that off you' if he ever saw her wearing it in the street. She continued to wear it, but if she ever caught sight of her cousin approaching, 'I acted like I don't see him!' He didn't recognize her.

A few months after our interview, Wafa started wearing the *niqab*—without the knowledge of her (Muslim) father, with whom she lived. For about a year, she maintained a routine of rolling up her *niqab*—which she had concealed in the collar of her black *jilbab*—on the doorstep each morning before setting out, then rolling it back down as she re-entered the premises in the evening. One day, her father recognized her in the street in her *niqab*, and promptly ordered her to leave the family home for good. Once he had calmed down, Wafa was able to reason with him, and was allowed to stay. Safia's family didn't know about her *niqab*, either, and she said that

> 90 percent of my friends, they have to sneak to wear it. . . . I know so many sisters that are scared of their parents finding out 'cause of what they might do to them. You know, a lot of sisters, their *jilbab*s are cut off—they're *born*-Muslims.

Some parents were anxious about their daughters' safety. Their concerns were not unfounded; research suggests that the frequency of experiences of Islamophobia is related to the degree to which a Muslim woman covers, with *niqab*-wearers at particularly high risk (Ameli and Merali, 2006, pp.36–37). A recent UK study revealed that those who wear the face veil suffer constant Islamophobic victimization that can have long-lasting psychological effects (Zempi and Chakraborti, 2014).

Nearly all of the women in my sample—including all those who wore face veils—reported being the victims of Islamophobic abuse from members of the public, though this was usually limited to comments, such as 'ninja!' or 'Batman!' But five reported having had objects thrown at them (such as bananas and eggs), five had been shoved or tripped up, three had been followed, two had been spat on, two had been threatened with violence, and one had had her *niqab* ripped off. While most women said that they had gradually become desensitized to such abuse, Saidah told me a couple of years later that she had become so tired of the constant insults that she was seriously considering moving to Saudi Arabia.

Fowsiya said that when a man followed her home one night, this proved to be 'the last straw for my mum'. Her mother accused her of being an extremist and started calling her 'a million times' whenever she went out. Fowsiya eventually buckled under this pressure and removed her *niqab*—but only after she had done some research and 'found out that [Shaykh] Albani said that it wasn't compulsory to wear the *niqab*'.

Unsurprisingly, migrant and refugee parents who had brought their children to Britain for better education and employment opportunities were severely disappointed by their daughters' decisions to adopt the *niqab*, and to some extent the *jilbab*, too. They feared that their daughters had jeopardized their career prospects in a Western, liberal society.

> My dad *hates* that I wear *niqab*, and he thinks that he brought me to this country . . . so he sees it as a barrier to like getting a job and stuff like that. So he . . . says, 'You know, you don't *have* to wear it—it is sunna [i.e., highly recommended]'. I take the opinion that it is sunna, but I wanna wear it . . . so a bit of a conflict with that. (Dania, Eritrean)

Dania compromised by removing her *niqab* while on her university campus. Indeed, several of the women abandoned the *niqab* altogether after family objections, but none caved into demands to remove their *jilbab*s. This was because the former is considered by most Salafi scholars to be sunna, while the latter is agreed to be *wajib*. Having learned the *ahkam* for different acts of worship at Salafi circles of knowledge, in books and on websites, the women weighed up the costs and benefits at stake when faced with the dilemma of whether or not to obey their parents—which is actually considered to be a *wajib* act, even if the parents are non-Muslims (so long as it does not involve disobeying God). This was precisely why Maryam, for instance, agreed to forgo the *niqab* but not the *jilbab*, despite her family's protests. However, she—along with Warda and Fowsiya—said she planned to adopt the *niqab* once married and no longer under her parents' roof.

Such cost-benefit evaluations were encouraged by Salafi teachers, who were often asked about how to deal with unsympathetic parents in the question-and-answer sessions after lessons. At the 2011 Al-Athariyyah conference, for instance, a lecturer read out the following question on a slip of paper passed from the women's section: 'I recently became Muslim and am wearing the *niqab*, but my father doesn't want anything to do with me. I've been giving him *da'wa* but he doesn't want to know. What should I do?' The lecturer responded by saying that according to Al-Albani, if a father tells his daughter not to wear the *niqab*, she is obligated to remove it. The vast majority of scholars held the *niqab* to be sunna, rather than *wajib*, so the 'obligation to your father takes precedence'. The lecturer added: 'Obey your father with everything if it doesn't contradict obedience to Allah.'*

Where a compromise could not be struck—that is, when obedience to parents clashed with *wajib* teachings, such as wearing the *jilbab* and not free-mixing—the women tried to give their families *da'wa*, calling them to 'true' Islam, in the hope of winning them around. *Da'wa* could involve explaining that certain practices do or do not conform to the Qur'an and sunna and encouraging others to act accordingly, or it could simply mean displaying good manners and patience in the hope of setting an example and improving others' perception of Salafism.

The women with Muslim backgrounds tended to interpret intergenerational disputes as clashes between culture and 'pure Islam', and regarded their parents as simply ignorant of the 'authentic' prescriptions in the Qur'an and sunna as a result of many years of implementing customs rooted in their countries of origin. Thus, they were in need of enlightenment. For example, Filsan said of her elder family members:

A lot of them will say, 'Yeah, I'm Muslim, I'm Sunni, that's it,' but do they really know the religion? No, it's just they've been brought up—'Oh, my father used to do that.' 'So why are you doing it?' ''Cause that's how I was taught.' 'But do you know why you were taught that way?—You don't know.' So there's no knowledge behind it.

Salafi teachers encouraged their students to give *da'wa* to non-Salafi family members, on condition that this be done gently and respectfully. Indeed, one of the Sisters of Tawheed speakers, Layla, encouraged her young Somali audience to use 'certain techniques'; notably, a practising Muslim woman should know how to 'soften' herself in order to win her parents round.

At the Al-Athariyyah conference, the speaker advised the convert whose father opposed her *niqab*-wearing to be persistent in giving him *da'wa* in a variety of ways, including rushing to open doors for him and giving him gifts to show that she had bettered herself. Hopefully, he said, this would prompt him to ask: 'Does Islam teach you that?' He also suggested that she leave CDs of talks and leaflets around the house and bring an older Salafi round to whom he is more likely to listen.

Time and again, teachers urged students to have the utmost respect for their parents—whether Muslim or not—for example, not eating before they do, forgoing leisure activities to help them, and speaking well of them. Not only is it obligatory to respect one's parents, but doing so may encourage them to see Salafism in a new light, and 'Eventually, they'll think: "My son or daughter wasn't like this before *Salafiyya*"' (guest speaker, Al-Athariyyah circle).

Four women said that they were gradually making progress in calling their (Muslim) parents to Salafism. Manal and Filsan's mothers started covering only after seeing their daughters do so. Amina said she was currently teaching her younger sister about Salafism, and Filsan said that she had already convinced all of her sisters to become Salafi.

In time, most of the women's families accepted their decision to become Salafis, though the majority did not sympathize with it fully; and in several cases, relatives softened their opposition after observing the positive effect Salafism seemed to have had on their daughters' manners and character. Nadia said that after embracing Salafism, her initially hostile family noticed a transformation from an outspoken and rebellious young woman into a helpful, respectful, and humble one.

> I come home early, I don't do anything bad, I'm always home, I help out. They're like, 'OK, she's not—she hasn't gone wild, you know, she's not doing drugs or, you know, doing this. She's not half-naked outside.' . . . So they were like, 'She's all right!' . . . They left me to it.

However, teachers were unequivocal about remaining stubborn in situations where obligatory teachings would be compromised, and even recommended correcting relatives' religious practices where necessary. This could cause heated, ongoing family arguments. When a new, young Salafi woman asked Umm Hamza during one of her lessons about how to deal with parents who tried to involve her in birthday and Christmas celebrations, the teacher answered:

> You've got to be firm, *ukhti* [i.e., my sister].... Say you're not upsetting Allah [in order] not to upset you.... Allah hates them things, so it's not for us to say: 'I'm not gonna do that 'cause my mum's gonna cuss [i.e., curse] me'.... And Allah will replace it with something better.

Yet a newly practising young, possibly overzealous, woman preaching to older relatives could invite outrage, scorn, and accusations of hypocrisy. Madeeha, who had embraced Salafism during the previous two months, said she was challenged fiercely by her Hanafi family when 'me, this non-practising girl, all of a sudden is practising, wearing the hijab and everything, and I come up with something [i.e., correcting their religious practice].... It's like, wow! They're not having it!' And Deqa's cousins, with whom she lived, started to call her 'the fun-killer' when, for example, she began asking that they change channels whenever a sex scene came on the television.

> All the things that I found normal one day, and I woke up the next day and I was like, 'That's not nice,' and they're like, 'Who are you to point fingers? Look at yourself.'

5.3 EDUCATIONAL DILEMMAS

Education is important—but the *din* [religion] comes first.* (Umm Mustafe)

In the winter of 2011, Sisters of Tawheed hosted a one-day conference attended by around seventy young Somalis aged about thirteen to twenty-four (with a few exceptions). Umm Mustafe and the other organizers clearly had this youthful audience in mind when they set the topics of the day, which included music, the media, smart phones, social networking sites, and celebrity role models, who were contrasted with the female *salaf.* But it was the first talk, on the subject of university, that became the main focus of the afternoon, dominating the subsequent question-and-answer sessions and demanding much elaboration.

Unlike the other topics, this was not an area in which the speakers could give clear-cut answers, so they spent time detailing different aspects of campus life and how each should be negotiated by a Salafi woman. Indeed, the speakers shied away from giving absolute rulings on the matter of whether women should attend university at all, probably realizing that most would go anyway, and that urging them not to do so would be unrealistic given the great value placed on higher education in the Somali community and in British society in general.

The speakers also knew they might incur the wrath of parents if they told teenagers to forget about their UCAS applications and ambitions of becoming doctors, lawyers, and biomedical scientists. Several women told me that among the first generation of Somali refugees in the West, ensuring one's children gained a Western university education was a matter of pride and an essential part of their mission for a 'better life' and to replace what was lost due to forced migration. In fact, four of the Somalis in my sample said that their decision to persevere with university or university applications was heavily tied to parental pressure.

The Salafi teachers placed the burden of responsibility firmly on the woman herself to consider her options. 'You need to decide whether to go to uni,' said Layla, who gave the talk. 'Don't take from the lecture, "I said this" or "Umm Mustafe said this"—you've got to decide for yourself.'*

Instead, the emphasis was on advising the women to consider their options carefully and to make arrangements to offset or decrease their exposure to the prohibited activities and surroundings associated with university. After all, Layla had gone to university herself—in order, she explained, to 'obey [her] parents'—and many campuses had thriving Salafi student societies that were effective *da'wa* bases. Preachers cannot ignore the fact that very often, it is on campuses that women are first introduced to Salafism by students and societies (see chapter 3.3). Some Salafi preachers, moreover, occasionally lecture for student societies.

'I'm not here to tell you "don't go",' Layla continued, 'but there are dangers, and you need to research it.'* As she spoke, some of the young women listened attentively, sitting cross-legged on the floor beneath her feet, while others tapped away on their BlackBerries, seemingly indifferent. Every now and then, Umm Mustafe, sitting next to Layla, would make a passionate interjection to add emphasis, answer a question, or translate a particularly pertinent point into Somali for the benefit of the mothers who had accompanied their teenagers and might, I surmised, be particularly keen for their offspring to take advantage of an education. Umm Mustafe later told me that the issue was incredibly delicate: many Somali parents, she said, 'push' their children to go to university, but that she thought it best to encourage them to make their own choices on such matters.

Layla advised the college students present to 'ask yourself: do I *really* need to go to university?' She added: 'If you go, make sure it's a necessity to put yourself in this environment, where half the things are haram.'* Such 'dangers' and 'haram' included free-mixing, student loans (because they incur interest), and exposure to liberal cultures, such as drinking and clubbing, as well as to 'deviated' Islamic groups, who may 'misguide' a Salafi woman by presenting themselves as practising Muslims, 'disguised' by the banner of an 'Islamic Society'.

As for those who were already university students, they should only do 'what is necessary'—attending lectures, completing assignments, and so on—and not 'go to the dining room when everyone is there, hanging around the corridors, high-fiving the brothers'.* Meanwhile, they should assess the amount of time and resources they were devoting to their religion (seeking knowledge, performing acts of worship, and so on), and aim to dedicate to it at least as much time and resources as they give to their studies. 'If these things match up with your *din* in your effort, then Allah will know about it,' she said.

Salafi teachings do not oppose higher education for women in theory; however, when it comes to universities in the West, there are so many points of conflict that it becomes a matter of a highly delicate balancing act at best, and at worst, something to be avoided altogether. On the one hand, as Umm Mustafe acknowledged at the conference, going to university may be seen as very important at a time of economic recession and high unemployment (though she said one should be preoccupied with the afterlife before matters of the *dunya*, i.e., worldly life, regardless of the recession). It can also train women to become good mothers who are able, ideally, to home-school their children so that they may forgo a non-Salafi education altogether. And Umm Mustafe, like all of the other teachers I encountered, always preached the importance of respecting one's parents, many of whom had cherished and well-mapped plans for their daughters' education and careers.

However, other than the above, I did not hear a positive word spoken about university (in the West) in Salafi circles, despite the fact that most of the young women I met seemed to have attended, be attending, or be planning to attend university. My interview sample reflects this apparent inclination for higher education among Salafis: five were contemplating whether or not to go to university; ten were students and negotiating campus life, with mixed results; seven had successfully completed degrees, some with reservations about the cost to their religion; and just one had never attended nor did she intend to go to university, lacking any inclination for higher education. It is to these women's struggles, sacrifices, and rationalizations I now turn.

A major issue for most of them was free-mixing. Unlike in Saudi Arabia, for example, where universities are segregated (with the exception of medical schools), students at British universities can expect to intermingle with the opposite sex in classes, lecturers' offices, on campus, and within student societies. Layla claimed that even some Islamic Societies permit a degree of free-mixing, so one cannot take for granted that there will be any totally men-free zones.

This consideration was so weighty that it put Warda off going to university altogether, though she had applied anyway in order to please her family.

At the time of interview, she was debating the best way of telling her parents that she had no intention of getting a degree, despite their hope that she would one day become a biomedical scientist. She said that she would have felt differently had there been women-only universities in the United Kingdom.

Others had devised or were devising practical solutions to reduce their exposure to the opposite sex while at university. Hayah was considering a distance-learning course at the Open University; and others, such as Deqa and Sagal, had chosen degree programmes for which the vast majority of students and tutors were female (nursing and primary school teaching, respectively).

However, even these choices could be problematic, as they nearly always involve work placements in mixed environments. At one of the Brixton Mosque circles, I met an Algerian mother-of-three who had been accepted on a teaching course at a London university, but had asked the staff to keep the place open for her until they could arrange a placement at an all-girls school. She seemed to realize that she had considerably reduced her chances of ever becoming a teacher, but remained hopeful and asked the other women at the circle to make *du'a* (personal prayers, supplications) for her.

For those already taking courses with men, a strategy of damage limitation seemed to be the only option, short of dropping out of university altogether. Restricting all interaction with men to that which is strictly necessary, however, is never a perfect solution and can offend and alienate others.

Bilan, in her third and final year at a London university, had tried to take this approach, but found that although *she* could avoid talking to men, her less practising friends did not wish to—so having friends came at the price of some free-mixing. Sometimes, when she ate lunch at the university canteen with her friends, men would pull up chairs to talk to them, making her feel awkward and unsure of how to act for fear of being considered rude. She said:

> What I do is I just finish what I'm doing and I go, 'Oh, I need to go,' and I go. . . .
> But the time that I have to sit there, it feels really weird, and I usually get quiet,
> like I look like I'm sulking. . . . But I don't want to offend them—and yet I feel
> uncomfortable sitting there.

Nadia, who became Salafi at about seventeen, initially abandoned her plans for university, but after two years decided to adopt a more practical outlook.

> So I went back to uni thinking, yeah, I need to, I follow certain rules. You know,
> I keep myself to myself . . . I don't mix with the men and stuff like that. Then
> it's OK. I did that anyway. Everyone thought I was extreme and nobody spoke
> to me anyway! [Laughs]

Prayer posed fewer problems at universities than at workplaces (see section 4, this chapter), and the women who mentioned the issue found that, although they felt awkward darting off to pray in the middle of a class, lecturers were tolerant or even accommodating. Shukri's lecturer even permitted her to pray at the back of the lecture theatre so that she did not have to dash across campus to the prayer room and back in order to pray on time.

Laboratory practical work and examinations posed far more problems than lectures, especially in the winter months, when the middle three of the five daily prayers are close together. Bilan had sat a three-hour exam starting at 2 p.m. the previous December, but had arrived several minutes late in order to pray *asr* (mid-afternoon prayer) on time. She had even planned on leaving early in order to catch *maghrib* (sunset prayer) at 3.50 p.m., but had lost track of time once she had started writing.

An increasingly pressing issue for British Salafis is how to afford university without obtaining a student loan, which would incur interest. The Qur'an (2:275) states that 'Those who eat *Riba* will not stand [on the Day of Resurrection] except like the standing of a person beaten by *Shaitan* [Satan] leading him to insanity,' and Salafis take this warning quite literally. During my fieldwork, the government increased tuition fees from around £3,000 to up to £9,000, starting in the academic year 2010–2011. It offset the hike by increasing the maximum student loan allowance so that no one would have to pay fees upfront. However, this measure could not benefit Salafis, for whom even this low-interest loan was intolerable.

Some women had already taken out student loans before they became Salafis, so could only adopt a 'damage limitation' option, resolving to pay them back as soon after graduating as possible in order to limit the amount of interest incurred. Others sought financial help from relatives and family friends. Yet others deliberately chose courses that were government-funded due to staff shortages—for example, Maryam did a course in dietetics—or were entitled to government income–assessed maintenance grants, so could avoid loans altogether. But for those who lacked these options, the only halal course was to take gap years or part-time jobs to help fund their studies.

A final area of concern was the ideological content of certain university courses. Salafi teachers warned their students about the dangers of subjects such as evolution theory and philosophy because of their supposed potential to sow the seeds of doubt that can eventually lead one to leave Salafism or even Islam altogether. Umm Hamza told her students that she knew 'many sisters' who went 'off *din* [i.e., astray]' after studying subjects such as philosophy and politics at university.

To compound the confusion, she added, a Muslim university student can expect to be 'pulled around by the isms and schisms' among her fellow Muslims on campus. Thus according to the scholars, one should not attend university without being firmly grounded in Islamic knowledge 'in order to decipher [that] this is nonsense'.

While some subjects, such as law and philosophy, are considered to be based on haram principles and therefore should be avoided or dropped if possible, other cases are less straightforward. For example, Sawdah, a second-year psychology student from Brixton Mosque, told me that she was concerned about attending classes on evolutionary psychology, as it was based on the 'false' theory of evolution. Most of her courses were not based on Darwinism, however, so she decided to continue with her degree. And Nadifa, a Somali in her early twenties from east London, started a course that was to all outward appearances compatible with her religion—a course about Muslim civilizations at the Islamic College, accredited by Middlesex University—but soon after decided that it had a 'Shia agenda' and promptly dropped out.

The women's responses to these dilemmas ranged from minor compromises—such as missing lecture time and alienating others by avoiding free-mixing—to major ones, such as changing degrees, changing institutions, dropping out, missing examination time, and postponing or avoiding university altogether. Especially when it came to major compromises, they tended to construct their decision-making processes as cost-benefit calculations. Bilan, for instance, explained her decision to miss part of her examination in terms of prioritizing an obligatory ruling, which carries reward if performed and punishment if not performed: 'Prayer is *wajib* upon me, whereas the exam is not. It's not compulsory for me to do the exam, but it's compulsory upon me to go and pray.'

This approach was encouraged by Salafi teachers, who constantly reminded the women not to be complacent as they would be accountable for every decision and every deed in the hereafter. Layla warned the young women gathered for the Sisters of Tawheed conference that the punishment for taking interest alone should deter them from taking out student loans. She said: 'A lot of sisters think, "Oh, it only raises half a percent, it's OK"— Allah doesn't want you to go to uni at the cost of a major sin.'

Meanwhile, aware that many women would enrol at or continue attending university anyway, she implied that any 'haram' in which the women engaged on campus—such as an inevitable degree of exposure to the opposite sex and non-Islamic ideologies—could be offset by shunning the company of less-practising Muslims and seeking knowledge with Salafi women instead. This, she said, maintained *iman* (personal faith) and earned reward.

The women took reassurance from the following hadith: 'You will never leave something for the sake of Allah, but Allah will give you something better in return.' (Ahmad 5:363). They interpreted this saying as proof that sacrifices made on God's behalf trigger compensation—not just in the afterlife, but in this life, too. Stories that 'proved' this rule circulated among the women. I heard one first hand: Nadifa, who gave up her 'Shia' degree in

Muslim civilizations, told me earnestly that she had done so 'for the sake of Allah,' despite 'really' wanting a degree, and that since then many doors had opened up for her. 'Like what?' I asked. Beaming, she said that she had since found the time to study the Qur'an regularly with a teacher and was making progress.

I also heard a story that seemed designed to deal with the dissonance that occurs when an apparent sacrifice is not followed up by compensation. It concerned a Somali who dropped out of university when she became depressed as a result of neglecting her religion and failing to turn up for circles of knowledge, meanwhile clubbing and drinking to 'fit into society'. She then decided to get back on track and apply for a job that would not compromise her religion, and could not understand why God did not give her one.

The story purported to show that on occasions when God does not provide, it is because one's intentions are not as pure as one originally thought. In this case, the woman had left university not for the sake of God, but out of exhaustion. Alternatively, her disobedience to God had disqualified her from compensation, due to the Qur'anic verse (13:11): 'Verily! Allah will not change the good condition of a people as long as they do not change their state of goodness themselves (by committing sins and by being ungrateful and disobedient to Allah).'

Such stories, of course, were open to much interpretation, but they were encouraging to those who faced difficult decisions about university, or indeed anything else.

5.4 NEGOTIATING A LIVING

Most people will not get a job that is 100 percent halal. . . . There is usually some haram in it, and it's for the *mu'min*, the believer, to distinguish. (Layla, Sisters of Tawheed conference 2011)

Although many of the women appreciated the freedom—as they saw it— that Salafism gave them to be full-time wives and mothers, most enjoyed the stimulation of work and were keen to launch and pursue careers. For many of the women, working was financially necessary anyway, and several were employed full-time (five) or part-time (eight), or looking for work. Most of the single women planned to maintain some form of employment once married, regardless of their financial need, and even the four married women worked or were making preparations to work by taking courses to gain qualifications.

However, employment was an area in which Salafi teachings posed great challenges by limiting the industries in which a woman is permitted to work and what she may wear and do in the workplace. Indeed, just five of the women in my sample said that their career plans were not at all disrupted by their embracement of Salafism. Another two were persevering with their careers despite difficulties reconciling them with their new religious practice.

All of the others identified a shift in their plans that was at least in part, if not wholly, related to their wish to fulfil Salafi teachings as strictly as possible. As the above quote illustrates, Salafi teachers expected their students—all young women yet to begin or in the early years of their careers—to weigh up the costs and benefits at stake when contemplating a career path or specific workplace dilemma, and to identify the most 'halal' path from the options available.

Naturally, these limitations compounded the effect of an already depressed job market. My fieldwork began soon after the onset of the world-wide financial crisis at the end of 2007. In Britain, this meant that plans for cuts to benefit payments were rolled out and unemployment rates rose, peaking at 8.1 percent in March 2012. Such conditions can particularly affect Salafi women, whose options are already severely limited.

There are certain career paths that Salafis feel obliged to exclude outright because these industries are founded on 'haram' principles. In such cases, there can be no room for compromise, so cherished ambitions and even existing careers have sometimes had to be discarded. 'Haram' sectors include the law—since the shari'a is the only 'correct' system—and jobs within the music and fashion sectors.

Shukri and Dania had wanted to become lawyers, but abandoned this ambition once they became practising. Fortunately for them, they had not already embarked upon a law degree. Another young (Somali) Brixton Mosque attendee, Nabila, embraced Salafism towards the end of her second year of law studies and promptly dropped out—despite her lecturers' protests that she was an excellent student who could go far. Manal had hoped to go into the music industry, and Humayrah into fashion, but both redirected their career paths once they became practising.

Other career decisions were more surprising. I met a Pakistani in her thirties at an Al-Athariyyah conference who had dropped out of her counselling degree after two (of three) years because she felt that she could not reconcile the 'man-made theories' students were expected to apply with Islamic teachings.

Most other careers posed no problems in principle, but in practice required compromise with Salafi teachings. Jobs that required travel, for example, could be problematic, given restrictions on women's mobility. Abyan, a Somali, had originally wanted to become a reporter, but changed her mind when she became practising because 'my brothers are not Arabs and they don't do the whole "I will follow you everywhere". . . . It's like, "Listen, you have legs, you go by yourself!"'

Travelling could also clash with a woman's role as wife and mother. Salma, a Jamaican *niqabi* (woman who wears the *niqab*) whom I met at a Tottenham

Da'wah conference, had abandoned her career as an aircraft engineer when she converted and opted for primary school teaching instead. She had realized that she would be expected to work in many different countries in order to familiarize herself with different types of aircraft, and was concerned that this would make tending to a family very difficult. I heard many other accounts of career-switching 'for the sake of my *din*', as the women invariably explained or implied.

Of course, all jobs that required employees to wear uniforms or to avoid wearing long and loose coverings, such as many positions in the medical profession, posed problems. The Equality Act (2010) in the United Kingdom is rather vague about employees' rights in this regard. An employee who is told she cannot wear an item of religious clothing may have grounds for legal challenge if she can prove that this puts her at a 'particular disadvantage'. In addition, she must be confident that her employer cannot show that banning such clothing would be a 'proportionate means of achieving a legitimate aim' (Equality and Human Rights Commission, 2011, p.59). The terms 'disadvantage' and 'legitimate aim' are not defined by the Act, however, and are left to judges to interpret—though possible grounds for banning religious symbols obviously include health, welfare, and safety reasons.

During my fieldwork, I did not encounter any women who said that they had been asked to remove their headscarves. But it was clear that the all-enveloping *jilbab* and *niqab* were far more vulnerable to challenges by employers.

Still, being unable to wear the *niqab* to work is relatively unproblematic, at least for those who agree with the scholarly majority that the face veil is recommended, rather than obligatory. One such woman was Abyan, who was happy to remove her *niqab* at her part-time job as a mental health support worker. The *jilbab*, however, is quite another matter; Salafi scholars agree that it is compulsory, so failing to wear it is considered sinful.

Fowsiya had worked as a laboratory researcher but had quit after a few months to become a teacher because her supervisor claimed that her *jilbab* was a health and safety hazard, even though she had covered it with a lab coat and hitched her *jilbab* above the floor. Her boss was also reluctant to let her pray on time—'Do that in your lunch break!' 'Obviously, I put my Islam before my career, so then I felt that it's time for me to leave,' she said. 'I need to work in an environment where I feel comfortable.'

Nadia and Warsan abandoned their plans to become doctors to work in schools instead (as a teacher and laboratory technician, respectively) because they did not want to compromise on what they wore. Similarly, Safia dropped out partway through her nursing degree when she started wearing the *jilbab*, partly due to the uniform requirements of the nursing profession.

Deqa was in the second year of her nursing degree and Madeeha already working as an operating theatre nurse when they became practising and started wearing *jilbabs*. But unlike Safia, they did not give up their ambitions. Both were aware that they were, strictly speaking, compromising Salafi teachings, but they reasoned that their uniforms were still modest and loose-fitting, and therefore obeyed the spirit of the law.

> They allow me to wear this t-shirt top and they allowed me to wear the trousers at the bottom of my dress, though they look at me weird, like: 'Why d'you wear all those clothes, it's really hot, twelve hours?' I'm like, 'I don't care,' because . . . nobody sees what I wear—they see the kind of confidence I have to do my job and to work on my patients . . . and the dress is quite big. (Deqa)

> I mean, I wear scrubs—it's really baggy. I wear like a great big long thing over it. It's not showing the shape of my arms or anything; it's really baggy. . . . We look horrible in it so . . . (Madeeha)

However, Deqa and Madeeha also had to take into account another issue, which was much harder to circumvent: free-mixing. Like the vast majority of jobs in Britain, theirs involved regularly intermingling with members of the opposite sex. This consideration, I soon realized, could wreak havoc with women's career plans; for example, it led Maryam eventually to turn her back on accounting, the subject in which she had graduated.

Khudeja, a black convert in her early twenties whom I met at an informal circle of knowledge in north London, told me she had abandoned her career in social work for the same reason. Although some jobs in her sector were women-focused—for example, supporting victims of domestic violence—the few positions available were coveted and rarely vacated, she said. Child protection was not an option either because it required home visits with men present.

She had since switched to a job supporting adults with learning difficulties, but was in the process of applying to become a teaching assistant for small children because her request to be placed in an all-female ward had not been granted. She had felt uneasy not only because of the sin she was committing by working in a mixed environment, but because, by then, she had internalized Salafi teachings on gender segregation to the point where she felt uncomfortable around unrelated men.

Deqa and Madeeha, on the other hand, decided to persevere with their professions in spite of their reservations. Their decisions, in contrast to those of Maryam and Khudeja, reflect in part differences in personal circumstances, rather than differences in how these obstacles were perceived. When I spoke to Khudeja about her career change, she was living with her parents and seeking marriage, and later expected to have her financial needs met by her husband. Maryam, too, was living under her mother's roof.

Madeeha, however, was new to Salafism and had already been working in the medical field for seven years. Having invested so much, she said she simply would not 'know what else to do'. For Deqa, continuing in her pro-fession was a clear case of financial necessity, as well as one of pride—re-lated to her status as a refugee with parents living in poorer circumstances in Kenya to whom she wished to send remittances. At the same time, she did not presume to dispute Salafi teachings on free-mixing and correct attire. Faced with this dilemma, she had approached a British Salafi preacher, who conceded that her circumstances may permit a temporary digression into a 'haram' work environment:

> He said to me, 'OK, if you have the intention of quickly getting your experi-ence'—'cause you need two years' experience as a nurse in this country—'and then go to a Muslim country then. Otherwise don't work, or otherwise get a job that you have your abaya, like a fertility clinic. But otherwise it's very dif-ficult, and Allah knows everybody's situation.' I said to him: 'Allah knows my situation, but if I don't work now, who's going to pay my rent?' Other girls will say, 'Oh it's haram,' and they stay at home because their mum pays the bill. I need to go work and pay my bills, that's why. And he said, 'OK, all right then. You know, Allah knows everybody's heart.'

The preacher's response highlights some of the tensions in Salafi teachings when applied in contemporary liberal, Muslim-minority contexts. According to the teachings, free-mixing and 'immodesty' of dress in front of the op-posite sex are haram, except in cases of dire necessity (*darura*), such as when an individual requires urgent medical attention or is in danger. The Qur'anic verse 2:286, 'Allah burdens not a person beyond his scope,' is often invoked in such discussions.

Since most jobs in Britain involve some 'haram', those who wish to work may attempt to define their circumstances in light of this criterion, such as a case of financial necessity. But this is no easy task, especially if a woman wishes to convince a religious authority before proceeding. Salafi teachers, who were often asked about these issues at circles of knowledge, tended to err on the side of caution by interpreting teachings as literally as possible, however impractical this might be for a young woman living in London, pos-sibly without financial support.

For example, a preacher at a 2011 Brixton Mosque conference said that it was better for parents to pay for their daughter's living costs than for her to work in a mixed environment. In another example, Amal, an Afro-Caribbean convert who worked as a nurse and had recently started to wear the *jilbab* and attend Salafi circles regularly, was beginning to have concerns about the compatibility of her work with her new religious practice. Intermingling with male colleagues and patients was inevitable, and exposing her forearms was mandatory.

She jotted down her questions on a slip of paper and asked me to pass them on to a Salafi preacher with whom I was in contact. The response was unequivocal: the preacher said that Amal's work involved dealing with men so she should 'fear Allah' and ask Him to give her something better, or else apply for a position in a Muslim country, such as Saudi Arabia. Finally, the preacher gave me the telephone number of a Saudi-based, English-speaking shaykh who could confirm the ruling, which I passed on to a now thoroughly perplexed Amal.

Similarly, Madeeha took steps to legitimize her decision to stay in her job after she embraced Salafism by seeking advice from a Salafi preacher. However, she did not receive the answer she was looking for when she asked about the permissibility of touching male patients—a necessary part of her job in a hospital.

'[She said,] "Under no circumstances." [Laughs] She goes, "If you were to know [the punishment], then you'd rather put your hand in the fire than touch a man."' Unwilling to accept this answer, Madeeha turned to a more liberal, non-Salafi preacher, who told her that her intentions were the over-riding factor. Thus, Madeeha reflected upon her intentions and another Islamic prescription—that of preserving life—and concluded that she could continue with her job, provided she kept physical contact with male patients to a minimum.

> Obviously, in Islam it's like, to let someone die, that's, like, haram innit. . . . But OK, to touch another man, that's haram as well. But what's more worse: to kill someone or to touch someone? . . . I'm not doing it with another intention, I'm doing it for the sake of I have to do it, you know? If I was to go into hospital, obviously, and I'm having an operation and I'm scared, I might want someone to comfort me. That's the way I feel, you know, and sometimes you might just pat them on their shoulder or something like that, you know. Obviously keep those things to a limit, and most are my elderly patients anyway—I wouldn't do it to a young, fit, hunky man, d'you know what I mean? [Laughs]

Madeeha, who was in her mid-twenties, was the only woman I met who openly challenged Salafi principles. This could be related to the fact that she was older than most of the women, and that she had only very recently become Salafi—approximately two months before the interview. Soon afterwards, however, she was offered a job in a ward for women and children and an even more modest uniform—a gown reaching her toes, in addition to scrubs. She accepted enthusiastically, seeing it as a God-given opportunity to pursue her beloved career without compromising her religion.

Only a minority of women seemed prepared to obey the spirit rather than letter of the law, like Deqa and Madeeha. The others, meanwhile, had to be very imaginative and flexible when looking for work and planning career paths. During fieldwork, I quickly lost count of the number of women I met who were in, or planning to enter, primary school teaching (including no fewer than ten of the women in my sample). In several cases at least, this was not the woman's first choice of career.

Working in a primary school with small children or at a girls-only secondary school does not require a uniform or much free-mixing, apart from occasionally with male colleagues. Even *niqabi*s find the profession appealing, since covering in front of children or girls is unnecessary. At an Islamic school, employers are likely to be more sympathetic to Salafi dress requirements, teachings on free-mixing, and strict prayer schedules, so these were particularly attractive places to work. In addition, the women said there were fewer ideological conflicts with the curriculum—for example, in religious studies, biology, and sex and relationship education.

However, only a tiny number of Salafi schools exist in Britain, so working in an Islamic school is likely to involve clashes of interpretation and practice that can make the working environment uncomfortable. Fowsiya, for instance, was happy to have found work in an Islamic school after her negative experience as a laboratory researcher, but said: 'I still have issues with them because they don't have the Salafi mentality.' The main issue, she said, was that the Hanafi South Asians who ran the school 'practically worship' a famous imam, by which she meant they seemed to attribute equal or more weighting to his words as to those of the Prophet and God Himself.

Fowsiya's employers did not take issue with her own interpretation of Islam, but Muna, a North African teacher at an Islamic secondary school whom I met at an Al-Athariyyah circle, said she felt under constant attack by her non-Salafi colleagues. For example, they would challenge her to defend her 'extreme' attire—'Why are you all in black?'—and her refusal to celebrate birthdays. 'What's wrong with giving a child a bit of happiness?' they had demanded.

Similarly, Hanifa, a bright twenty-something Somali whom I met at an Al-Athariyyah conference, had met resistance from non-Salafi Muslim volunteers in her work as a Muslim women's prison chaplain. After preaching that prayer beads were *bid'a* (reprehensible innovation), she was frustrated when volunteers undermined her authority by distributing them to prisoners anyway. In the end, she quit.

Other careers that circumvented Salafi prohibitions relatively well included midwifery (Safia's new career goal, after she dropped out of her nursing degree), out-of-hours office cleaning (Saidah's current part-time job), childcare (Hayah), and social work and healthcare in women-only wards (Shukri and Abyan). Safia and Filsan were currently working in call centres, which they justified on the basis that their dress and prayer times were accommodated (Safia was even allowed to wear her *niqab*). In addition, they said, the free-mixing required was less 'dangerous', since it was mostly by telephone, rather than face-to-face. Yet no job seemed to be entirely free from Salafi reservations; for instance, as a mental health support worker, Abyan could opt to work only with women, but she still had to deal with male visitors to the ward on a regular basis.

Having identified career paths that they could reconcile with their new religious practice and, with any luck, some relevant vacancies, women next faced the challenge of successfully applying for the few positions available. In addition to those self-imposed limitations, several women suspected that their opportunities had decreased further due to Islamophobia. Although experiences of prejudice and discrimination in the job application process can be extremely difficult to prove, they suspected that their Islamic appearance had prevented them from being successful. They acknowledged, however, that their suspicions could not be proved one way or the other and that it is always possible that another person is better qualified.

I often met women who had struggled for months, or even years, to obtain any employment, despite having the relevant qualifications. Maryam, who held a Bachelor's degree in accounting and finance, had been interviewed over the course of four years for numerous jobs in different sectors and at different levels, but without success. She suspected her *jilbab* played a role, especially after she was asked outright to 'simplify' her hijab—that is, just wear a short headscarf—when she applied to volunteer at a local hospital.

Sagal, who had been rejected for support teacher positions despite being told that she had all the right qualifications at interview, harboured similar suspicions. She said:

> When it comes to interviews, what you write on your application and what they see is two different things, and you can see the person's: 'Oh, it was you!' [i.e., surprised]. 'Cause you meet all the criteria and you have all the qualifications, but when they see you, it's a different story 'cause they weren't expecting someone like you to have these qualifications and to be applying. So you can see they're like looking at you in a certain way in interviews—they're quite shocked that it is actually someone wearing a hijab.

I wondered if, in some cases, these suspicions could be self-fulfilling because of the effect on confidence. Repeated rejections for part-time work over the past three years had damaged Firdaws' confidence and left her feeling depressed. Like most Salafi women, she regularly received verbal abuse on the street, and this compounded her pessimism when it came to job applications.

> It just makes me think yeah, if this is how people on the street are treating me, then how am I ever gonna get a job? 'Cause the minute I turn up, what are they

gonna be thinking? . . . It makes you get to the point where you start losing your self-esteem and your self-confidence.

Yet other women were more philosophical—and even accepted that employers might have valid reasons for not hiring a visibly Muslim woman. Shukri, who had applied in vain for numerous jobs over the years, and in the end settled for a job she disliked—carer for the elderly—said:

> I understand to a certain degree why companies or shops or whatever may feel a bit reluctant to employ you, simply because you might bring trouble their way. 'Cause I can demand certain things once I'm an employee, or like, for example, somewhere to pray, that it's my right to wear certain things, and they just don't want that trouble. They prefer not to deal with it, and I'm sure there's some prejudice behind it somehow but I don't know too much into it. If I don't get it [the job], what can you do?

Deqa said that Islamophobia simply made her more determined to prove herself:

> Sometimes when I go [for a] job interview, they're like, 'Y'all right, darling, are you lost?' and I'm like, 'No, no, no, I'm [here] for the job'. 'Oh.' . . . I'm so happy to prove them wrong.

Even if a Salafi woman successfully obtains a job that does not compromise her religion to an unacceptable degree, once employed, she may encounter problems with colleagues who do not sympathize with her strict religious practices—such as regular prayers at set times during the day. Several women said that they had wrestled with bosses who were unwilling to allow them to pray at the correct times, but had usually managed to resolve this by pointing out that other colleagues were permitted short cigarette breaks throughout the day. Humayrah had even negotiated with her bosses to cut her lunch breaks in half so that she could perform her midday and afternoon prayers at the correct times.

However, although the women were usually granted the right to pray more or less on time, this concession was sometimes only grudgingly given, and this could cause tensions in the working environment. Dania was allowed to pray at the correct times while she worked at a DIY store, but her manager would go out of his way to make her feel uncomfortable about it—'Look at her, she's getting an extra break.' Moreover, the women were conscious of ostracizing themselves by leaving the room at a time of their choosing, regardless of convenience to others.

5.5 CONCLUSION

All of the women encountered problems and contradictions as they tried to increase their participation in the community, openly practise Salafism within their households, and bring Salafi rulings to bear on their ambitions for higher education and future careers. Salafi teachings all but presupposed a segregated society in which women could work and study in women-only environments and have their financial needs met by their fathers or husbands. They were therefore an awkward fit for a career-minded woman living in London during an economic crisis. The teachings also envisioned a supportive household and united 'sisterhood', with every woman loving her fellow sisters 'for the sake of Allah', yet this was far from the reality for many women.

In these frustrating situations, rather than challenge the principles themselves, the women—with one exception—interpreted the clashes as resulting from human fallibility, whether that of oneself, other Salafis, or society as a whole. They thus took responsibility for negotiating their aspirations and commitments with Salafi teachings, and were encouraged to do so by their teachers. However, worldly priorities and necessities could not be ignored, so the women found imaginative and creative ways of navigating the teachings without abandoning their families or (present or future) livelihoods.

Where possible, the women resolved dilemmas by resorting to the simple *ahkam* classificatory system. For example, a woman may choose to obey her parents (*wajib*) over wearing a *niqab* (sunna, according to most scholars). However, when two rulings conflicted or when implementing a *wajib* ruling was impractical, the women had to be resourceful—or, as Warsan put it, 'you halal-ify it'.

If a woman was too busy or disinclined to go out to circles of knowledge, she could go online instead. Faced with stubborn, unsympathetic relatives, she might develop a discreet and diplomatic strategy for winning them round. Unwilling to forgo university, she might find a female-dominated course and alternative sources of funding to avoid a student loan. Likewise, she might forge a career path that does not involve 'too much' haram. And once in work, she could negotiate prayer breaks with her employer.

By mapping out her career path in this way, the Salafi woman is effectively pushed towards the traditionally 'feminine' professions such as nursing and school teaching, which attract a disproportionate number of women and therefore do not involve 'too much' free-mixing.

In some cases, a woman becomes Salafi after having already invested a great deal in her education and career. Some women felt able to retain their goals by obeying the spirit of the law, rather than the letter, reassuring themselves of the purity of their intentions and the modesty of their uniforms. Meanwhile, they tried to implement a strategy of damage control to limit their exposure to 'haram'; for example, by paying off student loans as soon as possible or avoiding conversations with male colleagues. At the same time, they could try to compensate for their digressions by attending circles of knowledge and performing other acts of worship.

Where sacrifice and perseverance were deemed necessary, the women employed the theodicies and other theological resources to which they had been introduced in circles of knowledge. They tried to interpret frustrating situations as 'tests' from God, and therefore opportunities to increase their rewards in this life and the next. Thus meaning could be bestowed upon difficult decisions, such as missing examination time, dropping out of university, or abandoning a career.

As a young woman gradually adopts a Salafi lifestyle and severs her ties to people, ideas, and practices that represent her former self, she may take what is possibly the most commitment-deepening and life-changing decision of all: to get married. The next chapter explores how Salafi women navigate the thorny process of match-making Salafi-style.

CHAPTER 6

◌✦◌

'Marriage Completes Half
Your Religion, Sister'

Salafi Match-Making

Imaam Ahmad (may Allah have mercy on him) said, 'Remaining single is not from Islaam, and anyone who introduces the idea of remaining single is introducing something other than Islaam.' Rejecting suitable men and delaying women from marriage jeopardises and endangers men, women and indeed the community as a whole. Suitable men are those who [*sic*] practise of Islaam is sound, whose manners are good and who are kind, honest and from a good family. The prophet (peace be upon him) said, 'Marry the one who has (i.e., practices) religion.' Al-bukhaari and Muslim. (BlackBerry Messenger 'broadcast' from Abeer, 2012)

On entering a Salafi community, a young woman will probably be confronted by the issue of getting married as never before. She will hear the subject mentioned frequently not only in sermons, classes, and lectures but also, above all, in conversations among women. Her peers will tell her thrilling stories—from the romantic to the ridiculous—about their meetings with suitors. They may pass on text messages containing religious advice on the subject, as above, or even suggestions for possible suitors.

Within a short time, the neophyte is likely to receive numerous wedding invitations and, quite possibly, marriage offers herself. Having adopted a visibly Salafi appearance—a *jilbab* and possibly a *niqab*, too—her comings and goings at Salafi mosques and other venues will probably attract the attention of men seeking brides. As a result, her thoughts may turn towards marriage far sooner than she had intended in '*jahiliyya*' (i.e., before she became practising/Salafi).

Marriage can serve as a highly effective commitment mechanism within a religious group. Indeed, David Bromley and Anson Shupe (1979, p.191), in their ethnography of the Unification Church in the United States, call it 'Perhaps the single most significant event' in maintaining members' commitment. They argue—and this could just as easily be said of Salafis—that

> [b]y marrying within the church the individual's family life also was tied to the movement. . . . If a member were to leave the church he or she would be giving up not only a religion but also a family because apostasy was primary grounds for divorce.

It is therefore not surprising that Salafis are encouraged to marry—and to marry within the group and in accordance with its teachings—as soon as possible. However, this is another area in which the tensions between Salafi ideals and social realities are brought into sharp relief.

Many of the young women I encountered during fieldwork were seeking husbands and had braced themselves for the challenges of Salafi-style match-making. Salafi teachings strictly prohibit free-mixing between the sexes, so potential spouses can meet only with a third party present and need to keep all communication business-like and to a minimum. Marriage after just a few short meetings is common. Defending this rigid approach, Salafis often recite the well-known hadith (Tirmidhi 3118): 'Whenever a man is alone with a woman, the Devil makes a third.'

This chapter places the Salafi match-making process in twenty-first-century London, where social realities intervene to render it highly impractical. It describes the strategies that young women devised to navigate the process smoothly and faithfully, and why they persevered.

Salafi teachings classify getting married as sunna. This means that marriage brings religious reward, though remaining single is not sinful per se. Nonetheless, as in some Christian fundamentalist groups (Brasher, 1998, p.145), singledom is not celebrated as a lifelong option, so adherents often feel a tacit if not palpable pressure to get married.

It is not only the act of marrying itself that brings reward; Salafis learn how marriage opens up the possibility of further, ongoing rewards. Rewardable acts associated with marriage range from increasing the *umma* (Muslim community) by having children to performing wifely duties, such as obeying one's husband and maintaining the home. Engaging in polygamy, like the Prophet and his wives did, also carries reward, and it is not uncommon in Salafi communities in Britain.

An oft-repeated phrase among Salafis is that 'marriage completes half your *din* [religion]', an expression taken from a hadith (Tirmidhi 3096). For Salafis, this indicates that marriage offers a particularly efficient route to a closer relationship with God and, ultimately, salvation. Saidah said:

I used to be like, huh! Gonna be with one person for the rest of my life! Aren't you gonna get bored? ... A lot of non-Muslims, they portray marriage as, like, the dead end of your life ... and that's how I used to think of marriage as well. ... But now, since the *din* and being a *salaf* [sic], I realize marriage is like something that's gonna put me 50 percent closer to God, *insha'Allah* [God willing]. It's like I was on this Earth and I took one hundred boxes—if I get married, that's fifty out of a hundred ... it's common sense! ... Everyone wants to achieve *janna* [Paradise], and it's like if you get married for the right reasons, for the sake of Allah, yeah, you're 50 percent closer to it.

Furthermore, the women were conscious that if they secured a pious, knowledgeable husband—ideally one who had studied in Saudi Arabia or Dammaj,[1] Yemen—they would acquire a (hopefully) permanent, freely available religious guide, who would help them to boost their *iman* (faith) and resist the temptations of modern life in the West. A devout husband may even whisk his wife off to a Muslim country, such as Saudi Arabia, in order to start a new life with dramatically reduced avenues to sin and improved opportunities to seek knowledge.

Abeer, a new Salafi and an Eritrean of Muslim background, said she had never considered marriage until she started practising her religion and became aware of the potential for spiritual benefit. 'A husband is ... responsible for his wife's religion, so I would love to have that support,' she said, echoing many other women I met. 'It's someone who's trying to guard my religion.' In this way, most Salafi women come to view marriage as a highly desirable step in their spiritual journeys.

Moreover, since free-mixing is forbidden, marriage is often viewed as a 'safety measure' that removes the temptation to sin. Many Salafi women—at least twelve of the women I interviewed[2]—had dated or had boyfriends in their '*jahiliyya*' pasts, and the temptation to return to old habits could be strong. Safia, who had embraced Salafism approximately ten months earlier, said she had resolved to marry as soon as possible for this very reason, even though it meant putting her university degree on hold. She said:

Sometimes you just feel weak and you don't wanna turn into haram, 'cause then it's easy to just call up your ex at some point, but it's like, you know, you need someone that's halal, Allah's pleased with it.

Some women already had long-term boyfriends when they embraced Salafism. It was not unusual for a woman to follow her Salafi boyfriend into Salafism, and in such cases, marriage became a matter of urgency to legitimize the relationship. Madeeha married her long-term Muslim boyfriend within a few months of becoming Salafi because she realized that 'it's haram to date and just live together'.

All nineteen of the unmarried women in my interview sample expressed a firm desire to get married (including one who had recently divorced after a three-month marriage)—and to go about it in the Salafi way, which they claimed was based on the Qur'an and sunna. Yet they were at different stages of the match-making process. Some felt that they were still relatively new to Salafism and not sufficiently versed in the rights and responsibilities of husbands and wives; some were still too nervous to start the process, which they found intimidating; and others wished to complete their education first.

At the other end of the spectrum, several were very active in investigating and attending meetings with suitors—two admitted to having had meetings with more than twenty men—and four were already engaged. Four others had recently married and were able to recall with precision their experiences of the match-making process. I also spoke informally to many other women during my fieldwork about their views on, and experiences of, the process, and these conversations also inform this chapter.

Women who had yet to embark on their quest for a husband were sometimes rather idealistic about it, confident that a few meetings would suffice. Meanwhile, those with some experience of it—either directly or through friends—were more realistic, and had devised imaginative solutions to minimize the risk involved in marrying a virtual stranger.

They all realized, however, that selecting a husband was a life-changing decision in which the stakes were higher than with conventional match-making. Marrying the 'right' man could not only bring great happiness but also generate religious rewards in this life and the next.

Conversely, marrying the 'wrong' man could be spiritually, as well as emotionally, harmful—and even traumatic. An unhappy and spiritually undernourished wife would struggle to fulfil her religious duties, which, according to Salafi teachings, include obeying her husband in everything that is religiously permissible—including even 'his request for intimacy' (i.e., sexual intercourse), whenever it is made (Ali Al-Utaybee, 2010, p.29).

Divorce is permissible—and, in fact, common in Salafi communities in Britain—but brings divine disapproval. It is also harder for a woman to initiate than it is for a man. Thus the women were anxious to use every resource at their disposal to secure a successful match.

6.1 'SISTER, ARE YOU INTERESTED?'
IDENTIFYING A SUITOR

The first obstacle husband-seekers faced was in identifying promising suitors while observing the tight restrictions on interaction between the sexes in Salafi communities. Direct approaches by women to men were strongly discouraged (Abu Khadeejah, 2009). However, women were frequently approached by men, usually via intermediaries—such as the suitor's sister or his friend's wife—in order to preserve strict gender segregation.

New Salafi women, particularly, tended to receive numerous offers. Amina, who had embraced Salafism about five months earlier, said: 'There's a lot of sisters that will come up to me, especially when you start practising. Yeah, you get asked like 24/7, "Are you interested? Are you interested?"'

Occasionally, women initiated the search themselves by asking married friends or their own *maharim* (men with whom they have close blood relationships) to 'get the word out'. Information would then be relayed back and forth via third parties to establish whether a match might be possible. Firdaws, a private person, called this process 'Chinese whispers'.

Some, like Firdaws, regarded this method as a bit 'hit-and-miss' and insisted on further quality control. As Sagal explained:

Some [sisters] are still like they're grown-up but they're kids at heart, so they'll just get you a kid. They won't look into the person a lot—they'll just say: 'Oh, he's really nice.' How do you know? 'Well, I saw him outside the masjid [mosque], that's how I know!'

Shukri found that zealous women would exaggerate prospective suitors' good qualities and 'might not give the real story'.

Abyan told me of her exasperation at being asked repeatedly by women in the community whether she would like to become 'the third wife to a brother who works in a bookshop', or consider a man who 'will be out of prison in two weeks'. 'When I say, "I don't think so," the sister says: "*Masha'Allah* [i.e., expression of joy], this brother's really religious."' She said she felt 'bullied' and under pressure from other women to consider any man that came along—otherwise, 'you're not seen as righteous'. She recalled being asked whether she would consider a twenty-three-year-old who already had a wife. Assuming that the man must be rich, Abyan had asked whether he came 'from a wealthy family with businesses or something', before being chastised: 'No he isn't, *ukhti* [my sister], don't judge him innit.'

Thus some women, such as Abyan, had resolved only to pursue leads that came from trusted friends and relatives. Fowsiya, Abeer, and Filsan agreed to meetings with their now-husbands after friends recommended them. Abeer said she would only investigate suitors suggested by her Salafi brother: 'I just wouldn't feel comfortable with the fact that this sister's husband knows a brother who knows a brother.' Likewise, Warsan had a Salafi cousin whom she would hold responsible for identifying suitors when the time came.

Yet even trustworthy friends and relatives could have faulty judgment— particularly where looks were concerned. Since photographs were impermissible, women often had to rely on descriptions of their prospective suitors, only to find them unattractive upon meeting them. Thus, while some women opted to break the rules on photographs, others took more active steps to identify pious and good-looking suitors.

The entrances of conferences and Salafi mosques after Friday prayers were places where large numbers of Salafi men and women emerged, and thus where initial interest could be sparked. From there, it was usually easy to identify and make contact with a person, thanks to the small size and insularity of the community. Nadia explained:

N: Say I go to a lecture, and then I see a couple of people, or say I might see my friend's brother and I'll be like, 'Ask that brother, who was that guy!' . . . Or I might see somebody about a lot, and I'll be like, who is that person? . . . So we all know each other really . . . 'cause there's not too much Salafis here. There's just certain gatherings, so you see the same people about.
ANABEL: Even though it's segregated?
N: Yeah, but like outside I might—you know, when we're leaving and stuff, I probably will see somebody. Or I might hear [someone] talking about somebody.

It was well known in the Brixton community that some young men and women deliberately hung back outside the mosque after Friday prayers in order to exchange flirtatious glances. Umm Reemah, a community elder, described such a scene thus: 'They stand and they're all, like, talking together and "hahahaha" [giggles], and then the brother walks past, they're all like, "Oh *astaghfirullah* [I seek God's forgiveness]!" [Touches her face with her hand, giggling].'

However, this approach, particularly if indiscreet, was frowned upon in the community. Umm Hamza repeatedly rebuked the younger women for such behaviour. At a 'sisters' seminar', she said:

> There are sisters gathering outside the masjid after *jum'a* [Friday midday congregational prayers], looking at men. And that's why I don't even go to *jum'a*, because I don't want to be lumped with those sisters. And I know they're doing it. . . . Why is everyone facing this way [looks to the left, as if towards the men's entrance] and fluttering their eyelids. . . . [They're] behaving loose. . . . The sisters who go to *jum'a* don't have manners. . . . Allah knows all that you're doing, so even if you're fooling the people that you're 'just looking out for sister Malika', He knows. I've even seen with my own eyes, sisters peeping through the curtain [that separates the men and women] to look at brothers. . . . [The *salaf*] Abu Sa'id said: 'Avoid sitting on the roadsides'— this is like standing outside after *jum'a*.*

Alternatively, Salafis could use technology to cast their net wider in the search for the perfect match, though such methods seemed to be more popular with men than women. Mass messages about men seeking wives were often circulated via social media such as BlackBerry Messenger.

Typically, a woman would 'broadcast' a message to all of her female contacts on behalf of a man to whom she or her husband had a connection. Each message included basic information about the man and his requirements for a wife, as well as the contact details of the woman acting on his behalf so that interested women could get in touch without free-mixing. The following 'broadcasts', which found their way to my own BlackBerry, reflect the men's perceptions of what the women were looking for (some details have been changed).

> Asalaam alaykum wa rahmatullahi wa barakatu [may the peace, mercy, and blessings of God be unto you], My dear sisters I hope your in great health and imaan. Is there any single, sisters looking for marriage? A brother who is 25 years old. Who has his own house, and also drives. He's a Jamaican revert [i.e., convert] brother. He's been a revert around 6 years. He's from East London. He prays & attends lectures in the masjid when he can. If interested contact Umm Mohammed 398477A.

> Asalamualykum sisters, There's a brother looking for marriage inshaAllah. The brothers Somali—Light skinned, upon the Sunnah. Age— 23. Sisters aged 21–25. Race wise preferably somali yemani arabic sisters, but would not mind as long as she has fear in Allah. And can guide me and help me with my deen [i.e., *din*]. InshaAllah in this life and Akhira [afterlife]! Seeking the reward of Allah. Is looking to one day make hijrah [migration for religious reasons] to Islmaic country where we can be in the laws of Allah and inshaAllah, by the will of Allah raise our Children in an islamic country. Job wise—work in a hotel. Born and raised Muslim. But in this society we can all fall into fintah [*sic—fitna*, i.e., trial, tribulation, temptation], especially us brothers. So I just want a new start and by the promise of Allah to be beneficial to each other. For fore there inquiry Add Shahana; 332553A (sister) and InshaAllah I will fill your interested. Serious sisters only please.

Such messages were then forwarded to friends. Yet I never heard of a marriage resulting from these rather haphazard efforts.

There was also a growing number of more organized Salafi match-making efforts that were designed to facilitate the process while preserving gender segregation. These services were usually free, forbade photographs, offered guidance such as quotes from Salafi scholars, and insisted that users follow Salafi teachings strictly throughout the process. For instance, the website 1Dawah Salafi Nikah allows women to browse the profiles of men 'upon the salafi manhaj [i.e., way]', but asks that they first obtain permission from their male guardians and that they pray *salat al-istikhara*—a prayer that is believed to aid a worshipper with important decisions.

Better known was an international, London-based website called Smatch, with thousands of Salafi men to choose from and a freely downloadable 'Marriage Guide' with advice from 'the Senior Scholars of our time', such as Shaykhs Al-Albani and Al-Uthaymin. Smatch asked women 'to refrain from any usage of this site, rather sufficing with their Walee [male guardian] registering on their behalf'.

I also encountered a BlackBerry Messenger service 'that deals with hundreds of people from inside and outside the UK', including sixteen- to forty-four-year-olds of Arab, Somali, Eritrean, Nigerian, and Jamaican origin living in London, Birmingham, Sweden, the Netherlands, Nigeria, Sri Lanka, and Saudi Arabia. Clients were accepted only if they 'are upon the Quran and Sunnah with the understanding of the Salaf' (though it was not clear how this was verified), and included women looking for co-wives for their husbands. In addition, some Salafi institutions, such as Brixton Mosque, offer their own match-making services, though none of the women said they used them.

I met two women from east London who had found husbands through Smatch, and several women said they had browsed such services. But the vast majority seemed to avoid these methods, or saw them as a last resort. This was largely due to an impression that they exposed women to yet more risk, since a man identified in this way could well be a stranger to the woman's immediate social circles. Another reason was embarrassment, particularly for Somalis. Many told me that they would feel ashamed to tell their families that they had relied on external networks when 'the system's already in place' (Sagal).

> What would I tell my family? Where did you meet this guy—Internet? . . . My family, they're very conventional, they're conservative . . . so I'd be embarrassed. (Nadia)

> With [Smatch] it's so awkward 'cause your parents would be, like, you came from a culture and you came from a Muslim group of people that can help you, why did you go somewhere else? . . . They would be very, almost, maybe even offended that you did that, so it's just an awkward conversation to have and you avoid it by not going on these sites. (Shukri)

There were also murmurs that marriage websites had been denounced by the Salafi scholars abroad. Such services, I suspect, are more in demand among converts and Salafis who live in sparsely populated areas.

Some women were also deterred by the detailed questions these services required their members to answer. For example, Smatch members had to rate their 'level' of Islam ('very Islamic', 'I must try harder', and so on) and answer questions about whether they could recite the Qur'an, how many suras (chapters of the Qur'an) or hadiths they had memorized, how often they attended circles of knowledge, and how much Arabic they knew. They were also given a short test on their Islamic knowledge ('Briefly define the Salafi dawah [call]', and so on)—partly, it seems, in order to weed out 'pseudo-Salafis'. Shukri was put off Smatch because of questions about which television programmes she watched and for how many hours per day. 'It's like, oh crap, I don't wanna expose this! . . . 'Cause imagine, one of the TV shows I watch is *X Factor*, it's a bit awkward! [Laughs]'

6.2 BACKGROUND CHECKS: BOX-TICKING AND WEEDING OUT 'BAD BROTHERS'

Once a suitor is identified, the woman must obtain enough information to enable her to decide whether or not to arrange a meeting. Meetings require the permission and presence of the woman's *wali* (male guardian) or an appointed substitute, so organizing them can be a complicated affair, involving the consultation of three people's schedules, as well as an awkward conversation with one's father or brother. Also, women may only have meetings with one man at a time, in accordance with hadiths such as Muslim 3294. Thus these meetings are usually only agreed to if there is serious interest.

Before this stage, women would ask around in order to determine how well their prospective suitors satisfied the most important criteria. Respected community figures, as well as the suitor's own relatives, friends, and even enemies, might be consulted about his character, appearance, family, and—crucially—which Islamic interpretation he adheres to. As Nadia put it:

> Background checks—it seems like FBI thing! I would ask people where he lives, what he does for a living, what uni he went to, what kind of people he hangs around with . . . for people to give me a reference on his character actually, or his religion.

Gathering references was a very popular technique; women took reassurance from the Islamic ruling that referees must be honest about a person's faults if approached about his or her suitability for marriage.

Aliyah, a trainee teacher who had had many meetings with suitors, had developed an efficient method. She would email the suitor (via her guardian) her 'profile' (see below), listing her own characteristics and requirements, then email any women connected to him a highly detailed and quasi-corporate 'reference' questionnaire, covering questions about everything from the man's piety to his spontaneity and generosity.[3]

Aliyah's marriage profile and reference questionnaire

This is my brief profile. Upon receiving the brothers' profile, and the response to the reference form [*below*] my wakil's [male guardian] number will be provided insha'Allah.

> Profile
> Aliyah
> I am 24
> Reverted to the deen in 2006 and Salafi (inshaAllah) (5 ½ years)
> Ivorian, born and raised in London
> Never been married, no children
> Ive been working in Muslim schools as a teacher for 4 years, and still in this profession.
> I am working towards becoming a qualified teacher, only with the hope that this qualification will bring benefit to my aakhiraah. Expected to qualify in 2012. If Allah wills.

Character

Please ask references for an unbiased account.

My friends that I love for His sake, and that know me closely are (in no specific order); [lists six names and telephone numbers].

(I have sought permission from all the above except some sisters have not replied my text yet—inshaAllah I shall provide them shortly.)

What I have to say for myself is that I can be very thorough and detailed I like precision. There are other personality traits that I am not keen on mentioning, as they are not praiseworthy. Though I will answer if asked. We ask Allah for good character.

Hijirah

I have no specific plans as to where and when I would love to make hijiraah to, though some thoughts have been given to Saudi, Nigeria, Egypt, Yemen—don't mind—I am happy with His decree.

I just pray Allah grants me an abode whereby the fitnah of living in the city, and in the midst of dunyaa [worldly life] is minimalized. I want to live it simple inshaAllah. I pray Allah grant me contentment in my heart. Ameen.

Children

It is not in my immediate plans, however, I would like children either from myself or fostered. I just want to do my duty of raising children in a way that Allah is pleased with. I love children, and I believe that I as a mother have the greatest responsibility—bringing up the ummah of Muhammad (saw). To nurture and care for them, I have experience with children Allahumdulillah [i.e., *Al-hamdulillah*; praise God] and I would love to have as many as possible.

Polygamy

I have absolutely no reservations of my husband having more than one wife, it is more desired to me. InshaAllah this is to be discussed further during the meeting.

Work

If the situation permits, I would like to be free from work (that is paid or contracted), rather I hope to spend my fee [*sic*] time volunteering in a hospital, school, or care home for the terminally ill.

I understand that my first priority is to serve Allah (swt) through fulfilling the obligations of my husband and children and my home is where I'd rather be as opposed to working. Additionally, I hope that as a wife, I can support my husband in his acquisition of knowledge and act of ibaadah [i.e., *'ibada*; worship] by fulfilling my duties in the home.

My duties to my husband are to

- Do everything that Allah loves and is Pleased with.
- Bring up the children. E.g., Making sure that they (and my husband) are well fed with a balanced diet, Tarbiyyah [i.e., nurturing in correct beliefs and practices] and Islamic personality.
- Maintain the house so that it is inviting and relaxing.
- Educate the children, ISLAMICALLY and academically.
- Support my husband through; obedience, compassion, consideration.
- Beautify myself with what pleases him.
- Not allow anyone to enter his household without his permission.
- Uphold good manners and etiquette.

- Respect and honour him in public and private.
- Will not fast nuwafl[4]—if I am told not to do so.
  (and perhaps more that I am unaware of).

I love to look after those who are personal to me (friends and family and neighbours), making sure that their needs are met, and that they are relaxed around me and happy to see me. I hate to burden people. I can be passionate and I have caring qualities, which I think is a prerequisite for marriage or any relationship.

I hope to raise children in the way that Allah is pleased and in a way that myself and my husband have mutually agreed.

I will aid my husband by maintaining etiquette, sharing my thoughts, supporting him, and by making the home an environment that is welcoming and inviting. I just want a simple relationship. I perform my duties and he performs his duties. (WITH TAQWA [i.e., fear of God, God-consciousness].)

My husband will have short comings, this is inevitable and I am ok with this, (as I will have more) so long as he is sincere.

What I'm looking for

- Alongside having taqwa, and being fair and just, I want that my husband is an inspiration to me.
- I want him to be able to understand Arabic so that we can converse in this language and that the noble Quran is better understood.
- First and foremost, I expect that my husband should teach me and help me to develop and grow in my deen.
- I expect he should pardon my short comings and advise me in the best manner.
- I expect that he is disciplined.
- I expect that he train me and look out for my welfare; (all aspects).
- I admire and respect a man who is disciplined.
- Who has hikmah [i.e., wisdom, discretion].
- A husband who is easily understood, even without words.
- A man who is not easily wavered by desire, but is balanced, level headed, considerate and takes into account all aspects.
- A man that will look out for me.
- A man that can train a woman.
- A man that can work as a team with his woman, (to be discussed further for clarification).
- A man that I can be shy of.

- A man that is reflective.
- I want to trust my husband, although I will never forget that it is in Allah the believers put their trust.

Above all, I want a husband who truly fears and loves Allah, loves the prophet and the sahaba [companions of the Prophet], emulates their ways, strives hard in Allah's cause, and aids his family and those under his responsibility in doing so.

My husband must teach me, my husband must teach me, my husband must teach me.

REFERENCE

Assalam alaikum wa rahmatullahi wa barakatuh jazzakhaAllahu khiran [i.e., may Allah reward you] sis . . . insha'Allah, if you could please forward this attachment to any of his closest friends, it would be most appreciated.

This is a brief account of my ideal;

- Aged between 24 and 34
- If already married I would like to speak to wife/ wives
- Must have the means to provide for a family
- Consistently attending class
- Own place
- Can speak, read and write Arabic
- Someone who has plenty of life experience

It would be nice that he possess these qualities

- Humble
- Masculine
- Patient
- Understanding
- Critical
- Amir [i.e., commander, general, or prince] type demeanour
- Just
- Optimistic
- Affectionate
- Passionate
- Above all, someone who has taqwa

Please rate from 1–5 (1 being strongly disagree, 5 being strongly agree) and give a concise account of the following characteristics

	0 = don't know, **1** = strongly disagree, **2** = not really, **3** = sometimes, **4** = mostly, **5** = strongly agree					
	0	**1**	**2**	**3**	**4**	**5**
Has limited understanding of the deen						
Fully applies his understanding of the deen in practical situations						
Has humour						
is quick to anger						
He is patient						
Is very stern						
Is very eager and strives hard						
He is steadfast in acts of worship						
Has taqwa						
Is responsible						
Is mature						
Is impartial						
He is absolutely honest and truthful						
He is liked by most						
He is well mannered						
He is good at managing stressful situations						
He is clean						
He is spontaneous						
He is generous						
He has a light, playful, easy going personality						
Has a low profile amongst people in the community						
He is humble						

	Never	sometimes	All the time
Would you ask him for advice?			
Does he talk a lot			
Is he very sociable			

What are his most appealing qualities?

If you were to give him a piece of advice, what would it be?

Any thing that strikes you about his character.

Thank you all for your time,

I understand that answering them, may take longer than 5 mins, but your support in this matter is very much needed, and appreciated.

May Allah reward you for your help, and increase you all in khair [i.e., goodness, good deeds].

Most important of all, for many women, was to determine which *da'wa* the man was upon, and the extent to which he could be considered 'practising'. A deficiency in this regard, along with a lack of chemistry, were common reasons for rejections. All of the single women specified that they could only marry a Salafi—with the exception of Saidah, who said she would reluctantly consider someone open to Salafism but not yet Salafi, and Sagal, who was actually concerned to avoid 'hardcore Salafis'.

Limiting suitors to Salafis was a natural step to facilitate compatibility but, more crucially, necessary to ensure that a woman, once married, would not face never-ending dilemmas about obeying her husband or obeying God—both obligatory duties.

The women cited scenarios to demonstrate the possible dangers of marrying a non-Salafi. A man who was not sympathetic to the *da'wa* might forbid his wife from attending Salafi circles or throw out her Salafi books, preventing her from fulfilling her obligatory duty of seeking knowledge. He might even insist that she accompany him to non-Salafi conferences or that she engage in a ritual that is not authorized by the Qur'an or sunna, which at worst could be tantamount to complicity in *bid'a* [reprehensible innovation] or *shirk* [polytheism].

There was also a common perception—particularly among the newer Salafis—that men who were genuinely Salafi and practising would treat their wives with respect, since they were aware of the eternal consequences of their actions. Dania had sought a man who was 'much more firmer than me' because

> in Islam, you have to obey your husband, so it would make it easier for me personally, 'cause you hear about some Muslim brothers who they're just interested in controlling their wife. They say do this, do that, da da da.

Dania's perception was that a 'practising' man would be gentle with his wife, while uncompromising where 'necessary', and said that this impression was confirmed when she married a Salafi. For example, her husband overrode her when she wanted to buy a television, she said, but she afterwards agreed with his decision because 'it's haram'. Safia, who was engaged, reasoned:

> I'm not gonna know the real him unless . . . I start living with him, unless I've experienced hardship and happiness with him. And it's true, I thought about

it, and then I thought: how do I know I can trust this person and how do I know he won't treat me wrong when I get married to him? And then I thought to myself: the way I see this brother, *masha'Allah*, he's God-fearing, and when someone is God-fearing, everything they do will be according to Allah's pleasure, isn't it. Like, before they do you wrong, they'll think twice about doing you wrong because in case of them gaining that sin, d'you get it?

Most women expected more than simply a practising Salafi man. Having internalized Salafi teachings about the role of the husband as head of his family and as responsible for teaching his wife, the women were determined to find a man who was *more* practising and knowledgeable in Islam than they were.

The man in the household is the breadwinner, he is the one that under his wings has his wife and his children. It's not me that looks after him; it's him that looks after me and my children, so you need someone that's gonna be just a *bit* more knowledgeable. . . . And what more can you want than a man that's gonna guide you to the highest level of *janna*? (Amina)

Sometimes these demands were very specific indeed. Aliyah (see Aliyah's marriage profile and reference questionnaire) specified that—among her many other requirements—her husband must know Arabic, be 'consistently attending class', and be able to 'train' her in her religion, thereby increasing her knowledge and *iman*. Others said that their future husband should pray his five daily prayers in the mosque—yet expected him to hold down a full-time job, too. Abeer said she wanted a man whose 'life revolves around Islam' and is 'more practising than I am, so they can help me with my religion'. Safia, too, dreamed of marrying a man who would rectify her religious shortcomings and help her to resist the constant temptations of life in a liberal, urban society.

It was also common for women to favour men who had studied abroad at recognized Salafi institutions, such as Madrasah Dar al-Hadith in Dammaj, Yemen, or the Islamic University of Madinah, yet such men were in short supply. Also important was 'good character', which many mentioned specifically. Typically, I was told that a husband must be well-mannered, calm, humble, kind, generous, non-judgmental, gentle, and patient, with a good sense of humour.

Besides religion and character, the women had more material considerations. Unsurprisingly, the women with university degrees were more likely to require a husband with similar qualifications—'someone that I can intellectually have conversations with' (Fowsiya). Far more important for most, however, was that a man be financially capable of supporting a wife and family. Several stated that they did not mind what kind of job he had, as long as 'I don't have to worry about money'. They said that they would be content as long as 'he can look after me', 'take responsibility', or 'support me in a comfortable manner'.

The women often mentioned that a husband is responsible for providing for his wife and family so that she is not obliged to work. Should she choose to work, any resulting income belongs to her alone. Many women seemed to look forward to marriage as an opportunity for leisure time and for abrogating all responsibility for finances after a period of struggling to find work (see chapter 5.4). A housewife could also devote more time to worshipping God, partly because wifely duties constituted acts of worship in themselves.

Indeed, the women's language often suggested that they craved *liberation* from employment in order to pursue leisure activities of their choice, as well as to become devoted mothers (all but one wanted children, and usually several). For example, Aliyah states in her profile (see Aliyah's marriage profile and reference questionnaire): 'I would like to be free from work (that is paid or contracted), rather I hope to spend my fee [*sic*] time volunteering in a hospital, school, or care home for the terminally ill.' In fact, they seemed to embrace Salafism's traditional gender roles eagerly. A few women were not career-minded, anyway. Others were keen to stay in employment but wanted the option of putting motherhood first.

Yet there was no suggestion that the women sought rich husbands to give them lives of luxury; on the contrary, several stated that they did not care about their standard of living as long as it was comfortable and sustainable, and some—such as Aliyah—idealized the 'simple' life as a means of getting closer to God.

All of the women seemed to have theorized at length about their ideal husbands. Some, particularly those who were new to Salafism and the matchmaking process, were confident of finding him. However, I met several more experienced women who confessed that they were highly cynical about the prospect of finding a 'genuinely' Salafi, God-fearing, and responsible man. They were passionately convinced that many supposedly Salafi men, especially in Brixton, had not truly left their '*jahiliyya*' pasts behind them.

There was particular concern about converts, many of whom were ex-offenders and had children from previous relationships. One middle-aged Somali Salafi told me that male Afro-Caribbean converts were known in the community for multiple divorces, something she put down to a mentality that they had never left behind of moving quickly from one woman to another. And when Somali Filsan joined the Brixton community, she formed the impression that many of the men were abusing Salafi teachings on polygamy to satisfy sexual desires. So many men seemed to be seeking second wives, yet she doubted that they could *all* be capable of fulfilling the conditions for polygamy, which include the ability to provide financially for another wife. These sentiments were not uncommon, particularly among the Somalis, and meant that many avoided converts altogether.

According to Brixton staff member AbdulHaq Ashanti, some of the blame actually lay with Somali men in the Brixton community, who had been 'scaremongering against the reverts'. He said they were 'behind the back of reverts advising Somali sisters: "Oh, don't marry the reverts, they don't treat women properly, and things like this."' In his opinion, this had unecessarily inflamed interethnic tensions within the community.

Yet this was a view also shared by some non-Somalis, converts, and born-Muslims alike. For instance, when I asked convert Firdaws whether she was hoping get married, she picked up my dictaphone to speak directly into it:

> I. Don't. Trust. The Brixton brothers! . . . There's too many *munafiqs* [hypocrites] in Brixton. . . . Too many brothers living double lives, and to be honest, a lot of brothers they don't provide for their wives. A lot of them can be abusive, a lot of them will just commit adultery, some of them are selling drugs—you never know what they're doing.

She said she knew a Salafi woman in Brixton whose husband was arrested at their home at 7 a.m. one morning for selling drugs, without the knowledge of his wife. At the mosque, women openly spoke of rumours that supposedly Salafi husbands were secretly drug-dealers. Such stories put Firdaws off husband-seeking almost entirely, though she was unusual in this respect.

I spoke to Kareem of Brixton Mosque about this issue. He acknowledged that some of the people—men and women—who had embraced Islam, and Salafism, had criminal pasts that they had struggled to leave behind. Nonetheless, he stressed that they were a small minority. Brixton Mosque, he added, is a public building open to all, and 'we can't police everyone regarding how they behave 24/7'.

When such cases are brought to the mosque's attention, the policy is to deal with it internally and 'Islamically'—without involving the police, said Kareem. The exception would be in cases of 'serious risk to life or property'—but he knew of no such occasions in the past. The first step is to advise the person involved to desist from their sinful activities. If that fails, the imam may 'expose' the person publicly in the Friday *khutba* (sermon). I have witnessed such exposures myself: no names are mentioned, but the details—of the theft, the back-biting, or the benefit fraud—are sufficient to alert at least those already aware of the situation, and potentially others. In such a small and tight-knit community, this can be a powerful weapon; but if that, too, fails, the fallen individuals are banned from the mosque and usually do not attempt to return. Kareem said that he knew of only two such bans—one on the grounds of suspicion of theft on the mosque premises, the other related to fighting in the mosque.

According to community elder Umm Reemah, who admitted to having heard 'horror stories' about husbands with double lives, the majority of men at Brixton who had previously been involved in crime had left it all behind: 'Usually, once they've been on the straight and narrow for a few years, they generally just continue to be good guys.'

The young women's negative perceptions of Salafi men, whether or not they were justified, undoubtedly had a great impact on their chances of finding a suitable match, since there was some unwillingness to risk marrying men with objectionable pasts. For example, Abyan said:

> I'm only open to a particular type of reverts, which may sound slightly snobby.... Just somebody that's from a similar background to me, who had a father, who had a mother, who had rules and regulations, than a person from the street, 'cause I think it's very difficult to shed that skin. You know, somebody who's in and out of prison, who comes from the gang culture.... It's very difficult to leave the street, even when we're Salafis and practising, it still kind of lingers on and follows you.

Safia turned down numerous offers when she started practising because she distrusted the men's pious appearances. 'I see them talking to other sisters.... I see them have two personalities—with me the holy, practising side; the other side, they still go out, they still do certain things.' She told me about a suitor she used to talk to on BlackBerry Messenger who proposed marriage while simultaneously trying to chat up her cousin.

Hindering the match-making process still further was the women's fear that unscrupulous men might—and do—take patriarchal Salafi teachings regarding relationships between the sexes too far. While Salafi teachings oblige wives to obey their husbands, the men must, for their part, treat their wives with respect. Yet the women volunteered many stories of disrespectful Salafi men and of women who had married controlling, even tyrannical men. Nadia had heard about a woman whose husband ordered her not to eat a cake that was right in front of her, and knew another woman who said her husband required 'references' for Nadia herself before he would permit his wife to visit.

Fowsiya said that 'most sisters complain' that some Salafi 'brothers' 'think they're all that and ... sometimes they act almost like they're higher than you'. She related an exchange at the Salafi mosque Daar Us Sunnah in Shepherd's Bush, west London, between herself and a man on the men's side of the curtain:

> The brother's like, 'Ah, it's past *maghrib* [sunset], what's the sisters doing here?' ... And I was like, 'What has it got to do with you?' ... All the other sisters were like, 'Shhh! Don't speak back to the brother!' I was like, 'I don't care!' [Laughs] And then he's like, 'Look, she's speaking back, what happened to her shyness and her *haya* [modesty, shyness]?'

Shukri and Abyan were worried that their future husbands might abuse their authority by preventing their wives from working. Their concerns were well founded: Shukri described a meeting with a Salafi man who admitted that it was permissible for wives to work, but said that 'my wife can't work, that's just my thing—if you marry me, you're not working'. Similarly, Abyan had a meeting with a Somali who told her: 'Basically, I don't want my wife to work.' Another said: 'Do you know that if I tell you you're not allowed to see your mum, you can't? I have the power to do that.' Both were rejected immediately.

However, despite their bleak assessment of men in the Salafi milieu, these women stubbornly refused to consider non-Salafis. They dealt with the cognitive dissonance by pointing out that the root of such attitudes and behaviour was not (Salafi) Islam, which they claimed was perfect and demanded the utmost respect for women. Rather, it was the misogynist views or violent predispositions that these men had never quite abandoned when they became Salafis. Firdaws pointed out that the problem was by no means limited to Salafi men:

A lot of people come to the *din* and they come to Brixton, but what they don't leave behind is their character from *jahiliyya*, like you've got a lot of ex-offenders, for example. . . . In *jahiliyya*, people deal with certain things in a certain way. A lot of the time they deal with it through violence. And, like, to be honest, like, I think if you was to ask non-Muslim women like in Brixton, for example, I think the majority of them would have got into a fight with a man. Them or someone they know would have experienced domestic violence, because that's just the way I think people in south London just deal with things, to be honest.

For most of the Somali, Eritrean, and Nigerian women, the basic pre-meeting requirements did not end here. The majority said they would try to restrict their search to men from the same race and, in some cases, even the same clan or sub-clan. This was primarily due to parental pressure. Many parents were part of close-knit networks of interconnected families that regarded marriage outside with apprehension. In particular, parents feared their role would be sidelined by a son-in-law with a different cultural background. For refugees, particularly Somalis, clanship had provided a crucial support mechanism for the newly arrived, and remained integral to their sense of identity and belonging (DCLG, 2009, p.35; El-Solh, 1991, p.544; Griffiths, 2002, pp.97–107)—despite also being a major source of division in the community (Rutter, 2006, p.175). In fact, after the influx of Somalis in the 1980s, there was a resurgence of clan-consciousness in Britain, despite the fact that it lost some of its effectiveness within the urban Somali context (El-Solh, 1991, pp.544–545).

There were also important practical considerations. Sagal explained that for Somalis, marriage signifies 'bringing two families together', so it is important that they gel. A woman who marries outside consigns herself to life as an interpreter. Warsan said that as her parents do not speak English, choosing a non-Somali would be tantamount to cutting them off from their own son-in-law and future grandchildren. Shukri required a fellow Somali so that he could communicate with her mother—to whom she was deeply attached—on both verbal and 'cultural' levels.

All of the Somalis and Eritreans faced parental pressure in this regard. Fowsiya even had to persuade her parents to accept a fellow Somali from a different sub-clan. They did so only because of their shared umbrella clan and origins in Somaliland, as well as the fact that 'he's a good brother, he comes from a good family'. Safia, too, had to convince her *wali* to let her marry a Somali from a different clan because 'they've got a completely different dialect to ours'.

Of course, some rebel. Many young Somali Salafis test their parents with non-Somali suitors, then seek assistance from open-minded imams in the event of opposition, claiming their parents are racist. It has been argued that Salafi leaders, in particular, are amenable in such situations (Birt, 2005, p.178), yet I found no evidence that they were actively facilitating 'runaway' marriages. Rather, leaders in Brixton and Birmingham said that they emphasized mediation and reconciliation with parents. Kareem of Brixton Mosque said: 'We don't marry anyone here unless it's clear the *wali*'s involved.' If there are problems with obtaining his consent, the mosque staff will involve a mediator from the family's community. If that does not work, they pass the case on to the Islamic Shari'a Council in Waltham Forest, east London.

One of the women's teachers, Umm Mustafe, speaking at a 'sisters' seminar' at Brixton, condemned 'runaway' marriages and advised young Somalis to be patient and respectful of their parents' wishes:

> In Brixton, a lot of young, Somali girls—a new thing that is creeping into the culture—go for black and white men, but if the family refuses, they say they're racist. So you abandon the parents who brought you into the world and go to a masjid and get an imam to marry you! . . . We need to stop this because I'm telling you, you *will* regret the consequences. The community will look down on you. Yes, parents are racist sometimes. But you will have to bear the consequences.*

However, most of my Somali interviewees, perhaps because they were older and more mature than some of the teenagers who were addressed at the Brixton seminar, seemed to have acquiesced to their parents' arguments in favour of Somali suitors. They were keenly aware of the potentially damaging consequences of intercultural marriages.

According to Daleela, who ran a Somali women's organization in east London and had connections with Brixton Mosque, there was a trend in around 2005 of Somali women marrying non-Somalis. But this trend gradually reversed after those women advised younger Somali women against it, relating their experiences of constant miscommunication and even hardship.

One Somali who did marry outside was Filsan. She struggled to get her family's cooperation when she declared her interest in a Nigerian Salafi convert. Her *wali* was 'stirring things up' by claiming her suitor was an extremist and continually postponing their pre-marriage meetings. Filsan said that her family would have been more accepting of a fairer-skinned suitor, such as an Arab, Canadian, or white European; and from what others told me, I formed the impression that this was true for many Somali and Eritrean parents. Filsan had eventually married the Nigerian with her family's blessing, but achieving harmony between the two families had involved 'a lot of work, a lot of understanding' over the years. Experiences such as hers—and far worse cases—had the effect of deterring others. Sagal, for instance, said she would stick to Somalis because 'I don't really want that headache'.

Endogamy was also a safety measure for the risk-averse. Given Salafism's tight restrictions on pre-marriage communication between couples, many women were not willing to take a chance with a man plucked from an entirely different community—for two reasons. First, many felt it would be much easier to relate to a man with the same cultural roots. Most of the women strongly and proudly identified with their inherited cultures, incorporating their specific values, etiquette, and cuisine, and wanted to share these with their future husbands.

Second, the insularity of some ethnic communities meant that the women could trust fellow ethnics' initial screening processes and depend on their support if there were problems down the line. Sagal explained:

> When they marry a Somalian, even if that Somalian is not from the same tribe as yours, they will find out in seconds—a phone call away, you know, what that person is. Tribe, sub-tribe, sub-tribe . . . whatever, parents, aunties, uncles, relatives in this country, outside the country. . . . OK, you told me that—another phone call: OK, tell me about this person, tell me about their character, tell me what they do. Another phone call: ah OK, has he ever been back home, does he go back home, does he send money back home? You know, within three phone calls, that person—sometimes only one phone call—they can find out that person's whole life. 'Oh yeah! I used to babysit him! Oh yeah, he was very difficult you know, we had him potty-trained at five'—you can find out the most ridiculous things about that person by a phone call.

Abyan, like many other women, was extremely concerned that marrying someone with whom she had had little contact would leave her vulnerable to deception. For her, marrying a fellow Somali would ensure that if her husband mistreated her, 'he couldn't get away with it 'cause he'd be scared of my family and his family'. A rocky marriage within the Somali community was likely to receive the attention and support of older relatives, ensuring that the wife would never be isolated or defenceless. For Abyan, marrying into another culture carried no such guarantees.

But restricting one's suitors in this way was problematic for both ideological and practical reasons. Salafi teachings urge a colour-blind approach to match-making (Abdul Waahid, 2006a), reflecting Salafism's general drive to purge Islam of all ethno-cultural accretions. Moreover, Salafis are proud of their ethnic variety, their success in bringing in converts, and their apparent ability to level out racial and tribal differences. Only piety ranks one person above another, they proclaim. Therefore Salafis who exclude suitors on ethnic or cultural grounds contradict Salafism's supposedly universalist thrust.

Amina, an Eritrean, seemed to be struggling with this contradiction:

> I can't see [myself] marrying any other cultural background guy. I don't know, I just, within myself, I love my culture as much as I love my *din*—of course, my *din* comes before my culture, but to me, I just—I wanna sit there with my mother-in-law and, you know, do the traditional stuff.

The women found various ways of resolving this ideological tension. One was to defer to one's parents as a mark of respect and obedience—itself an obligatory religious duty for Salafis. Fowsiya even suggested that a marriage conducted according to parents' as well as God's wishes would be blessed accordingly, such is the respect commanded by parents in Islam.

Also, many women said they would give preference to a suitor of the same race or clan to keep the peace, yet would not—in principle, anyway—reject a pious Salafi who fulfilled all of the other requirements. Shukri said: 'If, you know, a decent brother who wasn't Somali, he, you know, had everything going for him . . . and the only thing was his race, I cannot say no.'

Harder to resolve was the numbers problem that these preferences for endogamy created in Salafi communities. There were many male Afro-Caribbean converts at Brixton, probably outnumbering their female counterparts, and they tended to be open to mixed marriages. Yet they often found themselves repeatedly rejected by Muslim families as suitors for their daughters, due to these families' insistence on endogamy (Reddie, 2009, p.188). Meanwhile, it was commonly acknowledged that London's Somali, Eritrean, and Nigerian communities had produced fewer Salafi men than Salafi women.

In the case of Somalis, this gap seemed to be particularly stark. Daleela estimated that there were twice as many practising young Somali women as men in London. While young Somali men had high levels of unemployment and poor school grades (Aspinal and Mitton, 2010, p.42; Holman and Holman, 2003, p.2), with many falling into gang crime (DCLG 2009, p.8), their female counterparts outperformed them at school and many became religiously observant. They had expectations that many men simply could not fulfil.

This generation of Somalis had also witnessed how many Somali husbands, having struggled to obtain employment upon arrival in Britain, had drained, rather than added to, their families' resources (McGown, 1999, pp.17–18). Some of the Somali women I spoke to described Somali men as 'lazy', 'backward', and often abusive. Yet they were nonetheless determined to find a pious, provider Somali husband.

Daleela feared such women were unrealistic.

> [Young Somali women] aim very high and because they've done so exceptionally well for themselves. Why *should* they look at someone who hasn't academically achieved, who doesn't have a job, who isn't maybe got their head screwed on, they've gone into crime or whatever, you know, why *should* I go lower? . . . This is the mentality, and I think practising girls, definitely them, they are looking for someone who's academically achieved, practising on the same level as them and is of the *da'wa al-Salafiyya* [i.e., Salafism], 'cause they won't marry anyone else. So, really, they've narrowed it down *so* much.

Abdi Hasan, who headed another Somali community organization in east London, agreed that educated Somali women's unrealistic expectations were hampering match-making efforts. These expectations, in turn, deterred some Somali men, who were increasingly seeking non-Somali brides due to their perception that Somali ones, and the weddings they demanded, were prohibitively expensive. They also did not make for submissive wives.

> Men's perception is . . . if she's actually educated and knows what she's doing and can challenge you, she would be very difficult to control; she wants also much money. And women now think: 'Oh well, if that man is not in that category, if he's not earning £25,000, he's dumb, don't talk to him.' So it's both ways.

Abdi said he had noticed a local trend of Somali men marrying Pakistanis and white converts, including a number of men who had found brides via a match-making convert group in Germany.

In recent years, commentators have spoken of a 'Muslim spinster crisis' in the United Kingdom, as educated, career-focused women struggle to find husbands due to men's preference for 'submissive', 'domestic' wives (Janmohamed, 2013; Kinchen, 2012; Mohammed, 2012; Turner, 2012). This has led some men to look abroad: British Muslim men bring around 12,000 brides to the United Kingdom each year (Kinchen, 2012). Meanwhile, Muslim women, seeking men of an equal or superior socioeconomic status, are less inclined to consider grooms from 'back home'. This 'crisis' is usually linked to South Asian communities, but my findings suggest that a rather similar pattern is emerging among British Somalis.

With their long and specific lists of requirements, it is perhaps not surprising that many of the women struggled to find matches, though there were cases in which women appeared to have defied the odds. Fowsiya, for example, had ended up marrying a man with the desired character, piety, ethnicity, and clan—though he was not from the 'right' sub-clan. Others found few candidates in a city where 'genuinely' Salafi, comfortably well-off men of the same race seemed scarce. So, as time pressed on and suitors were successively rejected, some women began to widen their criteria to be more realistic.

Manal, for instance, who had been looking into potential husbands for several years, said she no longer regarded the process as a 'formula' or 'checklist', and had learned to moderate her expectations. She said she used to have what she called the 'younger girls' mentality'—that a man must be the perfect picture of piety and good prospects. 'I mean, you want him to attend every possible [Islamic] lesson there is out there in London, yet have an excellent career prospect.... It's not physically possible!' she said.

Once the women were satisfied that their most important requirements were met, they faced the next, much more daunting, part of the match-making process.

6.3 INTERVIEWS, INSURANCE POLICIES, AND '*WALI* FATIGUE'

At this point in the process, if not before, a woman needs to secure the cooperation of her male guardian (*wali*, or *wakil* in the case of those from non-Muslim families, who require guardians to whom they are unrelated) before she can proceed further. The guardian is charged with investigating the suitor, spending quality time with him (since the woman cannot), and arranging for the couple to meet.

He is supposed to be one of the woman's best tools for weeding out unscrupulous suitors, the theory being that he is likely to be fiercely protective and concerned for the well-being of the woman. However, since all but one of the women had non-Salafi families that were often unsympathetic to Salafi practices, this part of the match-making process was usually fraught with complications, delays, frustration, and compromise.

Few fathers, brothers, or uncles were prepared for the level of involvement and effort required. For women from non-Muslim families, the process was even more challenging because they had to find appropriate external guardians, such as Salafi preachers, who divided their time between numerous women, as well as their many other responsibilities.

Of my interviewees, four of the five converts appointed or said they would appoint external guardians, while the rest tried to find male family members who would take on the role. I turn first to the latter, larger group.

Guardianship automatically falls to the woman's father if he is Muslim and there are no major practical obstacles, but in nine cases he was absent— either dead (five) or abroad and with little or no contact with his daughter (four). In such cases, guardianship would be transferred to a brother or uncle. In Firdaws' case, her father was not Muslim so the guardianship fell to her older brother, a fellow convert.

The first obstacle, for several women, was convincing their guardians and other family members that they were ready for marriage, despite their relatively young age. Somali and Eritrean parents tended to encourage their daughters to complete higher education before marriage—unsurprising, given that many had come to Britain primarily to give their children access to a better education. The underlying, well-founded assumption was clearly that once married, their daughters were likely to become housewives and pregnant soon afterwards.

Fowsiya's parents had insisted that she complete her university degree before her wedding, and Bilan's family had for the same reason turned down all proposals on her behalf since they had started to flow in when she was just sixteen. She said her mother had urged her to 'educate yourself just in case' because 'you and the man could grow apart and then . . . you're uneducated, you've got kids, you need to be able to look after yourself, so just like an insurance for yourself'.

Bilan's mother had learned this the hard way; she had married a violent man in Somalia at a very young age, divorced him, and taken her children to Kenya, where she could not afford to have them educated. After finally negotiating visas for them all to come to Britain, she was determined to give her children the best opportunities, and worked in up to three jobs at once, including night shifts as a cleaner.

Bilan had eventually agreed with her mother's reasoning about marriage, but nonetheless maintained that her family should not reject proposals on this basis because 'marriage is more important than education'. This highlights a common tension with Salafi teachings: Salafi teachers urge their students not to delay marriage due to the *fitna* that can occur, particularly in a non-segregated, non-Muslim society, where avenues to sin are ubiquitous.

Bilan, who was in her final year of university, was certainly thinking along these lines. She admitted that 'it's getting harder and harder to repel people', particularly when it came to a certain young man with whom she was in contact.

> We have this friendly kind of vibe anyway. It might get—I could see myself getting carried away, and yeah, OK! Yeah, we'll have coffee or we'll go to a movie, or yeah, I'll stay over at yours—something like that extreme.

Dania, on the other hand, had eventually persuaded her parents to let her get married a year into her university degree—but only on the condition that, until graduating, she would disregard Salafi teachings that forbid contraception, apart from in exceptional circumstances (for example, risk to the health of the woman).

Once a woman has persuaded her *wali* that she is ready for marriage, she must gain his cooperation in investigating her suitor and arranging meetings. For most of the women, this was far from straightforward. As Abu Khadeejah put it, more and more (non-Salafi) Muslim fathers and brothers had 'relinquished their responsibility', refusing to take on the *wali*'s duties for their Salafi daughters and sisters.

For instance, most Somali parents favoured what women called the 'Somali approach' to pre-marriage proceedings: let your daughter identify and get to know her suitor free from family interference until she has accepted his proposals. Thus they were likely to balk at the suggestion that they be involved from the very start in identifying, investigating, and accepting—as well as rejecting—suitors.

Complicating matters further, it was not uncommon for Somali fathers to remain in Somalia, having little or no role in their daughters' upbringings. Even so, Salafi teachers insisted that young women in this position should ordinarily obtain their fathers' permission before proceeding with marriage offers. Moreover, some women had strained or minimal relationships with their guardians, which made securing their cooperation and trusting their judgment very difficult, if not impossible.

Shukri, a Somali, did not have much of a relationship with her non-practising father and struggled to gain his cooperation in arranging meetings with suitors. She recalled:

> Even getting him to the meeting was, oh my God, the hardest thing I had to do, 'cause in our culture, that's not OK, you can't just bring a guy that nobody knows to your house! [Laughs] . . . They were like, 'Hold on, you don't know the guy, I don't know the guy, *why* is he coming to our house?'

Some managed to elicit initial cooperation but soon faced the issue of 'wali fatigue'. After two suitors, Shukri's father refused to be involved anymore because 'I'd be like, "Dad, I'm not interested, tell them." And he was like, "This is embarrassing! How can I tell someone I've had coffee with, 'My daughter doesn't want you, go away!" [Laughs]' Since then, she had struck a compromise in order to keep her father happy yet stick to the spirit of the sunna.

> The last couple of times, it has been over email and ... not exposing it to my dad, but exposing it to my mum: this is the guy, this is who he is. And if she's OK with it, and I will get to know him more, I will tell [my dad] what he said, the questions that I've asked and what he said.... Then I'll say to my dad ... 'I'm thinking maybe, *maybe* I might wanna marry him. I want him to come over, I want you to see him.' Then I think he's gonna be a little bit more OK with that, 'cause it's not really him doing the work [laughs].

Somalis Abyan and Nadia both had to rely on non-practising brothers because their fathers had passed away. Abyan's brother found her approach 'a bit odd' and cooperated intermittently; Nadia's considered it plain 'ridiculous' and was reluctant to assist in any way. Abyan said of her brother, with whom she did not have much of a relationship:

> His involvement would just literally be, I bring somebody ... and I'd be like, 'OK, can you please call him and arrange a meeting,' and ... if he's having a good day, he'd be like, 'OK, fine.' Otherwise he'd be like, 'I don't know him, why don't *you* call him to arrange a meeting?'

Similarly, whenever Nadia asked her brother to 'check [a suitor] out for me', he complained that 'it ain't my business' and 'this is really embarrassing'.

Hardly anyone I spoke to seemed to have at their disposal the dutiful *wali* envisaged in Salafi teachings, and the women often had to devise imaginative solutions to circumvent the problem while sticking to the spirit if not letter of Salafi teachings. For instance, Fowsiya's father had preferred to postpone his involvement until after the engagement, but she had strategically roped in her Salafi brother to carry out most of the *wali*'s duties.

Several of the women who had yet to have meetings anticipated problems. Firdaws' brother was the only other Muslim in the family so would have to be her *wali*, but their relationship was strained so her expectations were very low. Warsan's parents lived abroad so she would have to rely on her uncle, who was an admirer of Islamist ideologues such as Sayyid Qutb and Hasan Al-Banna, so probably would not cooperate with all of her Salafi requirements.

Sagal, an orphan, was concerned that neither her brother nor her uncle (both non-practising) was equipped to protect her interests. She said she would effectively appoint her practising aunt as a 'behind-the-scenes *wali*': 'They [my brother and uncle] will probably do it, but she'll probably have her earpiece telling them everything: "Ask him that question!"'

In practice, unchaperoned meetings were common. According to Abu Khadeejah, difficulties getting guardians on board meant that more and more young Muslim women had postponed their fathers' involvement until the last minute—often only to be refused permission to marry.

> What they do is their father's alive, mother's alive, mother and father are Muslim, maybe they're not Salafi, so the first thing that they do is they— 'Oh forget that, they don't know what they're about, I'm old enough and wise enough to know what I'm looking for.' She registers herself on a website. Or that she goes out and starts—you know, goes to university and she bumps into a guy in the cafeteria and she decides . . . I'm gonna go up to him myself. . . . This type of behaviour, if it's tolerated, then it spreads like wildfire amongst our sisters.

By contrast, Bilan, Amina, and Saidah were confident about the level of support they could expect from their guardians. Bilan's older brothers were 'practising' and very protective so would 'automatically' investigate a suitor thoroughly, gathering references, so that she could feel fairly confident by the time she met him.

Saidah's father was not Salafi, but since she was 'my dad's favourite daughter', she felt she could trust him to research her suitors thoroughly. However, several months after our interview, her father suddenly became uncooperative when she proposed a non-Nigerian as her suitor, and she decided to ask an Islamic shari'a court to intervene.

Nonetheless, Saidah considered herself fortunate to have her father as her *wali*. She said that many divorced Salafi women from non-Muslim backgrounds had told her how lucky she was. Salafi women from non-Muslim families normally appoint Salafi imams or preachers as their guardians. Saidah said:

> They'd be like. . . . 'Brothers, when they know you ain't got no parents as *wali*, or someone like in your family as a *wali*. . .they kinda take the piss sometimes. . . they can be very like, oh yeah, tell you all these things,' and like . . . 'cause obviously there's [only] so much the imam can do, innit. But with someone like your father, he'd be more determined.

Indeed, Salafi women from non-Muslim families generally had to be much more proactive and alert to possible deception than the others. Two women gave emotional accounts of their struggles in negotiating the match-making process with a guardian who was not related to them. Both had found guardians who were well-respected, knowledgeable community figures and thus alert to the signs of a pious man. However, they were completely un-acquainted with the women's individual personalities and requirements. Remedying this ignorance was essential—yet awkward given the impermis-sibility of mixing between unrelated men and women.

Wafa, who considered her Muslim father not 'practising' enough to be her *wali*, had struggled to communicate effectively with her external guardian. He had thought it improper for her to have direct contact with him, so had asked her to pass on messages through his wife—who kept forgetting to do so. Frustrated, she switched to another *wakil*: a respected preacher in London whom she had never met.

Some community leaders had large numbers of women under their guardianship—one told me he was responsible for two hundred converts—so it was totally unrealistic to expect them to be as thorough as a family member, however well-intentioned they might be. Hayah, who was married to her third husband, reported positive experiences with one guardian, but found that others (Salafi and non-Salafi) seemed thoroughly indifferent to the process.

> They will just sit there while you're having your meeting ... they don't say a *word*. When the meeting's finished, they say: 'OK, you're finished, you're finished? [Claps hands together] OK, so *insha'Allah* you don't wanna meet up again next week?' Or 'whatever, whatever, that's it, *khalas*, *al-salamu 'alay-kum*, *al-salamu 'alaykum*'. That's it.... Sometimes there may be a fee—'Pay your fee, I'll do your *nikah* [i.e., Islamic marriage ceremony].' That's it. So this is why, as well, the divorce rate is very high because these people don't *know* each other.... Things really need to be researched—things like if they're from *jahiliyya* or even if they had previous partners beforehand, have they even taken a sexual transmitted disease test, or all these kinds of things.... Some of these guys—have they just been discharged from a *mental* institute?

From the *wakil's* perspective, searching for suitors and arranging meet-ings for women with whom they are barely acquainted could be an extremely time-consuming and burdensome role. Dawud, a Salafi preacher from south London, told me he had facilitated matches as a *wakil* for more than a hun-dred converts over the years, but gave up the role in 2013. 'It becomes a full-time job,' he said, adding:

> For a few sisters, there seems to be a chasm between expectations and real-ity. Some sisters expect you to be their father, and as such must be there for them at any time of the day or night! I've had calls at midnight. People have different personalities; some sisters seem to be understanding of the role and

responsibilities of an imam of a masjid in the UK, while a minority behave as if your only priority is to find a suitable spouse for them.

In any case, he said, regardless of the amount of time and effort the *wakil* devotes to a particular match, there is no guarantee of a marriage, as this route is far less successful than searching for matches through personal networks.

Once a woman has secured the consent of her guardian, the next step is usually a face-to-face meeting—also called an 'interview'—with her suitor. Those with less cooperative guardians, in particular, had to plan their meetings very carefully in order to maximize their effectiveness. Meetings normally take place at the home of one of the parties concerned (that of the woman if she comes from a cooperative Muslim family) and require the presence of the guardian. Under these carefully controlled conditions, women and men may freely yet respectfully exchange glances and conversation with one another in order to come to a decision.

The women, who were in the habit of segregating themselves entirely from men, were often extremely nervous about meeting under such unusual circumstances. A particular source of apprehension was the fact that a man is permitted, during the course of such a meeting, to request that the woman uncover herself, revealing her face and hair (though she would still be wearing modest clothing).

Meeting time is limited; they cannot go on indefinitely because this may lead to *fitna*, not to mention inconvenience for the guardian. Some guardians ask fewer questions than others, so the women usually compiled lists of their own in advance. They would also exchange advice with other Salafi women about the best questions to ask and what to watch out for. When Amina started to have meetings with a suitor, she consulted a married Salafi friend, who supplied a list of the questions that she herself had found most useful (below, with Amina's elaborations). Amina stuck to the list and said it generated useful—and pleasing—answers.

1. How long have you been practising?
    '—That'll give you an insight into how much knowledge he knows and whether he's beneficial for you and he can help you understand Islam more and more.'
2. Do you want to leave this country? *Hijra*?
3. Where do you want to live in this country?
4. Describe your relationship with your sisters and mother.
    '—She goes [her married friend]: "You're gonna really love this question."' And that's when he told me about his sisters, and he got one of his sisters

married, he's really close with his mum [in Saudi Arabia]. Even though he lives here, like, he's been back and forth to Saudi quite a few times. So that was a good thing, so our holidays can always be to Saudi [smiles]—I wouldn't wanna see any of the world, if that's the case!'
5. How do you make important and less important decisions in your life?
    '—And he gave me an excellent answer for that, it was something that I was definitely looking for, yeah. He goes, straight away: "Put my trust in Allah and pray *istikhara.*"'
6. How would you financially support your family? Work?
7. Where have you studied [Islam] and to what level?
8. What do you expect from your wife and children?
    '—'Cause there are some guys that say "I don't expect my wife to work— I expect my wife to be at home all day and, you know, do the duties of a woman". . . . But there are some guys that say: "I don't mind if you have a part-time job, you know, if you wanna go out there and make a little bit of money for yourself then that's fine, just as long as you know your roles and responsibilities within your household, it's up to you" . . . So I wanted to see how is he, does he want me to work?. . . 'Cause with me, I've only just started getting into what I really wanna do, so I wanna have that little bit of taste in career life. . . . He was quite open about it. . . .'
9. How would you react if your expectations are not met?
    '—. . . That was a really good answer from him as well. . . . "We're striving to get to *janna* at the end of the day, so if expectations are not met, you say *al-hamdulillah,* you carry on progressing," which is a very humble thing to say.'
10. What do you expect your wife's relationship to be with your family?
11. What do you expect your family's relationship to be with your wife?

Typical questions the women had asked, or said they would ask, at meetings included: Do you plan to make *hijra*? Where and from whom do you seek knowledge? How do you feel about your wife working? Would you want your wife to wear *niqab*? Would you consider taking a second wife? Such questions were aimed at identifying any potential sources of conflict, not least because once married, a woman would be obliged to obey her husband. They were also the sort of questions that might not occur to a non-Salafi guardian.
    But when the stakes were so high, could a Salafi woman trust the answers she received enough to proceed? Abyan said that she felt

like I'm not protected enough, just because he could easily lie. If I'm meeting somebody three times a week or two times a week, then he just has to pretend for a good two hours a week.

Dawud sympathized with such concerns. He compared the meetings process to job interviews. 'You're not gonna tell people about your weaknesses, you're not gonna tell people what you can't do—you'll tell people what you *can* do 'cause you want to get the job.' He added: 'In a marriage meeting, nobody will come out and say they have anger issues, or money problems, gambling addiction, etc. They hide their faults as much as possible and only show their best side.' Some women therefore devised additional strategies for getting to know their suitors better and ensuring against deception.

Maryam was determined not to ask the kind of direct questions popular among Salafi women, as above, because they made it easy for a man to tell a woman what she wants to hear. Instead of asking, for example, 'Do you get angry easily?', she said she would phrase questions in the form, 'Tell me about a situation where you . . .'—a technique reminiscent of job interviews. Shukri and Nadia's strategy was to ask the same questions again and again on different occasions to check for consistency, pretending to be ignorant of the fact that they had already asked them. Other women thought up hypothetical scenarios—for example, 'If my mum said that you weren't providing enough, what would you do?' (Fowsiya)—to get a clearer picture of the man's character.

Another strategy was to prolong the meetings stage, having numerous meetings over an extended period of time. However, this requires a very cooperative guardian in order to avoid turning into Western-style dating. Fowsiya and Dania, who both had numerous meetings with their now husbands over two years, took the imaginative step of holding meetings in the family home with the door open while their *wali* or brother was at home, thus minimizing the inconvenience to *maharim*, while sticking to the spirit of Salafi teachings. But even semi-private meetings such as these could be inconvenient to arrange, especially if the woman's guardian was not a relative or was a family member with whom she was not on good terms.

Instead, women often resorted to technology such as phone calls, text messages, instant messages, and emails in order to get to know their suitors better outside of meetings. Filsan, for example, struggled to gain the cooperation of her *wali* so could only arrange two meetings with her now husband, but they also exchanged numerous text messages. Some women admitted that such methods were frowned upon by some in the community as free-mixing in disguise, but used them anyway. Yet others embraced them as potentially instruments in God's plan. For example, Hayah, who began her acquaintance with her now husband via BlackBerry Messenger (often referred to as 'BB'), said that 'Allah sent this brother through on the BB'.

Others professed ignorance about whether or not such communications could be considered as 'meeting places' for men and women and therefore impermissible. Since such methods had obviously not existed at the time of the *salaf*, this was potentially a grey area. To be on the safe side, Wafa found the creative solution of copying in her guardian in all email correspondence to suitors.

In fact, community leaders generally advised the women against any phone or virtual communication with suitors because it was so easy for 'innocent' conversations to spiral out of control. Kareem warned his students about 'cases where people start chit-chatting [by telephone or other messaging methods] and guy says, "[I] wanna marry you," [they] chat for a long time, and next thing we know they meet in a café'. This then leads to meetings in houses and then *'shaytan* [i.e., the devil] comes in', leading to *zina* ('illicit' sexual acts), pregnancy, and abortion.

Similarly, community elders described Facebook and similar technologies disapprovingly to the younger women as 'Fitnabook' and 'deception of the *shaytan*', and advised new Salafi women to change their numbers in order to cut off men from '*jahiliyya*'. Such advice was not always heeded: three of the single women I interviewed admitted that they remained in contact with their ex-boyfriends via mobile phone.

Experienced *wakil* Dawud, however, had come to acknowledge that new technologies could legitimately play a small role in the match-making process. He had found that social media profiles could help build up trust before a meeting, since a comprehensive profile was unlikely to be faked. However, such tools should not be used for communication or swapping photos. Such methods, he said, 'open up a backdoor to a relationship which is virtual but still nonetheless not Islamic'.

Other women I interviewed were concerned to avoid the *fitna* associated with any form of communication, so they devised more extreme strategies to guard themselves against deception while speeding the marriage process along in an 'honourable' way. Wafa endorsed spying in order to verify whether, for example, the man really did pray his five prayers in the mosque every day. Abyan, inspired by friends who used the same technique, said she intended to use 'entrapment'—sending a female friend to approach the suitor for marriage via an imam. She felt uneasy about such underhand methods, but reasoned:

> I don't want to meet him and break all the conditions of, you know, the free-mixing, and I wanna fear Allah as much as I *can*. OK, I know this is entrapment, I know this is wrong . . . but it's just the best that I can do!

Once she is satisfied that she is not being deceived, a woman may nonetheless draw up a kind of insurance policy for added security. Mindful that obedience to husbands is obligatory, three women were deeply concerned about the possibility of being forbidden from working or seeing their families. Fowsiya knew other women whose husbands had prevented them from seeing their families ever again, so she was keen to establish some 'ground rules' with her fiancé before proceeding. Shukri and Nadia said they would actually make additions to their marriage contracts to forbid their husbands from preventing them from visiting their families and, in Nadia's case, from working, too.

Another sensitive area was polygamy, as the women knew that, Islamically, their future husbands would be entitled to remarry at any point. Yet interestingly, though most of my interviewees confessed that they struggled with the prospect of polygamy, only Humayrah and Abyan said they would stipulate in their contracts that their husbands would have to divorce them in order to remarry. While it was not taboo to admit to struggling with the idea of polygamy, since the Prophet's wives themselves were jealous of one another, taking action to prevent it when God made it permissible was another matter.

6.4 TRUSTING ALLAH—NOT MEN

The Salafi match-making process is risky, time-consuming, and fraught with obstacles at every stage. The women I encountered had theorized extensively about how to spot the ideal 'brother', but the reality involved negotiation and compromise.

Some did marry, but others remained single far longer than they had hoped they would, rejecting dozens of offers and attending numerous meetings in vain. Others ended up marrying men whom they had known in their pre-practising days, making the Salafi match-making process seem redundant.

For example, Safia got engaged to a man she had known for many years before becoming Salafi, reasoning that 'in all the years I've known him, I've never seen anything wrong, or any word of disrespect or anything at all and even when we weren't talking about marriage'. Similarly, Dania married an old family acquaintance. Firdaws and Saidah admitted that they would probably end up with their (Muslim) ex-boyfriends, as indeed Saidah later did (they are happily married with children now).

Yet others yielded to temptation, staying in contact with unrelated men, meeting their fiancés alone before marriage, concealing their suitors from their parents, and even having relationships. According to Umm Hamza, *zina* had increased significantly since she had entered the community over two decades ago, to the point where it had even become 'the norm'. At a Brixton 'sister's seminar', she said:

> In the last eight years, I've seen so many brothers and sisters commit *zina*, because it's become *fair-seeming* in the community. Back then [in the early 1990s], I only knew *one* sister who committed *zina*, it was so unheard of, and she was looked down upon and had to go away. This was nineteen years ago, and I only saw her again two years ago. She had to go from country to country.

But today, we see sisters with their bellies [i.e., pregnant] coming and sitting in the mosque like it's OK, and it becomes the norm.*

I was in close contact with two young women who got pregnant and had children out of wedlock during my fieldwork. Despite Umm Hamza's remarks that *zina* had become acceptable among Salafis, the reaction in the community to the women's pregnancies demonstrated that this was still a highly sensitive issue.

One of the women gave her consent for me to write about her situation in general terms. She had been very involved in her Salafi community, but fellow Salafis had started to distance themselves from her once her pregnancy began to show through her *jilbab*. She later revived some of these relationships, but only after she had had the baby and married the (Salafi) father.

When marriages do go ahead, it is far from certain that they will last. Divorce is reportedly common in Salafi communities. According to community elders at Brixton, the divorce rate among Salafis has increased since the 1990s, and it is not all that unusual to find Salafis who have already married at least twice by their mid-twenties. To put this in perspective, Kareem of Brixton Mosque said that the divorce rate within other communities—he mentioned South Asians in east London—was far higher, and that many of the divorce cases overseen by the mosque were from beyond the Brixton Salafi community.

Yet despite such problems, none of the women I encountered disagreed with any aspect of the Salafi match-making process in principle or tried to justify a superior alternative. The remainder of this chapter explains why.

The women had highly essentialized views of men and women that guided their perspective on relationships. Men, they often suggested, had higher sex drives than women and were inherently susceptible to infidelity. Thus, unless women forbade men sexual, visual, and verbal access to them outside of the committed marriage context, they were potentially vulnerable to disrespect, mistreatment, deception, and abandonment at their hands.

They often contrasted the status of the wife with that of the girlfriend or so-called baby mama (mother who is not married to her child's father). The wife commanded honour and respect, while the girlfriend or baby mama was more likely to be used for sex, cheated on, abandoned, or otherwise mistreated. One required a man to make a lifelong legal commitment, normally under the scrutiny of a woman's family, while the other was easily obtained and easily discarded.

The wife compared to a girlfriend, it's a *massive* difference. Like, the wife is someone you honour, it's somebody that you, you know, maybe take care of, that she has rights over you, your money is split, all those kind of things. . . . That's not always the case, but that is the understanding that most people have of the wife. Whereas a girlfriend's a bit more like, you know, I'm just trying to get to know you. . . . Maybe I might do certain favours for you, but it's not the way, like, you don't necessarily always live together and sometimes you find you're with someone for five years and you *still* don't feel like you can trust in certain aspects. (Shukri)

The best man is the man that wants to marry you and really respects you . . . I think a lot of the time, especially in the beginning, what they've got on their mind is, you know, to do *that*, rather than getting to know you. (Dania)

For these women, such was some men's capacity to beguile and deceive— and the woman's to be misled by emotion—that it was not enough to insist that a man commit to marriage from the outset. A woman also had to make sure that her dealings with him were entirely business-like, non-sentimen- tal, and overseen by a protective guardian. This would ensure that charm and good looks did not cloud her rational judgment, which prioritized other qual- ities in a husband—such as humility, piety, and stability. For this reason, the women generally wished to postpone 'falling in love' to after marriage— though a few said they wanted never to fall in love at all (or again), such was their fear of being misled by emotion.

The language women used when describing the match-making process conveyed their determination to maintain a business-like, rational ap- proach. Maryam referred to meetings between potential couples as 'inter- views'. Nadia spoke of performing 'background checks . . . like FBI thing!' And Sagal compared the process to a 'business deal' in which 'everything is ironed out, everything is looked at, nothing is overlooked, every situation that can come up . . . is looked at, anything that might be a conflict'. Getting to know one's suitor was referred to as 'doing research' or 'investigating'; and seeking others' opinions was called 'getting references'.

Rejections were formulated in a similarly business-like manner. Take, for example, an email Wafa sent via her *wakil* to a suitor, which she shared with me. Its tone is reminiscent of job rejection emails: 'Assalaamu alaykum wa rahmatullah wa barakatu, may Allaah reward this brother in all his ef- forts. There is nothing wrong with this brother, *masha'Allah*, but I feel that he does not meet my requirements.' By tightly restricting communication and expelling emotions from the match-making process, the women felt better equipped to distinguish serious suitors from time-wasters and deceivers.

It was difficult to judge the extent to which personal experiences had shaped these attitudes because I sensed a reluctance to talk about past relationships—partly, I expect, since Salafis believe it is wrong to reveal (and thereby risk promoting) one's sins to others (based on the hadith Bukhari 8:73:95). However, many, perhaps most, of the women had had relation- ships in the past, and several spoke about negative experiences that included heartbreaks, male infidelity, and, in one case, even attempted rape. Such experiences, of course, can profoundly affect future relationships with men.

Others had been deeply affected by friends' heartbreaks and abusive relationships, which had made them resolve not to become too easily emotionally attached to a man. For example, Filsan had been influenced by the experience of a friend who had married a man she was already in love with, yet he had gone on to commit adultery several times.

> So from that experience . . . I said to myself: 'I don't wanna go through that—I don't wanna be madly in love with someone that it makes me blind and he can just think he can do whatever he wants to do. I'd rather be rational and think clearly.'

A few of these accounts, I suspected, referred to themselves, rather than so-called 'friends'.

Yet others, particularly the Somalis, had internalized the values of a conservative upbringing, and seemed always to have opposed sex outside marriage and to have idealized a serious approach to relationships.

All, however, were conscious of living in a highly sexualized, 'over-permissive' society in which women were constantly objectified and under pressure to measure their self-worth in superficial terms. This awareness seemed crucial in shaping and confirming their attitudes towards relationships between the sexes. For instance, several mentioned that before their fully veiled days, they had attracted unwanted attention from men on the streets. Sometimes the attention was welcome and flattering at the time, but in hindsight, it was judged to be superficial and disrespectful. As Fowsiya said: 'They don't like you for who you are—they just like you for what they see.'

By contrast, they now felt respected by men, particularly Muslim men, who were generally more hesitant and gentlemanlike towards them. Amina said that after progressing from the headscarf to the all-enveloping *jilbab*, men started to make way for her in public places and she felt protected from sexual harassment. Others reported similar experiences:

> Before, people approached me or made a comment about the way I looked 'cause I wasn't wearing this [*jilbab*]. . . . Now, the only people that look at me would be people that are Muslims that are practising. . . . They'll be like, 'Sister, sister!' And they respect you, like 'sister', keeping the doors [open] for you, or help you. (Nadia)

> If I wear the [head]scarf, I would get ten guys, Somali guys, to talk to me on one day to ask me for my number. But if I wear the *jilbab* and I pass, they all look down, or look away 'cause obviously they assume I'm married, they respect me because I'm a practising sister—I'm not going to give them my number or go cinemas with them. (Deqa)

As their quotes indicate, the women tended to idealize the type of man they sought as a shy and chivalrous gentleman. They sought to revive a traditional notion of romance as a solution to the prevalence of heartbreak, infidelity, sexual harassment, sexually transmitted disease, single motherhood, family breakdown, and rape. This reflects the findings of other studies of conservative religious women, which highlight how rigidly defined standards for male behaviour influence women seeking a stable and cooperative union in societies where family breakdown prevails (Davidman, 1990, p.402; Davidman, 1991, p.43; Palmer, 1994; Reddie, 2009, pp.177–178; Sabirova, 2011, p.336; Woodhead, 2007a, pp.572–573).

But the women were well aware that, notwithstanding strict rules of conduct, both men and women were rebellious and capable of deception, so the Salafi match-making process was not foolproof. The reportedly high divorce rate was common knowledge in Salafi communities, and there were often rumours about unscrupulous husbands. Indeed, it may even be possible to construe that the Salafi process is *less* likely than conventional methods to guarantee a committed, respectful husband or long-lasting marriage.

Yet for these women, the process offered a reassurance that no other could: that the union would be blessed by God. Marrying for God-sanctioned reasons and using God-sanctioned methods guaranteed a positive outcome, because God's will was perfectly benevolent and rational. Similarly, by patiently trusting that God would bring her the right man at the right time, a woman could expect spiritual rewards and a blessed marriage when she was truly ready.

For women who had had unsuccessful relationships in the past, their failure was related, in hindsight, to their lack of divine authorization. Abeer said she was now determined to 'do it as correctly as possible' because a relationship from her pre-Salafi days, which she had hoped would lead to marriage, 'backfired in my face, it depressed me for ages'. Hayah said that after two unsuccessful marriages, she had finally resolved to approach match-making in a 'halal' way, and God had 'sent' her a wonderful man whom she would not normally have considered. I heard other similar stories during my fieldwork.

The overwhelming importance of ultimately entrusting match-making to God was illustrated by the great emphasis the women placed on the *istikhara* prayer. In this prayer, a Muslim entrusts a significant decision to God in order to determine the right path. Many of the women said they had performed the prayer in the past to ask God to bring their suitors closer to them if they were good for them, and to create a 'barrier' if they were not good matches. In this way, if a woman is shown no 'barrier', she can be certain that her prospective marriage will have God's authorization.

For some women, the outcome of the *istikhara* had constituted confirmation that their marriages should go ahead. This could be because of something specific that had occurred soon after praying the prayer. For example, a woman may dream that she is uncovered in front of her suitor, suggesting that she will indeed become his wife in the future. For all four of my married interviewees, however, it was simply the absence of obstacles following the praying of the *istikhara* that confirmed the suitability of their matches. Indeed, Dania said that this was how she 'knew' it was right to go ahead with her wedding.

Others explained how the *istikhara* had steered them away from unsuitable matches. Bilan said that after she prayed *istikhara*, God had exposed the mean and violent character of a man her parents were urging her to marry. Saidah had rejected a man she had been having meetings with because after praying *istikhara*, 'I started getting little signs about his attitude that he just had a little rude, boasty sort of ego about him, like he kinda belittled everyone'. Trusting in God's judgment paid off because 'then this brother ended up getting married . . . twice and got divorced! . . . Now he's been married five times and divorced [five times].' Amina was positive that after she had prayed *istikhara*, God had indicated to her that she should end a six-year relationship with a man she had hoped to marry someday.

> Every time I'd try and go out and see him, it was just something bad would happen, there was a barrier . . . *Al-hamdulillah*, I saw the light and I stopped it, and I'm in a better position now.

Salma, a Salafi of Pakistani origin in her mid-twenties from east London, told me how a six-week marriage to an abusive husband had taught her not to ignore the warning signs following the *istikhara*. After praying it, she had dreamed that the other man she had wanted to marry was dragging her suitor across the floor to a fire. At the time, however, she had dismissed this image, thinking that 'it's *shaytan* getting to me'.

The apparent anomaly of an unhappy, even abusive marriage conducted with meticulous reference to Salafi teachings and the guidance of the *istikhara* could be resolved by belief in *qadr* (divine decree). God allows marriages that were conducted 'correctly' to fail because of some greater purpose, such as the birth of righteous children. Moreover, God tests His followers with hardship, rewarding the steadfast in this life or the hereafter.

Hayah had married upon the guidance of the *istikhara*, only for the marriage to end in divorce. However, this did not deter her from following the same procedure for her current marriage:

> I prayed that *istikhara*, I got married, I got pregnant, I've had the baby, we got divorced. That's *qadr*. These children have a *reason* why they had to come. . . . There was a purpose for us to get together, make that child and that child. . . . [If] you truly believe in Allah, that if this brother is good for me or what have

you, then make us be joined in this marriage ... [then] whatever else happens from there happens from there.

Similarly, Amina knew a woman who had married 'purely for the sake of Allah' but divorced her husband after he turned violent. Yet this did not shake Amina's faith in the Salafi match-making process. 'That was her test, to get through it' was her reasoning.

Most of the women readily admitted that the prospect of marrying a virtual stranger was extremely nerve-racking. But God's dependability was a reassuring certainty that could potentially liberate them from their fears of deception or disappointment.

> No one's guaranteed to have a relationship that's not gonna end up badly, I can't say that—I can marry a brother who I think is the best brother that ticks all the boxes ... but I could end up in a divorce, *Allahu 'alam* [God knows best]. You know, you don't know, so I can't guarantee myself that, oh yeah, I'm gonna have the perfect Islamic marriage, no. But the fact that I trust in Allah before I trust in this man makes everything a lot easier.... If I'm doing it all correctly and it doesn't work out in the end, *al-hamdulillah*, it was better than if I didn't do it correctly and it didn't work out. (Abeer)

> It is kind of pure luck [laughs], like playing the lottery, 'cause obviously you don't know who you're getting yourself involved with. You put your trust in Allah, and whatever you go through it's just—it's a test anyways.... Ultimately, you put your trust in Allah, and He will guide you through it. (Filsan)

6.5 CONCLUSION

Having resolved to marry within the Salafi community, the women found themselves faced with a match-making process fraught with risks and impracticalities, and which clashed with social realities at every stage.

Salafi ideals envision a colour-blind, de-ethnicized, elect community, in which only piety determines the suitability of social and romantic attachments. The men, like the women, would be God-fearing, avid seekers of knowledge. Moreover, the true Salafi brother would constantly strive to embody the righteous traits of the Prophet who, according to Salafis, dealt with women kindly and justly. Parents would be practising Muslims, who understood the virtuousness of both marrying early and marrying for piety, and who would conscientiously guide their daughters through a risky process.

However, these ideals were disrupted by both internal and external social realities. Ethnic and cultural attachments were still instrumental in determining romantic—and, to some extent, social (see chapter 5.1)—attachments. After theorizing at length on their ideal husbands, the women often had to adjust their expectations, given the perceived shortage of 'genuinely' Salafi men with steady incomes and a shared ethnic background. And some found that Salafi guardians were too thinly spread to protect their interests. Beyond the Salafi milieu, many struggled to elicit the necessary cooperation from relatives to navigate the process smoothly.

As with the dilemmas described in chapter 5, the women tried to devise imaginative solutions that adhered to the spirit, if not letter, of Salafi teachings to address the obstacles as they appeared. The rules were often stretched to breaking point, or broken. Nonetheless, the women defended the Salafi match-making process as superior to any alternative. For them, the sexuality of men, the emotional nature of women, and the social ills brought on by an over-permissive, hyper-sexualized society called for a tightly controlled approach to dealings with men and the revival of a traditional notion of romance.

Many of the women were conscious of having made bad romantic choices in the past. Even those who had not were far from naïve about their potential vulnerability and the transience of modern-day relationships. All struck me as serious in their current approach to relationships, and unwilling to compromise on their ideal of a permanent, stable union, whatever the social uncertainties that surrounded them. For them, it was only by following a divinely sanctioned 'manual' as well as they could that they could guarantee a successful—and hopefully happy—match.

Conclusion

Salafism has attracted growing numbers of young British Muslims since the 1980s, intriguing—as well as alarming—many outside observers. An increasing proportion of these neophytes have been women, who now form a substantial component of Britain's Salafi communities. Salafi teachings, though never perfectly followed, guide all aspects of their lives—from mundane everyday habits to career choices and the selection of husbands.

But this kind of detail is lacking in academic accounts of Salafism in Britain, which have mostly focused on men, internal politics, doctrine, and security-related issues. The issues of *niqab*-wearing and radicalization continue to dominate media portrayals of Salafism, while the voices of Salafi women remain largely absent from the public sphere.

By contrast, this research has provided a grassroots view of the realities of ordinary Salafi women's lives. Thanks to my unprecedented degree of access to women's groups and long-term fieldwork, I have been able to provide a more comprehensive and detailed account of Salafism's appeal for women in the United Kingdom than what has been available so far.

Yet this study might well have failed at the first hurdle. Salafis, like many other Muslim groups post-9/11,[1] have been unwitting subjects of covert research, and many I approached were therefore hesitant to take part in any study, let alone such a deep one. While undercover investigations have, in certain cases,[2] raised important issues, they have also reduced opportunities for others to engage in transparent research that depends on honesty and mutual trust (Marranci, 2007). Several academics have reported facing major obstacles to access and acceptance in Muslim communities in Europe due to the sensitive political climate (Bolognani, 2007; De Koning et al., 2011; Dessing, 2013; Gilliat-Ray, 2005; Wiktorowicz, 2005a). Recent government drives against extremism appear to be having a similar silencing effect on potential subjects of research, who have become defensive under current conditions (Birt, 2015).

Covert research such as that in the *Undercover Mosque* documentaries also raises important ethical questions. For instance, is it morally justifiable, or even in the public interest, to secretly film Salafis—who condemn violent jihad and illegal activities—in their homes? This book is evidence that such underhand methods are also underproductive, as the overt methods employed here generated a much richer and more comprehensive picture of life in Salafi communities.

Although I have provided an account of Salafism's appeal and role in contemporary women's lives, I do not wish to suggest that there is any *single* explanation, or even that a complete account is possible. The women's conversion processes were varied and far from linear. Moreover, since my study was based on in-depth, qualitative methods, the women interviewed here are not necessarily representative of all Salafi women.

Yet a rather consistent picture has emerged from the data. The young Salafi women were unusually—though not uniquely—affected by the religious, moral, and gender ambiguities and uncertainties that characterize a contemporary, liberal, multifaith society. My research has identified three areas in particular of Salafi women's exposure to troubling uncertainties. Almost all had received some form of religious instruction from a young age, yet described it as incomplete, confusing, and even contradictory. As they grew up, they experienced and witnessed the vulnerability of women in a hyper-sexualized society, in which women were often left at a particular disadvantage. And at college and university, the women were exposed to a bustling, disorienting 'Islam market' of beliefs and practices, for which their limited religious education had left them unprepared.

Personal predispositions intensified the way these uncertainties were perceived and the urgency of resolving them. Interviewees mentioned personal crises and traumatic experiences of migration and resettlement as powerful contributing factors. Although they did not emphasize the experience of growing up with a minimal (or no) relationship with at least one parent—an experience shared by sixteen of the twenty-three women—this could also be significant. Some had experienced a conservative religious upbringing, which undoubtedly predisposed them to certain attitudes. Others were influenced by zealous friends.

Ethnic and social backgrounds, combined with local context, have also crucially influenced the making of Salafi women. Young people of Afro-Caribbean origin, among others, were pulled in by a local 'fashion' for converting to Islam during the mid-2000s that imbued conspicuous Islamic identity markers with street credibility—and led them to Brixton Mosque.

Young Somalis whose families fled the civil war (1991–present) form a newly dominant group in the London Salafi community. These women had spent many of their formative years in Britain and were conscious of a need to renegotiate the religious practices from their birth culture to suit the new environment. Certainly, they were proud of and attached to their Somali roots, but they had begun to question many of the 'cultural' practices they had grown up with and became dissatisfied with the apparent lack of textual support. They went to school in Britain and spoke English fluently—yet did not feel comfortable assimilating into what they saw as 'Western culture'.

Salafism provided a textually anchored, English- (and Arabic-) language faith system, with space for a sense of 'Somaliness'—so long as this did not override Islamic obligations. So, for instance, they could continue to wear a *dira* (Somali traditional dress) underneath their Salafi *jilbab*, and host loud and colourful *wala'im* (marriage banquets) with fellow Somali women. Some traditional practices associated with Somalia were incompatible, such as socializing with male cousins and visiting soothsayers. But the young women's progression to conservative Islam was undoubtedly smoothed by the fact that Islam was integral to their family lives, and often increasingly so since migration to the West.

Biographical factors and local, social, and ethnic contexts were wide-ranging and significant, but never sufficient for conversion to take place. My research reveals that social attachments to—and encounters with—Salafi groups were also more often a *barrier* than conducive to involvement, suggesting, against Lofland and Stark's model (1965, p.871), that affective bonds to the new group are not necessary for conversion. On the contrary, involvement often came despite poor relationships with adherents and after a prolonged period of resistance, experimentation, and reflection. I introduced the concept of *delayed conversion* to refer to this pattern, which is not accommodated by existing conversion frameworks.

The conversion narratives I recorded lacked uniformity and linearity, and often revealed the process of becoming Salafi to be interrupted and intermittent. Sometimes it was easy to identify a crisis that had preceded religious seeking; but with others, no such experience was evident. My research suggests that the main available stage models of conversion, such as those of Lofland and Stark (1965) and Rambo (1993), prove too restrictive to accommodate these varied and unstable patterns.

What appeared to be common to all of the women was the rational and deliberative process whereby they became convinced that Salafism alone could allay their uncertainties. With clear boundaries that were skilfully anchored in 'authoritative' sources—the Qur'an and sunna—and detached from others—emotion, reason, culture—Salafism provided a credible 'manual' for living that could 'guarantee' successful romantic relationships and, above all, an eternity of spiritual reward.

Among the tools employed by Salafi teachers to secure and reaffirm this conviction were constant references to the 'pure' sources and influential scholars, plus modest teaching delivery and boundary policing. Also, the notorious hadith of the 'saved sect' was regularly cited to elicit exclusive loyalty and draw clear lines between the saved and the damned.

Once they were won over, adherents described a sense of 'inner peace' on being liberated from what we can call the 'burden' of excessive choice, and upon finally appreciating the meaning of their Islamic practices. From that point on, competing interpretations of what it meant to be a good Muslim woman could confidently be shut out, and no acts of worship would go unrewarded.

The women also felt that their relationships with men were imbued with greater respect and security once they had embraced Salafism. Clearly divided domains for the sexes—both physically and ideologically—could stand guard against pervasive social ills and the uncertainties of emotional attachments outside marriage. The women believed in a traditional conception of romance and relationships that, thanks to rigid behavioural standards for both sexes, could ensure a stable and successful union. In this regard, they resemble conservatively religious women from other faith traditions.[3]

Yet as inhabitants of a liberal, multifaith society with competing attachments—such as friendships and familial ties—Salafis are not immune to the phenomenon of falling 'off *din*', or going astray. As with other modern forms of religiosity (Limbert, 2010, p.113), piety in Salafism must therefore be constantly nurtured and maintained through conscientious study and self-monitoring.

Teachers therefore encouraged the women to attend circles of knowledge on a regular basis. At these, they learned from teachers who were skilled in signalling their participation in a long chain of 'authentic' knowledge transmission going back to the Qur'an and sunna. This reassured the women that they were (finally) learning 'pure Islam' and could therefore trust their teachers. At the same time, other factors were significant, such as teachers' ability to relate to their students and project an approachable persona. These were also crucial in allowing female teachers to garner significant authority within their communities.

At circles of knowledge, the women learned about the fundamental importance of *tawhid*, underpinned by the *ahkam* classificatory system of reward and punishment. This system was conveyed effectively by the use of quantification and vivid descriptions of the hereafter, and backed up by theodicies. Meanwhile, teachers promoted a discourse of 'sisterhood'—both in their lesson content and by the encouragement of a shared etiquette, language, and identity markers—to nurture a deeper sense of belonging.

Thus, they employed circles to harmonize self-interest and the expectations of the group—in other words, to foster *commitment* in Kanter's (1972) sense of the term. At times, however, teachers displayed little awareness of, or sympathy with, the lived realities the women faced.

Having internalized a clear-cut framework for action, women scrutinized their lifestyles and attempted to bring them into line with Salafi teachings. Gradually, they increased their investment in the group by detaching from their former selves and forging new relationships, as well as adopting new practices and prohibitions.

However, as they did so, they faced disruptive realities from both within and outside the community. Many were disappointed to find that the spirit of 'sisterhood', idealized in circles of knowledge and by new Salafis, was often lacking. Dwindling participation in community events, partly due to practical difficulties in attending, was discouraging. To some, the Internet had demoted the value of the teacher, the texts being taught, and the 'physical' learning experience.

Judgmental attitudes, back-biting, and cultural differences had caused tensions in the sisterhood, leading some women to avoid socializing with other Salafis altogether, or to stick to mono-ethnic or mono-generational groups. And experiences and rumours of unscrupulous Salafi men, along with a numbers problem related to some women's preference for endogamy, had hindered women from taking the next crucial step in commitment—marriage.

Beyond the community, the adoption of a Salafi lifestyle could wreak havoc with women's educational and career ambitions, as well as with their familial relationships. At the point when they embraced Salafism, many already harboured cherished educational and career goals, which they later learned contradicted Salafi teachings.

Their parents were rarely sympathetic to Salafism, and many considered it to be a form of extremism. Those parents who were Muslim took a less conservative approach to Islam than their daughters, espousing practices rooted in their lands of origin. Refugee parents, in particular, had other priorities for daughters whom they had whisked to safety and—they had hoped—improved education and career prospects. They were reluctant to assist with a match-making process that they considered premature, unnecessarily complicated, and misguided.

Faced with these challenges, the women tried to subject their decisions to the cost-benefit calculus promoted by Salafi teachings. Punishable activities were to be avoided at all costs; *wajib* (obligatory) activities needed to be prioritized over sunna (highly recommended) ones.

Where possible, the women devised creative solutions to render Salafi ideals feasible. Sometimes they made major sacrifices; at other times, they adhered to the spirit rather than letter of the law—or broke it altogether. Yet, basking in their newfound certainty, rarely did women dispute the legitimacy of the teachings. In fact, they claimed that Salafi teachings promoted successful outcomes even when confronted with apparent evidence to the contrary. This was starkest in the case of match-making Salafi-style, which the women staunchly defended—despite not always conforming to it them-selves, and hearing reports of divorce and dishonourable husbands.

They remained confident that this system—as the only one underpinned by divine guarantees—would rein in men's 'unsavoury urges' and generate the best match. Since God's will was perfectly rational and benevolent, and His foresight and power unsurpassable, only conformity with His command-ments could liberate the women from their fears of deception, disappoint-ment, and life's many other uncertainties.

My ethnography has revealed the complexity of the construction and logic of a Salafi identity, so no one theory can accommodate my findings, though several can make valuable contributions. Elements of relative deprivation, resistance, the exercise of agency, and the pursuit of empowerment can all be detected in the accounts laid out here, yet a deprivation- or feminist-centred explanation would be too reductive and restrictive. As my research shows, the women's involvement in Salafism was far more than a mere coping mech-anism or reaction to social or other pressures. Moreover, an explanation rooted in feminist terminology seems inappropriate, given that the women were generally deeply suspicious of feminism, as they conceived it.

In some respects, Rational Choice Theory (RCT) can usefully illuminate the making of the Salafi woman. The theory suggests that individuals con-vert and commit to religious groups because, for them, the benefits out-weigh the costs. The theory has informed insightful studies of Muslim and Christian converts and revivalists (Brasher, 1998; Franks, 2001; Wohlrab-Sahr, 2006) and, more recently, shaped Social Movement Theory approaches to the study of Islamic activism (Wiktorowicz, 2004b, 2005a).

Rational Choice Theory portrays individuals as purposive, rational, and engaged in cost-benefit calculations aimed at preserving self-interest, and therefore counters passivist, pathologized perspectives on 'radical' Muslims and veiled women. Certainly, the women expressed their involvement in Salafism in terms of rational, deliberate decisions, and their constant ref-erences to reward and punishment are well accommodated by RCT. Divine reward had become, for them, a key motive for action and for strengthening commitment, while the fear of punishment was a powerful deterrent.

Of course, this does not mean that Salafi women did not often fall short of the divine standard, or that they always acted with (as they put it) 'puri-fied' intentions—meaning for the sake of pleasing God alone. Alongside the pursuit of long-term 'spiritual self-interest' (Wiktorowicz, 2005a, p.28), the women derived immediate cognitive relief from the 'certainties' of Salafism and—in some cases—a sense of togetherness, friendship, and belonging from participation in a 'sisterhood'.

On the other hand, Salafis' stubborn confidence in the efficacy of the Salafi match-making process in the face of evidence apparently to the con-trary could be considered the very definition of affective and *irrational*. Yet viewed within the system the women had internalized, such attitudes were seen as rational and articulated as such.

None of which is to suggest that Salafi women interpreted every situation in a purely rational manner, consciously weighing up the pros and cons. Academics have criticised RCT for failing to take into account the ways in which people are inhibited in their religious choices by ethnic, cultural, social, and other factors (Brasher, 1998, p.175; Bruce, 1999, pp.126–127). Moreover, an overly economics-based model would misrepresent the nature of religious choices.[4] A *rational* choice implies a calm calculation geared primarily towards self-interest, yet not only does this paint a rather bleak picture of human nature, but it also ignores the often emotional, confusing, and disordered aspects of religious experience—particularly conversion.

Much of the women's behaviour, attitudes, and decision-making—including the decision to become Salafi in the first place—was undoubtedly guided by unrecognized forces, 'deviant' impulses, and ethnic and social background, yet in the interview context was justified with reference to conscious, rational thought processes. Prolonged participant observation, however, enabled me to confirm and challenge aspects of the self-portraits they painted in interview settings.

Even a staunch conviction of the inherent rationality of one's beliefs can be shaken by new challenges if supporting commitment structures are inadequate. Indeed, a mixed picture of commitment has emerged from my research that raises questions about the women's future involvement.

THE FUTURE OF SALAFISM IN BRITAIN

Is Salafi commitment secure? This is a highly pertinent question in light of research on New Religious Movements (NRMs), which suggests that more than 90 percent of joiners tend to leave their groups within two years (Dawson, 2010, p.7).[5]

Kanter's (1972, pp.69–70) typology of commitment (see chapter 4) is helpful in sketching an answer. Where *instrumental* commitment is formed, she says, group participants will regard their ongoing involvement as more rewarding than leaving, so are likely to stay. Where *moral* commitment is present, demands on members are judged by them to be correct and moral, so such a group 'should have less deviance, challenge to authority, or ideological controversy.' Securing *affective* commitment implies a group cohesion and 'strong emotional bonds' (p.69) between adherents that should enable the community to withstand threats to its existence. Kanter (p.69) also observes that '[g]roups with all three kinds of commitment, that is, with total commitment, should be more successful in their maintenance than those without it.'

A picture of instrumentally committed adherents has undoubtedly emerged from this book. Once women have accepted the authorities on which Salafism rests, they tend to internalize fully the Salafi system of reward and punishment. With an eternity of spiritual reward at stake, the cost of leaving could never be justified. Moreover, as a woman increases her investment in Salafism by, for example, marrying a Salafi and starting a family, the negative consequences of leaving will become even more apparent. However, it is also true that new challenges can shake a believer's faith in this system, particularly if she fails to reaffirm her commitment through regular religious study and participation in the community.

Are these Salafis morally committed? Yes and no. Salafis constantly fall short of Salafism's stringent moral standards, and some even commit such 'major' sins as *zina* ('illicit' sexual acts). But adherents generally do not advertise—let alone boast of—their disobedience. Rather than blame the belief system, they blamed themselves or their circumstances as young women living in the West. This suggests that they accepted the group's right to control behaviour, and were unlikely to seek to undermine it.

Affective commitment (or lack of it), however, has emerged as a potential Achilles heel. In a liberal, Western society, Salafi teachings can be adopted only at the price of considerable social isolation, so it is important to replace old relationships with new ones. Strong relationships with fellow adherents promote a sense of belonging to the group and comfort in difficult times. They can also provide, as Barker (1983, pp.45–46) says in relation to NRMs,

> the deeper support of a social context within which the new language, concepts and vision of reality can be 'lived' through everyday interactions. The group, if it is to 'work through' its 'social policy' needs an environment that can both reinforce and keep alive its way of looking at the world, and protect it from the continual questioning and disbelief of those who still hold to the picture of reality from which the convert has defected.

In other words, plausibility structures (Berger, 1990, p.45)—without which a religious worldview is threatened—are strongly tied to affective commitment.

On the one hand, my research suggests that Salafism successfully promotes many shared identity markers and rituals, which help to maintain the plausibility of its beliefs. Indeed, even the somewhat harsh practice of giving *nasiha* to 'sisters' who have 'erred' can be regarded as a ritual that distinguishes Salafis from less 'hard-line' Muslims and reinforces the notion of belonging to a 'firm' and 'God-fearing' sisterhood.

On the other hand, many women were disheartened by the judgmental attitude of fellow adherents. They also struggled to form strong attachments to 'sisters' and to find suitable Salafi husbands. During my fieldwork, it was clear that—regardless of the repeated claim that piety trumps ethnicity—ethnic attachments competed with Salafi ones in followers' social and romantic lives.

Those who marry into the community are probably more likely to remain loyal to it, and it appears that many, if not most, Salafi women do end up married to Salafi husbands. Yet the efficacy of marriage as a commitment mechanism (Bromley and Shupe, 1979, p.191) can be questioned in a milieu in which divorce is reportedly common, and it cannot necessarily compensate for a lack of 'sisterly' ties. If Kanter is right, this lack of a 'we-feeling' may pose problems for the maintenance of the group if and when it encounters threats to its survival.

This lack of 'togetherness' was already taking its toll when I caught up with some of the Brixton women in 2015. Although the women I had remained in touch with were still active in the community, they told me that 'back-biting' and inter-clique tensions had meant that many women had stopped coming to the mosque altogether, or would make an appearance only for Friday prayers. Kareem's lessons still attracted few young women, and Umm Hamza no longer taught her weekend classes, so there were not many opportunities to socialize and make new friends. One woman tried to launch a mid-week 'coffee morning' to help revive the 'sisterhood', but it was short-lived due to poor attendance.

Umm Reemah said the women's section of the mosque now resembled a 'ghost town' most days, apart from the (non-Salafi) older Somali women downstairs. 'Sisters put me off coming,' some young women had told her. Another reason was that some women—including four of my interviewees—had emigrated, mostly to Saudi Arabia and other Gulf countries, where they hoped to suffer less prejudice and to have more job opportunities. Others had drifted towards other (quietist) Salafi mosques, or had lost their former religious zeal and swapped their *niqabs* and *jilbabs* for tight clothing, with their heads uncovered.

I have only encountered a few former Salafis who had totally renounced Salafism, and none was willing to be interviewed. But behavioural relapses were common—and indeed acknowledged in the London Salafi lexicon as 'going off *din*'. I spoke to Umm Hamza about this issue at some length. She said that she had never known anyone to admit to apostasy (which is, perhaps, unsurprising, given that Salafis advocate the death penalty for apostates under a legitimate Islamic state). Yet she did know women who 'still believe' yet are 'not practising'—for example, they no longer pray, cover, or attend circles. Relapses, she said, were triggered by the appearance of new problems and the resurfacing of old ones. Some women returned to old addictions, such as drinking, smoking, and drugs. But usually the catalyst was new problems, such as marital or financial issues. It can reasonably be assumed that some of these women will not return to the Salafi community.

The stream of young British-Somalis turning to Salafism shows no sign of abating, so will probably offset this loss. Salafi Publications told me that they anticipate soon the graduation of four British-Somali Salafis from the Islamic universities in Madinah and Riyadh, Saudi Arabia. All four, they hope, will join their preaching circuit within the next few years, joining a currently tiny pool of Somali Salafi preachers.

The number of Somalis being granted asylum in the United Kingdom has been in gradual decline since the turn of the millennium (Home Office, 2015a), but it is likely that Britain's Somali population has now reached at least 100,000 (Census 2011; International Organisation for Migration, 2006, p.5). It is a young community; according to the 2011 Census, 79 percent of the Somali-born population was aged under forty-five, compared with 58 percent of the population as a whole (ONS, 2014, p.10). It remains to be seen how this new Somali dominance will shape Salafi groups in the years to come.

Another possible area of growth is the *'petit muhajirun'* from European countries (see chapter 1.3), who were beyond the scope of this study and potentially worthy of future research. However, there are considerable challenges, both internal and external, on the horizon for UK Salafi communities. None appears to threaten the group's survival, but they could have destabilizing effects.

Internal Challenges

The UK Salafi community has already begun to deal with the challenges brought on by the maturation of its first generation. There is a range of factors that can account for the high turnover rates of NRMs, including disappointment with group leaders and members and simply moving on to another stage of personal development (Robbins, 1992, pp.91–92; Stark, 2003, pp.262–265). Also, as Barker (1995, p.170) suggests, as members complete their education, settle down, and take on additional work and family responsibilities, they are more likely to reconsider their commitment to the group:

> While idealistic young adults in their twenties may be eager to sacrifice themselves for a life of devotion . . . middle-aged parents are more likely to be worrying about such mundane matters as medical insurance, how to secure an education and a future for their families and, perhaps, how to pay the rent.

The comprehensiveness, rigour, and inflexibility of the Salafi lifestyle are undoubtedly vital in attracting adherents in their youth. But will Salafis maintain their zeal as they grow older?

In tune with Barker, Abdal-Hakim Murad (n.d.) suggests that Salafis are vulnerable to what he terms 'Salafi burnout'—'An initial enthusiasm, gained usually in one's early twenties, loses steam some seven to ten years later ... ultimately, a majority of these neo-Muslims relapse.' In fact, says Hamid (2009, p.400), even figures who were instrumental in the development of Salafism in the 1980s and 1990s—such as Abu Aliyah, Abu Muntasir, and Usama Hasan—'are no longer obsessed with defining themselves as Salafi.' Hamid (p.401) labels such former hard-liners 'post-Salafis', highlighting their more recent concern to bridge sectarian divides.

The zealous young people who became Salafis in the early to mid-1990s are now middle-aged, and even many of those who embraced Salafism in the 2000s are now faced with parental responsibilities. This raises the related issue of successfully transmitting Salafism to the first generation of 'born-Salafis', which began to emerge in the early 2000s. As these children grow up and interact with non-Salafis in a liberal, multifaith society, will they soften the rigidity and isolationism of the Salafi community that their parents formed, or even leave the community altogether? Like other NRMs, Salafi groups seem to be experiencing what Barker (1995, p.170) refers to as 'the challenge of a second generation'.

My conversations with community elders and leaders at Brixton revealed that parents have struggled to protect their children from the many sources of 'fitna' (trial, tribulation, temptation) in wider society. There are only about a dozen state-funded Islamic schools in Britain, and the few Salafi schools in Britain are fee-paying. Many staunchly Salafi parents therefore opted to home-school their children, which requires great sacrifices and considerable expertise. Kareem was concerned to see home-schooled children struggling to read out loud in his mosque classes. 'You have to be very dedicated to [organize home-schooling] ... [and] I don't think they [parents] were that dedicated,' he said. 'Also, they themselves didn't have the skills to educate their kids in a way which was appropriate.'

Whether home-schooled or not, Salafi adolescents may rebel. Community leaders at Brixton were concerned that, despite parents' efforts to instil Salafi values in their offspring, many of these young people had rejected aspects of the Salafi lifestyle, with some even turning to crime and ending up in prison. Compounding the problem, many had struggled to obtain a decent job due to their inadequate education. Those who wanted to go to university were forced to repeat some of their school years.

More recently, the mosque has started a weekly session for home-schooled children, which is taught by mothers with subject-specific skills. They were planning to hire a qualified teacher to teach some sessions. 'Hopefully, we've learned from the past,' said Kareem.

Those unable to home-school enrol their children at secular or non-Salafi Islamic schools. However, they often worry that their children's exposure to non-Islamic and 'deviant' Muslim ideologies and mixing with non-Salafis will draw them away from the Salafi community. Yet Shadee ElMasry (2010, pp.232–233) points out that such interaction need not signal the decline of Salafi groups. He uses the example of Hasidic Jewish communities in the United States, which have persisted through three or four generations despite some orders' regular interaction with non-Hasids.

Another threat is the possibility that Salafis may become disillusioned as a result of a number of recent accusations that male leaders and community members have behaved immorally towards women. Allegations of leaders' hypocrisy, if believed in the community, are potential defection triggers (Wiktorowicz, 2005, p.199). Over the past few years, several people claiming to be Salafis or ex-Salafis have written widely read blog posts 'exposing' male Salafi leaders and other Salafi men for allegedly inappropriate, even abusive, conduct towards Salafi women.[6] These accounts, which focus particularly on the Birmingham and Luton communities, portray Salafi leaders as self-serving, sex-obsessed, and misogynist, and describe in detail the alleged physical and emotional abuse of Salafi wives by their husbands. There are comparable accounts in the United States, which include allegations that Salafi leaders engaged in so-called 'hit-and-run' marriages (ElMasry, 2010). A preacher travelling to a city to give lectures over the weekend would marry one of the female attendees, it is claimed. He would then consummate the marriage, before leaving and sending a message to the woman informing her that they were now divorced.

Salafi women, these accounts suggest, are treated as disposable sex objects, as men divorce and cheat on them with ease, and marry additional wives for purely sexual motives. Many women, it is claimed, develop mental illnesses as a result of such abuse (Umm Amina, 2010). One former member of the Birmingham Salafi community has alleged that a mentally ill woman was publicly humiliated by one of the leaders (Umm Hawa, 2013)—an allegation emphatically denied by Salafi Publications (2013).

While I am unable to verify such accounts, which are often written under pseudonyms, they have undoubtedly damaged the reputations of the Salafi community and some of its leaders. However, it is unlikely that accusations against UK Salafi leaders, even if proven, could cause a mass exodus and threaten the group's survival. This is due to the structure of authority in Salafism. Certainly, such leaders could potentially lose their authority as it is partly based on their moral standing in the community (see chapter 4.2). But it is improbable that this would destabilize the community irrevocably because Salafis consider preachers' authority to be relative to—and subject to questioning from—the Qur'an, sunna, and other sources (Kühle and Lindekilde, 2010, p.86).

External Challenges

Salafis are also facing challenges to their religious practice from the society around them, particularly as a result of developments in UK government policies post ISIS. By making it harder to practise Salafism, these external challenges threaten the behavioural aspects of commitment—such as maintaining strict gender segregation and wearing the *niqab*. Such threats do not necessarily shake the cognitive aspect, but studies have shown that overly strict demands on members can trigger defection from NRMs (Stark, 2003, pp.262–264). Such pressures may also encourage Salafis to emigrate to countries where they feel freer to practise their faith.

The economic recession after 2008 and the huge hike in most British university tuition fees in 2012[7] had a particular effect on Salafi women. It became harder to find work, shrinking the already tiny pool of jobs available to women determined to follow Salafi teachings to the letter. In a depressed job market, extra qualifications can provide a competitive advantage—yet after the fee hike, going to university became an even greater moral dilemma, since few Salafis could afford it without taking out a student loan. Making matters worse, in 2015 the UK Chancellor of the Exchequer declared that he would scrap maintenance grants for poorer students and replace them with interest-bearing loans—making them 'haram' to Salafis. Umm Reemah said that some young Salafis had become disheartened at that time: 'Some have got it into their head that they can't be a Salafi and have a degree.'

But the specific problem regarding *riba* (usurious interest) may soon no longer be a factor. After a consultation in 2014, the UK government announced that it will work on the development of a shari'a-compliant alternative financial product to meet the needs of religious students, mainly Muslims (Department of Business, Innovation and Skills, 2014). This option will be introduced for the academic year 2016–2017, at the earliest.

Another external pressure is continuing political and public support for outlawing the *niqab* in Britain in the wake of nationwide bans in France and Belgium. Since the then Leader of the House of Commons Jack Straw ignited a public debate about the veil in 2006, calls for a ban have resurfaced periodically. Many Salafi women consider the *niqab* to be obligatory, meaning that every time a woman steps out in public without it, she 'earns' a sin—which is added to her 'account balance' on Judgment Day. For them, a public ban would be intolerable as it would effectively force them to disobey God constantly. Some told me that they would consider emigrating if they were forbidden to wear the *niqab*, or at least minimizing their excursions outside the home.

Former Prime Minister David Cameron did not support an outright ban but he signalled his support for institutions such as courts, schools, hospitals, and immigration centres to impose their own restrictions (Kirkup, 2013). Indeed, there is significant concern about the possible difficulties veils pose within specific professional, educational, and legal contexts. Yet a full ban on veils in public places seems unlikely in the near future. The European Court of Human Rights' decision in 2014 to uphold the French ban on face coverings prompted a short-lived revival of anti-*niqab* campaigning, led by Taj Hargey of the Muslim Educational Centre of Oxford. But his petition gathered only 2,030 signatures—far short of the 100,000 required to be considered for debate in parliament (Change.org, 2014).

The most recent challenge that UK Salafi communities have had to contend with relates to the newly intensified political climate. On 29 June 2014, the group calling itself the Islamic State of Iraq and the Levant—more commonly known in the West as ISIS—proclaimed itself to be a worldwide caliphate, with political, military, and religious authority over all Muslims in the world and 'Caliph' Abu Bakr al-Baghdadi at its helm. Thousands of European Muslims are thought to have travelled to Iraq and Syria to join ISIS, including hundreds from the United Kingdom. This has sparked fears that the recruits will instigate terrorist attacks in Europe if they return—fears that seemed justified when coordinated suicide attacks were launched in Paris on 13 November, 2015, killing 130 people.

Many commentators have pointed out the similarities between the religious behaviour of ISIS and that espoused by Salafism and/or Wahhabism in Saudi Arabia.[8] In particular, they point to patriarchal power structures, gender segregation, mandatory *niqab*-wearing, and the institutionalization of a religious police, and brutal shari'a punishments.[9] For the scholar Adis Duderija (2015), certain similarities can be accounted for by a shared approach to interpreting the Islamic sources that emphasizes the hadith, lacks contextualization, and rejects the traditional *taqlidi* method of following the established Sunni legal schools (*madhahib*).

The notion that Salafism is the ideological parent of, or inspiration for, ISIS is now widely accepted in the West. It is reinforced by the frequent and often unqualified use of the terms 'Salafi', 'Salafist', and 'Salafism' in the media in reference to ISIS and the radicalization pathways of terrorists. These terms were used, for instance, in connection with the alleged perpetrators of the terrorist attacks in Tunisia and France on 'bloody Friday' in June 2015, as well as the suspects behind the Paris attacks in November. The previous year, the *Times* newspaper ran a front-page story claiming that two British Jihadis who appeared in an ISIS recruitment video 'were followers' of 'the ultra-conservative Salafi wing of Islam' (Kennedy, 2014).

The ideological origins of ISIS are a complex issue beyond the scope of this book, so I will confine myself to two important points that are rarely stated in most treatments of this topic. First, while there are some similarities between the beliefs and practices apparently endorsed by Salafis and

ISIS, some of these are also shared by mainstream Sunni traditionalists. For example, other non-violent Muslim groups—such as the Deobandis and Tablighi Jamaat activists—practise gender segregation and the *niqab*, and even mainstream Sunni traditionalists uphold the obligatory nature of women's veiling[10] and immutability (though not necessarily applicability) of the corporal punishments of classical Islamic law, such as stoning to death for adultery (Cole, 2009, p.96; Duderija, 2015, p.239).[11] Duderija also points out that Sunni traditionalists share with the Salafi/ISIS interpretational methodology essentially the 'same gender ideologies pertaining to the nature of female sexuality which is used as raison d'etre for advocating women's confinement, seclusion and gender segregation' (2015, pp.238–239).

Second, there are also crucial doctrinal differences between the (mainstream) Salafis and ISIS. These run so deep that one prominent Salafi preacher, Abu Khadeejah, was happy to be quoted as saying: 'There is a *war* between the Salafis and ISIS.' The latter have said of the Saudi Salafi 'ulama: 'Their apostasy is even grosser than any other, having studied the clear texts proving their collapse into kufr [disbelief].' (Islamic State, 2016, p.7)

Salafi preachers in the United Kingdom have actually been among the most vocal and prolific opponents of ISIS and Jihadism in the British Muslim community, devoting sermons and articles to 'refuting' the militant group, and warning Muslims not to associate with it. For example, in mid-2014, AbdulHaq Ashanti of Salafi Manhaj publishing house, which is associated with Brixton Mosque, translated numerous Arabic statements by Salafi scholars condemning ISIS and telling Muslims not to join them. He made the compilation freely available online (Ashanti, 2014). These scholars condemn ISIS on many fronts, ranging from matters of creed—such as their understanding of *takfir* and established principles of *fiqh*—to specific practices, such as suicide missions and the killing of aid workers. Shaykh Sa'd al-Shithri is quoted as saying: 'It is incumbent on anyone who is a part of them [ISIS] to leave them immediately.'

Meanwhile, Abu Khadeejah has delivered haranguing sermons[12] to his congregations in Birmingham and elsewhere, accusing ISIS of using Islam as a 'smokescreen' for the pursuit of power and wealth, and warning Muslims not to be fooled by them. He has also urged Muslims to be alert for signs that their children may have been radicalized. In addition, he wrote a leaflet outlining the Salafi position on jihad and how ISIS has deviated from it, which he made freely available online for Muslims to 'mass distribute' in their communities (Abdul Waahid, 2014). He ends the leaflet with advice that British Muslims should 'inform the authorities' if they become aware of 'those who incite or plan terrorist acts such as suicide bombings, kidnapping or killing'.

It is important to note that by preaching so vociferously and constantly against Jihadi groups, Salafi leaders knowingly open themselves up not only to accusations of 'selling out' but also to real risks to their personal safety.

Abu Khadeejah, for example, has been subject to a constant stream of online abuse from ISIS-sympathizers—often identifiable by the tell-tale black flag on their social media profile pictures—ever since the so-called caliphate was declared in June 2014. He showed me a few of these messages, some of which included direct or veiled threats—for example, tweets declaring him to be an apostate who deserves death. One man tagged him in a selfie while driving up a motorway towards Birmingham, where the preacher is based. The caption read: 'Driving up the M6 to smash some Salafis.' Abu Khadeejah understood it as a direct threat.[13] He was therefore exasperated by the constant suggestion that the Salafis and ISIS were kindred spirits.

The Salafi critique of Jihadism is not new. Salafi scholars and UK-based organizations and preachers have spoken out against Jihadi ideologies and atrocities since the early 1990s, with some even receiving public funds to lead counter-extremism initiatives in the mid-2000s (see chapter 1). But in 2011, the coalition Conservative-Liberal UK government cut funding to Salafi organizations and others it suspected of fostering so-called non-violent extremism—not directly promoting violence, but supposedly propagating the 'intolerant' ideology that fostered it.

In October 2015, the newly elected Conservative government introduced sweeping extensions to the UK counter-extremism strategy, which were aimed at limiting the activities of anyone deemed 'extremist', regardless of whether they supported or condemned violence. The controversial[14] new measures included a statutory duty for public institutions such as schools and universities to monitor and report 'extremism', as well as powers to ban 'extremist' organizations and to 'restrict the harmful activities of the most dangerous extremist individuals' (Home Office, 2015b, p.34). Under the government's definition of extremism, anyone who vocally or actively opposes 'fundamental British values', such as 'democracy, the rule of law, individual liberty and the mutual respect and tolerance of different faiths and beliefs' (p.9), is a potential target.

It is highly likely that, despite their stance against ISIS and terrorism, the Salafis will fall foul of this definition. Salafis in the United Kingdom often oppose voting in a parliamentary democracy, and believe in the supremacy of shari'a over man-made law. Their patriarchal gender ideology includes pro-*niqab* teachings, the permissibility of polygamy, and strict segregation of the sexes—which, as this book has shown, proves extremely limiting for women who wish to work or study in Western societies. Also, Salafi preachers encourage Salafis to self-segregate from wider society to some extent by not befriending non-believers and Muslim 'deviants'. Some Salafi preachers also teach hatred of non-Muslims—though the dominant view is that this should be qualified to hatred of disbelief.

On the other hand, Salafi organizations, preachers, and publications also prescribe obedience to the law of the land. Although some do use the existing

UK shari'a tribunals for personal matters, Salafis do not campaign for shari'a to become the law of the land—nor do they want a worldwide caliphate. Also, patriarchy does not necessarily entail unwilling subjugation: all of the women interviewed for this research embraced this conservative gender ideology as a matter of personal choice. And although Salafis preach a degree of separation from non-believers, they believe in treating everyone with kindness and good manners, and many do actually have non-Salafi (Muslim and non-Muslim) friends.

Despite the above beliefs and ideals, Salafi preachers, organizations (such as mosques and schools), teachers, social workers, and student societies are likely to come under greater scrutiny under the new counter-extremism strategy. It is not yet clear how this will affect Salafi communities, but two scenarios—which are not mutually exclusive—seem possible.

Scenario one is that Salafis will isolate themselves further from wider society and move discussions of the more controversial teachings out of mosque circles and student events at university and restrict them to informal gatherings in their homes and on online discussion forums. One leader I spoke to in late 2015 said that this shift towards greater isolation had already started to happen.

After the new government strategy was announced, another preacher who is regularly invited to speak on campuses told me that in future he would, if necessary, stick to topics that 'won't get me banned'—avoiding discussions of sensitive issues such as polygamy or gender segregation. In his view, the strategy will 'drive beliefs underground' and, if taken to further extremes, could make Salafis reconsider their future in the United Kingdom and even emigrate. Needless to say, scenario one would contradict the counter-extremism strategy's avowed aim of building 'more cohesive communities' and tackling segregation and feelings of alienation (Prime Minister's Office, 2015).

A second scenario is that the strategy may encourage Salafis to reconsider how their strict teachings should be propagated and applied in a Western context. They may, for example, become more engaged with wider society, and more open to a degree of flexibility on gender segregation and dress rules, given the practical difficulties of applying these in the United Kingdom.

The findings of this study suggest that this second scenario is less likely, given how categorical teachers were about the *ahkam* and punishments that awaited rule-breakers in the hereafter. Obsessed with preserving the 'chain of authentic knowledge', Salafis in Britain have tended to be reluctant to rationalize exceptions to strict rules. The Salafis who participated in this study took for granted that one could not justify any deviation from the teachings without an explicit ruling from a scholar—or else a 'clear' case of 'dire necessity' (*darura*). Salafi scholars, who are based in non-Western countries like Saudi Arabia, do sometimes make exceptions on a case-by-case basis,[15] but often do not. This is hardly surprising, since they are far removed from the social realities of living in a Western society, where it is virtually impossible to avoid intermingling with non-Muslims and the opposite sex.

However, some British Salafi preachers and community figures are already encouraging Salafis to take a more flexible, rational approach than before. They argue that there has always been room for some pragmatism within Salafi doctrine, but overzealous and excessively literalist followers have often failed to recognize this fact. Dawud, for example, who gives talks across south London, told me in November 2015:

> There needs to be a change in the attitudes. . . . For example, in the community there can be this understanding that you must wear black and *niqab*, and there's no way you can go to university even as a man, let alone a woman, 'cause of free-mixing. But you go to school, college—why can't you be free-mixing [at university]? It's something you can't avoid. It comes down to learning [your religion]. The religion is flexible. . . . You're not going to say it's permissible to free-mix, but this is the society in which you live, so there's bound to be a level of free-mixing—though some of it is needless.

He also believes that Salafis need to engage more with the political process in order to participate more in their local communities, albeit in a limited way. While democracy, for Salafis, is fundamentally 'un-Islamic', he said there was no harm in—and much to be gained from—community leaders developing cooperative relationships with their local MPs.

To justify their flexible stance, these leaders point, for example, to the principle that one should not seek to 'remove an evil' (for example, isolating oneself from non-Muslims to avoid too much intermingling)[16] if it leads to a greater evil (such as state interference, antagonism towards Salafis, and disharmony within families and society).[17]

According to Abdul Haqq Baker, UK Salafis' 'excessive' literalism and 'blind following'[18] of the scholars has meant that

> over the years, Salafi women and men have pulled out of society, withdrawn themselves from society because 'we don't want to be mixing'. So they ghettoize themselves—and they've ghettoized their children in the process.

A further consequence of this ultra-conservatism has been a vulnerability to accusations of extremism in the post-9/11 age, he said.

These critical comments may seem surprising, coming from the former chairman of one of Britain's most important Salafi mosques. Abdul Haqq Baker still regards himself as Salafi; but since the late 1990s, he has gradually reconsidered how Salafis should contextualize the teachings, particularly in Western environments. He told me in November 2015 that UK Salafis, having more knowledge of their personal circumstances than the scholars do, should judge for themselves how far to apply strict Salafi teachings in Britain. If unsure, they should consult the scholars.[19] But they should challenge the rulings of the scholars if they fail to recognize the realities of the Western context.

For example, if a woman wants to practise strict gender segregation—not mixing with men and wearing a full *jilbab*—but understands clearly that doing so will rob her of the opportunity to gain qualifications or make a living, she should decide for herself to modify her religious practices accordingly. Such an approach would not only help empower Salafi women and encourage greater participation in society; it would also represent the true spirit of Salafism, he said.

Abdul Haqq says that 'dozens and dozens' of British Salafis are coming round to his more flexible way of thinking. But his approach is still considered rather radical by many Salafis because it elevates the role of the lay intellect, which is seen as a key instrument for the corruption of 'pure' Islam.

It is difficult to assess how influential these more moderate voices will become within the Salafi community. But any wider tempering of rigid attitudes would probably happen organically, rather than as a result of external pressure or interference, which could simply displace or even harden them—as per scenario one.

In the 'micro' world of the everyday, however, compromise, adaptation, and intermingling is already happening. We should not assume that all Salafis share the same beliefs and behaviours, or that these are anywhere near as black and white, inflexible, or coherent as Salafi texts and pulpit preachings often suggest. As the academic Meredith McGuire points out, everyday lived religion is not necessarily *logically* coherent—but it is *practically* coherent, in that it makes sense in the context of an individual's everyday life (2008, p.15). The 'authorized', elite Salafism of its official spokespeople—scholars and preachers—is not the same as the Salafism of the ordinary believer, which is constantly changing, adapting, and developing in response to challenging everyday realities.

This book has shown how, despite the literalism and legalism for which Salafism is notorious, ordinary Salafi women relate to the texts and live out their religion in diverse ways. Some are hyper-cautious, preferring to sacrifice their ambitions in order to avoid the cognitive dissonance caused by grey areas. But many others drop practices that are unworkable and creatively adapt others to suit their everyday lives and ambitions. Moreover, adherents adopt new, often more nuanced positions over time—and some leave the community altogether.

It is a far more dynamic and complex picture than the essentialist one often suggested by media stereotypes, on the one hand, and Salafi preachers and texts, on the other.

NOTES

INTRODUCTION

1. Emphasis added.
2. *Undercover Mosque: The Return*, 2008. Directed by Andrew Smith. Channel 4, Dispatches, 1 September.
3. Amghar, 2007, p.42. This does not mean that they are pacifists. More detail to follow.
4. See, for example, Mondal (2008), Tarlo (2010), Franks (2000, 2001), Contractor (2012), and Zempi and Chakraborti (2014).
5. I use the term 'black' inclusively to cover Somalis and Eritreans, though this is problematic in that some East Africans do not identify with it. As I learned from interviews, some Somalis prefer to describe their ethnic identity as 'Somali' or 'African'. Likewise, some Eritreans considered their ethnicity as 'Eritrean'. Yet many did understand themselves to be 'black Muslims', and were often considered as such by other Muslims. Brixton Mosque is seen as a 'black' mosque (though not necessarily exclusionary or exclusively so) by both 'black' and non-black Muslims alike, and has a large East African contingent.
6. This conception has gained academic currency since Lofland and Stark's (1965) pioneering analysis of conversion as a complex series of events. It has largely replaced the previously dominant Pauline model—that is, the pattern suggested by St. Paul's conversion on the road to Damascus (i.e., mystical and characterized by sudden 'understanding'). See, for example, Rambo (1993), Roald (2004), McGuire (2001), Al-Qwidi (2002), Brasher (1998, p.37), Nieuwkerk (2006a), and Zebiri (2007).
7. See, for example, Finney (1978), Glock (1962), Kanter (1972), and McGuire (2001, p.84).
8. Strictly speaking, the correct term is 'polygyny', which refers to the practice of men taking multiple wives but not vice versa. I use the more inclusive term, 'polygamy', as it is much more widely understood.
9. Correspondence with Abu Muntasir (25.11.15), JIMAS founder and chief executive. He no longer considers himself a Salafi.
10. Under exceptional circumstances, voting is allowed—for example, if voting could help keep out an Islamophobic candidate.
11. See, for example, Adraoui (2009), Amghar (2007), Bowen (2014), Hamid (2009), Hasan (2007), Haykel (2009), Meijer (2009b), and Roex (2014).
12. A political manifestation of Salafism originating in Saudi Arabia and associated with the `Awakening Shaykhs', Safar al-Hawali (b.1950) and Salman al-`Awda (b.1955).

13. See, for example, Bangstad and Linge (2015) and De Koning (2012a).
14. I am not suggesting that we should necessarily adopt insider terminology and reportive definitions in academic analyses, but rather pointing out some of the weaknesses of the prevailing typological model for studying Salafis in the West today. Neither am I saying that the typology has no value as an analytical tool and should be scrapped altogether. On the contrary, it has in some ways facilitated the understanding of Salafi trends in the West. Notably, it helped authors to clarify the complex debates and splits that emerged around the time of the Gulf War in Saudi Arabia, Britain, and elsewhere (see, e.g., Bowen, 2014; Hamid, 2009). But its analytical value is highly context-dependent; as Hegghammer (2009, p.251) points out, 'it is very problematic to assume that all actors known as Salafis in their respective contexts can be analysed as parts of a single transnational Salafi movement'.
15. See De Koning (2012) for more on the issue of Salafis' political engagement.
16. In support of this, Salafis cite a hadith in which the Prophet stood up as a Jew's funeral passed by, saying: 'Is she not a soul?' (Muslim 2224; Bukhari 1312–13).
17. Kharijites; an early sectarian group in Islam that revolted against Caliph Ali ibn Abi Talib. Salafis use the term to refer to contemporary Jihadis.
18. For more details on how Salafism has taken the form of political parties post-Arab Spring, see Cavatorta and Merone (2016), which was in press at the time of writing.
19. Svensson (2012).
20. For more on Salafi hermaneutics, see Duderija (2007).
21. Not all hadiths are considered 'authentic', by any means—in fact, thousands are forgeries (Wiktorowicz, 2006, p.215). Salafis believe that these traditions must undergo a process of 'authentication' by hadith scholars.
22. See Adraoui (2009), Amghar (2007, 2009), Baker (2011), Bangstad and Linge (2015), Baylocq and Drici-Bechikh (2012), Becker (2009, 2011), Birt (2005), De Koning (2009, 2012), Dogan (2012), Geelhoed (2014), Hamid (2009), Kühle and Lindekilde (2010), Lambert (2011), Martensson (2012), Olsson (2012, 2014), Özyürek (2015), Roy (2004), Shanneik (2011, 2012), and Wiedl (2012).
23. Notable exceptions include De Koning (2012) on Dutch Salafis. The articles in the 2012 edition of *Comparative Islamic Studies* also responded to the over-emphasis on Salafism's doctrinal aspects by examining its social aspects, too.
24. Geelhoed spent three-and-a-half months in 2009 attending Brixton Mosque on Friday afternoons and occasionally South Bank University Islamic lectures.
25. For example, Contractor (2012), Franks (2001), Piela (2012), Roald (2001), and Zebiri (2007).
26. See Abou El Fadl (2001, 2005), Baker (2011), Cesari (2008), International Crisis Group (2004), Kühle and Lindekilde (2010), Lambert (2011), Moussalli (2009), Murad (2001, 2005), and Oliveti (2002).
27. See Birt (2005) and Hamid (2009); also Elmasry (2010) on Salafis in the United States.
28. But see Elmasry (2010) on African American Salafis.
29. See Baker (2011 and 2013); Churches Together in England (2013); Young, Muslim and Black (2011); and Young Muslims Becoming 'Radicalised' (2013).
30. See, for example, Adnan (1999), Birt (2002), Brice (2010), Haleem (2003), Köse (1996), Nieuwkerk (2006), Roald (2004), and Zebiri (2007).
31. See Adraoui (2009), Amghar (2007), Birt (2005), De Koning (2009), Hamid (2009), Kepel (1994), and Roy (2004).

32. Scholars have classified explanations fitting this mould as 'sociopsychologi-
cal' (Wiktorowicz, 2004a, p.6)—characteristic of the first generation of Social
Movement Theory, before it was replaced by rational actor models—or as influenced by Relative Deprivation Theory (Dawson, 2010, p.5) or Henri Tajfel's (1978,
1979) Social Identity Theory (SIT). The latter stresses adherents' quest for certainty and self-esteem, which 'fundamentalism' seems to provide, given its clearly
defined beliefs and values based on 'inerrant' texts, as well as the promise of being
first in God's eyes (Marranci, 2009, p.42). According to Marranci (2009, p.44), SIT
has become the dominant approach in studies of 'fundamentalism', particularly
the Islamic variety, though this is rarely acknowledged by the authors themselves.

33. The collection of groups that campaigned against NRMs that they deemed to be
'cults'.

34. See Singer and Lalich (1996) for an example of this narrative.

35. See, for example, Barker (1984), Dawson (2008, pp.95–124), and Richardson
(1993).

36. To a lesser extent, comparisons with NRMs also informed Sageman (2004). Roel
Meijer's (2009a) edited volume refers to Salafism as 'Islam's new religious movement' in its title, but its actual analysis does not engage with studies of NRMs.

CHAPTER 1

1. Including the Netherlands (De Koning, 2009), Denmark (Kühle and Lindekilde,
2010), France (Adraoui, 2009), the Gulf states, Somalia, Nigeria, South Africa
(Dumbe and Tayob, 2011), Palestine (Hroub, 2009), Indonesia (Hasan, 2007),
Pakistan, Sudan, Egypt, Yemen, and Ethiopia.

2. While Orientalists once viewed Ibn Taymiyya as being violently opposed to reason,
more recent scholars have tended to view his project as not entirely at odds with
the intellectual world of his day. For a contextual study of Ibn Taymiyya's reform-
ism as a unique and complex vision of theology, rather than an attempt to purify
Islam from the rational sciences, see, for example, Hoover, 2006. For an overview
of diverse scholarly readings of Ibn Taymiyya, see Bazzano, 2015a and 2015b.

3. See Al-Rasheed (2007) on the Saudi variant of Salafism and its contemporary
contestations.

4. Some of his followers founded the Ahl-e-Hadith movement in India in the early
1870s. This movement took root in Britain under the leadership of Moulana Fazal
Karim Asim, with the first signs of activity appearing in 1962 (Gilliat-Ray, 2010,
p.107)—long before the spread of Salafism in the United Kingdom in the 1980s
and 1990s. Today, however, the two groups have a degree of overlap; for example, Green Lane Mosque in Birmingham is considered as one of the Ahl-e-Hadith
headquarters but also as a Salafi mosque.

5. Conversation with British Madinah graduate, 21 October 2015.

6. However, Griffel (2015, pp.215–216) argues that this was probably due to a limitation of the Arabic language during their time: '–isms (or rather—iyyas) were
introduced much later than the ideologies they describe,' he says.

7. Nonetheless, it is important to acknowledge that there may have been overlaps in
the late nineteenth and early twentieth centuries. Griffel (2015) argues that in its
early years, the Salafist reform movements' various protagonists had relationships
with each other, as illustrated by the case of the Salafiyyah Press and Bookstore in
Cairo (est. 1909), which was closely committed to 'Abduh's programme of reform,
yet 'also had connections to the more conservative, Ibn Taymiyya-inspired circles
of reform in Damascus' (p.201). However, Salafis today reject any historical connections between the two groups.

8. For detailed accounts of the history of Islam in Britain, see Ansari (2000) and Gilliat-Ray (2010).

9. The Rushdie Affair was the controversy that erupted following the publication of Salman Rushdie's novel *The Satanic Verses* in the United Kingdom in 1988. Many Muslims saw the novel as blasphemous, and the Ayatollah Ruhollah Khomeini of Iran issued a fatwa ordering Muslims to murder Rushdie. Muslim anger was manifest in protests, book-burnings, killings, attempted killings, and bombings.

10. Hizb ut-Tahrir, meaning 'the Party of Liberation', is a Sunni Islamist movement that seeks to re-establish the caliphate. It was founded in 1953 by Taqi al-Din al-Nabhani in Jerusalem and now has a presence in around forty countries.

11. A revivalist Islamic movement founded by Abul A'la Mawdudi (1903–1979) in British India in 1941. Its emphasis on political activism and on the creation of an Islamic state has led it to be described by outside observers as 'Islamist'.

12. For an overview of some of the main Islamic reform movements that have emerged in Britain, see Gilliat-Ray (2010).

13. See Bowen (2014, pp.60–69) on the early JIMAS years.

14. The Deobandi Islamic revivalist movement originated in Deoband, northern India, in 1867 and focuses on the practice of Sufism alongside observance of (Hanafi) Islamic law (Gilliat-Ray, 2010, p.87). The Deobandis have a larger network of mosques than any other Islamic faction in Britain (Naqshbandi, 2015).

15. The Barelwi movement promotes practices such as the veneration of saints, visiting the tombs of holy Muslims, and the following of Sufi teachers. The name comes from the north Indian town of Bareilly, the hometown of the movement's main leader Ahmed Riza Khan (1856–1921).

16. Interview with the author.

17. Interviews with the author.

18. See, for example, Abou El Fadl (2006).

19. See, for example, Bowen (2014), De Koning (2009), Elmasry (2010), Hamid (2009), Hasan (2007), Hroub (2009), and International Crisis Group (2004).

20. I do not mean to suggest that all Madinah graduates came to adopt a Salafi or Wahhabi interpretation.

21. There were also bitter intra-Salafi disputes in the United States during the 1990s; see ElMasry (2010).

22. Correspondence with Abu Muntasir (25.11.15).

23. See Philip Johnston (2007).

24. See BBC News Online (2006).

25. See BBC News Online (2001).

26. Interview with Abdul Haqq Baker, former director of IMPACT.

27. See Lambert (2011), *Countering Al-Qaeda in London: Police and Muslims in Partnership*, and Baker (2011), *Extremists in our Midst: Confronting Terror.*

28. The only earlier convert-managed mosques of which I am aware are Abdullah Quilliam's Liverpool Muslim Institute (est. 1889) and possibly Dr Gottlieb Wilhelm Leitner's mosque at Woking (est. 1889), though it is not known whether Dr Leitner converted to Islam.

29. Commonly used terminology among Muslims to refer to converts to Islam. The term 'revert' emphasizes Muslims' belief that everyone is born with a natural predisposition to Islam, but may be brought up to accept different belief systems.

30. The Nation of Islam is an Islamic movement founded by Wallace D. Fard in Detroit, Michigan, in the 1930s. He believed that Islam was the true religion for blacks, who were superior to whites. The group mixes Islam with black nationalism and is criticized for being 'black supremacist'.

31. *Salla Allahu 'alayhi wa-sallam*—may God honour him and grant him peace.
32. See Lambert (2011), especially chap. 8.
33. Militant Islamist cleric of Egyptian origin who preached at and around Finsbury Park Mosque in north London between 1997 and 2004. In 2015 he was sentenced to life in prison in the United States for terrorism offences.
34. Interview with Brixton Mosque leaders.
35. Spokesman of Al-Muhajiroun successor organizations.
36. Former head of Al-Muhajiroun.
37. American-Yemeni preacher (1971–2011) believed to have inspired terrorists and would-be terrorists.
38. Note that the STREET project had no direct relationship to Brixton Mosque.
39. See also George Mavrommatis (2010).
40. Naqshbandi, 2015 (www.MuslimsInBritain.org). Note these are estimates based on the mosques, halls, prayer rooms, and mosques under construction of which Naqshbandi was aware as of November 2015. Naqshbandi identifies Salafi mosques through a combination of criteria: *fiqh* practice observed first hand; the mosque self-defining as Salafi or Ahl-e-Hadith; references (books in the mosque or links on the website) that are exclusive to Salafi sources and scholars; affiliation to a Salafi umbrella organization; and the contributions and corrections received from users of his directory website.
41. Some of Geelhoed's (2011, p.167) 'fundamentalist' Dutch Muslim interviewees expressed a desire to migrate to Britain for the same reasons, and four did so.

CHAPTER 2

1. I spoke to many women informally, and have given some of them pseudonyms. However, they do not appear in 'Information on Interviewees' because I was unable to collect data systematically about them.
2. These twenty-three interviewees are Abeer, Abyan, Amina, Bilan, Dania, Deqa, Filsan, Firdaws, Fowsiya, Hayah, Humayrah, Iman, Madeeha, Manal, Maryam, Nadia, Safia, Sagal, Saidah, Shukri, Wafa, Warda, and Warsan. For more information about them, see 'Information on Interviewees'.
3. General regions are given where reference to a specific country could compromise anonymity.
4. According to Charlie Ball (2013), only around 27 to 40 percent of the UK population had degrees around the time fieldwork was conducted, compared with 70 percent of my interview sample (including degrees the women were in the process of completing).
5. There is already an extensive body of literature that has convincingly demonstrated the agency of conservative or 'fundamentalist', hijab-wearing Muslim women (e.g., Ahmed, 2011; Amir-Moazami, 2010; Badran, 2006; Contractor, 2012; Franks, 2000, 2001; Mahmood, 2005; Tarlo, 2010).
6. The only exception of which I am aware is Geelhoed (2014), who did three-and-a-half months of fieldwork in the United Kingdom.
7. Anne Akeroyd (1984, p.147) and Marta Bolognani (2007, p.284) also point out the problems consent forms pose in sensitive research settings.
8. For example, Davidman, 1991, p.54.
9. See also Davidman (1991, p.53) and Luhrmann (1989, p.15).
10. Salafis see themselves as a minority 'saved sect', the only one saved from Hell in the afterlife, referring to hadiths such as Tirmidhi 2565, Abu Dawud 3980, and Ibn Majah 3982–83.

CHAPTER 3

1. I use 'parents' as shorthand for 'parents or guardians' hereafter. One interviewee, Sagal, is an orphan and was raised by her aunt.

2. *Jahiliyya* usually refers to the pre-Islamic historical age, but in the British Salafi lexicon it typically refers to an individual's 'pre-Salafi' days.

3. For information on the psychological effects of the migration experience for Somali refugees in the United Kingdom, see McCrone et al. (2005) and Warfa et al. (2012).

4. See Tesfagiorgios (2005) for background on Eritrean refugees in Britain and Thiollet (2007) for information on Eritrean migration to the Arab world, including Saudi Arabia.

5. I.e., the *shahada*, five daily prayers, zakat (annual charitable payment of a fixed portion of one's wealth), fasting during Ramadan, and the hajj (pilgrimage to Mecca, Saudi Arabia).

6. See Baker (2001, ch.2), for details of other confrontations.

7. See Hosken (2012).

8. See BBC News Online (2005) and Ashford, France, and Bonnici (2007).

9. Hamid (2007, 2009) gives an overview of the main Islamic groups popular among Muslim youth in Britain, and the competitive atmosphere in which they operated, during the 1990s and 2000s.

10. Based on a hadith in which the Prophet is reported to have said that just one sect will be saved from Hell (Tirmidhi 2565, Abu Dawud 3980, and Ibn Majah 3982–3983).

11. Also see Peter Hopkins' (2011) study of Muslim students in Britain regarding their alienation from the drinking culture. In 2012 London Metropolitan University considered introducing alcohol-free areas to cater for students, particularly Muslims, who consider alcohol to be immoral (BBC News Online, 2012).

12. Sometimes Salafis of the 'exclusivist' variety, for example, set up splinter groups to promote their *da'wa*, separate from ISOCs, which they see as too inclusive.

13. Abdulmutallab was a Nigerian who tried to bomb a passenger aircraft on Christmas Day in 2009. He was found to have connections with Al-Qa'ida in the Arabian Peninsula and the radical preacher Anwar Al-Awlaki.

14. See, for example, The Centre for Social Cohesion (2010), Quilliam (2010), Home Office (2011), and Sutton and Stuart (2012).

15. See, for example, Allen (2011) and the Caldicott Report (2010).

16. See Baker (2011) and Lambert (2011). However, Baker told me that, at least during his time as chairman of the mosque (1994–2009), 'we have never worked for any government or received funding from governments here or abroad. We've never spied or informed on Muslims for the authorities.'

17. This is the Islamic doctrine of *hisba*, taken from various Qur'anic verses and hadiths, which Salafis interpret to mean that Muslims are Islamically obligated whenever they are able to advocate 'good' and repudiate 'evil' by their actions, speech, and 'heart' (except where this would lead to a greater evil). Repudiating evil 'with the hand' (i.e., taking action to stop it) carries a greater reward than doing so 'with the tongue' (i.e., speaking against it), which is preferable to hating the evil 'in the heart'.

18. In the sense of putting forward the refutations of scholars and preachers.

19. *My Brother, the Islamist*, 2011. Directed by Robb Leech. BBC3, 11 April.

20. See, for example, Barker (1984), Dawson (2008, p.77), De Koning (2009), and Wiktorowicz (2001, 2005a).

21. Peter Berger (1990, p.45) coined the expression 'plausibility structure' to refer to the social processes that construct and maintain a particular religious (or any other) reality.
22. As quoted in Abdul-Waahid (n.d.a).
23. Correspondence with two ex–Al-Muhajiroun associates.
24. Though not eternally for those who remained in the fold of Islam.

CHAPTER 4

1. See, for example, Barker (1984).
2. Charity: zakat is an Islamically obligatory annual payment of a fixed portion of one's wealth, whereas *sadaqa* is any non-obligatory donation. These sums may be paid by husbands on behalf of wives, and are proportionate to what adherents can afford.
3. This term reflects the terminology used by Salafis: such gatherings are referred to as *halaqat*, literally 'circles'.
4. Al-Hilaalee, n.d., pp.20–21, cited in Brixton Mosque e-newsletter, 5 October 2010.
5. *Subhanahu wa-ta'ala*—may He be glorified and exalted.
6. I could not estimate the number of male attendees because of gender segregation.
7. See, for example, Barker (1993) and Wiktorowicz (2005a).
8. See Meijer (2011, p.379) and Wiktorowicz (2001, pp.120–146).
9. An example from one of my circles: the Qur'an (2:219) forbids *khamr*, usually understood as wine or substances that intoxicate; therefore, by analogy, spirits and other intoxicants are also impermissible, despite not being explicitly mentioned in the Qur'an.
10. See also Gauvain (2013, pp.115–122) on authority in Egyptian Salafism.
11. See, for example, Ammerman (1987, p.183).
12. See Messick (1993), especially chap. 4.
13. Theodicies are attempts to reconcile God's omnipotence, omniscience, and omnibenevolence with the existence of evil or suffering in the world. See Weber (1964, pp.138–150).
14. I.e., *yarhamuk Allah* (may Allah have mercy on you).
15. Referring to BlackBerry instant messaging.
16. See Becker (2009) on Salafi online forums.

CHAPTER 5

1. David Bromley and Anson Shupe Jr. (1979, pp.178–179) and Thomas Robbins (1992, p.91) made this observation about other NRMs.
2. Firdaws, Iman, and Wafa all had siblings who had also converted to Islam, like their sisters.
3. 'Brainwashing' is an explanation commonly given by parents who are concerned about their children's engagement with new religions (Barker, 1989).
4. For more on Salafi interpretations of veiling, see Bin Baaz et al. (2008).

CHAPTER 6

1. A small town in north-west Yemen where the famous Salafi shaykh Muqbil bin Hadi al-Wadi'i established Madrasah Dar al-Hadith, an Islamic educational institution.
2. Some women seemed reluctant to talk about this, so the number may well be higher.

3. Some details have been changed or omitted to maintain anonymity.
4. I.e., *nafl*; voluntary fasting. According to Salafi teachings, wives must seek permission from their husbands before doing voluntary (i.e., non-compulsory) fasts. This is related to the husband's right to sexual relations with his wife, since sex is forbidden during fasting periods (Ahmad Abu Saif, 2004, pp.116–117).

CONCLUSION

1. For example, the first *Undercover Mosque* documentary (2007); the documentary *Lessons in Hate and Violence* (2011); and Theo Padnos' book *Undercover Muslim: A Journey into Yemen* (2011).
2. For example, *Lessons in Hate and Violence* led to the imprisonment of a religious teacher for assaulting boys; and another documentary, *Secrets of Britain's Sharia Councils* (2013), revealed how a shari'a court had discouraged domestic abuse victims from involving the police.
3. See, for example, Davidman (1990, p.402; 1991, p.43), Palmer (1994), Reddie (2009, pp.177–178), Sabirova (2011, p.336), and Woodhead (2007a, pp.572–573).
4. For this criticism of RCT and many others, see Bruce (1999).
5. See, for example, Barker (1984) on the Unification Church.
6. See, for example, Adan_1 (2009), Johnpi (2009), Umm Amina (2010), and Umm Hawa (2013). Also, the US-based site http://protectmuslimsisters.com.
7. Many students now pay £9,000 in tuition fees per year. Before 2012, they paid a maximum of £3,290.
8. 'Salafism' and 'Wahhabism' are often used interchangeably.
9. See, for example, Alvi (2014).
10. Veiling the head, but not necessarily the face.
11. See also Bowen (2014b).
12. See, for example, Abdul Waahid (2015a, 2015b).
13. See also video of Abu Haleema (2015), an associate of Anjem Choudary, and three masked men standing threateningly on the rooftops of a take-away one block from the Salafi Mosque in Birmingham. He was later banned from using social media to promote his views.
14. For criticisms of the new policy see, for example, Kazmi (2015), Anderson (2015), Dodd and Travis (2015), and Anon (2015).
15. For an example of this, see Bazmul (2015). Here, the Mecca-based scholar Muhammad bin 'Umar Bazmul advises a young woman studying in a mixed university not to abandon her studies unless 'she is unable to maintain her hijab or she fears for her religion'.
16. Note that intermingling with non-Muslims is not inherently an 'evil'; under certain conditions, it is wholly in accordance with Salafi teachings (see introduction).
17. See, for example, hadith 34 of Al-Nawawi's *Forty Hadith* and accompanying commentary (Zarabozo, n.d., p.994).
18. His use of this expression implies that he detects an element of hypocrisy here, as this is the same accusation Salafis make about other Muslims who, for example, 'blindly follow' the *madhahib*.
19. Abdul Haqq bases this on the Qur'anic verse 16:43: 'So ask of those who know the Scripture [learned men of the Taurat (Torah) and the Injeel (Gospel)], if you know not.'

GLOSSARY

'Alim	Scholar
'Awra	Intimate parts of the body that should not be exposed to the opposite sex (or, for certain body parts, the same sex) for reasons of modesty
'Ibada	Worship
'Ilm	Knowledge of Islam
'Ulama	Scholars trained in Islamic sciences
'Umra	The lesser hajj
Abaya	Women's robe-like dress
Ahkam	Plural of *hukm*
Ahl al-batil	People of falsehood
Ahl al-bid'a	People of *bid'a*
Akhira	Afterlife
Al-amr bi-l-ma'ruf wa-l-nahy 'an al-munkar	Doctrine of enjoining good and forbidding evil
Al-firqa al-najiya	The saved sect
Al-hamdulillah	Praise God
Allahu 'alam	Allah knows best
Al-salaf al-salih	The pious predecessors, namely the first three generations of Muslims
Al-salamu 'alaykum wa rahmatullahi wa barakatuh	May the peace, mercy, and blessings of God be unto you; full version of the Islamic greeting, the first part of which means 'peace be unto you'

Al-wala' wa-l-bara'	Doctrine of loyalty and disavowal
Amir	Commander, general, or prince; historically, the caliph's title
Asr	Mid-afternoon prayer
Astaghfirullah	I seek God's forgiveness
Aya	Verse of the Qur'an
Ayaah	Alternative spelling of *aya*
Batil	False, falsehood
Bid'a	Reprehensible innovation of Islamic beliefs and practices
Dalil	Evidence or proof from the Qur'an and/or sunna
Darura	A state of dire necessity, when one can omit doing something *wajib* or do something *haram*
Da'wa	Call; Preaching to call others (Muslim or non-Muslim) to 'true' Islam
Deen	Alternative spelling of *din*
Din	(Islamic) religion
Dira	Somali traditional dress
Du'a	Personal prayers, supplications
Dunya	Worldliness, worldly life
Fajr	The dawn prayer; the first of the five daily prayers
Fatwa	Advisory opinion issued by a recognized Islamic legal authority in response to a specific question
Fiqh	Islamic jurisprudence; the Islamic science that is the product of human efforts to decipher the shari'a
Firdaws	The highest level of Paradise
Fitna	Trial, tribulation, temptation
Free-mixing	Intermingling of the sexes; excludes interactions between close family members and spouses
Ghiba	Back-biting
Hadith	Reports of the sayings and actions of the Prophet and other early Muslims
Hajj	Pilgrimage to Mecca, Saudi Arabia
Halal	Islamically permissible
Halaqa	Circle, gathering for Islamic knowledge-seeking around a teacher
Halaqat	Plural of *halaqa*
Haqq	Truth

Haram	Islamically forbidden; a *hukm*
Hawza	Seminary where Shi'a Muslim clerics are trained
Haya	Modesty, shyness
Hijab	Muslim women's head coverings; may also refer to larger coverings (such as the *jilbab*)
Hijra	Migration for religious reasons, usually from a non-Muslim country to a Muslim one
Hikma	Wisdom, discretion
Hizbi	Partisan
Hizbiyya	Partisanship
Hukm	Ruling (as applied to actions)
Iftar	The breaking of the fast at sunset during Ramadan
Ijma'	Consensus of Muslim scholars
Ijtihad	Reasoning about Islamic law independently of any school of jurisprudence by an Islamic scholar
Ikhlas	Sincerity, a purified intention; i.e., an intention to do something for the sake of God
Iman	Personal faith, which is proportionate to the soundness of a person's beliefs, words, and deeds
Insha'Allah	God willing
Jahiliyya	Pre-Islamic age of ignorance or a person's sinful, pre-practising, or pre-conversion past
Janna	Paradise
Jazak Allahu khayra	May God reward you; expression of gratitude
Jilbab	All-enveloping (apart from the face and hands) one- or two-piece Muslim women's outer garment in a plain colour
Jum'a	Friday midday congregational prayers
Kafir	Non-Muslim, used both descriptively and occasionally derogatorily
Kafiyyat	Traditional Arab headdresses
Khair	Alternative spelling of *khayr*
Khalas	Enough, that is all
Khawarij	Kharijites; an early sectarian group in Islam that revolted against Caliph Ali ibn Abi Talib. Salafis use the term to refer to contemporary Jihadis
Khayr	Goodness, good deeds
Khutab	Plural of *khutba*

Khutba	Sermon, usually referring to those delivered during *jum'a*
Kuffar	Plural of *kafir*
Kufr	Disbelief
Madhahib	Plural of *madhhab*
Madhhab	School of Islamic law, one of the four schools of Sunni jurisprudence
Madrasa	Muslim religious school
Maghrib	Sunset, sunset prayer
Maharim	Plural of *mahram*
Mahram	Husband or male with a close blood relationship to a woman
Makruh	Hated, detested; a *hukm*
Manhaj	Programme of action, way
Masha'Allah	Literally, 'whatever God wills'; expression of joy
Masjid	Mosque, place of worship
Mawlid	Celebrations marking the birth of the Prophet Muhammad
Minhaj	Alternative spelling of *manhaj*
Mu'alim	Teacher
Mubah	Islamically permissible; a *hukm*
Mu'min	(Muslim) believer
Munafiq	Religious hypocrite
Mustahabb	Highly recommended; a *hukm*
Nafl	Voluntary fasting
Nar	(Hell)fire
Nasiha	Sincere, Islamically sound advice
Nikah	Islamic marriage ceremony
Niqab	Muslim woman's face veil
Niqabi	A woman who wears a *niqab*
P.b.u.h.	Peace Be Upon Him, respectful phrase following mention of the Prophet's name
Qadr	Divine decree
Qat	Mild stimulant commonly grown in East African and Middle Eastern countries

Rakat	Prescribed prostrations and words accompanying ritual prayers
Rasul (-ullah)	(The) Messenger (of God), often used to refer to the Prophet Muhammad
Revert	Convert to Islam; preferred terminology for Muslims who believe that everyone is born Muslim
Riba	Usurious interest
Sadaqa	Non-obligatory charity
Sahaba	Companions of the Prophet Muhammad
Salafiyya	Salafism, the Salafi methodology, Salafi teachings collectively
Salam	(Colloquial) Islamic greeting; used by some British Muslims as a verb; to '*salam*' a Muslim is to say '*al-salamu 'alaykum*' to him or her
Salat	Compulsory prayers conducted five times a day
Salat al-istikhara	Prayer believed to aid the worshipper with important decisions
S.a.w.	*Salla Allahu 'alayhi wa-sallam*, i.e., may God honour him and grant him peace; respectful phrase following mention of the Prophet Muhammad's name
Shahada	Profession of faith that makes someone a Muslim if uttered under certain conditions
Shari'a	Islamic law
Shaytan (fem. *shaytana*)	Devil
Shirk	Associating partners with God or assigning uniquely divine qualities to something other than Him
Shirk al-akbar	Major *shirk*
Shirk al-asghar	Minor *shirk*
Shura	Consultation (committee)
Subhanallah	Glory to God
Sunna	The 'authenticated' speech, actions, silent approval, and characteristics of the Prophet; or a *hukm* (*see mustahabb*)
Sura	Chapter of the Qur'an
hisba	*See al-amr bi-l-ma'ruf wa-l-nahy 'an al-munkar*

S.w.t.	*Subhanahu wa-ta'ala*, i.e., may He be glorified and exalted; respectful phrase following mention of God's name
Tabi' al-tabi'in	The successors of the *tabi'in*
Tabi'in	The successors of the Prophet's companions
Tajwid	Art of Qur'anic recitation
Takfir	Pronouncement on somebody that he or she is no longer a Muslim
Talib al-'ilm	Student of knowledge, i.e., someone who has studied with 'ulama for lengthy periods
Taqlid	Following a *madhhab* (exclusively and uncritically)
Taqwa	Fear of God, God-consciousness
Tarawih	Night prayers during Ramadan
Tarbiya	Nurturing (individuals) in 'correct' beliefs and practices
Tawba	Repentance
Tawhid	Oneness of God, doctrine of absolute monotheism
Thawb	Muslim men's robe-like garment, raised above the ankles
Ukht(i)	(My) sister; respectful address to a fellow Muslim woman
Umma	Muslim community
Wahy	Revelation
Wajib	Obligatory; a *hukm*
Wakil	Male guardian of an un-related female (usually a convert) engaged in the match-making process
Wala'im	Plural of *walima*
Walaykum al-salam	And unto you peace; standard response to Islamic greetings
Wali	Male guardian of a female relative engaged in the match-making process
Walima	Marriage banquet
Wallahi	I swear to God
Wudu	Cleansing rituals
Yawm al-qiyama	The Day of Judgment
Zakat	Annual charitable payment of a fixed portion of one's wealth
Zina	'Illicit' sexual acts, especially sex outside marriage and adultery

INFORMATION ON INTERVIEWEES

Table A. SALAFI WOMEN INTERVIEWED (CORRECT AT TIME OF INTERVIEW). THOSE ASSOCIATED WITH SISTERS OF TAWHEED ARE INDICATED WITH AN ASTERISK (*), WHILE THE OTHERS WERE ASSOCIATED WITH BRIXTON MOSQUE

Pseudonym	Age bracket	National background	Muslim background/ convert? (M/C)	Employment (FT = full-time; PT = part-time)	Education	Single, engaged, married, or divorced (S/E/M/D); children?	Dress (J = *jilbab*; A = abaya with headscarf; N = *niqab*)
Abeer	19–23	Eritrea	M	FT	BTech	S	J; wears N for trips to mosques and conferences
Abyan	19–23	Somalia	M	PT	Doing BSc	S	J and N (removes N for work)
Amina	24–29	Eritrea	M	Volunteer	Doing BA	S	J
Bilan	19–23	Somalia	M	Volunteer	Doing BSc	S	J
Dania	19–23	Eritrea	M	n/a	Doing BA	M	J; wears N when not at university
Deqa*	24–29	Somalia	M	FT	BSc	S	J but headscarf and uniform for work
Filsan	24–29	Somalia	M	PT	BTech and doing Access course	M (with children)	A
Firdaws	19–23	Not disclosed	C	n/a	Doing BSc	S	J
Fowsiya*	19–23	Somalia	M	FT	BA	E	J

Name	Age	Origin		Employment	Education	Marital	Dress
Hayah	24–29	Jamaica	C	n/a	NVQs	M (with children)	J
Humayrah	19–23	Kenya	C	PT	Doing BA	S	A for mosque; otherwise headscarf and loose Western clothing
Iman	19–23	Southern Africa	C	n/a	Diploma	M	J and N
Madeeha*	24–29	South Asia	M	FT	Diploma	E	J and N but A for work
Manal	24–29	Eritrea	M	PT	BA	S	A
Maryam	24–29	Nigeria	M	n/a	BA and doing Access course	S	J
Nadia	19–23	Somalia	M	n/a	Doing BA	D	J
Safia	19–23	Somalia	M	PT	BTech	E	J and N
Sagal	19–23	Somalia	M	n/a	Doing BA	S	J
Saidah	19–23	Nigeria	M	PT	MA	S	J and N
Shukri	19–23	Somalia	M	PT	Doing BA	S	J
Wafa	19–23	Nigeria	C	PT	Doing foundation degree	S	J
Warda	19–23	Somalia	M	n/a	Doing BTech	S	J
Warsan	24–29	Somalia	M	FT	BSc	S	J; wears N for trips to mosques and conferences

Table B. LEADERS INTERVIEWED

Name	Male/female (M/F)	Associated organization
Abdi Hasan (real name)	M	Somali community organization, east London
AbdulHaq Ashanti (real name)	M	Administration, Brixton Mosque, since 2002
Abdul Haqq Baker (real name)	M	Chairman, Brixton Mosque, 1994–2009
Abu Khadeejah (real name)	M	A leader of Salafi Publications, Birmingham
Ahraz	M	Staff member, Brixton Mosque
Daleela	F	Somali women's organization, east London
Dawud	M	Salafi preacher, south London
Kareem	M	Teacher, Brixton Mosque
Khalid	M	Al-Athariyyah, east London
Umm Hamza	F	Long-time community member and teacher, Brixton Mosque
Umm Mustafe	F	Teacher, Sisters of Tawheed
Umm Reemah	F	Long-time community member, Brixton Mosque
Uthman	M	Salafi Publications, Birmingham

INTERVIEW QUESTION GUIDE
FOR SALAFI WOMEN

PERSONAL DETAILS
General
1. Date of birth
2. Place of birth
3. Age when came to Britain (if applicable)
4. Revert/born-Muslim? Age when reverted/became practising
5. Ethnicity and national origin
6. Current residence (London borough), including cohabitants
7. What kind of work do you do for a living, if any?
8. Highest educational qualification

Family
1. Where were your parents born? (Reasons for migration, if applicable)
2. Which languages are spoken in your family?
3. What do/did your parents do for a living?
4. Did your parents identify with any particular religion(s)?
5. What about your grandparents?
6. What about your siblings (if any)?

Husband/children
1. Marital status
2. When did you get married? (if applicable)
3. Ethnicity of husband (if applicable)
4. Religious background of husband (if applicable)
5. Religious identity of husband (if applicable)
6. Occupation of husband (if applicable)
7. Children? Ages of children (if applicable)

BECOMING PRACTISING/SALAFI

1. What does being Muslim mean to you?
2. What makes your approach to Islam different to those of other Muslims, who may interpret their religion in different ways?
3. Can you tell me about your religious upbringing (if any)?
4. Can you tell me about how you became practising/interested in Salafism (if mentioned)?
5. How did your family feel about you becoming practising/Salafi in this way? How about other people who were important in your life at the time?
6. Did you have any (other) experiences of other religious groups before becoming Muslim/Salafi?
7. Looking back on these experiences, why did you decide to move on to your current understanding of religion?
8. Going back to your conversion to Islam/embracement of Salafism, which aspects of this change were easiest? Hardest?

DAILY LIFE

1. What do you like most about the Salafi way of life? Least?
2. Do you have questions? Who/what do you turn to if you have questions in your *din* [religion]?
3. Have your career plans changed since becoming practising/Salafi? What about your family plans? What about your education plans?
4. How does the work that you do for a living/your current education fit with your religious practice (if applicable)?
5. What meaning does wearing hijab/*jilbab*/*niqab* have for you (if applicable)?

SEEKING RELIGIOUS KNOWLEDGE

1. How do you go about learning more about your religion?
2. Do you go to classes/events, for example at a mosque? Why/what prevents you from attending them?
3. Are there any particular mosques/*da'wa* groups you identify with and seek religious knowledge at? Why?
4. Are there any particular religious teachers you seek knowledge from? Why?

MARRIAGE
Single women

1. Have you ever been married? What happened (if applicable)?
2. Do you hope to get married some day? Why?

3. Are you taking steps towards marriage at the moment? Why/why not? What kind of steps/how are you going about it?

4. Where/from whom did you learn about this way of approaching marriage? Why did it make sense to you?

5. How do you find out about potential husbands? What sort of husband do you want?

6. How did you choose your *wali/wakil* (male guardian) (if applicable)? What is his role? Is he happy to take on this role? In your view, does he perform it in a way that meets your requirements and those of the sunna?

7. Have you had meetings with brothers in the past? Can you tell me about them?

8. For you, what are the benefits of looking for a husband in this way? What are the main challenges?

9. How does this approach to relationships with men differ from your approach before you became Muslim/practising?

10. Would you consider using/have you used a (Salafi) marriage website? Why?

11. In your future household, would you distinguish between male and female roles? How? Why?

Married women

1. How did you meet your husband?

2. Who was your *wali* (if applicable)? Was he happy to take on this role? In your view, did he perform it in a way that met your requirements and those of the sunna?

3. How did your family feel about your choice of spouse?

4. How did you get to know him better?

5. What were the benefits for you of finding a husband in this way? And what were the challenges?

6. Where/from whom did you learn about this way of approaching marriage? Why did it make sense to you?

7. What sort of husband were you looking for?

8. At what point were you sure you wanted to marry him? Why? What lengths did you go to to make sure he was the man for you?

9. Did you previously meet other prospective husbands? What happened? Why did you decide not to go forward? What were the main challenges you experienced?

10. How did this approach to relationships with men differ from your approach before you became Muslim/practising?

11. In your household, do you distinguish between male and female roles? Why? How does this work on a day-to-day basis?

Both

1. What do you think about women's and men's roles in Salafism?
2. Would you like to have children one day (if applicable)? Why?
3. Would you consider/have you considered or engaged in polygamy?

OTHER RELATIONSHIPS

1. Have your friendships changed since you became practising/Salafi?
2. Are your closest friends Salafis or non-Salafis? Do you have friends who are non-Salafi Muslims/non-Muslims?
3. Is it important to you to maintain contact with sisters/fellow Salafis?
4. Do you think there is a sisterhood at [name of Salafi institution]?
5. Do you want to live in a Salafi/Muslim neighbourhood in the future? (If yes) would you move to a Muslim country? Which? Why? Do you consider *hijra* (migration for religious reasons) to be *wajib* (obligatory)?
6. Thinking about your relationships with non-Muslims in London today, whether strangers or people you know, are there any particular experiences, positive or negative, that come to mind? Describe them. If negative, how did they affect you?

AND FINALLY ...

1. Anything else you wish to add?
2. Anyone you know who may like to be interviewed?

BIBLIOGRAPHY

Abbas, Tahir ed., 2005. *Muslim Britain: Communities under Pressure*. London: Zed Books.

Abbas, Tahir ed., 2007. *Islamic Political Radicalism: A European Perspective*. Edinburgh: Edinburgh University Press.

Abdel Haleem, Harfiyah, 2003. Experiences, Needs, and Potential of New Muslim Women in Britain. In: H. Jawad and T. Benn, eds. 2003. *Muslim Women in the United Kingdom and Beyond*. Leiden: Brill. Ch.6.

Abou El Fadl, Khaled, 2001. Islam and the Theology of Power. *Middle East Report* 221, pp.28–33.

Abou El Fadl, Khaled, 2005. *The Great Theft: Wrestling Islam from the Extremists*. New York: HarperSanFrancisco.

Abou El Fadl, Khaled, 2006. Corrupting God's Book. In: K. Abou El Fadl, ed. 2006. *The Search for Beauty in Islam: A Conference of the Books*. Lanham, Md.: Rowman & Littlefield. Ch.57.

Abu-Lughod, Lila, 1999. *Veiled Sentiments: Honor and Poetry in a Bedouin Society*. 2nd ed. Berkeley: University of California Press.

Adnan, Adlin, 1999. *New Muslims in Britain*. London: Ta-Ha.

Adraoui, Mohamed-Ali, 2008. Purist Salafism in France. *ISIM Review* 21/Spring, pp.12–13.

Adraoui, Mohamed-Ali, 2009. Salafism in France: Ideology, Practices and Contradictions. In: R. Meijer, ed. 2009. *Global Salafism: Islam's New Religious Movement*. New York: Columbia University Press, pp.364–383.

Ahmed, Akbar S. and Donnan, Hastings, 1994. Islam in the Age of Postmodernity. In: A. S. Ahmed and H. Donnan, eds. 1994. *Islam, Globalization, and Postmodernity*. London; New York: Routledge, pp.1–20.

Ahmed, Akbar S. and Donnan, Hastings, eds., 1994. *Islam, Globalization, and Postmodernity*. London; New York: Routledge.

Ahmed, Leila, 2011. *A Quiet Revolution: The Veil's Resurgence, from the Middle East to America*. New Haven: Yale University Press.

Akeroyd, Anne V., 1984. Ethics in Relation to Informants, the Profession and Governments. In: R. F. Ellen, ed. 1984. *Ethnographic Research: A Guide to General Conduct*. London: Academic Press, pp.133–154.

Alexiev, Alex, 2002. The End of an Alliance: It's Time to Tell the House of Saud Goodbye. *National Review* 54/20, pp.38–42.

Ali Musawi, Mohammed, 2010. *Cheering for Osama: How Jihadists Use Internet Discussion Forums*. [pdf] Quilliam. Available at: <www.quilliamfoundation. org/wp/wp-content/uploads/publications/free/cheering-for-osama-how-jihadists-use-the-internet-forums.pdf> [Accessed 13 November 2015].

Allen, Charles, 2006. *God's Terrorists: The Wahhabi Cult and the Hidden Roots of Modern Jihad*. London: Little, Brown.

Allen, Chris, 2011. Against Complacency. *Soundings: MCB Policy Matters for Muslims in Britain* [online], June 15. Available at: <http://soundings.mcb.org.uk/?p=33> [Accessed 26 August 2013].

Allen, Christopher and Nielsen, Jørgen S., 2002. *Islamophobia in the EU after 11 September 2001: Summary Report on Behalf of the EUMC European Monitoring Centre on Racism and Xenophobia*. European Monitoring Centre on Racism and Xenophobia.

Allievi, Stefano, 2006. The Shifting Significance of the Halal/Haram Frontier: Narratives on the Hijab and Other Issues. In: K. van Nieuwkerk, ed. 2006. *Women Embracing Islam: Gender and Conversion in the West*. Austin: University of Texas Press. Ch.5.

Almond, Gabriel A., Appleby, R. Scott, and Sivan, Emmanuel, 2003. *Strong Religion: The Rise of Fundamentalisms around the World*. Chicago: University of Chicago Press.

Almond, Gabriel A., Appleby, R. Scott, and Sivan, Emmanuel, 2004. Fundamentalism: Genus and Species. In: M. E. Marty and R. S. Appleby, eds. 2004. 2nd ed. *Fundamentalisms Comprehended*. Chicago and London: University of Chicago Press, pp.399–424.

Al-Qwidi, Maha, 2002. *Understanding the Stages of Conversion to Islam: The Voices of British Converts*. PhD. University of Leeds. Available at: <http://etheses.whiterose.ac.uk/485/1/uk_bl_ethos_250876.pdf> [Accessed 13 November 2015].

Al-Rasheed, Madawi, 1998. *Iraqi Assyrian Christians in London: The Construction of Ethnicity*. Lewiston, N.Y.: Edwin Mellen Press.

Al-Rasheed, Madawi, 2005a. Saudi Religious Transnationalism in London. In: M. Al-Rasheed, ed. 2005. *Transnational Connections and the Arab Gulf*. Oxford: Routledge, pp.149–167.

Al-Rasheed, Madawi, ed., 2005b. *Transnational Connections and the Arab Gulf*. Oxford: Routledge.

Al-Rasheed, Madawi, 2007. *Contesting the Saudi State: Islamic Voices from a New Generation*. Cambridge: Cambridge University Press.

Al-Rasheed, Madawi, 2008. The Local & the Global in Saudi Salafism. *ISIM Review* 21/Spring, pp.8–9.

Al-Rasheed, Madawi, 2011. *A History of Saudi Arabia*. 2nd ed. New York: Cambridge University Press.

Alvi, Hayat, 2014. The Diffusion of Intra-Islamic Violence and Terrorism: The Impact of the Proliferation of Salafi/Wahhabi Ideologies. *The Middle East Review of International Affairs*, 18(2), pp.38–50.

Ambrose, Kenneth P., 1983. Function of the Family in the Process of Commitment within the Unification Movement. In: G. G. James, ed. 1983. *The Family and the Unification Church*. New York: Unification Theological Seminary, pp.23–33.

Ameli, Saied R. and Merali, Arzu, 2006. *Hijab, Meaning, Identity, Otherization and Politics: British Muslim Women*. [pdf] London: Islamic Human Rights Commission; Impeks Publishing.

Ameli, Saied Reza and Merali, Arzu, 2015. *Environment of Hate: The New Normal for Muslims in the UK*. [pdf] Islamic Human Rights Commission, 17 November. Available at: <www.ihrc.org.uk/attachments/article/11559/Executive%20Summary-UK-ll-02.pdf> [Accessed 17 November 2015].

Amghar, Samir, 2007. Salafism and Radicalisation of Young European Muslims. In: S. Amghar et al., eds. 2007. *European Islam: Challenges for Public Policy and Society*. Brussels: Center for European Policy Studies, pp.38–51.

Amghar, Samir, 2009. Ideological and Theological Foundations of Muslim Radicalism in France. In: M. Emerson, ed. 2009. *Typologies of Radicalisation in Europe's Muslim Communities*. Brussels: Centre for European Policy Studies, pp.27–50.

Amghar, Samir, Boubekeur, Amel, and Emerson, Michael eds., 2007. *European Islam: Challenges for Public Policy and Society*. Brussels: Center for European Policy Studies.

Amir-Moazami, Schirin, 2010. Avoiding 'Youthfulness?': Young Muslims Negotiating Gender and Citizenship in France and Germany. In: L. Herrera and A. Bayat, eds., 2010. *Being Young and Muslim: New Cultural Politics in the Global South and North*. New York: Oxford University Press. Ch.12.

Ammerman, Nancy Tatom, 1987. *Bible Believers: Fundamentalists in the Modern World*. New Brunswick, N.J.: Rutgers University Press.

Ammerman, Nancy T. ed., 2007. *Everyday Religion: Observing Modern Religious Lives*. Oxford; New York: Oxford University Press.

Anderson QC, David, 2015. The Terrorism Acts in 2014 (September 2015). Independent Reviewer of Terrorism Legislation, 17 September. Available at: <https://terrorismlegislationreviewer.independent.gov.uk/terrorism-acts-report-published-today> [Accessed 13 November 2015].

Anon., 2015. PREVENT will have a chilling effect on open debate, free speech and political dissent. *The Independent*, 10 July. Available at: <www.independent.co.uk/voices/letters/prevent-will-have-a-chilling-effect-on-open-debate-free-speech-and-political-dissent-10381491.html> [Accessed 13 November 2015].

Ansari, Humayun, 2000. *The Infidel Within: Muslims in Britain since 1800*. London: C. Hurst & Co.

Anwar, Muhammad, 2005. Issues, Policy and Practice. In: T. Abbas, ed. 2005. *Muslim Britain: Communities under Pressure*. London; New York: Zed Books, pp.31–46.

Armbruster, Heidi and Laerke, Anna eds., 2008. *Taking Sides: Ethics, Politics and Fieldwork in Anthropology*. New York; Oxford: Berghahn Books.

Ashford, Ben, France, Anthony, and Bonnici, Tony, 2007. Shot Billy had a gun too. *The Sun*, 7 September. Available at: <www.thesun.co.uk/sol/homepage/news/18522/Shot-Billy-had-a-gun-too.html> [Accessed 13 November 2015].

Aspinall, Peter J. and Mitton, Lavinia, 2010. *The Migration History, Demography, and Socio-Economic Position of the Somali Community in Britain*. New York: Novinka/Nova Science.

Atay, Tayfun, 2008. Arriving in Nowhere Land: Studying an Islamic Sufi Order in London. In: H. Armbruster and A. Laerke, eds. 2008. *Taking Sides: Ethics, Politics and Fieldwork in Anthropology*. New York; Oxford: Berghahn Books, pp.45–64.

Austin-Broos, Diane, 2003. The Anthropology of Conversion: An Introduction. In: A. Buckser and S. D. Glazier, eds. 2003. *The Anthropology of Religious Conversion*. Lanham, Md.: Rowman & Littlefield. Ch.1.

Badran, Margot, 2006. Feminism and Conversion: Comparing British, Dutch, and South African Life Stories. In: K. van Nieuwkerk, ed. 2006. *Women Embracing Islam: Gender and Conversion in the West*. Austin: University of Texas Press. Ch.8.

Baker, Abdul Haqq, 2011. *Extremists in our Midst: Confronting Terror*. [e-book] Houndmills, Basingstoke: Palgrave Macmillan.

Baker, Abdul Haqq, 2013. Islam's ability to empower is a magnet to black British youths. *The Guardian Comment Is Free*, 19 August. Available at: <www.

theguardian.com/commentisfree/2013/aug/19/islam-empower-magnet-black-british-youths> [Accessed 13 November 2015].

Ball, Charlie, 2013. Most people in the UK do not go to university—and maybe never will. *The Guardian*, 4 June. Available at: <www.theguardian.com/higher-education-network/blog/2013/jun/04/higher-education-participation-data-analysis> [Accessed 13 November 2015].

Bangstad, Sindre and Linge, Marius, 2015. 'Da'wa is Our Identity'—Salafism and IslamNet's Rationales for Action in a Norwegian Context. *Journal of Muslims in Europe* 4(2), pp.174–196.

Barker, Eileen, 1983. Doing Love: Tensions in the Ideal Family. In: G. G. James, ed. 1983. *The Family and the Unification Church*. New York: Unification Theological Seminary, pp.35–52.

Barker, Eileen, 1984. *The Making of a Moonie: Choice or Brainwashing?* Oxford: Basil Blackwell.

Barker, Eileen, 1989. *New Religious Movements: A Practical Introduction*. London: H.M.S.O.

Barker, Eileen, 1993. Charismatization: The Social Production of 'an Ethos Propitious to the Mobilisation of Sentiments'. In: E. Barker, J. A. Beckford, and K. Dobbelaere, eds. 1993. *Secularization, Rationalism and Sectarianism: Essays in Honour of Bryan R. Wilson*. Oxford: Clarendon Press, pp.181–201.

Barker, Eileen, 1995. Plus ça change. *Social Compass* 42(2), pp.165–180.

Barker, Eileen, 2013. Doing Sociology: Confessions of a Professional Stranger. In: T. Hjelm and P. Zuckerman, eds. 2013. *Studying Religion and Society: Sociological Self-Portraits*. Abingdon; New York: Routledge. Ch.4.

Bartlett, Jamie, Birdwell, Jonathan, and King, Michael, 2010. *The Edge of Violence: A Radical Approach to Extremism*. London: Demos.

Bayat, Asef, 2010. Muslim Youth and the Claim of Youthfulness. In: L. Herrera and A. Bayat, eds. 2010. *Being Young and Muslim: New Cultural Politics in the Global South and North*. New York: Oxford University Press. Ch.2.

Baylocq, Cedric and Drici-Bechikh, 2012. The Salafi and the Others: An Ethnography of Intracommunal Relations in French Islam. In: B. Dupret, T. Pierret, P. Pinto, and K. Spellman-Poots, eds. 2012. *Ethnographies of Islam: Ritual Performances and Everyday Practices*. Edinburgh: Edinburgh University Press. Ch.10.

Bazzano, Elliott A., 2015a. Ibn Taymiyya, Radical Polymath, Part I: Scholarly Perceptions. *Religion Compass* 9(4), pp.100–116.

Bazzano, Elliott A., 2015b. Ibn Taymiyya, Radical Polymath, Part II: Intellectual Contributions. *Religion Compass* 9(4), pp.117–139.

BBC News Online, 2001. Who is Richard Reid? *BBC News Online*, 28 December. Available at: <http://news.bbc.co.uk/1/hi/uk/1731568.stm> [Accessed 13 November 2015].

BBC News Online, 2005. 'Muslim' gangs target vulnerable. *BBC News Online*, 12 August. Available at: <http://news.bbc.co.uk/1/hi/england/london/4145198.stm> [Accessed 13 November 2015].

BBC News Online, 2006. Profile: Zacarias Moussaoui. *BBC News Online*, 25 April. Available at: <http://news.bbc.co.uk/1/hi/world/americas/4471245.stm> [Accessed 13 November 2015].

BBC News Online, 2012. London Metropolitan University's alcohol-free zone plan. *BBC News Online*, 13 April. Available at: <www.bbc.co.uk/news/uk-england-london-17701963> [Accessed 13 November 2015].

Becker, Carmen, 2009. 'Gaining Knowledge': Salafi Activism in German and Dutch Online Forums. *Masaryk University Journal of Law and Technology* 3(1), pp.79–98.

Becker, Carmen, 2011. Muslims on the Path of the Salaf Al-Salih. *Information, Communication & Society* 14(8), pp.1181–1203.

Berger, Peter L., 1990. *The Sacred Canopy: Elements of a Sociological Theory of Religion.* 3rd ed. New York: Anchor Books.

Berkey, Jonathan P., 2007. Madrasas Medieval and Modern: Politics, Education, and the Problem. In: R. W. Hefner and M. Q. Zaman, eds. 2007. *Schooling Islam: The Culture and Politics of Modern Muslim Education.* Princeton, N. J.: Princeton University Press. Ch.2.

Bernard, H. Russell, 2006. *Research Methods in Anthropology: Qualitative and Quantitative Approaches.* 4th ed. Lanham, Md.: AltaMira Press.

Birt, Jonathan, 2005. Wahhabism in the United Kingdom: Manifestations and Reactions. In: M. Al-Rasheed, ed. 2005. *Transnational Connections and the Arab Gulf.* Oxford: Routledge, pp.168–184.

Birt, Yahya, 2002. Building New Medinas in These Sceptred Isles. *Q-News*, May–June pp.21–23.

Birt, Yahya, 2007. Wahhabi Wrangles. [blog] 2 November. Available at: <https://yahyabirt1.wordpress.com/2007/11/02/wahhabi-wrangles> [Accessed 13 November 2015].

Birt, Yahya, 2015. Telling or Censoring our British Muslim Stories? [blog] 21 August. Available at: <www.everydaymuslim.org/#!Telling-or-Censoring-Our-British-Muslim-Stories/c1h40/55d6f4940cf20831ee3a705e> [Accessed 13 November 2015].

Bolognani, Marta, 2007. Islam, Ethnography and Politics: Methodological Issues in Researching amongst West Yorkshire Pakistanis in 2005. *International Journal of Social Research Methodology* 10(4), pp.279–293.

Bourque, Nicole, 1998. Being British and Muslim: Dual Identity amongst New and Young Muslims. In: A. Jones, ed. 1998. *University Lectures in Islamic Studies, Vol 2.* London: Altajir World of Islam Trust, pp.1–18.

Bourque, Nicole, 2006. How Deborah Became Aisha: The Conversion Process and the Creation of Female Muslim Identity. In: K. van Nieuwkerk, ed. 2006. *Women Embracing Islam: Gender and Conversion in the West.* Austin: University of Texas Press. Ch.9.

Bowen, Innes, 2014a. *Medina in Birmingham, Najaf in Brent: Inside British Islam.* London: Hurst & Company.

Bowen, Innes, 2014b. British mosques aren't that moderate after all. *The Spectator,* 14 June. Available at: <http://new.spectator.co.uk/2014/06/who-runs-our-mosques> [Accessed 5 December 2015].

Brasher, Brenda E., 1998. *Godly Women: Fundamentalism and Female Power.* New Brunswick, N.J.; London: Rutgers University Press.

Breen-Smyth, Marie, 2009. The Challenge of Researching Political Terror Critically. *Arches* 3/4, pp.65–70.

Brice, M. A. Kevin, 2010. *A Minority within a Minority: A Report on Converts to Islam in the United Kingdom.* [pdf] Faith Matters. Available at: <http://faith-matters.org/images/stories/fm-reports/a-minority-within-a-minority-a-report-on-converts-to-islam-in-the-uk.pdf> [Accessed 13 November 2015].

Bromley, David G. and Shupe Jr., Anson D., 1979. *'Moonies' in America: Cult, Church, and Crusade.* Beverly Hills, Calif.; London: Sage Publications.

Bruce, Steve, 1987. The Moral Majority: The Politics of Fundamentalism in Secular Society. In: L. Caplan, ed. 1987. *Studies in Religious Fundamentalism*. Albany: State University of New York Press, pp.177–194.

Bruce, Steve, 1993. Religion and Rational Choice: A Critique of Economic Explanations of Religious Behavior. *Sociology of Religion* 54(2), pp.193–205.

Bruce, Steve, 1999. *Choice and Religion: A Critique of Rational Choice Theory*. Oxford: Oxford University Press.

Buckser, Andrew and Glazier, Stephen D. eds., 2003. *The Anthropology of Religious Conversion*. Lanham, Md.: Rowman & Littlefield.

Caldicott Report, 2010. *Umar Farouk Abdulmutallab: Report to UCL Council of independent inquiry panel*, September. [pdf] Available at: <www.ucl.ac.uk/caldicott-enquiry/caldicottreport.pdf> [Accessed 13 November 2015].

Callaway, Helen, 1992. Ethnography and Experience: Gender Implications in Fieldwork and Texts. In: J. Okely and H. Callaway, eds. 1992. *Anthropology and Autobiography*. London; New York: Routledge, pp.29–49.

Camber, Rebecca, 2013. You must take off your veil: Judge rules that Muslim defendant can wear niqab during trial but NOT when giving evidence. *The Daily Mail*, 16 September. Available at: <www.dailymail.co.uk/news/article-2421893/Judge-Peter-Murphy-rules-Muslim-woman-REMOVE-face-veil-evidence.html> [Accessed 13 November 2015].

Cameron, David, 2011. Full transcript; David Cameron; Speech on radicalisation and Islamic extremism; Munich; 5 February 2011. *New Statesman*, 5 February. Available at: <www.newstatesman.com/blogs/the-staggers/2011/02/terrorism-islam-ideology> [Accessed 13 November 2015].

Cameron, David, 2015. Speech on extremism; Birmingham; 20 July 2015. Available at: <www.gov.uk/government/speeches/extremism-pm-speech> [Accessed 13 November 2015].

Campbell, Colin, 1972. The Cult, the Cultic Milieu and Secularization. In: M. Hill, ed. 1972. *A Sociological Yearbook of Religion in Britain*. London: SCM Press Ltd, pp.119–136.

Caplan, Lionel, 1987. Fundamentalism as Counter-culture: Protestants in Urban South India. In: L. Caplan, ed. 1987. *Studies in Religious Fundamentalism*. Albany: State University of New York Press, pp.156–176.

Caplan, Pat, 1992. Spirits and Sex—a Swahili Informant and His Diary. In: J. Okely and H. Callaway, eds. 1992. *Anthropology and Autobiography*. London; New York: Routledge, pp.64–81.

Cavatorta, Francesco and Merone, Fabio eds., 2016. *Salafism after the Arab Awakening: Contending with People's Power*. London: Hurst & Co.

Cesari, Jocelyne, 2008. Muslims in Europe and the Risk of Radicalism. In: R. Coolsaet, ed. 2008. *Jihadi Terrorism and the Radicalisation Challenge in Europe*. Aldershot: Ashgate, pp.97–107.

Change.org, 2014. British Muslims launch historic campaign to ban the burka in the UK, Muslim Educational Centre of Oxford. Available at: <www.change.org/p/british-society-the-uk-electorate-and-members-of-parliament-british-muslims-launch-historic-campaign-to-ban-the-burka-in-the-uk> [Accessed 13 November 2015].

Chrisafis, Angelique, 2001. British followers back Afghan people but condemn violence. *The Guardian*, October 26. Available at: <www.theguardian.com/uk/2001/oct/26/afghanistan.terrorism1> [Accessed 13 November 2015].

Churches Together in England, 2013. Christians consider ways to stem the flight of black British youths to Islam and radicalisation. [press release] 18 July. Available at: <www.

cte.org.uk/Articles/364457/Churches_Together_in/Working_Together/Minority_
Ethnic_Christian/Church_response_to.aspx> [Accessed 13 November 2015].

Clark, Janine A., 2004. Islamist Women in Yemen: Informal Nodes of Activism. In:
Q. Wiktorowicz, ed. 2004. *Islamic Activism: A Social Movement Theory Approach.*
Bloomington: Indiana University Press, pp.164–184.

Cohen, David, 2005. The Rise of the Muslim Boys. *Evening Standard*, 3 February.

Cole, Juan, 2009. *Engaging the Muslim World.* New York: Palgrave Macmillan.

Coleman, Simon, 2003. Continuous Conversion? The Rhetoric, Practice, and
Rhetorical Practice of Charismatic Protestant Conversion. In: A. Buckser and
S. D. Glazier, eds. 2003. *The Anthropology of Religious Conversion.* Lanham, Md.:
Rowman & Littlefield. Ch.2.

Contractor, Sariya, 2012. *Muslim Women in Britain: De-mystifying the Muslimah.*
Abingdon, Oxon; New York: Routledge.

Cooke, Miriam and Lawrence, Bruce B. eds., 2005. *Muslim Networks from Hajj to Hip
Hop.* Chapel Hill; London: University of North Carolina Press.

Coolsaet, Rik ed., 2008. *Jihadi Terrorism and the Radicalisation Challenge in Europe.*
Aldershot: Ashgate.

Crewe, Ben and Maruna, Shadd, 2006. Self-Narratives and Ethnographic Fieldwork.
In: D. Hobbs and R. Wright, eds. 2006. *The SAGE Handbook of Fieldwork.*
London: SAGE, pp.109–123.

Croft, Stuart, 2012. *Securitizing Islam: Identity and the Search for Security.* Cambridge:
Cambridge University Press.

Daschke, Dereck and Ashcraft, W. Michael, 2005. Introduction. In: D. Daschke and
W. M. Ashcraft, eds. 2005. *New Religious Movements: A Documentary Reader.*
New York; London: New York University Press, pp.1–21.

Davidman, Lynn, 1990. Women's Search for Family and Roots: A Jewish Religious
Solution to a Modern Dilemma. In: T. R. D. Anthony, ed. 1990. *In Gods we Trust:
New Patterns of Religious Pluralism in America.* 2nd ed. New Brunswick, N.J.;
Oxford: Transaction. Ch.20.

Davidman, Lynn, 1991. *Tradition in a Rootless World: Women Turn to Orthodox Judaism.*
Oxford; Berkeley: University of California Press.

Dawson, Lorne L., 2008. *Comprehending Cults: The Sociology of New Religious
Movements.* 2nd ed. Don Mills, Ont.; Oxford: Oxford University Press.

Dawson, Lorne L., 2010. The Study of New Religious Movements and the
Radicalization of Home-Grown Terrorists: Opening a Dialogue. *Terrorism and
Political Violence* 22, pp.1–21.

Deeb, Lara, 2006. *An Enchanted Modern: Gender and Public Piety in Shi'i Lebanon.*
Princeton: Princeton University Press.

De Koning, Martijn, 2007. Salafism as a Transnational Movement. *ISIM Review* 20/
Autumn, p.64.

De Koning, Martijn, 2009. Changing Worldviews and Friendship: An Exploration of
the Life Stories of Two Female Salafis in the Netherlands. In: R. Meijer, ed.
2009. *Global Salafism: Islam's New Religious Movement.* New York: Columbia
University Press, pp.404–423.

De Koning, Martijn, 2012a. The 'Other' Political Islam: Understanding Salafi Politics.
In: O. Roy and A. Boubekeur, eds. 2012. *Whatever Happened to the Islamists?
Salafs, Heavy Metal Muslims and the Lure of Consumerist Islam.* London: Hurst
and Company, pp.153–178.

De Koning, Martijn, 2012b. Between the Prophet and Paradise: The Salafi Struggle
in the Netherlands. *Canadian Journal of Netherlandic Studies* 33.2/34.1,
pp.17–34.

De Koning, Martijn, 2013a. How Should I Live as a 'True' Muslim? Regimes of Living among Dutch Muslims in the Salafi Movement. *Etnofoor, The Netherlands Now* 25(2), pp.53–72.

De Koning, Martijn, 2013b. The Moral Maze: Dutch Salafis and the Construction of a Moral Community of the Faithful. *Contemporary Islam* 7(1), pp.71–83.

De Koning, Martijn, Bartels, Edien, and Koning, Daniëlle, 2011. Claiming the Researcher's Identity: Anthropological Research and Politicized Religion. *Fieldwork in Religion* 6(2), pp.168–186.

Della Porta, Donatella and Diani, Mario, 1999. *Social Movements: An Introduction.* Oxford: Wiley-Blackwell.

DeLong-Bas, Natana J., 2004. *Wahhabi Islam: From Revival and Reform to Global Jihad.* Oxford: Oxford University Press.

Department for Business, Innovation and Skills, 2014. *Sharia-Compliant Student Finance: Government response to consultation on a Sharia-compliant alternative finance product.* [pdf] Available at: <www.gov.uk/government/uploads/system/uploads/attachment_data/file/349899/bis-14-984-government-response-to-a-consultation-on-a-sharia-compliant-alternative-finance-product.pdf> [Accessed 13 November 2015].

Department for Communities and Local Government (DCLG), 2009. *The Somali Muslim Community in England.* [pdf] Available at: <http://karin-ha.org.uk/wp-content/uploads/2013/01/1210847.pdf> [Accessed 13 November 2015].

Dessing, Nathal M., 2011. Thinking for Oneself? Forms and Elements of Religious Authority in Dutch Muslim Women's Groups. In: M. Bano and H. Kalmbach, eds. 2011. *Women, Leadership, and Mosques: Changes in Contemporary Islamic Authority.* Leiden: Brill, pp.217–233.

Dessing, Nathal M., 2013. How to Study Everyday Islam. In: N. M. Dessing, N. Jeldtoft, J. S. Nielsen, and L. Woodhead, eds. 2013. *Everyday Lived Islam in Europe.* Surrey; Burlington, Vt.Vt.: Ashgate. Ch.3.

DeWalt, Kathleen M. and DeWalt, Billie R., 2002. *Participant Observation: A Guide for Fieldworkers.* Walnut Creek, Calif.; Oxford: AltaMira Press.

Dodd, Vikram, 2002. Sect opposes protests and brands terrorists as sinners. *The Guardian,* 31 August. Available at: <www.theguardian.com/uk/2002/aug/31/september11.religion> [Accessed 13 November 2015].

Dodd, Vikram and Travis, Alan, 2015. Anti-extremism drive puts British values at risk, says police chief. *The Guardian,* 19 October. Available at: <www.theguardian.com/uk-news/2015/oct/19/government-extremism-crackdown-hurt-uk-values-peter-fahy-manchester> [Accessed 13 November 2015].

Dogan, Güney, 2012. Moral Geographies and the Disciplining of Senses among Swedish Salafis. *Comparative Islamic Studies* 8(1–2), pp.93–112.

Donnelly, Laura and Williams, Rhiannon, 2013. Secret ban on face veils for staff at 17 hospitals. *The Daily Telegraph,* 19 September. Available at: <www.telegraph.co.uk/health/nhs/10319264/Secret-ban-on-face-veils-for-staff-at-17-hospitals.html> [Accessed 29 December 2013].

Douglas, Mary, 1966. *Purity and Danger: An Analysis of Concepts of Pollution and Taboo.* London: Routledge.

Dresch, Paul, 2000. Wilderness of Mirrors: Truth and Vulnerability in Middle Eastern Fieldwork. In: P. Dresch, W. James, and D. Parkin, eds. 2000. *Anthropologists in a Wider World.* New York; Oxford: Berghahn Books, pp.109–127.

Dresch, Paul, James, Wendy, and David, Parkin eds., 2000. *Anthropologists in a Wider World.* New York; Oxford: Berghahn Books.

Duderija, Adis, 2007. Neo-traditional Salafi Qur'an-Sunnah Hermeneutic and the Construction of a Normative *Muslimah* Image. *Hawwa* 5(2–3), pp.289–323.

Duderija, Adis, 2015. The "Islamic State" (IS) as Proponent of Neo-Ahlhadith Manhaj on Gender Related Issues. *Journal of Women of the Middle East and the Islamic World* 13, pp.198–240.

Dumbe, Yunus and Tayob, Abdulkader, 2011. Salafis in Cape Town in Search of Purity, Certainty and Social Impact. *Die Welt des Islams* 51, pp.188–209.

Dwyer, Claire, Shah, Bindi, and Sanghera, Gurchathen, 2008. 'From Cricket Lover to Terror Suspect'—Challenging Representations of Young British Muslim Men. *Gender, Place & Culture* 15/2, pp.117–136.

Eade, John, 1996. Nationalism, Community, and the Islamization of Space in London. In: B. D. Metcalf, ed. 1996. *Making Muslim Space in North America and Europe*. Berkeley; Los Angeles; London: University of California Press, pp.217–233.

Eickelman, Dale F. and Piscatori, James, 2004. *Muslim Politics*. 2nd ed. Princeton, N.J.; Oxford: Princeton University Press.

ElMasry, Shadee, 2010. The Salafis in America: The Rise, Decline and Prospects for a Sunni Muslim Movement among African-Americans. *Journal of Muslim Minority Affairs* 30(2), pp.217–236.

El-Or, Tamar, 1994. *Educated and Ignorant: Ultraorthodox Jewish Women and their World*. Translated from Hebrew by H. Watzman. Boulder; London: Rienner.

El-Solh, Camillia Fawzi, 1991. Somalis in London's East End: A Community Striving for Recognition. *New Community* 17(4), pp.539–552.

El-Solh, Camillia Fawzi, 1993. 'Be True to Your Culture': Gender Tensions among Somali Muslims in Britain. *Immigrants & Minorities* 12(1), pp.21–46.

Emerson, Michael, 2009. *Ethno-Religious Conflict in Europe: Typologies of Radicalisation in Europe's Muslim Communities*. [e-book] Centre for European Policy Studies. Available at: <www.ceps.eu/book/ethno-religious-conflict-europe-typologies-radicalisation-europes-muslim-communities> [Accessed 13 November 2015].

Equality and Human Rights Commission, 2011. Employment Statutory Code of Practice. [pdf] Available at: <www.equalityhumanrights.com/uploaded_files/EqualityAct/employercode.pdf> [Accessed 13 November 2015].

Esposito, John L. 2003. *The Oxford Dictionary of Islam*. Oxford: Oxford University Press.

Evans, Jonathan, 2010. John Evans' terrorism speech. *The Daily Telegraph*, 17 September. Available at: <www.telegraph.co.uk/news/uknews/terrorism-in-the-uk/8008252/Jonathan-Evans-terrorism-speech.html> [Accessed 13 November 2015].

Farquhar, Michael, 2015. Saudi Petrodollars, Spiritual Capital, and the Islamic University of Medina: A Wahhabi Missionary Project in Transnational Perspective. *International Journal of Middle Eastern Studies* 47, pp.701–721.

Finney, John M., 1978. A Theory of Religious Commitment. *Sociological Analysis* 39(1), pp.19–35.

Franks, Myfanwy, 2000. Crossing the Borders of Whiteness? White Muslim Women Who Wear the Hijab in Britain Today. *Ethnic and Racial Studies* 23(5), pp.917–929.

Franks, Myfanwy, 2001. *Women and Revivalism in the West: Choosing 'Fundamentalism' in a Liberal Democracy*. New York: Palgrave.

Freilich, Morris ed., c1970. Toward a Formalization of Field Work. In: M. Freilich, ed. 1970. *Marginal Natives: Anthropologists at Work*. New York: Harper & Row, pp.485–594.

Gardham, Duncan, 2011. 7/7 inquest: plot leader Mohammed Sidique Khan 'was raised a liberal Muslim'. *The Telegraph*, 6 May. Available at: <www.telegraph.co.uk/news/uknews/terrorism-in-the-uk/8497217/77-inquest-plot-leader-Mohammed-Sidique-Khan-was-raised-a-liberal-Muslim.html> [Accessed 13 November 2015].

Gauvain, Richard, 2013. *Salafi Ritual Purity: In the Presence of God*. New York: Routledge.

Geaves, Ron, 2005. Negotiating British Citizenship and Muslim Identity. In: T. Abbas, ed. 2005. *Muslim Britain: Communities under Pressure*. London, New York: Zed Books, pp.66–77.

Geelhoed, Fiore, 2011. *Purification and Resistance: Glocal Meanings of Islamic Fundamentalism in the Netherlands*. PhD. Erasmus University Rotterdam. Available at: <http://repub.eur.nl/pub/31685> [Accessed 13 November 2015].

Geelhoed, Fiore, 2014. *Striving for Allah: Purification and Resistance among Fundamentalist Muslims in the Netherlands*. The Hague: Eleven International.

Gellner, Ernest, 1992. *Postmodernism, Reason and Religion*. London: Routledge.

Gilliat-Ray, Sophie, 2005. Closed Worlds: (Not) Accessing Deobandi *dar-ul-uloom* in Britain. *Fieldwork and Religion* 1(1), pp.7–33.

Gilliat-Ray, Sophie, 2010. *Muslims in Britain: An Introduction*. Cambridge: Cambridge University Press.

Gilligan, Andrew, 2012. Security services 'failing' to stop British jihadis heading to Syria. *The Sunday Telegraph*, 25 August. Available at: <www.telegraph.co.uk/news/uknews/terrorism-in-the-uk/9499202/Security-services-failing-to-stop-British-jihadis-heading-to-Syria.html> [Accessed 13 November 2015].

Githens-Mazer, Jonathan, 2009. Mobilization, Recruitment, Violence and the Street: Radical Violent *Takfiri* Islamism in Early Twenty-First-Century Britain. In: R. Eatwell and M. J. Goodwin, eds. 2009. *The New Extremism in 21st Century Britain*. London: Routledge. Ch.2.

Githens-Mazer, Jonathan, 2013. Why Woolwich Matters: The South London Angle. Royal United Services Institute [online], 31 May. Available at: <https://rusi.org/commentary/why-woolwich-matters-south-london-angle> [Accessed 29 March 2016].

Githens-Mazer, Jonathan and Lambert, Robert, 2010. *Islamophobia and Anti-Muslim Hate Crime: UK Case Studies 2010*. Exeter: European Muslim Research Centre and University of Exeter.

Gledhill, Ruth, 2013. Cameron stands firm on Muslim veil bans despite U-turn by Birmingham college. *The Times*, 13 September. Available at: <www.thetimes.co.uk/tto/faith/article3868064.ece> [Accessed 13 November 2015].

Glendon, Mary Ann, 1981. *The New Family and the New Property*. Toronto: Butterworths.

Glock, Charles Y., 1962. On the Study of Religious Commitment. *Religious Education* 57(S4), pp.98–110.

Glock, Charles Y., 1964. The Role of Deprivation in the Origin and Evolution of Religious Groups. In: R. Lee and M. E. Marty, eds. 1964. *Religion and Social Conflict*. New York: Oxford University Press, pp.24–36.

Goodhart, David, 2007. Open letter to Tariq Ramadan. *Prospect* 135, June 30. Available at: <www.prospectmagazine.co.uk/magazine/openlettertotariqramadan/#.UhShtZLVB8E> [Accessed 13 November 2015].

Gov.uk, 2015. PM's Extremism Taskforce: Tackling extremism in universities and colleges top of the agenda. Available at: <www.gov.uk/government/news/pms-extremism-taskforce-tackling-extremism-in-universities-and-colleges-top-of-the-agenda> [Accessed 13 November 2015].

Goward, Nicola, 1984. Personal Interaction and Adjustment. In: R. F. Ellen, ed. 1984. *Ethnographic Research: A Guide to General Conduct.* London: Academic Press, pp.100–118.

Griffel, Frank, 2015. What Do We Mean by 'Salafi'? Connecting Muhammad 'Abduh with Egypt's Nur Party in Islam's Contemporary Intellectual History. *Die Welt Des Islams* 55, pp.186–220.

Griffiths, David J., 2002. *Somali and Kurdish Refugees in London: New Identities in the Diaspora.* Aldershot: Ashgate.

Haddad, Yvonne Yzbeck, 2006. The Quest for Peace in Submission: Reflections on the Journey of American Women Converts to Islam. In: K. van Nieuwkerk, ed. 2006. *Women Embracing Islam: Gender and Conversion in the West.* Austin: University of Texas Press. Ch.1.

Hafez, Sherine, 2011. *An Islam of Her Own: Reconsidering Religion and Secularism in Women's Islamic Movements.* New York and London: New York University Press.

Hamid, Sadek, 2007. Islamic Political Radicalism in Britain: The Case of Hizb-ut-Tahrir. In: T. Abbas, ed. 2007. *Islamic Political Radicalism: A European Perspective.* Edinburgh: Edinburgh University Press, pp.145–159.

Hamid, Sadek, 2008. The Development of British Salafism. *ISIM Review* 21/ Spring, pp.10–11. Available at: <https://openaccess.leidenuniv.nl/bitstream/handle/1887/17235/ISIM_21_The_Development_of_British_Salafism.pdf?sequence=1> [Accessed 13 November 2015].

Hamid, Sadek, 2009. The Attraction of 'Authentic' Islam: Salafism and British Muslim Youth. In: R. Meijer, ed. 2009. *Global Salafism: Islam's New Religious Movement.* New York: Columbia University Press, pp.384–403.

Hamid, Sadek, 2011. British Muslim Young People: Facts, Features and Religious Trends. *Religion, State and Society* 39(2–3), pp.247–261.

Hammond, Andrew, 2012. *The Islamic Utopia: The Illusion of Reform in Saudi Arabia.* London; New York: Palgrave Macmillan.

Hasan, Noorhaidi, 2007. The Salafi Movement in Indonesia: Transnational Dynamics and Local Development. *Comparative Studies of South Asia, Africa and the Middle East* 27/1, pp.83–94.

Hasan, Usama, 2014. *Expert Witness & Personal Testimony, USA vs. Babar Ahmad, USA vs. Syed Talha Ahsan.* [pdf] Quilliam, 15 April. Available at: <www.quilliam-foundation.org/wp/wp-content/uploads/publications/free/expert-witness-statement-usama-hasan-150414.pdf> [Accessed 13 November 2015].

Hashem, Mazen, 2006. Contemporary Islamic Activism: The Shades of Praxis. *Sociology of Religion* 67(1), pp.23–41.

Hassan, Harun, 2002. 'Not housekeepers any more': Somali women of the diaspora. *Open Democracy*, November 7. Available at: <www.opendemocracy.net/people-africa_democracy/article_692.jsp> [Accessed 13 November 2015].

Hawley, John Stratton, 1994. *Fundamentalism and Gender.* New York: Oxford University Press.

Haykel, Bernard, 2003. *Revival and Reform in Islam: The Legacy of Muhammad al-Shawkani.* Cambridge: Cambridge University Press.

Haykel, Bernard, 2009. On the Nature of Salafi Thought and Action. In: R. Meijer, ed. 2009. *Global Salafism: Islam's New Religious Movement.* New York: Columbia University Press, pp.33–57.

Hefner, Robert W. and Zaman, Muhammad Qasim, 2007. *Schooling Islam: The Culture and Politics of Modern Muslim Education.* Princeton, N.J.: Princeton University Press.

Hegghammer, Thomas, 2009. Jihadi-Salafis or Revolutionaries? On Religion and Politics in the Study of Militant Islamism. In: R. Meijer, ed. 2009. *Global Salafism: Islam's New Religious Movement*. New York: Columbia University Press, pp.244–266.

Herriot, Peter, 2007. *Religious Fundamentalism and Social Identity*. New York: Routledge.

Hjelm, Titus and Zuckerman, Phil eds., 2013. *Studying Religion and Society: Sociological Self-Portraits*. Abingdon; New York: Routledge.

Hobbs, Dick and Wright, Richard eds., 2006. *The SAGE Handbook of Fieldwork*. London: SAGE.

Holman, Christine and Holman, Naomi, 2003. *First steps in a new country: baseline indicators for the Somali community in LB Hackney*. Available at: <apps.hackney.gov.uk/servapps/Reports/s_ViewRptDoc.aspx?id=1173> [Accessed 13 November 2015].

Home Office, 2011. *Prevent Strategy*. [pdf] June. Available at: <www.gov.uk/government/uploads/system/uploads/attachment_data/file/97976/prevent-strategy-review.pdf> [Accessed 13 November 2015].

Home Office, 2015a. Immigration statistics, April to June 2015. Available at: <www.gov.uk/government/statistics/immigration-statistics-april-to-june-2015> [Accessed 13 November 2015].

Home Office, 2015b. *Counter-Extremism Strategy*. [pdf] October. Available at: <www.gov.uk/government/uploads/system/uploads/attachment_data/file/470088/51859_Cm9148_Accessible.pdf> [Accessed 13 November 2015]

Hoover, Jon, 2006. Ibn Taymiyya as an Avicennan theologian: a Muslim approach to God's self-sufficiency. *Theological Review* 34–46(1), pp.34–46

Hopkins, Gail, 2010. A Changing Sense of Somaliness: Somali Women in London and Toronto. *Gender, Place & Culture* 17(4), pp.519–538.

Hopkins, Peter, 2011. Towards Critical Geographies of the University Campus: Understanding the Contested Experiences of Muslim Students. *Transactions of the Institute of British Geographers* 36(1), pp.157–169.

Hosken, Andrew, 2012. The rise and fall of Brixton's GAS gang. *BBC News Online*, 12 June. Available at: <www.bbc.co.uk/news/uk-18398190> [Accessed 13 November 2015].

Hroub, Khaled, 2009. Salafi Formations in Palestine: The Limits of a De-Palestinised Milieu. In: R. Meijer, ed. 2009. *Global Salafism: Islam's New Religious Movement*. New York: Columbia University Press, pp.221–243.

Husain, Ed, 2007. *The Islamist: Why I Joined Radical Islam in Britain, What I Saw Inside and Why I Left*. London: Penguin Global.

Information Centre about Asylum and Refugees, July 2007. *ICAR Briefing: The Somali Refugee Community in the UK*. [pdf] Available at: <www.icar.org.uk/ICAR_briefing_on_Somali_Community.pdf> [Accessed 13 November 2015].

Inge, Anabel, 2008. *Salafism in Britain: The New Generation's Rebellion*. Master's dissertation. SOAS, University of London.

Inge, Anabel, 2014. The Draw of Certainty: Salafism and Young Women in London. *The Middle East in London*, 10:5, October.

Inge, Anabel, 2015. In Search of 'Pure' Islam: Conversion to Salafism among Young Women in London. In: Y. Suleiman, ed. 2015. *Muslims in the UK and Europe I*. Cambridge: Centre of Islamic Studies, University of Cambridge, pp.119–129. Available at: <www.cis.cam.ac.uk/assets/media/muslims_in_the_uk_and_europe_i_1.pdf> [Accessed 13 November 2015].

International Crisis Group, 2004. *Indonesia Backgrounder: Why Salafism and Terrorism Mostly Don't Mix*. [pdf] *ICG* Asia *report* 83. Available at <www.seasite.niu.edu/ Indonesian/Islam/83_indonesia_backgrounder_why_salafism_and_terrorism_don_t_mix_web.pdf> [Accessed 13 November 2015].

International Organization for Migration, 2006. *Somali Regions: Mapping Exercise*. [pdf] London: International Organization for Migration. Available at: <http:// unitedkingdom.iom.int/sites/default/files/doc/mapping/IOM_SOMALI_ MR.pdf> [Accessed 13 November 2015].

Islamic State, 2016. Kill the imams of kufr. *Dabiq*, Rabi' Al-Akhir 1437.

Janmohamed, Shelina, 2013. Boris Johnson was right about Muslim women struggling to find husbands. *The Daily Telegraph*, 10 July. Available at: <www.telegraph.co.uk/ women/womens-life/10171595/Boris-Johnson-was-right-about-Muslim-women-struggling-to-find-husbands.html> [Accessed 13 November 2015].

Jansen, Willy, 2006. Conversion and Gender, Two Contested Concepts. In: K. van Nieuwkerk, ed. 2006. *Women Embracing Islam: Gender and Conversion in the West*. Austin: University of Texas Press. Foreword.

Jawad, Haifaa and Benn, Tansin eds., 2003. *Muslim Women in the United Kingdom and Beyond*. Leiden: Brill.

Jihad—A British Story, 2015. Directed by Deeyah Khan. ITV, Exposure, 15 June, 22:40.

Johnston, Philip, 2007. July 7 preacher Abdullah El-Faisal deported. *The Daily Telegraph*, 25 May. Available at: <www.telegraph.co.uk/news/uknews/1552580/July-7-preacher-Abdullah-El-Faisal-deported.html> [Accessed 13 November 2015].

Jones, Alan ed., 1998. *University Lectures in Islamic Studies, Vol 2*. London: Altajir World of Islam Trust.

Jouili, Jeanette S., 2009. Negotiating Secular Boundaries: Pious Micro-Practices of Muslim Women in French and German Public Spheres. *Social Anthropology* 17(4), pp.455–470.

Kandiyoti, Deniz, 1988. Bargaining with Patriarchy. *Gender & Society* 2(3), pp.274–290.

Kanter, Rosabeth Moss, 1972. *Commitment and Community: Communes and Utopias in Sociological Perspective*. Cambridge, Mass.: Harvard University Press.

Kazmi, Zaheer, 2015. The United Kingdom's Extreme Anti-Extremism Policy: Why It Won't Work. *Foreign Affairs*. Available at: <www.foreignaffairs.com/articles/ united-kingdom/2015-08-05/united-kingdoms-extreme-anti-extremism-policy> [Accessed 13 November 2015].

Kenna, Margaret E., 1992. Changing Places and Altered Perspectives: Research on a Green Island in the 1960s and in the 1980s. In: J. Okely and H. Callaway, eds. 1992. *Anthropology and Autobiography*. London; New York: Routledge, pp.147–162.

Kennedy, Dominic, 2005. Radical al-Muhajiroun group is behind most UK terror plots. *The Times*, 21 March. Available at: <www.thetimes.co.uk/tto/news/uk/ crime/article4390086.ece> [Accessed 13 November 2015].

Kennedy, Dominic, 2014. British Muslims flock to join jihadists' hardline sect. *The Times*, 21 June. Available at: <www.thetimes.co.uk/tto/news/uk/article4128318.ece> [Accessed 13 November 2015].

Kepel, Gilles, 1994. *The Revenge of God: The Resurgence of Islam, Christianity, and Judaism in the Modern World*. Cambridge: Polity Press.

Kepel, Gilles, 1997. *Allah in the West: Islamic Movements in America and Europe*. Stanford: Stanford University Press.

Kepel, Gilles, 2002. *Jihad: The Trail of Political Islam*. Cambridge, Mass.: Harvard University Press.

Kerbaj, Richard, 2009. Government gives £1m to anti-extremist think-tank Quilliam Foundation. *The Times*, 20 January. Available at: <www.thetimes.co.uk/tto/news/politics/article2026766.ece> [Accessed 13 November 2015].

Kinchen, Rosie, 2012. Muslim high-flyers share a husband. *The Sunday Times*, 11 March. Available at: <www.thesundaytimes.co.uk/sto/news/uk_news/Society/article991378.ece> [Accessed 13 November 2015].

Kingsley Brown, Thomas, 2003. Mystical Experiences, American Culture, and Conversion to Christian Spiritualism. In: A. Buckser and S. D. Glazier, eds. 2003. *The Anthropology of Religious Conversion*. Oxford: Rowman & Littlefield, pp.133–145.

Kirkup, James, 2013. David Cameron supports Muslim veil ban in schools and courts. *The Daily Telegraph*, 29 September. Available at: <www.telegraph.co.uk/news/politics/david-cameron/10342501/David-Cameron-supports-Muslim-veil-ban-in-schools-and-courts.html> [Accessed 13 November 2015].

Köse, Ali, 1996. *Conversion to Islam: A Study of Native British Converts*. London: Kegan Paul International.

Kühle, Lene, 2012. Excuse Me, Which Radical Organization Are You a Member Of? Reflections on Methods to Study Highly Religious but Non-organized Muslims. In: N. Jeldtoft and J. S. Nielsen, eds. 2012. *Methods and Contexts in the Study of Muslim Minorities: Visible and Invisible Muslims*. Abingdon; N.Y.: Routledge, pp.77–91.

Kühle, Lene and Lindekilde, Lasse, 2010. *Radicalization among Young Muslims in Aarhus*. [pdf] Centre for Studies in Islamism and Radicalisation, Department of Political Science, Aarhus University. Available at: <www.ps.au.dk/fileadmin/site_files/filer_statskundskab/subsites/cir/radicalization_aarhus_FINAL.pdf> [Accessed 13 November 2015].

Kundnani, Arun, 2008. Islamism and the Roots of Liberal Rage. *Race & Class* 50(2), pp.40–68.

Lacroix, Stéphane, 2008. Al-Albani's Revolutionary Approach to Hadith. *ISIM Review* 21/Spring, pp.6–7. Available at: <https://openaccess.leidenuniv.nl/bitstream/handle/1887/17210/ISIM_21_Al-Albani-s_Revolutionary_Approach_to_Hadith.pdf?sequence=1> [Accessed 13 November 2015].

Lacroix, Stéphane, 2009. Between Revolution and Apoliticism: Nasir al-Din al-Albani and his Impact on the Shaping of Contemporary Salafism. In: R. Meijer, ed. 2009. *Global Salafism: Islam's New Religious Movement*. New York: Columbia University Press, pp.58–80.

Lambert, Robert, 2008. Empowering Salafis and Islamists against Al-Qaeda: A London Counterterrorism Case Study. *PS: Political Science and Politics* 41(1), pp.31–35.

Lambert, Robert, 2011. *Countering Al-Qaeda in London: Police and Muslims in Partnership*. London: Hurst & Company.

Lauzière, Henri, 2010. The Construction of *Salafiyya*: Reconsidering Salafism from the Perspective of Conceptual History. *International Journal of Middle East Studies* 42, pp.369–389.

Lessons in Hate and Violence, 2011. Channel 4, Dispatches, 14 February, 20:00.

Lewis, Philip, 2007. *Young, British and Muslim*. London: Continuum.

Limbert, Mandana E., 2010. *In the Time of Oil: Piety, Memory, and Social Life in an Omani Town*. Stanford, Calif.: Stanford University Press.

Lofland, John and Skonovd, Norman, 1981. Conversion Motifs. *Journal for the Scientific Study of Religion* 20(4), pp.373–385.

Lofland, John and Stark, Rodney, 1965. Becoming a World-Saver: A Theory of Conversion to a Deviant Perspective. *American Sociological Review* 30(6), pp.862–875.

Luhrmann, T. M., 1994. *Persuasions of the Witch's Craft: Ritual Magic and Witchcraft in Present-day England.* London: Picador.

MacEoin, Denis, 2007. *The Hijacking of British Islam: How Extremist Literature is Subverting Mosques in the UK.* London: Policy Exchange.

Mahmood, Saba, 2005. *Politics of Piety: The Islamic Revival and the Feminist Subject.* Princeton, N.J.: Princeton University Press.

Malik, Jamal ed., 2004. *Muslims in Europe: From the Margin to the Centre.* New Brunswick, N.J.: Transaction.

Malik, Shiv, 2007. My Brother the Bomber. *Prospect* 31, June 30. Available at: <www.prospectmagazine.co.uk/magazine/my-brother-the-bomber-mohammad-sidique-khan/#.UhT9g5LVB8E> [Accessed 13 November 2015].

Malinowski, Bronislaw, 2014 [1922]. *Argonauts of the Western Pacific.* London; New York: Routledge.

Marranci, Gabriele, 2007. Policy Exchange hijacks professional research. [blog] 31 October. Available at: <http://marranci.com/2007/10/31/policy-exchange-hijacks-professional-research> [Accessed 13 November 2015].

Marranci, Gabriele, 2009. *Understanding Muslim Identity: Rethinking Fundamentalism.* Hampshire: Palgrave Macmillan.

Martensson, Ulrika, 2012. Norwegian Haraki Salafism: 'The Saved Sect' Hugs the Infidels. *Comparative Islamic Studies* 8(1–2), pp.113–138.

Marty, Martin E. and Appleby, R. Scott eds., 2004. 2nd ed. *Fundamentalisms Comprehended.* Chicago; London: University of Chicago Press.

Mavrommatis, George, 2010. A Racial Archaeology of Space: A Journey through the Political Imaginings of Brixton and Brick Lane, London. *Journal of Ethnic and Migration Studies* 36(4), pp.561–579.

Mavrommatis, George, 2011. Stories from Brixton: Gentrification and Different Differences. *Sociological Research Online* 16(2). Available at: <www.socresonline.org.uk/16/2/12.html> [Accessed 13 November 2015].

McCrone, P., Bhui, K., Craig, T., Mohamud, S., Warfa, N., Stansfeld, S. A., Thornicroft, G., and Curtis, S., 2005. Mental Health Needs, Service Use and Costs among Somali Refugees in the UK. *Acta Psychiatrica Scandinavica* 11(5), pp.351–357.

McGuire, Meredith B., 2001. *Religion: The Social Context.* 5th ed. Belmont, Calif.; London: Wadsworth.

McGuire, Meredith B., 2008. *Lived Religion: Faith and Practice in Everyday Life.* Oxford; New York: Oxford University Press.

Meijer, Roel ed., 2009a. *Global Salafism: Islam's New Religious Movement.* New York: Columbia University Press.

Meijer, Roel, 2009b. Introduction. In: R. Meijer, ed. 2009. *Global Salafism: Islam's New Religious Movement.* New York: Columbia University Press, pp.1–32.

Meijer, Roel, 2011. Politicising *al-jarh wa-l-ta'dil*: Rabi' b. Hadi al-Madkhali and the Transnational Battle for Religious Authority. In: N. Boekhoff-van der Voort, K. Versteegh, and J. Wagemakers, eds. 2011. *The Transmission and Dynamics of the Textual Sources of Islam: Essays in Honour of Harald Motzki.* Leiden; Boston: Brill, pp.375–399.

Mercury, Sunday, 2008. Birmingham Robber Given £10,000 to Fight Terror. *Birmingham Mail*, 29 November. Available at: <www.birminghammail.

co.uk/news/local-news/birmingham-robber-given-10000-to-fight-236489>
[Accessed 13 November 2015].

Messick, Brinkley, 1993. *The Calligraphic State: Textual Domination and History in a Muslim Society*. Berkeley; Los Angeles; Oxford: University of California Press.

Mitchell, J. Clyde, 1984. Case Studies. In: R. F. Ellen, ed. 1984. *Ethnographic Research: A Guide to General Conduct*. London: Academic Press, pp.237–241.

Mohammed, Syma, 2012. Why British Muslim Women Struggle to Find a Marriage Partner. *The Guardian*, 18 January. Available at: <www.theguardian.com/commentisfree/belief/2012/jan/18/british-muslim-women-marriage-struggle> [Accessed 13 November 2015].

Mondal, Anshuman A., 2008. *Young British Muslim Voices*. Oxford: Greenwood World.

Moussalli, Ahmad, 2009. *Wahhabism, Salafism and Islamism: Who Is The Enemy?* [pdf] Conflicts Forum, January. Available at: <http://conflictsforum.org/briefings/Wahhabism-Salafism-and-Islamism.pdf> [Accessed 13 November 2015].

Murad, Abdal-Hakim, n.d. Islamic Spirituality: The Forgotten Revolution. [online] Available at: <www.masud.co.uk/ISLAM/ahm/fgtnrevo.htm> [Accessed 13 November 2015].

Murad, Abdal-Hakim, 2001. Recapturing Islam from the Terrorists. [online] September 14. Available at: <www.masud.co.uk/ISLAM/ahm/recapturing.htm> [Accessed 13 November 2015].

Murad, Abdal-Hakim, 2005. Islam's Heart of Darkness. *The Tablet*, 23 July. Available at: <http://archive.thetablet.co.uk/article/23rd-july-2005/4/islams-heart-of-darkness> [Accessed 13 November 2015].

My Brother, the Islamist, 2011. Directed by Robb Leech. BBC3, 11 April.

Naqshbandi, Mehmood, 2015. Muslims in Britain. [online] Available at: <www.MuslimsInBritain.org> [Accessed 13 November 2015].

National Commission on Terrorist Attacks, 2004. *The 9/11 Commission Report: Final Report of the National Commission on Terrorist Attacks upon the United States*. [pdf] Available at: <http://govinfo.library.unt.edu/911/report/911Report.pdf> [Accessed 13 November 2015].

Nawaz, Maajid and Husain, Ed, 2010. *Preventing Terrorism: Where Next for Britain?* [online] Quilliam. Available at: <www.scribd.com/doc/34834977/Secret-Quilliam-Memo-to-government#archive_trial> [Accessed 13 November 2015].

Nielsen, Jørgen S., 1995. *Muslims in Western Europe*. 2nd ed. Edinburgh: Edinburgh University Press.

Nieuwkerk, Karin van ed., 2006a. *Women Embracing Islam: Gender and Conversion in the West*. Austin: University of Texas Press.

Nieuwkerk, Karin van, 2006b. Gender and Conversion to Islam in the West. In: K. van Nieuwkerk, ed. 2006. *Women Embracing Islam: Gender and Conversion in the West*. Austin: University of Texas Press, pp.1–16.

Nieuwkerk, Karin van, 2006c. Gender, Conversion, and Islam: A Comparison of Online and Offline Conversion Narratives. In: K. van Nieuwkerk, ed. 2006. *Women Embracing Islam: Gender and Conversion in the West*. Austin: University of Texas Press, pp.95–119.

Nomis Official Labour Market Statistics, 2013. All people—Economically active—Unemployed (Model Based) Lambeth. Office for National Statistics, March. Available at: <www.nomisweb.co.uk/reports/lmp/la/1946157253/subreports/ea_time_series/report.aspx?> [Accessed 13 November 2015].

Office for National Statistics (ONS), 2014. *2011 Census Analysis: How do Living Arrangements, Family Type and Family Size Vary in England and Wales?* [pdf]

Available at: <www.ons.gov.uk/ons/dcp171776_366963.pdf> [Accessed 13 November 2015].

Office for National Statistics (ONS), 2015. Population by Country of Birth and Nationality, Reweighted data for calendar years 2004 to 2013. Available at: <www.ons.gov.uk/ons/rel/migration1/population-by-country-of-birth-and-nationality/revisions-to-population-by-country-of-birth-and-nationality---calendar-years-2004-to-2013/index.html> [Accessed 13 November 2015]

Okely, Judith, 1992. Anthropology and Autobiography: Participatory Experience and Embodied Knowledge. In: J. Okely and H. Callaway, eds. 1992. *Anthropology and Autobiography*. London; New York: Routledge, pp.1–28.

Okely, Judith and Callaway, Helen eds., 1992. *Anthropology and Autobiography*. London; New York: Routledge.

Okruhlik, Gwenn, 2004. Making Conversation Permissible: Islamism and Reform in Saudi Arabia. In: Q. Wiktorowicz, ed. 2004. *Islamic Activism: A Social Movement Theory Approach*. Bloomington: Indiana University Press, pp.250–269.

Olden, Anthony, 1999. Somali Refugees in London: Oral Culture in a Western Information Environment. *Libri* 49, pp.212–224.

Oliveti, Vincenzo, 2002. *Terror's Source: The Ideology of Wahhabi-Salafism and Its Consequences*. Birmingham: Amadeus Books.

Olsson, Susanne, 2012. Swedish Puritan Salafism: A Hijra within. *Comparative Islamic Studies* 8(1–2), pp.71–92.

Olsson, Susanne, 2014. Proselytizing Islam—Problematizing 'Salafism'. *The Muslim World* 104(1–2), pp.171–197.

Omaar, Rageh, 2006. *Only Half of Me: Being a Muslim in Britain*. London: Viking.

Open Society Foundations, 2014. *Somalis in London*. [pdf] Available at: <www.opensocietyfoundations.org/sites/default/files/somalis-london-20141010.pdf> [Accessed 13 November 2015].

Özyürek, Esra, 2015. *Being German, Becoming Muslim: Race, Religion, and Conversion in the New Europe*. Princeton; Oxford: Princeton University Press.

Padnos, Theo, 2011. *Undercover Muslim: A Journey into Yemen*. London: Bodley Head.

Palmer, Susan Jean, 1994. *Moon Sisters, Krishna Mothers, Rajneesh Lovers: Women's Roles in New Religions*. Syracuse, N.Y.: Syracuse University Press.

Peach, Ceri, 2005. Muslims in the UK. In: T. Abbas, ed. 2005. *Muslim Britain: Communities under Pressure*. London: Zed Books, pp.18–30.

Peach, Ceri, 2006. Islam, Ethnicity and South Asian Religions in the London 2001 Census. *Transactions of the Institute of British Geographers* NS 31, pp.353–370.

Piela, Anna, 2012. *Muslim Women Online: Faith and Identity in Virtual Space*. London; New York: Routledge.

Piela, Anna, 2014. You've been framed! How niqabis are pictured in the British mass media. *Publicspirit*, 22 January. Available at: <www.publicspirit.org.uk/assets/Anna-Piela-Niqab-10th-Jan.pdf> [Accessed 13 November 2015].

Prime Minister's Office, 2015. PM: New counter-extremism strategy is a clear signal of the choice we make today. 19 October. Available at: <www.gov.uk/government/news/pm-new-counter-extremism-strategy-is-a-clear-signal-of-the-choice-we-make-today> [Accessed 13 November 2015].

Puttick, Elizabeth, 1999. Women in New Religious Movements. In: B. Wilson and J. Cresswell, eds. 1999. *New Religious Movements: Challenge and Response*. London; New York: Routledge, pp.143–162.

Quilliam, 2010. *The Threat of Radicalisation on British University Campuses: a case study*. [pdf] September. Available at: <www.quilliamfoundation.org/wp/wp-content/

uploads/publications/free/the-threat-of-radicalisation-on-british-university-campuses.pdf> [Accessed 13 November 2015].

Ramadan, Tariq, 2004. *Western Muslims and the Future of Islam.* Oxford: Oxford University Press.

Rambo, Lewis R., 1993. *Understanding Religious Conversion.* New Haven, Ct.; London: Yale University Press.

Rambo, Lewis, 1999. Theories of Conversion: Understanding and Interpreting Religious Change. *Social Compass* 46(3), pp.259–271.

Raymond, Catherine Zara, 2010. *Al-Muhajiroun and Islam4UK: The group behind the ban.* [pdf] International Centre for the Study of Radicalisation and Political Violence. Available at: <http://icsr.info/wp-content/uploads/2012/10/1276697989CatherineZaraRaymondICSRPaper.pdf> [Accessed 13 November 2015].

Reddie, Richard S., 2009. *Black Muslims in Britain: Why Are a Growing Number of Young Black People Converting to Islam?* Oxford: Lion.

Richardson, James T., 1993. A Social Psychological Critique of 'Brainwashing' Claims about Recruitment to New Religions. In: D. G. Bromley and J. K. Hadden, eds. 1993. *Religion and the Social Order: The Handbook on Cults and Sects in America.* Volume 3(B). Greenwich, Ct.; London: Jai Press, pp.75–97.

Roald, Anne Sofie, 2001. *Women in Islam: The Western Experience.* London; New York: Routledge.

Roald, Anne Sofie, 2004. *New Muslims in the European Context: The Experience of Scandinavian Converts.* Leiden: Brill.

Roald, Anne Sofie, 2006. The Shaping of a Scandinavian 'Islam': Converts and Gender Equal Opportunity. In: K. van Nieuwkerk, ed. 2006. *Women Embracing Islam: Gender and Conversion in the West.* Austin: University of Texas Press. Ch.2.

Robbins, Thomas, 1992. *Cults, Converts and Charisma: The Sociology of New Religious Movements.* London; Newbury Park; Beverly Hills; New Delhi: SAGE Publications.

Robert, Na'ima B., 2005. *From My Sisters' Lips.* London: Bantam Press.

Roex, Ineke, 2014. Should We be Scared of All Salafists in Europe? A Dutch Case Study. *Perspectives on Terrorism* 8(3), pp.51–63.

Rose, Susan D., 1987. Women Warriors: The Negotiation of Gender in a Charismatic Community. *Sociological Analysis* 48(3), pp.245–258.

Roy, Olivier, 2004. *Globalised Islam: The Search for a New Ummah.* London: Hurst & Co.

Roy, Olivier, 2010. *Holy Ignorance: When Religion and Culture Diverge.* Translated from French by Ros Schwartz. London: C. Hurst.

Rutter, Jill, 2004. Refugee Communities in the UK: Somali Children's Educational Progress and Life Experiences. [briefing paper] London Metropolitan University. Available at: <http://open.tean.ac.uk/handle/123456789/716> [Accessed 13 November 2015].

Rutter, Jill, 2006. *Refugee Children in the UK.* Maidenhead: Open University Press.

Sabirova, Guzel, 2011. Young Muslim-Tatar Girls of the Big City: Narrative Identities and Discourses on Islam in Postsoviet Russia. *Religion, State and Society* 39(2–3), pp.327–345.

Sageman, Marc, 2004. *Understanding Terror Networks.* Philadelphia: University of Pennsylvania Press.

Salomon, Noah, 2009. The Salafi Critique of Islamism: Doctrine, Difference and the Problem of Islamic Political Action in Contemporary Sudan. In: R. Meijer, ed.

2009. *Global Salafism: Islam's New Religious Movement*. New York: Columbia University Press, pp.143–168.

Secrets of Britain's Sharia Councils, 2013. BBC 1, Panorama, 22 April, 20:30.

Seddon, Mohammed Siddique, Hussain, Dilwar, and Malik, Nadeem eds., 2002. *British Muslims: Loyalty and Belonging*. Leicester: Islamic Foundation.

Sedgwick, Mark, 2000. Sects in the Islamic World. *Nova Religio* 3(2), pp.195–240.

Sedgwick, Mark, 2007. Jihad, Modernity, and Sectarianism. *Nova Religio* 11(2), pp.6–27.

Sedgwick, Mark, 2010. The Concept of Radicalization as a Source of Confusion. *Terrorism and Political Violence* 22(4), pp.479–494.

Sedgwick, Mark, 2012. Salafism, the Social, and the Global Resurgence of Religion. *Comparative Islamic Studies* 8(1–2), pp.57–70.

Shanneik, Yafa, 2011. Religion and Diasporic Dwelling: Algerian Muslim Women in Ireland. *Religion and Gender* 2(1), pp.80–100.

Shanneik, Yafa, 2012. Conversion and Religious Habitus: The Experiences of Irish Women Converts to Islam in the Pre-Celtic Tiger Era. *Journal of Muslim Minority Affairs* 31(4), pp.503–517.

Shterin, Marat and Yarlykapov, Akhmet, 2011. Reconsidering Radicalisation and Terrorism: the New Muslims Movement in Kabardino-Balkaria and its Path to Violence. *Religion, State and Society* 39(2–3), pp.303–325.

Siddiqui, Ataullah, 2004. Muslim Youth in Britain: Cultural and Religious Conflict in Perspective. In: J. Malik, ed. 2004. *Muslims in Europe: From the Margin to the Centre*. New Brunswick, N.J.: Transaction, pp.49–59.

Silvestri, Sara, 2012. Faith Intersections and Muslim Women in the European Microcosm: Notes towards the Study of Non-organized Islam. In: N. Jeldtoft and J. S. Nielsen, eds. 2012. *Methods and Contexts in the Study of Muslim Minorities: Visible and Invisible Muslims*. Abingdon; New York: Routledge, pp.121–138.

Singer, Margaret Thaler with Lalich, Janja, 1996. *Cults in Our Midst*. San Francisco: Jossey-Bass.

Smith, Jacqui, 2008. Our shared values—a shared responsibility. Speech to the first International Conference on Radicalisation and Political Violence, 17 January. Available at: <http://tna.europarchive.org/20061101012820/http:/press. homeoffice.gov.uk/Speeches/sp-hs-terrorism-keynote-jan-08> [Accessed 13 November 2015].

Song, Miri, 2012. Part of the Mainstream? British Muslim Students and Islamic Student Associations. *Journal of Youth Studies* 15(2), pp.143–160.

Soria, Valentina, 2012. *Global Jihad Sustained through Africa*. [pdf] *UK Terrorism Analysis* 2, Royal United Services Institute.

Spradley, James P., 1980. *Participant Observation*. New York; London: Holt, Rinehart and Winston.

Stark, Rodney, 2003. Why Religious Movements Succeed or Fail: A Revised General Model. In: L. L. Dawson, ed. 2003. *Cults and New Religious Movements: A Reader*. Malden, MA; Oxford; Carlton, Victoria: Blackwell, pp.259–270.

Suleaman, Nasreen, 2006. Restless convert in quest for jihad. *BBC News Online*, May 3. Available at: <http://news.bbc.co.uk/1/hi/uk/4942924.stm> [Accessed 13 November 2015].

Sutton, Rupert and Stuart, Hannah, 2012. *Challenging Extremists: Practical frameworks for our universities*. [pdf] Henry Jackson Society. Available at: <http://henryjacksonsociety.org/wp-content/uploads/2012/05/SRSocialMedia.pdf> [Accessed 13 November 2015].

Svensson, Jonas, 2012. Mind the Beard! Deference, Purity and Islamization of Everyday Life as Micro-factors in a Salafi Cultural Epidemiology. *Comparative Islamic Studies* 8(1–2), pp.185–210.

Tajfel, Henri ed., 1978. *Differentiation between Social Groups: Studies in the Social Psychology of the Inter-group Relations.* London: Academic Press.

Tajfel, Henri, 1979. Individuals and Groups in Social Psychology. *British Journal of Social and Clinical Psychology* 18, pp.183–190.

Taji-Farouki, Suha, 1996. *A Fundamental Quest: Hizb al-Tahrir and the Search for the Islamic Caliphate.* London: Grey Seal.

Tarlo, Emma, 2010. *Visibly Muslim: Fashion, Politics, Faith.* Oxford; New York: Berg.

Tesfagiorgios, Petros, 2005. *Refugees and the Development of Africa: The Case of Eritrean Refugees in the UK.* [pdf] Available at: <www.irr.org.uk/pdf/eritrean_refugees. pdf> [Accessed 13 November 2015].

The Centre for Social Cohesion, 2010. *Radical Islam on UK Campuses.* [pdf] Available at: <http://conservativehome.blogs.com/files/1292336866_1-1.pdf> [Accessed 13 November 2015].

The Guardian, 2001. Mosque leader warns over extremist converts. *The Guardian*, 26 December. Available at: <www.theguardian.com/world/2001/dec/26/september11.uk> [Accessed 21 August 2013].

Thiollet, Hélène, 2007. *Refugees and Migrants from Eritrea to the Arab World: The Cases of Sudan, Yemen and Saudi Arabia 1991-2007.* [pdf] Migration and Refugee Movements in the Middle East and North Africa, Forced Migration & Refugee Studies Program, American University in Cairo, Egypt. Available at: <www.aucegypt.edu/GAPP/cmrs/Documents/HeleneThiollet.pdf> [Accessed 13 November 2015].

Tiilikainen, Marja, 2013. Illness, Healing, and Everyday Islam: Transnational Lives of Somali Migrant Women. In: N. M. Dessing, N. Jeldtoft, J. S. Nielsen, and L. Woodhead, eds. 2013. *Everyday Lived Islam in Europe.* Surrey; Burlington, Vt.: Ashgate. Ch.10.

Tiilikainen, Marja, 2015. Looking for a Safe Place: Security and Transnational Somali Muslim Families. *Journal of Religion in Europe* 8, pp.51–72.

Torab, Azam, 1996. Piety as Gendered Agency: A Study of *Jalaseh* Ritual Discourse in an Urban Neighbourhood in Iran. *Journal of the Royal Anthropological Institute* 2(2), pp.235–252.

Torab, Azam, 2002. The Politicization of Women's Religious Circles in Post-revolutionary Iran. In: S. Ansari and V. Martin, eds. 2002. *Women, Religion and Culture in Iran.* Richmond, Surrey: Curzon. Ch.9.

Turner, Hossein, 2012. Is there a marriage crisis in the British Muslim community? *Weekly Zaman*, 7 January. Available at: <http://ingiltere.zaman.com.tr/en/newsDetail_getNewsById.action?newsId=547> [Accessed 13 November 2015].

Undercover Mosque, 2007. Directed by Andrew Smith. Channel 4, Dispatches, 15 January, 20:00.

Undercover Mosque: The Return, 2008. Directed by Andrew Smith. Channel 4, Dispatches, 1 September.

United Nations Development Programme (UNDP), 2009. *Somalia's Missing Million: The Somali Diaspora and its Role in Development.* [pdf] Available at: <www.so.undp. org/content/dam/somalia/docs/Project_Documents/Poverty_Reduction/Somalia%20Missing%20Millions.pdf> [Accessed 13 November 2015].

Vallely, Paul, 2007. Wahhabism: a deadly scripture. *The Independent*, November 1. Available at: <www.independent.co.uk/news/uk/home-news/wahhabism-a-deadly-scripture-398516.html> [Accessed 13 November 2015].

Vanderwaeren, Els, 2012. *Muslimahs'* Impact on and Acquisition of Islamic Religious Authority in Flanders. In: M. Bano and H. Kalmbach, ed. 2012. *Women, Leadership, and Mosques: Changes in Contemporary Islamic Authority.* Leiden; Boston: Brill, pp.301–322.

Wagemakers, Joas, 2009. The Transformation of a Radical Concept: *al-wala' wa-l-bara'* in the Ideology of Abu Muhammad al-Maqdisi. In: R. Meijer, ed. 2009. *Global Salafism: Islam's New Religious Movement.* New York: Columbia University Press, pp.81–106.

Warfa, Nasir, Curtis, Sarah, Watters, Charles, Carswell, Ken, Ingleby, David, and Bhui, Kamaldeep, 2012. Migration Experiences, Employment Status and Psychological Distress among Somali Immigrants: A Mixed-Method International Study. *BMC Public Health* 12(749), pp.1–12.

Watson, Helen, 1994. Women and the Veil: Personal Responses to Global Process. In: A. S. Ahmed and H. Donnan, eds. 1994. *Islam, Globalization, and Postmodernity.* London; New York: Routledge, pp.141–159.

Weber, Max, 1964. *The Sociology of Religion.* 4th ed. Translated from German by Ephraim Fischoff. Boston: Beacon Press.

Weiss, A. M., 1994. Challenges for Muslim Women in a Postmodern World. In: A. S. Ahmed and H. Donnan, eds. 1994. *Islam, Globalization, and Postmodernity.* London; New York: Routledge, pp.127–140.

What's Wrong with Polygamy? 2011. BBC Asian, 26 September, 18:00.

Wickham, Carrie Rosefsky, 2002. *Mobilizing Islam: Religion, Activism, and Political Change in Egypt.* New York: Columbia University Press.

Wickham, Carrie Rosefsky, 2004. Interests, Ideas, and Islamist Outreach in Egypt. In: Q. Wiktorowicz, ed. 2004. *Islamic Activism: A Social Movement Theory Approach.* Bloomington: Indiana University Press, pp.231–249.

Wiedl, Nina, 2012. *The Making of a German Salafiyya: The Emergence, Development and Missionary Work of Salafi Movements in Germany.* [pdf] Aarhus: Centre for Studies in Islamism and Radicalisation, Aarhus University.

Wiktorowicz, Quintan, 2001. *The Management of Islamic Activism: Salafis, the Muslim Brotherhood, and State Power in Jordan.* Albany: State University of New York Press.

Wiktorowicz, Quintan, 2004a. Introduction. In: Q. Wiktorowicz, ed. 2004. *Islamic Activism: A Social Movement Theory Approach.* Bloomington: Indiana University Press, pp.1–33.

Wiktorowicz, Quintan ed., 2004b. *Islamic Activism: A Social Movement Theory Approach.* Bloomington: Indiana University Press.

Wiktorowicz, Quintan, 2005a. *Radical Islam Rising: Muslim Extremism in the West.* Lanham, Md.: Rowman & Littlefield.

Wiktorowicz, Quintan, 2005b. The Salafi Movement: Violence and the Fragmentation of Community. In: M. Cooke and B. B. Lawrence, eds. 2005. *Muslim Networks from Hajj to Hip Hop.* Chapel Hill; London: University of North Carolina Press, pp.208–234.

Wiktorowicz, Quintan, 2006. Anatomy of the Salafi Movement. *Studies in Conflict & Terrorism* 29, pp.207–239.

Wilson, Bryan R., 1982. The New Religions: Some Preliminary Considerations. In: E. Barker, ed. 1982. *New Religious Movements: A Perspective for Understanding Society.* New York; Toronto: Edwin Mellen Press, pp.16–31.

Wohlrab-Sahr, Monika, 2006. Symbolizing Distance: Conversion to Islam in Germany and the United States. In: K. van Nieuwkerk, ed. 2006. *Women Embracing Islam: Gender and Conversion in the West.* Austin: University of Texas Press. Ch.3.

Woodhead, Linda, 2007a. *Gender Differences in Religious Practice and Significance.* In: J. A. Beckford and J. Demerath, eds. 2007. *The Sage Handbook of the Sociology of Religion.* Los Angeles; London; New Delhi; Singapore: Sage, pp.550–570.

Woodhead, Linda, 2007b. *Sex and Secularisation.* In: G. Loughlin, ed. 2007. *Queer Theology: Rethinking the Western Body.* Oxford: Blackwell, pp.230–244.

Woods, Orlando, 2012. The Geographies of Religious Conversion. *Progress in Human Geography* 36(4), pp.440–456.

Yaghi, Adam, 2014. On the Altar of ISIS: Difference, Plurality, and the Roots of Contemporary Violence in the Middle East. *Just Peace Diplomacy Journal,* 9 November, pp.1–18.

Young, Angry and Muslim, 2005. Directed by Julian Hendy. Channel 4, Dispatches, 24 October.

Young, Muslim and Black, 2011. BBC World Service, Heart and Soul, 3 February. Available at: <www.bbc.co.uk/programmes/p00d872v> [Accessed 13 November 2015].

Young Muslims 'becoming radicalised', 2013. Robert Pigott, BBC Radio 4, Today, 19 August. Available at: <www.bbc.co.uk/news/uk-23753325> [Accessed 13 November 2015].

Zaman, Muhammad Qasim, 2007. Epilogue: Competing Conceptions of Religious Education. In: R. W. Hefner and M. Q. Zaman, eds. 2007. *Schooling Islam: The Culture and Politics of Modern Muslim Education.* Princeton, N.J.: Princeton University Press. Ch.11.

Zebiri, Kate, 2007. *British Muslim Converts: Choosing Alternative Lives.* Oxford: Oneworld Publications.

Zempi, Irene and Chakraborti, Neil, 2014. *Islamophobia, Victimisation and the Veil.* Hampshire: Palgrave Macmillan.

Zubaida, Sami, 2003. Islam in Europe. *Critical Quarterly* 45(1–2), pp.88–98.

Primary Textual, Online, and Audio Sources

1Dawah Salafi Nikah, n.d. Why 1Dawah Salafi Nikah? [website] Available at: <salafinikah.1dawah.com> [Accessed 13 November 2015].

'Abdul 'Azeez Aali Shaykh, Saalih bin, 2008. A Warning against Extremism. [pamphlet] Translated from Arabic by AbdulHaq al-Ashanti. Amman: Jamiah Media.

'Abdur-Rahman, Abu Ameenah and al-Ashanti, AbdulHaq, n.d. 7 Reasons Why Al-Muhajiroun are Deviants. [pamphlet] London: Jamiah Media.

Abdul Waahid, Abu Khadeejah, n.d.a. Who Are the Salafis and Are They from Ahlus Sunnah wal-Jamaa'ah? [leaflet] The Salafi Press.

Abdul Waahid, Abu Khadeejah, n.d.b. Common Doubts Regarding the Prophet Muhammad. [leaflet] Salafi Publications.

Abdul Waahid, Abu Khadeejah, n.d.c. Magic Explained in Light of the Qur'an & Sunnah. [leaflet] Salafi Publications.

Abdul Waahid, Abu Khadeejah, 2006a. Forced Marriage and Racism. [CD] 10 March. Salafi Publications.

Abdul Waahid, Abu Khadeejah, 2006b. 7/7 A Year On. [CD] 7 July. Salafi Publications.

Abdul Waahid, Abu Khadeejah, 2008. A Brief Word on How to Deal with Differences of Opinion amongst the Salafees. [2 CDs] Salafi Publications.

Abdul Waahid, Abu Khadeejah, 2009a. The Veiling of the Muslim Woman & Its Conditions. [leaflet] Salafi Publications.

Abdul Waahid, Abu Khadeejah, 2009b. O Youth Marry Whoever Pleases You of Women! [3 CDs] Birmingham Winter Conference, December, Masjid as Salafi. Salafi Publications.

Abdul Waahid, Abu Khadeejah, 2009c. Islaam: Between Extremism & Neglect. [leaflet] Salafi Publications.

Abdul Waahid, Abu Khadeejah, 2009d. Mankind's Greatest Need & Mankind's Gravest Sin. [leaflet] Salafi Publications.

Abdul Waahid, Abu Khadeejah, 2010. Do Not Prevent the Youth from Marriage. [CD] 15 October. Salafi Publications.

Abdul Waahid, Abu Khadeejah, 2013. May 1996: OASIS & Salafi Publications—Spreading Salafi Da'wah. 18 December. Available at: <www.abukhadeejah.com/may-1996-oasis-salafi-publications-a-new-approach-to-salafi-dawah> [Accessed 13 November 2015].

Abdul Waahid, Abu Khadeejah, 2014. FREE Flier: Combatting ISIS Al-Qaeda & "Islamist" Insurgencies Worldwide. [leaflet] 20 September. Salafi Publications. Available at: <www.abukhadeejah.com/free-leaflet-combatting-isis-al-qaeda-islamist-insurgencies-worldwide> [Accessed 13 November 2015].

Abdul Waahid, Abu Khadeejah, 2015a. Understanding The Terrorist Insurgency in Light of ISIS and the Paris Attacks. Lecture delivered at 'The Anti-Terrorism Conference' at Markaz Muadh bin Jabal, Slough, on 21 January 2015. Available at: <www.salafisounds.com/understanding-the-terrorist-insurgency-in-light-of-isis-the-paris-attacks-by-abu-khadeejah> [Accessed 13 November 2015].

Abdul Waahid, Abu Khadeejah, 2015b. Sisters! Do not be deceived by ISIS and the Khawaarij, do not travel to them! Friday sermon. Available at: <www.salafisounds.com/sisters-do-not-be-deceived-by-isis> [Accessed 13 November 2015].

Abu Aliyah, 2013. Socalled Madkhali Salafi Exposed by Abu Aliyah (MUST SEE). [video] 18 March. Available at: <www.youtube.com/watch?v=JlnbhGdoQ7E> [Accessed 13 November 2015].

Abu Haleema, 2015. Madkhali Village. [video] Available at: <www.youtube.com/watch?v=bMDAYQXvZO0> [Accessed 13 November 2015].

Adam, Ben, 2006a. The Veil Unveiled: The True Status of Women in Islam. [leaflet].

Adam, Ben, 2006b. The Punished. [leaflet].

Adam, Ben, 2006c. United Colors of Islam. [leaflet].

Adan_1, 2009. Salafi fitna on the somali sisters. [online] 9 May. Available at: <www.somalinet.com/forums/viewtopic.php?f=63&t=209164&sid=ad2c1ac0f73c4f2b4bbb028a32d23a4b> [Accessed 13 November 2015].

Ahmad Abu Saif, As-Sayyid bin, 2004. *The Choice of Every Woman*. Riyadh; Jeddah; Sharjah; Lahore; London; Houston; New York: Dar-us-Salam.

Al-'Uthaymeen, Muhmmad ibn Saalih, 1997. *Explanation of the Three Fundamental Principles of Islaam*. Translated from Arabic by Aboo Talhah Daawood ibn Ronald Burbank. Birmingham: Al-Hidaayah Publishing and Distribution.

Al-Atharee, Fawzee, 2002. Treatment of Non-Muslims in Their Lands. Translated by Abu Uwais. Available at: <www.salafipublications.com/sps/downloads/pdf/LSC010002.pdf> [Accessed 13 November 2015].

Al-Barbahaaree, Abu Muhammad al-Hasan ibn 'Alee ibn Khalf, 1995. *Explanation of the Creed*. Translated from Arabic by Abu Talhah Daawood Ibn Ronald Burbank. Birmingham: Al-Haneef Publications.

Al-Jaabiree, 'Ubayd, 2007. And from His Signs is that He Created for You from Yourselves, Spouses that You May Dwell with, and He Put Between You Love & Mercy. [2 CDs] Winter Conference 2007, 29 December. Salafi Publications.

Al-Hanbali, Ibn Rajab and Al-Ajurri, Abu Bakr, 2009. *The Journey of the Strangers*. Birmingham: Daar Us-Sunnah

Al-Madkhalee, Rabee' Ibn Haadee, 1997. *The Methodology of the Prophets In Calling to Allaah: That is the Way of Wisdom & Intelligence*. Translated from Arabic by Aboo

Talhah Daawood ibn Ronald Burbank. Birmingham: Al-Hidaayah Publishing and Distribution.

Al-Sa'di, 'Allamah 'Abd al-Rahman, 2003. *An Explanation of Muhammad ibn 'Abd al-Wahhab's Kitab Al-Tawhid.* Translated by Abu Khaliyl. Birmingham: Al-Hidaayah Publishing and Distribution.

Al Salman, Mashur Hasan, 2010. *The Noble Women Scholars of Hadith: Women's Concern with the Prophetic Hadith.* Translated from Arabic by Abu Hayyan Salal bin 'AbdulGhafur and AbdulHaq al-Ashanti. London: Jamiah Media.

Al Salman, Mashhur bin Hasan, 2011. *The Fiqh Madhhab of Ahl ul-Hadith: The Legitimacy of its Features.* Translated from Arabic by AbdulHaq al-Ashanti. London: Jamiah Media.

Al-Utaybee, Badr bin Ali, 2010. *20 Pieces of Advice to my Sister Before her Marriage.* 2nd ed. Translated from Arabic by Team Riwayah. Jersey City, N.J.: Riwayah Publications.

Al-Wasaabee Al-'Abdalee, Abu Ibraheem Muhammad bin 'Abdul-Wahhab bin 'Ali, 2009. *Beneficial Speech In Establishing The Evidences Of Tawheed.* Translated from Arabic by Abu Naasir Abid bin Basheer. Birmingham: Salafi Publications.

Anon., 2010. *The Rise of Jihadist Extremism in the West: An Analysis of Extremist Ideologies and the Most Notable Figureheads of Radicalisation.* Birmingham: Salafi Publications.

Ar-Rayyis 'Abdul-Aziz, 2010. *The Beautiful Advice to the Noble Salafis of the West.* [pamphlet] Translated from Arabic by AbdulHaq Al-Ashanti. London: Jamiah Media.

Ashanti, AbdulHaq, 2014. *The ISIS Papers.* Available at: <www.salafimanhaj.com/?p=318> [Accessed 13 November 2015].

As-Salafi, Abū Ameenah 'AbdurRahmān and al-Ashantī, 'AbdulHaq, 2009. *A Critical Study of the Multiple Identities and Disguises of 'Al-Muhajiroun'.* London: Jamiah Media.

As-Salafi, Abū Ameenah 'AbdurRahmān and al-Ashantī, 'AbdulHaq, 2011. *'Abdullah El-Faisal al-Jamayki: A Critical Study of his Statements, Errors and Extremism in Takfeer.* London: Jamiah Media.

As-Salafiyyah, Umm Salamah, 2005. *Supporting the Rights of the Believing Women.* Dallas, Texas: Tarbiyyah Bookstore Publishing.

Badawi, Abdul-Azeem, 2007. *The Concise Presentation of the Fiqh of the Sunnah and the Noble Book.* 3rd ed. Translated from Arabic by Jamaal al-Din M. Zarabozo. Riyadh: International Islamic Publishing House.

Bajwa, Hamza A., 2009. Foreword. In: A. A. A. As-Salafi and A. Al-Ashanti, 2009. *A Critical Study of the Multiple Identities and Disguises of 'Al-Muhajiroun'.* London: Jamiah Media.

Bazmul, Muhammad bin 'Umar, 2015. Facebook post, 6 June. Translated by AbdulHaq al-Ashanti. Available at <www.facebook.com/mohammadbazmool/posts/828171750634646> [Accessed 13 November 2015].

Bin Abdul Aziz, King Fahd, n.d.a. Introduction. [website] Available at: <www.king-fahdbinabdulaziz.com/main/m000.htm> [Accessed 13 November 2015].

Bin Abdul Aziz, King Fahd, n.d.b. Provision of Copies of the Holy Quran. [website] Available at: <www.kingfahdbinabdulaziz.com/main/m600.htm> [Accessed 13 November 2015].

Bin Baaz, 'Abdul-'Azeez bin 'Abdillaah, Al-'Uthaimeen, Muhammad bin Saalih, Al-Fawzaan, Saalih bin Fawzaan, and Al-Madkhalee, Zayd bin Haadee, 2008.

Four Essays on the Obligation of Veiling. 3rd ed. New York: Al-Ibaanah Book Publishing.

Call to Islam, n.d.a. Tawheed & Shirk. [leaflet] Masjid Ghurabaa, Luton.

Call to Islam, n.d.b. The Shias & The Sahabah. [leaflet] Masjid Ghurabaa, Luton.

Ghudayyaan, Abdullaah bin, 2005. Importance of Da'wah & the Characteristics of a Caller. [2 CDs] 12 June. Salafi Publications.

Ibn Katheer Dimashqi, Al-Hafiz, 2006. *Book of The End: Great Trials and Tribulations.* Translated from Arabic by Faisal Shafiq. Riyadh: Dar-us-Salam.

JIMAS, 2015. About us. [website] Available at: <www.jimas.org/about-us> [Accessed 13 November 2015].

Johnpi, 2009. Report from the UK: Exposing the UK Salafi's Part 1. [website] Available at: <http://talkislam.info/2009/07/16/report-from-the-uk-exposing-the-uk-sala> [Accessed 2 July 2015].

Kamaludin, Mohammad, 2015. History: Summary of the History of the Brixton Masjid Community. [website] Available at: <http://brixtonmasjid.co.uk/about-us/history> [Accessed 13 November 2015].

Madinahstudent, n.d. Benefits Available to Students. [website] Available at: <http://admission.iu.edu.sa/Advantages.aspx> [Accessed 13 November 2015].

Mahdi, A. R., n.d. Who Is Allah? [leaflet] Brixton Mosque: Masjid Ibnu Taymeeyah.

Masjid Ibnu Taymeeyah, Brixton, 2012. A Call from the Towers about the Ignorance of Yusuf Bowers! A Critical Analysis of the Lecture Entitled 'The History of the Salafi Da'wah in the UK'. [internal document] London: SalafiManhaj.

Muhammad, Abu Idrees, 2009. The Rights of Women within Islaam. [CD] 15 May, Masjid as-Salafi. Salafi Publications.

Salafi Events, 2011. Words of Benefit. [CD] London.

Salafi Publications, n.d.a. The Corruption of Terrorism & Suicide Bombings: Exposing the Perpetrators of Evil. [leaflet].

Salafi Publications, n.d.b. THINK for Yourself: Do You Really Believe Evolution is True??? [leaflet].

Salafi Publications, n.d.c. The State of the Ummah: Causes of Weakness & Means for Revival. [leaflet].

Salafi Publications, n.d.d. Seven Fundamental Questions Regarding Islam. [leaflet].

Salafi Publications, 2009. Women in Islaam: Separating Fact from Fiction. [leaflet].

Salafi Publications, 2013. A challenge to the slander against the honor of Abu Khadeejah by an unknown, nameless & shameless person. 4 September. Available at: <https://twitter.com/SalafiTalk/status/375218079984541696/photo/1> [Accessed 13 November 2015].

Salafitalk.net, 2011. Hijrah to Birmingham—Shaikh Ubaid Clarifies! January 19. Available at: <http://salafitalk.net/st/printthread.cfm?Forum=9&Topic=12027> [Accessed 13 November 2015].

Sloan, Abū Ameenah 'AbdurRahmān and al-Ashantī, 'AbdulHaq, 2011. *A Critique of the Methodology of Anwar al-Awlaki and his Errors in the Fiqh of Jihad.* London: Jamiah Media.

Smatch, 2007. Marriage Guide. Available at: <http://smatch.net/download.cfm> [Accessed 30 August 2013].

Strategy To Reach Empower and Educate Teenagers (STREET), n.d. STREET. [leaflet].

The Islaamic Awareness Society U.K., n.d.a. Women in Islaam: Ignore the Propaganda Find out the Truth. [leaflet].

The Islaamic Awareness Society U.K., n.d.b. The Man Muhammed (May God's Peace Be Upon Him). [leaflet].

The Noble Qur'an. Translated from Arabic by Muhammad Taqi-ud-Din Al-Hilali and Muhammad Muhsin Khan. Available at: www.dar-us-salam.com/TheNobleQuran [Accessed 13 November 2015].

Umm Amina, 2010. The Salafi exploitation of young British Muslim women. [online] 29 December. Available at: <www.spittoon.org/archives/8466> [Accessed 16 January 2014].

Umm Hawa, 2013. How Abu Khadeejah Drove A Sister Away From Her Deen. [online] 7 August. Available at: <http://refutingmadkhalis.wordpress.com/2013/08/07/how-abu-khadeejah-drove-a-sister-away-from-her-deen> [Accessed 13 November 2015].

Zarabozo, Jamaal al-Din M., n.d. Commentary on the Forty Hadith of al-Nawawi Volume 2. N.p.: Al-Basheer Publications and Translations.

Websites and Webpages Consulted

www.abdurrahman.org
www.abukhadeejah.com
www.al-athariyyah.com
http://brixtonmasjid.co.uk
www.croydonict.com
http://dhlearningcentre.org
http://dusunnah.com
www.fatwa-online.com
www.freekoran.co.uk
www.healthmeanswealth.co.uk
www.hmcc-uk.org
www.islamqa.info
www.jimas.org
www.kingfahdbinabdulaziz.com
www.madeenah.com
www.madinahstudent.co.uk
http://protectmuslimsisters.com
www.salafievents.com
www.salafimanhaj.com
www.salafimedia.com
http://salafinikah.1dawah.com
www.salafipublications.com
www.salafitalk.net
www.facebook.com/Salafiyah.nikah
http://smatch.net
www.thewahhabimyth.com
www.facebook.com/pages/Tottenham-Dawah-Salafiyyah/201322089892982

INDEX